PRAISE FOR TOM BISSELL'S
APOSTLE

"Expertly researched and fascinating. . . . Bissell is a wonderfully sure guide to these mysterious men. . . . This is a serious book about the origins of Christianity that is also very funny. How often can you say that?"

—*The Independent* (London)

"A writer of restless curiosity and lively wit. . . . Bissell has mastered his source materials in a meticulous and open-minded manner."   —*The Seattle Times*

"Bissell's apostolic journeys create a fascinating and quirky blend of contemporary travel narrative and scholarly investigation into the New Testament."

—BBC.com, "Nine Books to Read in March 2016"

"*Apostle* is a fine mash-up. Certainly, early Christianity is its subject, but storytelling is its object, how we call our world into existence and try to make sense of it."

—*The Philadelphia Inquirer*

"The book . . . is not a diatribe against Christianity. . . . Rather, it attempts to examine the stories and legends of the apostles and the development of church teaching about Jesus on the basis of current historical, theological and archaeological evidence. . . . The person of Christian faith who is willing to navigate the currents Bissell is riding will be rewarded with startling new insights."

—*The Wichita Eagle*

TOM BISSELL
APOSTLE

Tom Bissell was born in Escanaba, Michigan, in 1974. He is the author of eight previous books, including *Chasing the Sea*, *The Father of All Things*, and *Extra Lives*, all available in Vintage paperback, and has been awarded the Rome Prize and a Guggenheim Fellowship. Two of his short stories were adapted into the feature films *The Loneliest Planet* (directed by Julia Loktev) and *Salt and Fire* (directed by Werner Herzog); *The Disaster Artist* (cowritten with Greg Sestero) is currently being adapted into a feature film by James Franco. He lives in Los Angeles with his partner, Trisha Miller, and their daughter, Mina.

Chasing the Sea (2003)

Speak, Commentary (with Jeff Alexander) (2003)

God Lives in St. Petersburg and Other Stories (2005)

The Father of All Things (2007)

Extra Lives (2010)

The Art and Design of Gears of War (2011)

Magic Hours (2012)

The Disaster Artist (with Greg Sestero) (2013)

APOSTLE

OR
BONES THAT SHINE LIKE FIRE

· *Travels Among the Tombs of the Twelve* ·

TOM BISSELL

VINTAGE BOOKS
A Division of Penguin Random House LLC
New York

FIRST VINTAGE BOOKS EDITION, FEBRUARY 2017

Portions of this work originally appeared, in different form, in *The
Lifted Brow*, *Virginia Quarterly Review*, and *The Best American Travel
Writing 2010*.

The author gratefully acknowledges the American Academy
in Rome, the Black Mountain Institute, and the John Simon
Guggenheim Memorial Foundation for their support.

Photographs of Judas Iscariot and Jesus Christ courtesy of Marco
Ronchin; all other photographs © Marie-Lan Nguyen /
Wikimedia Commons

The Library of Congress has cataloged the Pantheon edition
as follows:
Bissell, Tom.
Apostle : travels among the tombs of the twelve / Tom Bissell.
pages ; cm
Includes bibliographical references and index.
1. Apostles.   2. Church history—Primitive and early Church, ca.
30–600.   3. Christian pilgrims and pilgrimages.   4. Bible—New
Testament—Criticism, interpretation, etc.   I. Title.
BS2440.B57 2016   225.9'22—dc23   2015023269

Vintage Books Trade Paperback ISBN: 978-0-307-27845-6
eBook ISBN: 978-1-101-87097-6

Author photograph © Joanna DeGeneres
Book design by Soonyoung Kwon

www.vintagebooks.com

Printed in the United States of America
10 9 8 7 6 5 4 3 2 1

Again and always for Trisha Miller,
and for Heather Schroder

An argument arose among them as to which one of them was the greatest.

—LUKE 9:46

CONTENTS

Author's Note

My religion makes no sense
and does not help me
therefore I pursue it.

—Anne Carson, "My Religion"

I grew up Catholic in a moderately churchgoing household and was an enthusiastic altar boy until I was sixteen. Along with my Sunday Mass duties, I showed up two or three times a week for the impossibly early, poorly attended, and much shorter daily Mass, which priests otherwise performed alone. The enjoyment I received from being an active participant in the various rituals of Catholic observance—slipping the bone-white robe over my head, cinching a red rope belt around my waist, ferrying the chalices, pouring ablutions over sacerdotal hands—was real, and I have never once looked back on those years with anything but fondness.

My loss of faith was nonetheless sudden and decisive. I will spare the reader any emotional archaeology of that event, other than to say that during my junior year of high school, while doing a report on a national newsweekly's annual Easter-timed "Who Was Jesus?" cover story, I read a book that forced me to recognize that what I had previously accepted as an inviolate block of readily understandable scripture was the product of several cultures intergalactically different from my own. Moreover, these scriptures contained all manner of textual and translational difficulties, many of which grew more, not less, bewildering as new manuscripts and findings came historically to light. A true understanding of God via scripture suddenly seemed beyond the power of anyone I could imagine. I stopped attending Mass and soon enough abandoned Christian belief altogether. I realize that others have pondered the same quandaries and doubts and come to different conclusions; some of them have written books you will find in my bibliography. *Est modus in rebus.*

I have few certainties about early Christianity; I hope nothing here serves to advance fringe theories fattened by scholarly table scraps. As often as possible, I try to summarize and quantify scholarly views, though I sometimes identify those that seem to me the most reasonable. One of my goals was to try to capture something of early Christianity's doctrinal uncertainty and how it affected the first Christian storytellers. The earliest Christian stories were about Jesus, and at least some of those telling them were presumably related to his earliest followers. Tradition has assigned a term for the most elite circle of his earliest followers: "Twelve Apostles." Soon enough, stories were being told about them.

From 2007 to 2010, I traveled to the supposed tombs and resting places of the Twelve Apostles. In doing this, I visited nine countries (one of which I literally walked across) and more than fifty churches and spent many hours talking to the people I met at and around these sites. Most of the Twelve have more than one tomb or reliquary, but I decided early that I would limit myself, at least in narrative terms, to one site each. This book has no interest in determining which sites have the greatest claim to a given apostle's remains. It is instead an effort to explore the legendary encrustation upon twelve lives about which little is known and even less can be historically verified.

Popular understanding holds that after Jesus's ascension to Heaven the Twelve Apostles, working initially out of Jerusalem, quickly moved to establish identifiably Christian churches throughout the Roman world and beyond. Eusebius, one of the earliest Christian writers to attempt a proper historical account of his faith, wrote that the "chief matter" of his history was to establish the "lines of succession from the holy apostles." But Eusebius, who lived three centuries after the apostles themselves, "failed to find any clear footprints of those who have gone this way before me." There are few facts about the apostles in Eusebius's pages, and as often as not they come from outside the New Testament. Indeed, since the very beginning of Christian history, the Twelve Apostles have wandered a strange gloaming between history and belief.

After the gospels, the Twelve are featured prominently within the New Testament only in the first few chapters of the Acts of the Apostles, when "divided tongues, as of fire . . . rested on each of them." These divine tongues apparently grant the apostles the ability to speak in other languages. The "amazed and perplexed" people of Jerusalem wonder if these unaccountably polyglot Galileans might not be "filled with new wine," but Peter, their spokesman, assures the crowd that the apostles are not drunk, "for it is only nine o'clock in the morning." The Twelve Apostles go on to perform many "signs and wonders" before the people of Jerusalem. With this, save for a few brief later appearances in which they referee interfaith disputes and supply general community guidance, the Twelve as a group sink from sight within the New Testament.

How to account for the sudden disappearance of Jesus's specially privileged followers in the only extant primary source of Christianity's rise? The church fathers, working off a strange passage in chapter 10 of Luke, seized on talk of Seventy Disciples*—unmentioned in the other gospels—who are chosen by Jesus to spread his word "to every town and place where

---

* The numbers seven and seventy recur throughout scripture. In this case, seventy apparently mirrored a concomitant Jewish belief related to the number of languages thought to have been spoken around the world; by coincidence or design, it was also close to the number required to assemble the supreme administrative Jewish council known as the Sanhedrin.

he himself intended to go." Jesus even claims to have "watched Satan fall from heaven like a flash of lightning" during their travels. According to Eusebius and other church fathers, the Seventy Disciples were Christianity's chief proselytizers.

The authors of the New Testament are not consistent in their use of the terms "disciple" and "apostle," but in most cases they have clear differences in terms of theological responsibility. (Later use of the terms was looser. Irenaeus referred to the Seventy as apostles, and Jerome confidently bestowed the title of "apostle" upon the Jewish prophet Isaiah, who lived seven centuries before Jesus.) The term "disciple" occurs far more frequently in the gospel tradition, though it is usually unclear whether it is intended to describe followers of Jesus generally or a smaller, more privileged group within those followers. Among New Testament writers, only Paul and Luke seem to view the title "apostle" as applicable to those outside the Twelve, though Luke's expansion of the term is fleeting. Paul had obvious self-interested reasons for seeing the title "apostle" extended to those outside the Twelve, because he himself was outside the Twelve and did not begin to follow Jesus until several years after his death.

Most of the church fathers attempted to keep the Seventy Disciples separate from the Twelve Apostles, an effort that resulted in much confusion. Clement of Alexandria, for instance, seemed to number the apostle Thaddaeus among the Seventy. He also included among them a certain Cephas. This is Peter's special nickname in the Gospel According to John, bestowed by Jesus himself, yet Clement appeared to argue that Cephas was, in fact, a different man from Peter. Eusebius, following Clement, wrote that Cephas was "one of the seventy disciples, who happened to have the same name as Peter the Apostle." Paul mentions Cephas several times in his letters, and while it is highly probable Paul is actually discussing Peter, it is not certain. A few hundred years after his death, even the most famous member of the Twelve had moved beyond accountable certainty.

Like the Seventy and much else that distinguished the beliefs and self-understanding of the first Christians, the notion of the Twelve is Jewish in origin and concerns one of Judaism's first historical traumas: the capture, deportation, and "loss" of ten of Israel's twelve tribes following the Assyrian destruction of the northern kingdom of Israel in the eighth century BCE. In his time, Jesus would not have been unique if he believed that the tribes would one day reunite in Jerusalem upon Yahweh's final victory over the forces of unrighteousness, whereupon a new Temple would be constructed, allowing all the nations of the world to worship him. But Jesus would certainly have been unique, and radical, if he foresaw his own followers sitting "on twelve thrones, judging the twelve tribes of Israel," as he says in the Gospel According to Matthew. This suggestion that the Twelve will in some way rule some form of a somehow reconstituted Israel is as explicit as Jesus gets in the canonical gospels about the role of the Twelve.

Most scholars believe the historical Jesus's concerns were quite a bit more modest. They look to his stories, teachings, and parables—tales of dying beggars, angry sharecroppers, quarrelsome peasants, and hungry landowners ordering around their slaves—as indications of these more local concerns. "Jesus was not teaching some sort of new lifestyle to individuals," the scholar Richard Horsley notes, "but addressing local communities about their disintegrating socio-economic relations." While the precise nature of Jesus's relationship to Judaism is a question that will never be resolved, it is difficult, nevertheless, to read the gospels without seeing the hand of the later Gentile church.

In the Gospel According to Mark, for instance, we are told that Jesus is understood to have "declared all foods clean" by instructing his disciples, "It is what comes out of a person that defiles." We can safely assume Jesus had some basic connection to his culture and religion, which means that his tacit endorsement of shellfish, pork, and improperly butchered meat is probably not the voice of a first-century Galilean speaking—

especially when, in another gospel, that of Matthew, Jesus explicitly says he intends to abolish "not an iota, not a dot" from Jewish Law. In Acts, Peter is celestially prodded to "kill and eat" unclean beasts during a vision. Peter's response: "I have never eaten anything that is profane or unclean." Not until the next day does the Peter of Acts realize his religion's dietary laws have been divinely rendered void. The vision allows Peter a clear conscience as he makes his first non-Jewish convert: the Roman centurion Cornelius.

Such seeming scriptural contradictions, especially those involving Judaic observance, are why the Twelve were, and continue to be, regarded as important to Christians. Whatever they believed must have been similar to what Jesus believed. The church fathers recognized that the Seventy might have played a more active role in spreading the faith, but the Twelve came to be seen and safeguarded as guarantors of legitimacy. This was a long process—in fact, its full realization took centuries— and became less a matter of learning what the apostles believed and more a matter of retroactively assigning to them the prevailing beliefs of a later time. Clement of Rome, in his supposed letter to the Corinthians, also known as *1 Clement* and written around the turn of the first century, was the first to explicitly make the case of doctrinal purity based on succession from the Twelve. A few years later, Ignatius of Antioch argued that the apostles belonged on a spiritual plane above that of lowly bishops and deacons, who were intended merely to follow apostolic teachings rather than initiate their own. Thus, by the turn of the first century, Christian teachers such as Clement and Ignatius were already discussing the apostles as part of an honored era now concluded.

Who were the Twelve Apostles, and what, exactly, did they believe? Were they wanderers and preachers conscious of creating a new faith or largely observant Jews who stayed mostly around Galilee and Judaea? Or were they some combination of the two? The church fathers wondered over such matters themselves, and what the Acts of the Apostles told them was not always complimentary to what they wished to believe. Peter and John are shown in Acts to engage in some limited missionary work with non-Jews, but what we are clearly expected to understand as a typical day finds them "going up to the [Jewish] temple at the hour of prayer, at three o'clock in the afternoon." When the apostles are depicted as operating together in Acts, it is often as men whom the people of Jerusalem hold "in high esteem."

Acts shows them riling the Jerusalem authorities, of course, much as Jesus had, but the Pharisee Gamaliel urges his outraged colleagues and co-religionists to "let [the apostles] alone, because if this plan or this undertaking is of human origin, it will fail; but if it is of God, you will not be able to overthrow them." Gamaliel's plea for mercy is accepted, and the apostles are not killed but rather suffer group flogging before the Sanhedrin; afterward, they are told "not to speak in the name of Jesus." The apostles briefly withdraw, rejoice "that they were considered worthy to suffer dishonor," and head right back to the Temple. Eusebius, noting such matters, wrote with evident discomfort that the apostles "were of Hebrew stock and therefore, in the Jewish manner, still retained most of their ancient customs."

The Greek word the New Testament gives us as *apostolos* (one who is sent) is the noun form of the then more commonly used compound verb *apostellein* (to send from). "Apostle" can mean one who is an "agent" or "envoy" of a particular message, though to Greek speakers the word might have had a militarily nautical overtone, as it was sometimes used in reference to naval forces dispatched on the errands of a city-state. Scholars debate whether the New Testament's twelve envoys were actual historical figures, or were created by the authors of the Christian canon (written between 50 and 120 CE), or some combination thereof. Paul, who again was not a member of the Twelve Apostles, writes in his first letter to the Corinthians that his resurrected Lord first appeared to "Cephas, then to the twelve." This provides crucial evidence that some notion of twelve specially chosen followers existed from Christianity's earliest days, though Paul appears to view the Twelve as separate from the apostles. Either way, it is the lone mention of the Twelve in any of Paul's surviving letters. What cannot be denied is that the Twelve play an important role—one, moreover, that would have been difficult to insert after the fact—in three of the four gospel traditions. Most notably, the Twelve became the first to partake of the Eucharistic tradition during the Last Supper, which alone guaranteed their significance.

And yet, amazingly, the New Testament lacks complete agreement about who the Twelve actually were. When Eusebius wrote, "The names of our Savior's apostles are in the gospels for all to read," he was passing over the fact that the gospels' apostle lists have small but important variations. Mark, in all likelihood the first gospel to have been written, lists the Twelve as "Simon (to whom [Jesus] gave the name Peter); James son of Zebedee and John the brother of James (to whom he gave the name Boanerges, that is, Sons of Thunder); and Andrew, and Philip, and Bartholomew, and Matthew, and Thomas, and James son of Alphaeus, and Thaddaeus, and Simon the Cananaean, and Judas Iscariot, who betrayed him." Matthew gives a near identical list (though he mentions that Matthew was a "tax collector" and that Andrew was the brother of Peter), and Luke follows it closely but for adding "Judas of James," dropping Thaddaeus, and giving "Simon the Cananaean" a new epithet: "Simon, who was called the Zealot." John gives no list of the Twelve but mentions among Jesus's inner circle one "Nathanael of Cana," who appears nowhere else in the New Testament. An early Christian text known as *The Epistle of the Apostles,* which may date from the second century and was discovered only in 1895, gives this list, obviously influenced by John, of not twelve but eleven apostles: John, Thomas, Peter, Andrew, James, Philip, Bartholomew, Matthew, Nathanael, Judas Zelotes, and (interestingly distinct from Peter) Cephas. Such inconsistencies both undermine and support the Twelve's basis in history. As one scholar writes, "That the lists preserve the names of some of the companions of Jesus during his ministry is beyond doubt. But the fluctuation in the names reveals that they were not all precisely remembered as time wore on."

Equally amazing is that "Twelve Apostles," a phrase that today has the resonance of a beloved hymn, appears exactly once in the New Testament, in Matthew 10:2. Its familiarity is rather the result of a kind of synthesis. Matthew's use of "apostle" in the above-mentioned passage is the only time the word appears in his gospel; he prefers "the twelve" or "the twelve disciples." Mark, too, uses "apostle" only once. It is Luke's frequent use of "apostle" that allowed the term its later prominence, though he uses "the twelve" relatively infrequently. John prefers the catchall "disciple," never uses "apostle" (though he does refer to a "sending" [*apostellein*] in 4:38), and contains only four mentions of "the twelve."

If their differing labels and names were not enough, the gospels offer portrayals of the Twelve that are sometimes difficult to reconcile with one another. In Matthew, Jesus does not call the Twelve until after he has begun his public ministry to Israel. He sends them out across the land "like sheep into the midst of wolves.... Whoever welcomes you welcomes me." As in Mark, special attention is given to the "authority" Jesus grants the Twelve over "unclean spirits." Matthew's Jesus tells the Twelve this: "What I say to you in the dark, tell in the light; and what you hear whispered, proclaim from the highest housetop." John's Jesus, too, shuns secrecy, telling the high priest of Jerusalem, "I have said nothing in secret." According to Luke, however, the Twelve are told by Jesus "sternly" not to tell anyone that he is the Messiah.

Both Mark's and John's gospels seem to view the Twelve,

and especially Peter, in an unenthusiastic light. In Mark, the Twelve are chronically unable to understand his teachings. "Do you have eyes, and fail to see?" Jesus asks them. "Do you have ears, and fail to hear?" One scholar sums up Mark's bizarre portrayal of the Twelve "as moving from a lack of understanding to complete failure to understand." Mark even writes of the apostles' hearts being inexplicably hardened against Jesus after witnessing one of his most astounding miracles!

Within the canon of the New Testament, the apostles are rarely described as fully formed characters, but then few characters in first-century texts were. The few members of the Twelve lavished with any attention at all are often represented by certain iconic traits. The rest are, to modern readers' frustration, absent of personality. The Twelve are often depicted in the gospels and Acts as speaking as one and then in ways that disappoint Jesus, such as when he asks them, in Mark, "Who do people say that I am?" "They" answer him: "John the Baptist; and others, Elijah; and still others, one of the prophets." Jesus presses them: "But who do you say that I am?" It is Peter, the most discernible of the apostles in all of the gospels, who answers: "You are the Messiah." This is followed by one of the New Testament's most puzzling moments: Peter rebukes Jesus, which in turn moves Jesus to publicly liken Peter to Satan. The brothers Zebedee, James and John, are shown to be aggressive and quick to anger, such as when they ask Jesus if he would like them "to command fire to come down from heaven and consume" a Samaritan village, thereby earning Jesus's scolding; they later demand to know if they can sit at his right and left hand in Heaven. Thomas, of course, doubts Jesus's resurrection, and the conniving Judas betrays him. The rest of the Twelve are largely anonymous, mouthing dialogue of no distinction.

There is also the matter of the odd doublings of their names: the two Simons, two Jameses, and two Judases among the Twelve (to say nothing of the numerous other Simons and

Jameses strewn throughout the gospels) have long confused even the gospels' most brilliant readers. Christianity's appeal is largely fueled by its claims of historical legitimacy: *These events* happened *at this time* before *these eyewitnesses.* Yet the existence of the faith's most crucial eyewitnesses is uncertain, for nothing outside the New Testament confirms the Twelve's existence as individuals.

It is apparent from the simultaneously idealized and obscure account of early Christian history in Acts that very early something happened to the Twelve that either broke their fellowship or diminished their authority. When Paul first visits Jerusalem, no fewer than four years after the death of Jesus, he speaks of meeting not the Twelve but rather only "apostles," among whom he seems to include James the brother of Jesus. By his next trip to Jerusalem, a decade later, these apostles have vanished. In their place are what Paul now calls Pillars, of whom he has not much good to say. The title "apostle" itself had faded from use, which indicates it was probably intended to refer only to the Jerusalem circle of Jesus's original followers.

In the early 40s CE, James son of Zebedee, the brother of the apostle John, was supposedly executed, for reasons unknown, by Herod Agrippa I. It is the only recorded martyrdom of one of the Twelve in the New Testament. The ruling authority of the Twelve can, within the narrative context of Acts at least, be judged to have begun to end around this time. When Judas dies, according to Acts, the Eleven recruit community members and restore themselves to Twelve by drawing lots. Yet James's death merits no such emergency restoration, and the Twelve is no longer Twelve. Because James's death "pleased the Jews," Agrippa has Peter arrested. Peter escapes from Agrippa's prison with angelic assistance, and after leaving instructions to tell the other apostles what has happened, "he left and went to another place" and is mentioned again in Acts only once.

An ancillary explanation for the Twelve's diminishment

has to do with the growing prominence of Christians with little or no connection to the Twelve. In 1 Corinthians, written between 50 and 60, Paul takes issue with growing factionalization within Corinth's Christian community. "'I belong to Paul,'" he writes in scornful mimic, "or 'I belong to Apollos,' or 'I belong to Cephas,' or 'I belong to Christ.'" (Note that only one faction attaches itself to an apparent member of the Twelve.) There was also the challenge of absorbing a growing number of Gentiles into what was still a sect of Judaism. The author of Acts plays down the trauma of Gentile impact on the early church, but Paul's letters suggest that eager Gentile entrants into a Jewish sect created problems that not every prominent early Christian knew how to deal with. The Twelve Apostles are said to have enjoyed the personal instruction of Jesus himself. Despite that, the Christian community they led was, according to scripture, confused about and sometimes even bewildered by the issue of Gentiles. This may be why record of the Twelve's prominence within the early church is so fragmentary and uncertain, for history does not record a single member of the Twelve, with the possible exception of Peter, as having had any particular impact on early Christianity. It is only Christian legend that tells us otherwise.

Even after I lost my religious faith, Christianity remained to me deeply and resonantly interesting, and I have long believed that anyone who does not find Christianity interesting has only his or her unfamiliarity with the topic to blame. I think, in some ways, I wrote this book to put that belief to the test.

With few exceptions, the biblical quotations throughout these pages are from the New Revised Standard Version; the translations I have used for other keystone texts (Eusebius, Josephus) can be found in the bibliography. I avoid using the word "Gnostic," a blanket term that scholars who study the diverse theological variations within early Christianity have largely abandoned; instead, I refer to "heterodox" Christianity. For early Christian beliefs in line with those that, in the second, third, and fourth centuries, became the foundation of Christian orthodoxy, I use the scholar Bart D. Ehrman's term "proto-orthodoxy." In matters of dating, I have opted for BCE (before the Common Era) and CE (Common Era). Unless it is within an appropriate theological context, I refer in these pages to Jesus rather than Jesus Christ.

Finally, as a nonspecialist writing about one of the most complicated and widely studied subjects in all of humanity, I do not doubt that this book contains mistakes of fact and interpretation. I have done my best not to distort the biblical, historical, and theological scholarship that now informs my understanding of early Christianity. Thus, any and all mistakes should be blamed on the tares of the Devil, he who does not sleep.

—TCB
Los Angeles
January 4, 2015

JUDAS ISCARIOT

Hakeldama: Jerusalem, Israel

KIDRON & HINNOM • HELL ON EARTH • THE FIELD
OF BLOOD • THE PILGRIMS OF NEW ULM • "FRIEND,
DO WHAT YOU ARE HERE TO DO" • THE HORRIBLE
DEATH • NAZAR THE SHEPHERD • THE DE QUINCEY
THEORY • THE MYSTERY OF THE BETRAYAL • STREET
FIGHTING

I.

The first apparent mention of Jerusalem is found on a piece of thirty-eight-hundred-year-old Egyptian pottery. For the vast majority of time since, Jerusalem has been perceived as a remote, baffling place—a kind of world-historical Salt Lake City. Much of its soil is friably poor, and the nearest meaningful river or harbor is a journey of many miles. That this tactically worthless city became the Finland Station of monotheism was one of history's stranger accidents. God would never have chosen Jerusalem, and so Jerusalem chose God.

Topographically, Jerusalem has nothing to recommend it other than two pretty, undulating valleys, known as Kidron and Hinnom, on its southern and eastern flanks. Both are deep and desertic, stubbled with little merkins of shrubbery and lined with low gray trees that look squashed and drained of chlorophyll. While these naturally occurring moats offered Jerusalem's early inhabitants considerable protection against invaders, later epochs would nullify their efficacy, allowing Jerusalem to become one of the world's more frequently occupied cities.

The sun did strange things to the landscape here, vivifying the dominating grays and sands, weakening the greens, and walling off thousands of hillside houses behind shimmering heat-haze force fields. Somewhere ahead of us, the Hinnom valley crossed the Kidron valley, which had a storied past. David traversed the Kidron valley in flight from his traitorous son Absalom. A young Galilean healer named Jesus navigated his donkey along the Kidron valley during his initially triumphal journey up to Jerusalem. Located within the Kidron valley were many of the first century's most spectacular surviving burial sites—columnar audacities carved directly into the valley's rock walls—along with the supposed tombs of the prophets Zechariah and Isaiah.

The Hinnom valley—which begins on the western side of the Old City, close to the Jaffa Gate, and turns sharply to slither along the base of Mount Zion—emanated more sinister historical vibrations. According to a fairly obscure verse in 2 Kings, the Hinnom valley is where children were apparently burned alive as offerings to stubbornly enduring Canaanite gods. Jeremiah goes further, quoting the Lord's fulmination against those who spill the "blood of the innocent" in this "valley of Slaughter." Later it was used as a place to dump things considered unclean (a rather overarching category for ancient Jews), whereupon all such refuse, including unclean corpses, was burned. These fires' greasy soot and smoke, some of it redolent of barbecued human flesh, blew through the streets of Jerusalem, dirtying cloaks and staining buildings.

By the first century CE, the Hinnom valley was no longer used as an open-air furnace, but apparently certain associations proved difficult to shed. In Greek, Hinnom becomes *Gehenna,* a word employed several times in the New Testament. In the Gospel According to Matthew, Jesus claims it as a place the "scribes and Pharisees" will be unable to escape, while in the Gospel According to Mark, Jesus refers to its "unquenchable fire." Here was the rare religious tradition whose creation could be tracked virtually step-by-step. Begin with a site, at the base of a city, associated with child sacrifice and municipal incineration. End with a fiery transdimensional prison imagined as being located *beneath* the physical world. The Hinnom valley was a place where you could literally, rather than figuratively, walk through Hell.

It was also home to a site of profound but ambiguous importance to early Christianity, though its precise location was becoming increasingly difficult to verify. Jay and I peered together at our foldout map. On it, the boldfaced place-names (Herod's Gate, Solomon's Stables, Dome of the Rock, Western Wall) were packed together so plentifully it invited despair of ever seeing them all. Down near the bottom of our map, however—stark and alone but for an italicized *HINNOM VALLEY*—was our destination: HAKELDAMA. We had been looking for it for close to an hour. Jay suggested we try yet another path. This was his first visit to Jerusalem. It was mine, too, but he was a historian, so I followed him.

A shin-high wall of pale brown stones lined the new path. Some of the previous paths we had explored were blacktopped; this one was not. Not many feet had been this way: the path's gravel was still loose and crunchy. To the left was the base of Mount Zion, the southern face of which was bare and undeveloped. To the right were rocky cliffs, atop which were quite a few sandstone apartment buildings. That morning it had rained. In a few places, thick spouts of collected runoff rainwater drained into the valley, as though someone were emptying a series of high-capacity pitchers. Along the path were several shallow caves, most of which were barred. We passed a few apparent dig sites fenced off with thin wire barriers. These little excavations all had an ongoing, archaeological neatness to them, but there were no archaeologists working here this afternoon who could help us find Hakeldama.

Jerusalem's Old City is a place in which even the alleys claimed sites of world-changing historical consequence. Most of such sites are purported at best. Hakeldama was one of the few places named in the New Testament whose present-day location scholars are reasonably sure is accurate, and yet there were no plaques that commemorated it, no signs that announced it, no obvious paths that led to it. Only caves, mud, and bushes.

From where we now stood, we could see at least ten pathways through the Hinnom valley. All of them were empty. Jay, far ahead of me now, found a sandal and, a few steps later, a rubber ball. We jumped off a small ledge onto an exceedingly thin trail that led muddily toward a new clearing. Finally, Hakeldama. Exposed stones the shape of mandibular canines stuck up out of the clearing's weedy grass. A dead tree, a rampike as gray and hard as concrete, stood near the middle of the clearing, all of its naked branches pushed one way, as though arranged by millennia of wind. A Palestinian woman in a white head scarf and carrying a plastic shopping bag was walking along the ridge above us.

Very little of the Old City could be seen from Hakeldama. We could see the Mount of Olives, whence Jesus is said to have ascended to Heaven and which was crowned with a glittering salt-white diadem of over 150,000 Jewish tombstones. Parts of the mount's slope were striped with tall, shaggy spears of cedar and blotted with shorter, rounder olive trees, but large portions of the mount were bare. (The Romans cut down nearly every tree in the region during the Jewish War [66–73 CE] in order to build siege engines; the mount had apparently never fully recovered.) Jesus was arrested somewhere on or at the base of the Mount of Olives, in the Garden of Gethsemane, the present location of which is at best an informed guess. According to Christian scripture, one of Jesus's own disciples guided the arresting party to Gethsemane, and Hakeldama was traditionally believed to be the place where that betrayer met his end.

II.

In the various ancient copies of the New Testament texts that mention it, Hakeldama goes by many names: Akeldama, Acheldemach, Akeldaimach, Haceldama. It is a transliteration from the Aramaic *haqel dema* and means "field of blood."

The Gospel According to Matthew and the Acts of the Apostles (universally credited to the evangelist Luke) are the only New Testament texts to mention the Field of Blood. They offer contradictory etymologies of its name, but the apostle Judas, Jesus's betrayer, is central to both versions. Papias of Hierapolis, one of the early second century's most prominent Christians,* also linked Judas to a field and described its ineradicable stench, though he did not refer to it as the Field of Blood.

Something happened to the disciple who led the authorities to Jesus. It had something to do with a field. Two thousand years later, Jay and I stood in the middle of a place that had a reasonably valid claim of being that field. Here, many believed that a mysterious and calamitous fate laid its word across the most despised betrayer in human history. Yet once the initial frisson of its notoriety had passed, Hakeldama was lonely and unendurably dull. This was disappointing, but so was much else about Jerusalem.

The zonated nature of the city was perhaps its most alienating feature. No one is allowed entrance to as much as a coffee shop without being passed over by a security guard's explosive-detecting wand. This is expected, of course. Less expected are the church doors hung with signs that read ABSOLUTELY NO FIREARMS and the Israeli police horses whose agitated eyes were shielded by wraparound Plexiglas visors. The city's people, meanwhile, lived in something short of obvious amity. Jerusalem's crowded streets had the phobic, elbowy feeling of a convention no one was particularly happy to be attending. Greek Orthodox priests in black robes and rope belts sullenly ate ice cream beside glum Franciscan priests in sunglasses and floppy hats. Hasidim and

---

* Although his name comes up relatively frequently in the work of the church fathers, Papias is a man of whom not much is known, other than that his church was connected to one of Paul's lieutenants, a man named Epaphras.

head-scarfed Arab women hurried through the streets as though in flight from modernity itself. On King David Street, vendors stepped out into the passing crowd, found someone with whom to make eye contact, offered unbidden directions, then demanded as a reciprocal favor that their new friend look inside their stores and spend fifty dollars.

The markets themselves were largely a gallows of shoddy merchandise: bowls of beads, body stockings, stuffed camels, plastic toy sniper rifles, pirated Arab-language copies of *Toy Story,* carbon-datably dried pineapple. At one corner, an Evangelical tour group led by a man with a thick southern accent argued over the opening line of the Twenty-Third Psalm, while a few feet away a Roman Catholic tour group led by a young, sunburned priest stopped at one of the stations of the Via Dolorosa. Meanwhile, M16-bearing Israeli soldiers looked upon them all with unmistakable irritation. A little farther down the street, mouthy Palestinian schoolkids shouted down insults from atop the wall of the Aqsa school. Nearby, tourists gawked at the gargantuan crown of thorns around the dome of the Church of the Flagellation, while others posed for photographs while struggling beneath its freestanding photo-op cross. Young Palestinian men manned T-shirt stands that sold FREE PALESTINE! shirts alongside shirts emblazoned with FOR THE SAKE OF ZION—I WILL NOT BE SILENT!

Jerusalem might have been an easy city to love, but it was virtually impossible to like. As Jay pointed out, its tendencies toward the excessive should not have been surprising. During the second century BCE, a Jewish nationalist movement overthrew the region's stridently Hellenizing Seleucid overlords and went on to found the Hasmonaean dynasty—a regime that became as cruel and appalling as that of any Greek-styled warlord. In the first century CE, Jewish Zealots devoted to the Temple led a doomed revolt against the Romans that ensured the destruction of that Temple, which was never rebuilt. Christians have never behaved more barbarously than during their various attempts, successful and unsuccessful, to control Jerusalem. Medieval Muslims once sacked the supposed tomb of Jesus itself, and today their twenty-first-century heirs are sent marching in the streets by an errant editorial.

A German Dominican priest who visited Jerusalem in the late fifteenth century was already questioning whether the shrines he kneeled before had any relationship to the locations they claimed to commemorate. The places where Jesus was imprisoned, flogged, and finally condemned by Pilate have been in Brownian motion for centuries, often based on nothing more empirical than where a freshly arrived crusader felt like pointing his sword. In this respect, the Church of the Holy Sepulchre, Christianity's holiest place, was both an exception and not. While its location is not based completely in fantasy (the first devotional building constructed on its grounds, raised by Constantinian architects in the fourth century, was built in recognition of an early local tradition), many of the claims made for the Sepulchre's other contents (such as Adam's tomb and the literal center of the earth) were puzzling, to say the least. The building that stands today is, by and large, a half-restored, half-reconstructed version of a church first erected in the twelfth century by crusaders. Weakened by various calamities over the last thousand years, the Holy Sepulchre of today only *looked* as though it were about to collapse and kill everyone inside.

Many Christians face a challenging emotional experience in the Holy Sepulchre. They come to see the spot on which Jesus was crucified and peer into the nearby cave in which his body was entombed. What they find instead is hooded, frowning Copts, villainously bearded Armenians, medieval darkness, and gagging clouds of incense. The Holy Sepulchre is divided into various areas overseen by six Christian sects for whom agreement is a once-in-a-millennium occurrence. (Unsightly scaffolds once stood within the church for the better part of a century because none of its caretakers could agree on the form some badly needed repairs would take.) The key keepers of the church are, famously, a Muslim family—the only ones who can be trusted to let everyone inside.

The Church of the Holy Sepulchre was merely one radioactive particle whirling within the spiritual fallout of the city that contained it. For decades, the troubles of Jerusalem have held our world hostage. This sad reality becomes most evident at the Western Wall, the one surviving piece of the Second Temple, which was destroyed by the Romans near the end of the Jewish War in 70 CE. Visually, it is striking: its crenellated baby-teeth ramparts, the fright wigs of bright evergreen that grow from its cracks, the irregular size of its constituent bricks, the glowy manner in which it catches and holds the slanted late-afternoon light. Many of the Jews who today came to the Wall prayed for the annihilation of the Aqsa Mosque and Dome of the Rock* built above it, and within the latter one can find the following written around its inner dome: "God is but One God; utterly remote is He in His glory from having a son." While we watched people pray at the Western Wall, Jay said, "Jerusalem is a city of contradictions. Three of them."

Before our search for Hakeldama began that day, Jay and I had stopped for an early lunch in what had become our favorite falafel restaurant. Near the end of our meal, nearly three dozen pilgrims from New Ulm, Minnesota, invaded the otherwise empty restaurant. Their Palestinian guide remained outside, pensively smoking. After the owner explained to them what falafel was, all thirty ordered hamburgers. A Santa-like man with a thick white nicotined beard and intensely merry eyes sat next to Jay; his short-haired, nervously smiling wife sat next to me. Both were eager to chat with whom they were delighted to learn

---

* The Dome of the Rock was briefly reconsecrated as a church in 1099. It was re-Islamized in 1187 when the armies of Saladin conquered Jerusalem. Christians would hold the Holy Land again between 1229 and 1244, whereupon they faced another defeat by the forces of Islam. Christianity has enjoyed no formal rule over the land of Jesus since.

were fellow Americans. They had been in Israel six days. What had they seen? Bethlehem, of course. Galilee, where they had gazed upon the very place where Jesus once trod on water. This morning had brought them to the shore of yet another amazement: the dungeon in which Jesus had been beaten, even though the New Testament does not record such a dungeon. And us? We described our plan to find Hakeldama, which Judas supposedly purchased with the money he had earned by betraying Jesus. Husband and wife shifted uncomfortably and shared a bridge-partner glance. Jay quickly explained that he was a professional historian. His area was the Crusades, generally, but his particular specialty was the study of how Jerusalem was perceived by those who had never been there. He described to our new friends how nearly all of the first travel guides about Jerusalem were written by crusader-era scribes who routinely failed—to the frustration of modern historians—to take note of the contemporaneous reality of the city around them and instead focused on imagining they had found the exact spot where Jesus had saved the adulterous woman from stoning or where Mary had learned her Psalter.

Our new friends nodded politely and for a while did not speak. Finally, the man looked up and asked, "Why the heck would you want to see where Judas killed himself?"

III.

"The figure of Judas Iscariot," one popular Christian writer has said, "is the most tragic in all the Bible." Another writes, "He committed the most horrible, heinous act of any individual, ever." Yet another writes that Judas "is the greatest failure the world has ever known." The name Judas Iscariot* has become an electromagnet of wickedness.

---

* The ancient copyists of the New Testament texts render "Iscariot" at least ten different ways. What it was intended to mean, no one knows, but theories abound. The

Who Judas was, what he did, why he did it, and what he ultimately means have been debated within Christianity from its first decades. In the centuries since, many—believers and nonbelievers alike—have attempted to discern in his few scriptural appearances a personality complicated and large enough to merit the crime of which he is condemned. This has resulted in many imagined Judases. We have been presented with a Judas who is tormented and penitent, a Judas possessed by devils, a Judas possessed by the Devil, a Judas who is diseased, a Judas who is loyal, a Judas who does what he has to do, a Judas who wants Jesus to act against Rome, a Judas who is confused, a Judas who is loving, a Judas who loves women, a Judas who kills his own father, a Judas who works as a double agent, a Judas who does not understand what he has done, a Judas who kills himself, a Judas who lives to old age, a Judas who loves Jesus "as cold loves flame," a Judas who is the agent of salvation itself.

The scholar Kim Paffenroth, one of Judas's more astute contemporary judges, writes that all of this imaginative toil has been for naught. "We will never see Judas," he writes, "and we will never not see him because, like every historical or literary

---

notion that Iscariot means "man of Kerioth" has a solidly ancient acceptance among scribes and church fathers. Indeed, many early manuscripts of John have "from Kerioth" in place of "Iscariot." John also mentions that Judas has a father, one Simon Iscariot, which further suggests a place-of-origin name. Theories that Judas's name signals his ultimate intention (Iscariot meaning "man of lies," for instance, or "ruddy-colored one," which reflects an ancient cultural revulsion toward redheads) have, over the centuries, proved popular but unconvincing. The most common understanding of Iscariot is that it refers to the Sicarii, a violent band of Jewish extremists. According to Josephus, the Sicarii carried small swords that resembled curved Persian daggers, which the Romans called *sicae*. The problem is that Josephus explicitly places the rise of the Sicarii in the time of the Roman procurator Festus, who ruled in the 50s CE, and never mentions them as existing—much less active—during the time of Pilate. Some have argued that the gospel writers nevertheless intended Judas's name to be redolent of Sicarii villainy, for few who were alive during the first century would have been fondly disposed to the murdering and kidnapping Sicarii.

character, he is found everywhere and in everyone." One of the first Christian martyrdom documents, written in the mid-second century, proclaims that those who betray their fellow Christians have "received the punishment of Judas himself." By the third century, Christians were warning in their epitaphs that any violators or grave robbers would "share the lot of Judas." By the time of the medieval Passion play—a performed reenactment of Jesus's arrest, trial, and crucifixion, the nature of which allowed for frequent extra-scriptural editorialization—Judas had become synonymous with Jews as a people.

The color used to symbolize him is that of contagion: yellow. His symbols have been the scorpion, money, coins, and the noose. In obedience to the many prescriptions of early Christian art, Judas was almost always turned away from the viewer, or beardless, or wearing an unusually colored robe, his halo extinguished. Even as these prescriptions faded from the Western tradition, Judas was often painted as a vile, apelike man. Leonardo da Vinci's *Last Supper* defied centuries of tradition when it depicted Judas not as leaving the table, or already absent, but as sitting near Jesus, his face obscured by shadow. While at work on the painting, Leonardo had difficulty with Judas's face. In the end, he made Judas resemble a prior he hated.

IV.

The greatest failure the world has ever known is mentioned twenty-two times in the New Testament. The Gospel According to John mentions him the most; the Gospel According to Mark, which was probably the first gospel to have been written, mentions him the least. In Mark, Judas is little more than plot spot welded to a name. Matthew and Luke, which most scholars accept as having used Mark as their narrative foundations, depart in different ways from their source when it comes to Judas.

It is important to understand that when we speak of Matthew, Mark, Luke, and John as being the authors of the gospels,* we are speaking less of what one scholar calls a "detectable mind" and more of a complicated, even competitive, process of composition and interpretive overlay. None of the gospels are signed, and all show evidence of having been edited in the interests of theological refinement. Authors were not officially assigned to the gospels until the late second century by Irenaeus of Lyon, one hundred years after the last of them was completed. (Whether the gospels were *intended* to be anonymously written texts is a much more difficult and obviously unresolved question.) When Irenaeus attached names to the gospels, it was not necessarily out of the belief that men named Matthew, Mark, Luke, and John had written them.† "Authorship" did not have the same conceptual or moral framework in ancient times as it does for us today. Arguments based on who wrote which gospel in many cases hinged on the *authority* thought to stand behind that gospel—this is especially true in Matthew's and John's cases—rather than the person who actually, physically wrote them. This is very similar to the traditions of early Judaism, in which Moses is regarded as the "author" of the first five books of the Hebrew Bible not because he wrote them but because the traditions they contained were believed to wend back to him.

The idea that the writers of the gospels were self-conscious

---

* In New Testament Greek, the word used for "gospel" is *euangélion,* which means "good news." Early Latin-speaking Christians used *evangelium* for "gospel," but in the Middle Ages an Anglo-Saxon neologism was coined: *god spel* (good news), which was eventually and stylishly shortened to "gospel."

† The first scholar to seriously question the traditional identities of the New Testament's authors was John Toland, a once-Catholic Irish convert to Protestantism. His argument held that the New Testament was mostly composed of essentially anonymous documents. He also argued that the church fathers' attribution of texts to authors was in almost every case demonstrably spurious. In 1699, Toland was threatened with execution for his trouble. Shockingly, the next intellectually serious study of the formation of the New Testament canon did not occur until the nineteenth century.

newshounds going out and reporting or remembering the story of Jesus is somewhat anachronistic. The Gospel According to Luke's opening lines claim that its author has "decided, after investigating everything carefully from the very first, to write an orderly account" about the events of Jesus's life and ministry, but many writers of historical narrative in the Greco-Roman world opened with portrayals of themselves as paradigms of reliability. The first-century historian Josephus, for instance, places early stress on his cool-mindedness—"I shall state the facts accurately and impartially"—yet he is widely viewed as one of the most gratuitously self-serving historians who ever lived.

"Matthew," "Mark," "Luke," and "John" were probably not individual authors writing by candlelight, their memories aglow and their sources scattered around them. The writing of the gospels was, in all likelihood, subsidized by various Christian communities, making their earliest forms compromise-driven. This is not to imply any purposeful dishonesty on the part of the early Christians who wrote and circulated the gospels. It is merely to acknowledge the gospels' nature, which, as any scholar who has studied their most ancient surviving forms can attest, is distinguished by literally thousands of copyist errors, editorial intrusions, and regional peculiarities. Thus, to speak of the Judas of Matthew, Mark, Luke, or John is to speak of Judas as he was understood according to different traditions embedded within imperfectly understood processes undertaken by sometimes vastly different Christian communities.

In writing his gospel, Mark clearly had no great designs on establishing Judas's meaning or in interpreting his actions. Thus, any questions surrounding Mark's portrayal of Judas are in many ways codicils to larger questions about Mark's gospel itself. The available evidence overwhelmingly indicates that an oral tradition concerning Jesus existed before Mark was first composed anywhere from three to four decades after the death of Jesus. Does Mark's gospel indicate a break with that oral tradition, or is Mark's gospel the literary consummation of that oral tradition? Did Mark invent key aspects of the Jesus story or merely preserve them? Was Mark the first to join two separate strands of Jesus material (a "words" strand and a "deeds" strand) into what is called a gospel? Did Mark *invent* the gospel form by combining these two strands? These questions are so difficult to answer in no small part because we cannot be sure if Mark *was* the first gospel.

The early-second-century Christian Papias, who recorded an expanded form of Judas's death unlike anything in the gospels, famously noted that he preferred hearing stories about Jesus to reading them. If that was the case, what, exactly, was Papias hearing? Was it our familiar gospels, now-lost gospels, an earlier oral tradition of the sort that Mark might have based his gospel on, or the stories of people who actually knew Jesus and his disciples? Because Papias knew of a version of Judas's death quite different from that of the gospels, we can assume that other parts of the Jesus story were still in flux in the early second century. Actually, we do not have to assume. Works by Clement of Rome, Clement of Alexandria, and Polycarp, all of whom lived around the same time as Papias, refer to sayings they attribute to Jesus that have no precise parallel in our versions of the gospels.

Mark's story of Judas's betrayal begins with Jesus and the disciples in Bethany at the home of Simon the leper. An unnamed woman sits at Jesus's feet and opens "an alabaster jar of very costly ointment," which she proceeds to pour over Jesus's head. According to Mark, "some who were there" grow angry and demand to know why the ointment was wasted. These unnamed people begin to scold the woman. Jesus tells them to leave her alone, because she "has performed a good service for me. For you always have the poor with you . . . but you will not always have me." Immediately after this, Mark goes on, Judas "went to the chief priests in order to betray [Jesus] to them." The chief priests, in turn, promise to pay Judas when the betrayal is enacted. Shortly thereafter, Jesus announces at the Last Supper,

"One of you will betray me, one who is eating with me," though he does not name Judas. Jesus then takes the disciples to the Mount of Olives, where he prays alone at Gethsemane and asks his father to "remove this cup from me." When he returns from his prayer and finds the disciples sleeping, he upbraids them ("Enough!"), before suddenly announcing, "See, my betrayer is at hand."* Judas arrives alongside "a crowd with swords and clubs, from the chief priests, the scribes, and the elders." Judas has told the chief priests that he will identify Jesus with a kiss, which he does while fulsomely calling Jesus "Rabbi!" There Mark's haunting, skeletal account of Judas's betrayal ends.

Mark leaves a number of things unclear. Was Judas actually inspired to betray Jesus over the issue of wasted ointment? Why did the chief priests need Judas's help, exactly? At which point did Judas leave the Last Supper? How did Judas know where to find Jesus once he did leave the Last Supper? All are questions that would occur to any careful reader. Few have read Mark more carefully than Matthew and Luke, and both evidently found Mark's handling of the betrayal either wanting or incomplete. Matthew was probably written between 70 and 80 CE, while Luke was probably written between 80 and 100 CE, so both had access to repositories of narrative and legendary material the earlier Mark was apparently unaware of, or at least did not use. Some of this unique material concerned Judas.

Like Mark, Matthew begins the story of Judas's betrayal in Bethany. Again a woman pours ointment over Jesus's head. This time, however, it is specifically "the disciples" who grow angry. Once more Jesus attempts to abate their anger with instruction similar to that in Mark, after which Judas goes to the chief priests and asks them, "What will you give me if I betray him to you?"

---

* Mark is many things; narratively sophisticated is not one of them. He was known in antiquity as "stump-thumbed" due to his clumsiness and love of redundancy. His idea of an elegant transition is "and." Yet with Jesus's in-dialogue narration of his own arrest, Mark manages an atypical literary stylishness.

The chief priests provide Judas his answer: thirty pieces of silver. (This is an apparent riff on the Hebrew scripture Zechariah. Matthew, more than any other gospel writer, worked with various pieces of scripture flattened out next to him,* extracting as much exegetical serum as possible.) Already the picture is more complicated than in Mark, for Matthew has made money Judas's motivation rather than his reward.

Matthew also changes Jesus's Last Supper proclamation to the Twelve that one of them will betray him, expanding it to indicate that Jesus is aware of the identity of his betrayer— something Mark does not explicitly do—and that the betrayer himself knows he has been discovered. The second-century pagan philosopher Celsus, the first person whom Christianity irritated enough to inspire a book-length denunciation, pointed to Jesus's betrayal as a powerful indictment of his divinity: "Would a god . . . be betrayed by the very men who had been taught by him and shared everything with him?" Mark provided no protection from the criticism that Jesus was too humanly stupid to foresee his own betrayal. Matthew seems to want to show that Jesus was not surprised by the betrayal, thereby shielding him from accusations of fallibility. Unlike Mark's, Matthew's Judas speaks up after Jesus's announcement: "Surely not I, Rabbi?" Matthew also has Jesus address Judas during the betrayal: "Friend, do what you are here to do." After witnessing Jesus's condemnation, Matthew writes that Judas "repented" to such a degree that he brings his payment back to the chief priests. "I have sinned by betraying innocent blood," Judas tells them and, in a move reminiscent of the wicked shepherd of Zechariah, casts his money into the Temple. He then departs and hangs himself. Matthew's Judas

---

* So intent is Matthew on tying Jesus's every action and word to Hebrew scripture that he misinterprets Zechariah 9:9 to nonsensically portray Jesus riding into Jerusalem on both a colt *and* an ass. The church father Jerome ingeniously argued that this obvious flub was symbolic of Jesus's relationship to the Jewish and Gentile worlds.

publicly and unambiguously acknowledges his sin, attempts to disavow those with whom he collaborated, and doles out to himself the most extreme possible penalty. This is not Mark's cipher, or a placard of evil, but a human being whose actions Matthew has at least attempted to comprehend.

Luke apparently struggled hardest with the notion of one of the Twelve being a betrayer. To account for this unfathomable turn of events, Luke opted for an explanation that would long affect Christian thinking: Judas betrayed Jesus because of Satan.* This vastly expanded the reach, efficacy, and anthropological interest of Satan, hitherto an infrequently glimpsed enigma in human consciousness. Luke, like Matthew, was in all likelihood trying to counter the potent question of how the Messiah could have been betrayed by one of his own, but his thinking landed him on a radically different plane.

Luke abandons the Bethany portion of the betrayal narrative and merely notes that as Passover in Jerusalem begins, "Satan entered into Judas called Iscariot, who was one of the twelve." Judas confers with the authorities and once again is paid for his services. His motivation, however, remains demonic; money is a worldly afterthought. At the Last Supper, as in Matthew, Luke's Jesus makes clear that he knows he must be betrayed to fulfill scripture ("For the Son of Man is going as it has been determined") but wishes a woe, similar to that of Mark, on the one who will give him over. Judas, though, is not named. Nor does Judas, when he leads the authorities to his master, apparently get to kiss Jesus. Instead, Jesus stops him short with these words:

---

* Luke was obviously more mindful than Matthew or Mark of the implications inherent to Jesus's having granted to the Twelve the "power and authority over all demons and to cure diseases." This means that Judas, at one point during Jesus's ministry, was believed to have performed miracles. A shocking notion even to the wholly secular, and yet there it is in Christian scripture. Perhaps, in Luke's mind, a man granted by Jesus the ability to corral demons and cure disease could be corrupted only by a force of contending power.

"Judas, is it with a kiss that you are betraying the Son of Man?" This is the only time in the gospel tradition that Jesus addresses Judas by name.

John appears just as bewildered as Luke that one of Jesus's own followers was a traitor. "Did I not choose you, the twelve?" Jesus says to his disciples in the Gospel According to John. "Yet one of you is a devil." Like Mark, John contains a story of Jesus's trip to Bethany, though he lodges there in the home of Lazarus (not, as in Mark, Simon the leper). Lazarus lives with his sisters Mary and Martha, and whereas Mark and Matthew have an unnamed woman anointing Jesus, John tells us it is Mary who takes "a pound of costly perfume made of pure nard" and applies it to Jesus's feet with her hair. In an additional touch of verisimilitude, the house soon fills "with the fragrance of the perfume." John provides other extra details. In Mark, unnamed people get upset at this profligate use of expensive fragrance. In Matthew, it is the disciples. In John, it is *Judas* who complains, "Why was this perfume not sold for three hundred denarii and the money given to the poor?" But John's Judas is no man of conscience. "Judas said this," John writes, "not because he cared about the poor, but because he was a thief." According to John, Judas has been stealing from the common purse since Jesus's ministry began. Interestingly, though, money will have no place in John's version of Judas's betrayal.

This leaves us with John's rendering of the betrayal itself, which is, of all the gospels, the most dramatically compelling. As Passover begins, we learn that the Devil has "already" entered "into the heart of Judas son of Simon Iscariot." Jesus knows this, for "the Father had given all things into his hands." John's Last Supper, which lacks the Eucharistic tradition found in the other gospels, mainly consists of Jesus's talking. One of the first things Jesus says is "Very truly, I tell you, one of you will betray me." The alarmed apostles look about the table and ask who it might be. Jesus answers, "It is the one to whom I give this piece of bread when I have dipped it in the dish." Jesus gives the bread to Judas. The rest of the passage deserves full citation:

> After [Judas] received the piece of bread, Satan entered into him. Jesus said to him, "Do quickly what you are going to do." Now no one at the table knew why he had said this to him. Some thought that, because Judas had the common purse, Jesus was telling him, "Buy what we need for the festival"; or, that he should give something to the poor. So, after receiving the piece of bread, he immediately went out. And it was night.

It is a scene of spooky, inarguable power and scalp-clawing mystification. Why do the disciples not understand Jesus's words to Judas when he has plainly identified him as his betrayer? What is the difference between the earlier Devil that "already" entered Judas and the "Satan" that penetrates him here? This brand of narrative impenetrability is infrequent in John. Unlike the other evangelists, John has the proper storytelling sense to portray Judas's departure from the Last Supper and to explain that Judas knew the postprandial gathering place to which Jesus would lead the Twelve (though John does not name it as Gethsemane). And yet, after subjecting Judas to such close narrative attention, John is content during the betrayal scene to leave Judas "standing with" the authorities and provide him with nothing to say or do. John also has a "detachment" of Roman soldiers there to do the arresting, whom Jesus forces to the ground in an apparent display of his power. The word translated as "detachment" is, in Greek, actually the technical military term for a cohort, which is to say six hundred soldiers, a number that would have been close to every available Roman soldier in Jerusalem. Whether John was simply confused by the terminology or intended to portray six hundred soldiers searching for one man is unclear, though none of the other gospels indicate the presence of Roman soldiers during Jesus's arrest. John, turning his back on the unlovely spectacle, never mentions Judas again.

V.

All these questions and contradictions raise a fundamental question: Was Judas real? Those who believe Judas was real must shadowbox a few small pertinences: There is little information about him in the New Testament; what information it does contain is contradictory; the first generation of church fathers said almost nothing about Judas. Paul, our earliest* Christian commentator, writes in his first letter to the Corinthians of "the night when [Jesus] was betrayed"—literally, "handed over"—and embeds that betrayal within the Last Supper/Eucharist tradition, as do the gospels. But *who,* if anyone, betrayed or handed Jesus over is not specified by Paul.

The scholar Kim Paffenroth writes that Paul "shows that it is quite possible to proclaim an idea of Jesus, his mission, and his passion without any idea of his betrayer," but very smartly goes on to note that it is "practically impossible to have a *story* of him that lacks the crucial poignancy of the betrayer." Paul had a much stronger theological mind than the gospel writers. What he did not have is their storytelling inclination or skills. The difference between them is similar to the difference between an essayist and a fiction writer. If Jesus is an idea in Paul and a character in the gospels, Judas may be an example of the key difference between ideas and stories. Stories need characters, and characters need motives.

---

* Paul, who is sometimes called an "apostle not of the Twelve," wrote his letters decades before the gospels were written. Because standard arrangement of the New Testament places Paul's letters after the gospels and Acts, the temporal relationship between Paul's letters and the gospels is sometimes lost on average Christians. The New Testament was not always arranged in this way. In some of the earliest codices of the New Testament, the Pauline epistles are sandwiched *between* the gospels and the Acts.

Matthew and Luke both attempted to deal with the betrayal as a fulfillment of scripture, but these attempts, even by the wooden-nickel standards of prophecy, are some of the least convincing bits of exegesis found in the gospel tradition. Consider the matter of Hakeldama, the Field of Blood. In Matthew, after Judas has thrown his money into the Temple, the chief priests gather it up out of the belief that it is "not lawful" for such money to be placed in the treasury. To cleanse the sum, they use it "to buy the potter's field as a place to bury foreigners." Matthew writes that this "fulfilled what had been spoken through the prophet Jeremiah." The prophecy being fulfilled here does not exist in any surviving form of Jeremiah. Matthew appears to be mixing various bits of Hebrew scripture, some of it perhaps from Zechariah. This has long baffled Christian commentators, who have generated all manner of explanations and excuses for the inconsistency. Meanwhile, in Acts, Luke refers to Judas's having "acquired a field with the reward of his wickedness" and allows Peter to claim scriptural precedence for the occurrence: "For it is written in the book of Psalms, 'Let his homestead become desolate, / and let there be no one to live in it.'" This is apparently a citation of Psalm 69:25, which no longer contains the words Peter cites.

Leaving aside the fact that Matthew and Luke refer back to passages of Hebrew scripture that are no longer extant, it is impossible for both accounts to be simultaneously true. In Matthew, the priests buy the field. In Acts, Judas buys the field himself. In Matthew, it is to serve as a foreigners' burial place. In Acts, there are no burial overtones (though some scholars have suggested *Hakeldama* is a distant Greek corruption of "sleeping place" or "cemetery"). In Matthew, the "blood" of the field refers to that of blood money. In Luke, the "blood" appears to refer to that which Judas spilled onto its ground.

Luke also opted for a more economical placement of Judas's death, saving it for the beginning of his Acts of the Apostles. Here, the death (not the suicide) of Judas comes during Peter's

address to the believers in Jerusalem. We are told that Judas, after
acquiring his field, fell "headlong" and "burst open in the middle
and all his bowels gushed out." A somewhat similar account of
Judas's death can be found in fragments of a second-century
work by Papias of Hierapolis:

> Judas wandered in this world, a great example of impi-
> ety. His flesh swelled so much that where a cart went
> through easily, he was not able to go through, not even
> the mass of his head; they say that his eyelids swelled
> so much that he could not see any light at all. . . . His
> genitals were more enlarged and unsightly than any
> other deformity, while blood and worms flowed from
> all over his body, necessarily doing great harm just
> by themselves. . . . [T]hey say that he died on his own
> property, and that on account of the stench that place
> is desolate and uninhabited even until now.

Note the fixation on stench, the wormy corruption of the
body's sensual parts, the prolonged nature of the suffering. Note,
too, what has been lost from Acts: the name of the field, how
Judas came to possess it, and any notion of scriptural fulfillment.
The accounts of Judas's death in both Acts and Papias have much
in common with an ancient genre that might be called the Horrible Death, in which a deserving fiend suffers a pustular and
often disintegration- or worm-related end.*
    Scribes working throughout Christianity's first five centu-

---

* In Acts, Herod Agrippa I is "eaten by worms." In the apocryphal Jewish work 2
Maccabees, the Hellenizing ruler Antiochus IV Epiphanes falls out of his chariot so
"as to torture every limb"; soon "the ungodly man's body" is aswarm "with worms." In
Josephus, Herod the Great suffers from something described as "mortification of the
genitals," and a Sicarii accomplice named Catullus sees his bowels "eaten through"
before falling out of his body. In Eusebius, a Christian tormentor has a "suppurative
inflammation" afflict "the middle of his genitals," while his bowels are overtaken by
"a teeming indescribable mass of worms." Etc.

ries were troubled by the New Testament's discrepancies when it came to Judas's end, and several changed a number of passages to bring them into agreement, but the invasive solutions provided by devout editors were eventually judged unsatisfactory. In time, a process called harmonization emerged within Christian thought, which involves taking contradictory passages from different gospels and explaining away the differences by creative imagining. In Judas's case, this meant positing a death by hanging, as Matthew writes, but then a rope breaks, and a swollen, distended body falls and breaks open on the ground, as Luke writes. When one chooses to view the gospels not as singular texts with different points of view and distinct literary and historical contexts, the New Testament becomes a story as seamless as serial television, which is probably why harmonization remains the prevalent mode among conservative Christian apologists. Yet we can thank the gormless convolutions of harmonization for one aspect of the Judas story. Matthew never indicates that Judas was remembered as having used Hakeldama as his place of self-murder or being buried there, and Luke's account as to where exactly Judas expired is vague. Only through harmonization did Hakeldama become known as the last earthly place on which Judas set eyes.

VI.

Let his homestead become desolate,
and let there be no one to live in it.

Luke was citing scripture he believed fulfilled prophecy; he might as well have been forecasting Hakeldama's future. Desolate? Lunar. Let there be no one to live in it? Neither Jay nor I had seen anyone for hours. It was the sort of hot, quiet day in which one could almost hear the faint sizzle of solar combustion. While Jay sat on a stone and read a book, I filled my notepad with doodles of the hilltop Old City's skyline. We were as mutually oblivious and silently occupied as castaways who had given up all hope of rescue. I had planned to ask all those we encountered at Hakeldama what moved them to come here. Morbid curiosity or historical inquisitiveness? Spiritual openness or angry righteousness? Sadness expressed or vengefulness savored? As it happened, my only visitor thus far had been a small gray lizard. It approached, stopped next to my shoe, and locked into a pose of alert stillness. The moment I lifted my foot, the lizard shot away, a living bullet.

Jay suddenly said my name and told me to look up. On the ridge above Hakeldama, standing behind a barbed-wire fence, three sheep stared down at us with dull, domesticated half interest. They had approached along the same path earlier used by the Palestinian woman, who remained the only human being we had seen in the immediate area. One of the sheep was adobe brown and wore a bright, many-colored collar. The other two were collarless and white, or approximately white: clumps of dirt and dung dangled from their thick wool coats. A man came up behind the sheep, speaking to them in Arabic. It appeared that he was their shepherd, an occupation that came with certain sartorial expectations, all of which he atomized. He wore dusty jeans and a green-and-black Windbreaker with a prominent tear on one sleeve. He said nothing; neither did we. Two small children came up behind the shepherd, both carrying long wooden switches. One of the children began to apply his switch, harmlessly but repeatedly, to the backside of the brown sheep, which somehow seemed to sigh.

The shepherd appeared neither friendly nor unfriendly, and I debated whether or not to say hello. Jay had already returned to his book. Without saying anything, I returned to my doodles. A few minutes later, I looked up again. The shepherd, his small flock, and the children were still standing there, the cloudless sky behind them a wall of brilliant, wet-paint blue. I wondered if this man regarded us as trespassers. Was this perhaps his land? Did his children play here? Did his sheep graze here? All seemed remote possibilities. The land probably belonged to the nearby monastery, if anyone, and the only game I could imagine being played at Hakeldama was who could run away from it the fastest.

Below us, on the road that snaked along the bottom of the Hinnom valley, a hip-hop-blaring white sedan motored toward Silwan. A historically Arab neighborhood adjacent to the Old City, Silwan had lately become the object of a considerable settling effort by Jewish Israelis. One large Jewish development there is named for Jonathan Pollard, the convicted American spy who gave U.S. military secrets to Israel.

I looked up at the shepherd and waved. To my surprise, he smiled and waved back. To him I made another, more complicated gesture that involved pointing at myself, a two-fingered walking pantomime, and then pointing at him. Once he figured out what I was trying to suggest, he nodded and waved us up. We circled our way toward the ridge, stepping over what had to be the most halfhearted barbed-wire fence in all of Israel.

From the top of the ridge, we could see more of Silwan. I had read that parts of this neighborhood, which filled a valley and swept handsomely up its hillsides, were lovely, but many of its muddy and squatly woeful facing buildings resembled nothing so much as a charmless San Francisco. We could see something far more charmless, however, and this was a section of what the Israelis called the Separation Barrier and the Palestinians called the Racial Segregation or Apartheid Wall. The Israeli government proposed a limited barrier to separate Jewish Israelis from Palestinians in the early 1990s, during the first intifada. Construction on a barrier between the Gaza Strip and Tel Aviv began in 1994, but as Israeli-Palestinian relations worsened and finally ruptured in 2000 with the beginning of the second intifada, which killed more than eight hundred people, the Israeli government called for a far more comprehensive barrier.

The majority of the barrier was found in rural areas, and in those places it was, for the most part, a militarized chain-link fence. In urban areas, the barrier took the form of an eight-foot-high concrete wall, which was purportedly intended to frustrate snipers. The portion of the barrier we now looked upon was of the concrete-wall variety and lay close to Silwan's southern edge. It was nearly finished. Another proposed portion of the barrier would brush the edge of the neighborhood of Givat Hananya or Abu Tor, which was found directly to the south of Hakeldama and had the distinction of being one of Jerusalem's only mixed Jewish-Arab neighborhoods. As far as I could figure from the barrier's currently planned coordinates, Hakeldama would be hemmed in on at least two sides but would not fall inside it. On one older, outdated map, the barrier's proposed path seemed purposely altered to avoid enclosing Hakeldama—a place, it appeared, no one had any wish to claim.

The shepherd welcomed Jay and me to his ridge with a handshake, his left hand placed over his heart. His name was Nazar, and he claimed to be thirty-four years old. If he had said his shoes were thirty-four years old, I might have believed him. Nazar looked at least fifty and seemed unwell in the purest diagnostic sense of the word. One of his eyes had the cloudy opaqueness of a mood ring, and his mouth was filled with the stained and broken teeth of a fairy-tale goblin.

Nazar spoke halting English. I asked him if the children with him were his. They were not. He did not know whose they were. Sometimes, he said, they walked with him while he grazed his sheep. I looked at the children. They were ten or eleven, black-haired, brown-eyed, their faces just beginning to shift from adolescent roundness to preteen angularity. I said hello. One smiled, but neither responded. The smiling boy was wearing a Darth Maul T-shirt and had a large half-moon scar under his eye. The other boy shifted his gaze from me to Jay and back again in the sad way of someone who had come to take his invisibility for granted.

When I asked Nazar if many people came to Hakeldama, he did not seem to know what I was talking about. I pointed down toward the field. Hakeldama. The Field of Blood. Suddenly he was nodding. I asked, "Do you know the story of this place?"

"I know the story," he said. "Yes."

"Judas?"

"Yehuda. Yes. I know the story." To prove it, he jerked an imaginary noose around his neck and smiled. "Yehuda."

"Do many people visit Yehuda's field?"

"Yes, some America, some Britannia. Not many people. One day, people come. Two day, no people."

"What do you think of the field?"

Nazar thought for a moment. It was clear he regarded this question as odd. "Nothing."

"Nothing?"

"Yes. Nothing."

"Do these children know the story of the field?"

He spoke to them in Arabic. The children emphatically shook their heads. He looked back at me. "They don't know."

It seemed apt that of the three people I encountered at Hakeldama, one did not care two figs about its associations, and the others knew nothing about it. Nazar's brown sheep bleated irritably. One of the children hit the brown sheep on its rump with his switch. The sheep trundled along down the ridge, stopped, and bleated again. "These are your sheep?" I asked.

"Yes," he said. But I already knew that, because Nazar had already told me.

Our conversational oscillograph was flatlining. Out of this straining awkwardness, Nazar suddenly pulled a question. "How big is your stay?"

"A few days."

"Yes? Good."

"And how about you?" I asked him. "Do you live nearby?"

"Yes, I live." He swept his hand toward Silwan, into which a lone red motorcycle with an unhelmeted driver was flying up a path.

"Can you see your house from here?"

Nazar did not answer. Instead, he turned and pointed to the southwest, where the keg-like King Solomon Hotel rose up from the horizon. "You live?"

"No," I said, pointing to the west. "Over there. Yemin Moshe." This was a tiered residential complex of apartment buildings, all of them architecture-school elegant and well tended. It was, needless to say, a Jewish neighborhood.

Nazar nodded glumly and seemed to weigh the advisability of bringing up something else he wished to address. I waited. "Before," he said finally, "I live two houses." He was vaguely aggrieved now, began to speak faster, and his grammar quickly became a casualty. These two houses were also in Silwan, but neither was a house he currently lived in. Apparently, a Britannia had wanted to help him with one of his homes, his home, which is under the ground, on the other side, which big shot came to help, help, help, but he come now away, and no help. And three hundred, which is three hundred? Three zero zero, which is this? Three hundred. Yes, Britannia help three hundred, he try but no help. And then Israelis take his home.

I stood there, nodding in a careful, piecing-it-together way. Jay and I would spend the next four days exchanging theories as to the precise nature of these described machinations.

Once again Nazar pointed off into the distance, toward the Separation Barrier/Apartheid Wall, which suddenly looked to me less like a wall and more like a dam, which, I supposed, it was. He began to say something about the barrier but did not have the words. His hand dropped. He shook his head and looked at the ground. He had said as much as he could.

"What is this little fence for?" I asked him, placing my hand atop one of the barbed-wire fence's wooden stakes.

Nazar looked up. "For small people and animal not come here. No fence, maybe big fall."

I thanked Nazar for his time. "No problem," he said, and again, fumblingly, we shook hands. As Jay and I started away, the muezzins of Jerusalem's many mosques began the *adhan,* or call to prayer. They did not begin simultaneously. At first, there were four distinct voices, at least one of which did not sound prerecorded, but they were soon joined by others, and more after that. I had heard the *adhan* in many cities of the world and had never found it anything other than an ideal of sonic beauty. The call to prayer made mornings less lonely, made late afternoons more melancholy, and filled the evening with strange, silvery omens. But I had never heard a call to prayer quite like this growing gale of sound. The voices—another had just joined— lost their lovely spirals of individuality and overlapped into a formless meteorological whole, something everywhere at once but nowhere specifically. I was not sure if this sensation was due to the acoustics of the valley or the sheer number of voices or was a simple acknowledgment of the hostility these calls to prayer both provoked and gave voice to. For a moment, it felt as though the Hinnom valley's every ghost had turned banshee in anger and now sang and swirled around us. When we looked back at Nazar, he was using a large, flat rock to drive the fence stake I had touched deeper into the ground.

VII.

It was difficult not to be frustrated by the barrenness of Hakel-dama, as well as by the myriad contradictions and uncer-tainties surrounding Judas's betrayal of Jesus. Of course, the greatest mystery was the central one: Why? Why did Judas betray Jesus? Any attempted explanation for Judas's actions is limited by the paucity of the source material (not that this has stopped anyone). The earliest Christian writers to inch beyond the gospels' minimalist portrayal of Judas sought answers in his childhood. A work today known as *The Arabic Infancy Gospel,* written around the fifth or sixth century, is the first sur-viving piece of Christian literature to have imagined Judas as a boy. For its author, the seeds of evil were planted deep: the nasty tyke, already possessed by Satan, strikes his fellow toddler Jesus (on the very spot a Roman lance will later penetrate) and makes him cry. For this writer, evil was a matter not of behavior, or even choice, but of being. Such a villain had to suffer, yet the suffering of Papias's and Luke's Judas, however extreme and loathsome, is also somewhat impersonal—a scary, vaguely ludicrous bedtime story. In the following centuries, Judas found himself pushed down on ever more horrifying nail beds. The most famous example is contained in the *Inferno* section of *The Divine Comedy,* wherein Dante marvels at the sight of a three-headed Satan, each of his mouths filled with a sinner "torn up by teeth . . . that stripped their backs to show the bones beneath." One of these sinners is Judas, his extruding legs kicking helplessly and eternally. Virgil tells Dante,

> With just his legs
> He signals pain. His head is not on show.
> We do not see or hear the way he begs
> For that same mercy he did not bestow.

One of the strangest and most elaborate retellings of the Judas story can be found in Jacobus de Voragine's *Golden Legend,** an audacious churchman's attempt to collate, curate, and expound on the lives of literally hundreds of figures from the first Christian millennium. (It is, essentially, Christian legend encyclopedized.) According to Jacobus, Judas's mother, Cyborea, has a

---

* Jacobus was born around 1230 in Varazze, a town on the Gulf of Genoa in northwestern Italy. He became a Dominican friar early in his life and was eventually elected archbishop of Genoa in 1292, six years before his death. The historical trustworthiness of his two-volume masterwork is questionable, to say the least, and some of its information is based on sources that might not have existed outside Jacobus's mind. *The Golden Legend*'s popularity during medieval times is attributable to its energetic, sometimes witty, and often quite bizarre re-creations of saintly lives and deaths. During the Renaissance, however, *The Golden Legend* was suppressed due to its (in Erasmus's words) "strange lies," which is unfair: Jacobus displays not a little skepticism in his accounts and often includes contrasting stories in the interest, one assumes, of his conception of impartial inquiry.

dream that she will bear a son "so wicked" he might destroy the Jewish people. When Judas is born, his alarmed parents put him in a basket and push him out to sea. The queen of an island called Scariot happens to be walking along the beach when the basket washes ashore. Barren of an heir, the queen decides to raise Judas as her own, "in royal style." Then the queen unexpectedly becomes pregnant; once her child is born, "Judas frequently maltreated the royal child and made him cry." The queen, in frustration, tells Judas he was a foundling; Judas, in turn, kills the queen's son and flees to Jerusalem to "the household of Pilate, who was then governor of Judea." Pilate adores Judas, treating him "as a favorite." One day, Pilate, while strolling around his palace, sees a nearby orchard and sends Judas to fetch some fruits. The orchard's owner comes out and confronts Judas. They argue; Judas kills him, quickly disposes of the body, and marries the man's wife. Of course, the man he has killed is his father, and the woman he has married is his mother. When this Judas discovers his life is plagiarized Sophocles, he turns to Jesus and begins to follow his ministry.

Accounts such as Jacobus's contain an implicit rehabilitation of Judas, if only because he is shown to be the victim of forces beyond his comprehension. Although Jacobus wrote at roughly the same time as Dante, we can see a differently perceived Judas taking shape. The first-century minds of the gospel writers imagined a Judas who caused the tumblers of prophecy to fall into place. Jacobus's freer mind was able to inject agency into the Judas story, if only to cruelly drown it. Being evil, Jacobus seems to suggest, is not the same thing as being cursed. Amid the spearlike certainties of medieval Christian thought, this Judas comes as something of a respite, and his fate might have struck many of Jacobus's readers as being much like their own: resoundingly unfair, difficult to comprehend, and pointless to resist.

The most prominent form of Judas rehabilitation imagines him in terms that could be called heroic, if tragically misguided. This Judas is typically a reluctant traitor who turns Jesus over to the authorities for reasons ranging from frustration to impatience to the certainty that a captured Jesus will finally act, take up his Davidic crown, and drive the Romans from Palestine. Even though the gospels contain nothing to support this view, the Judas of ardent nationalism has been a popular one since the nineteenth century and became even more popular in the latter half of the twentieth, when post-Holocaust sensitivities to the conspicuously Jewish role Judas had long played in the Christian narrative intensified.

The idea that Judas betrayed Jesus in order to save Israel is often called the De Quincey theory, so-named for the opium-eating memoirist Thomas De Quincey, the first writer to popularize (though not originate) the notion. He published his views in an essay titled "Judas Iscariot" in 1857, a time when textual criticism, unaligned with any religious creed and much of it German, was beginning its first invasion of the New Testament. De Quincey argues that the Twelve were guilty of the "delusion" that peaceful means could succeed in bringing the Kingdom of Heaven down to earth. He goes on to refer to Jesus as "sublimely over-gifted" and "like Shakspere's [sic] great creation Prince Hamlet, not correspondingly endowed for the business of action." In De Quincey's excitable mind, Judas was the only member of Jesus's circle willing to take the necessary action to place Jesus "at the head of an insurrectionary movement."

This is, in many ways, the Judas contemporary audiences are left with, a man who can be imagined only as having acted out of hope for insurrection or some other ostensibly rational purpose. Perhaps this merely reveals a reasonable human dissatisfaction with the Judas story, which centuries of pogroms, many of them driven by Christian determination to blame the death of Jesus on Jews, have made morally appalling. The Son of God, betrayed by the son of the Jews. This was the view of Augustine and many other early Christian thinkers, but only in the sludgier corners of the Internet could one dare publicly entertain such thoughts today.

In 2006, the public received yet another ideation of Judas when the lost* *Gospel of Judas,* a work written in the mid-second century, was finally translated and published by a team of scholars working for the National Geographic Society. This gospel—a self-applied misnomer, in that it is structured not like a gospel but rather as an interminable cosmic dialogue between Jesus and Judas—had in some manner come to the attention of the church father Irenaeus, who condemned it for its portrayal of Judas "as knowing the truth as none of the others [that is, the Twelve] did."

In *The Lost Gospel,* one of many quickly published books about *The Gospel of Judas,* the journalist Herbert Krosney writes, "This version of Judas's story was too controversial for early Church leaders like Irenaeus. By condemning it, they erased it from history, never to be seen again." Krosney also argues that "Jesus Christ arranges his own execution" in this controversial gospel by asking Judas to betray him, without remembering that in the canonical gospel tradition Jesus implicitly does the same thing. Krosney refers to *Judas* as being "unlike anything that you have read before," which is simply not true. Many dozens of novels, plays, stories, poems, and films have presented essentially the same story that Krosney spells out.

Despite these insinuations, *The Gospel of Judas* is a piece of sectarian polemical literature aimed at rival Christians. It is not, and does not pretend to be, an account of the life and death of Jesus. As the scholar April D. DeConick has established, *The Gospel of Judas* makes no claims for a heroic Judas acting in concert with Jesus and in fact condemns him more harshly than the gospels. "Our modern consciousness appears to need a 'good' Judas," DeConick writes. "We have generated plot after plot, character after character, story after story, to exonerate Judas, to figure out his motivations, to make him our friend and hero."

* "Lost" must be qualified: *Judas* had drifted around the antiquities underground for decades, its existence known to several scholars, though its contents were not.

To find this man in *The Gospel of Judas* required considerable effort. The gospel came out of the traditions of Sethian
Christianity, so named for Adam and Eve's son Seth, whom
these ancient Christians believed had secret rituals and guidance written on stone tablets that they alone possessed. Sethian
Christians additionally regarded the now widely accepted Christian theology of atonement (which presupposes that Jesus died
for our sins) as little more than child sacrifice. DeConick refers
to the Sethians as the "most confrontational" group among the
second century's many heterodox Christians, as they apparently
viewed Christians who claimed direct descent from apostolic
teaching with special disgust.*

DeConick argues, in fact, that *The Gospel of Judas* is basically an anti-apostolic parody. Here, the apostles are presented
as having dreams involving child sacrifice and sodomy, which
Jesus tells them are representative of the "people that you lead
astray." Judas, who in the work receives both illumination and
condemnation, is merely Jesus's cosmological sounding board—
though the gospel's elliptical presentation of the betrayal, with
which it concludes, is undeniably powerful: "And [the scribes]
approached Judas. They said to him, 'What are you doing here?
Aren't you the disciple of Jesus?' He answered them as they
wished. Then Judas received some money. He handed him over
to them."

---

* From our modern viewpoint Sethian beliefs are more or less incomprehensible,
but here goes nothing: Sethian Christianity's "prime creator god" was known as Ialdabaoth (an apparent corruption of "Yahweh, Lord of the Sabbath"), and his agents
were called archons, all of whom were thought to employ adjutant angels as gov-
ernors of their respective realms. The god worshipped by apostolic Christians was,
to Sethians, a lesser god in thrall to Ialdabaoth. Jesus's crucifixion was a trick on
Ialdabaoth, who sought to capture Jesus's dying soul. Jesus, however, eluded capture, and the release of his soul resulted in the defeat of the archons and terminated
Ialdabaoth's control over humanity. This sounds preposterous, but so do many of
orthodox Christianity's more difficult postulations. The difference is that orthodox
Christianity has an available and highly esteemed record of philosophical inquiry to
burnish it. No doubt the Sethians had their Augustine, too.

VIII.

To early Christians, a horribly punished Judas reaffirmed order. To modern Christians, a horribly punished Judas questions the very nature of Christian redemption. Irenaeus, in his dismissal of *The Gospel of Judas,* referred to "the mystery of the betrayal," and it is a mystery, one deep and confounding enough to have taxed the best minds of Christianity. In the Gospel According to John, Jesus says, "I lay down my life in order to take it up again. No one takes it from me, but I lay it down of my own accord." If this is the case, if Jesus died willingly, how, then, can Judas be blamed for the betrayal? What, exactly, was betrayed?

One early Christian named Marcion pondered this very question. A rich Greek shipping mogul and bishop's son, Marcion rejected every apostle but Paul as false; his conception of Jesus's divinity was, incredibly, even higher than that of what became Christian orthodoxy. Marcion's Jesus was an entirely new god, a "stranger" god, who had no relation to the Jewish God. To gather support for his beliefs, he relocated to Rome and cobbled together his own proto–New Testament, which contained most but not all of the Pauline letters and what is believed to have been a heavily redacted form of the Gospel According to Luke, though Marcion dispensed with Luke's Acts.* One of the most powerful, successful, and influential Christian heterodoxies of its or any other time, Marcionism remained active three hundred years after its founder's death—smaller Marcionite communities endured until the *tenth* century—and some of its beliefs traveled as far as Afghanistan. Marcion himself was excommunicated by the Roman church in the mid-140s; the church even bit the bullet and returned his many tithes and alms. Marcion's conception of Jesus nevertheless prompts serious theological questions. If

---

* This was the first known assemblage of New Testament writings, though almost all textual evidence of Marcion's canon was destroyed. Marcion was also the first to identify Paul as the author of 2 Thessalonians, Colossians, and Ephesians.

Jesus truly was who he said he was, for instance, could he be betrayed? To a Marcionite, the answer was obvious. Marcion's "gospel" thus contained no mention of the Judas tradition.

In the third century, Origen, early Christianity's greatest theologian, asked similar questions about Judas, and one of his answers came out of the belief, which he helped formulate, in what is called universal reconciliation, which holds that all souls, including demonic ones, will eventually receive salvation, in part because the fall of humankind into sin was a universal event beyond the control of those who were not yet born. (Universal reconciliation was declared anathema by the church in the mid-sixth century, and Origen himself was named a heretic—though an often fondly regarded heretic whose work many thoughtful Christians enjoyed on the sly for centuries.) Origen believed that Judas began as a faithful, believing disciple of Jesus but suffered some crisis of faith that allowed Satan to influence him. Judas was, all the same, saved. To support this view, Origen noted the manner in which Judas behaved after the betrayal, as well as his "agonizing remorse when he repented of sins that he could no longer bear even to live." This showed that Judas "could not utterly despise what he had learnt from Jesus."

One of Origen's most moving struggles was his attempt to reconcile Jesus's apparent foreknowledge of Judas's betrayal with the freedom of choice supposedly granted by God. Origen, who was deeply conversant with Greek philosophy and litera-ture, used the example of Oedipus to show that foreknowledge did not overrule free will because foreknowledge was not caus-ative and prognostication was not instigation: "For it does not follow from the fact that Jesus correctly predicted the actions of the traitor and of the one who denied him, that he was respon-sible for their impiety and wicked conduct." While Origen acknowledged that citing a story from mythology was somewhat unusual ("historicity does not affect the argument"), he did not have many other places to turn. Judas was forcing even the most brilliant Christians to confront questions that the faith seemed ill-equipped to answer.

Why was Judas's soul the price of God's vacation into mortality? What does that mean—not only for Judas, but for all his fellow mortals? Does this not mean we are merely divine playthings? How can God love any of us if he was willing to so carefully arrange the condemnation of one of us?

IX.

On our last day in Jerusalem, Jay decided during breakfast that he would regret leaving Jerusalem without seeing the Garden of Gethsemane. I had seen enough sites of invented significance over the last few days and opted to stay behind in our rented apartment in Yemin Moshe and read. Jay set out. Forty minutes later, he returned. "Something's going on over by the Aqsa Mosque," he said. "Something noisy and violent."

We turned on the television. Whatever was happening near the Aqsa Mosque, CNN International was already on the scene. Apparently, during the afternoon prayer, a cleric at the Aqsa Mosque addressed the Israeli restoration effort that was under way directly beneath Jerusalem's largest and most famous mosque. The Israelis were repairing the mosque's entrance ramp, which had become badly weakened. Jay and I had passed by the site several times during our walks around the city, and the amount of earth the restoration had broken was significant. Understandably, many of Jerusalem's Muslims were curious about what, exactly, was being done beneath their holy acreage, from which, they believed, Muhammad had commenced his Night Journey. The Israelis had installed twenty-four-hour observation cameras around the restoration site to allay local Muslim fears, but not many Palestinians had the wherewithal, impetus, or patience to see for themselves what the cameras were broadcasting.

During the afternoon prayer, the Aqsa cleric convinced a number of young men that the Israelis were not, in fact, restoring an entrance ramp but rather *dismantling* the mosque's foundation. Several dozen—perhaps as many as a hundred— keyed-up young Palestinians shortly emerged from the Aqsa Mosque and began hurling rocks and bottles at the first Israeli soldiers and police officers they encountered. The Israeli security forces responded with tear gas and rubber bullets. The Palestinians responded with more rocks. Eventually, one enterprising Palestinian got his hands on a deadlier weapon—a pistol of some kind—and fired back, to the result of some extended, sporadically exchanged gunfire. A few Palestinians—including some armed ones—had in the meantime barricaded themselves within a nearby building. I suggested to Jay that we hail a cab and figure out a way to get to the top of the Mount of Olives, which looks down on the Old City. From there, we would have a good view of the standoff.

Right outside Yemin Moshe's security gate we found a forty-year-old Palestinian man glumly sitting on the curb beside his Mazda. That he was a freelance cabbie was clear from the plain, detachable TAXI sign affixed to his roof, but his car seemed well maintained. We raised our hands to him, at which he sprang to his feet and waved us over. I told him where we wanted to go.

"It will be hard to visit the top of the Mount of Olives today," he said. "There's trouble in the Old City."

I was a journalist, I said. My friend here was a historian. Trouble in the Old City was precisely what we wanted to see.

The man looked us over. He was wearing a thick brown sport coat, the arms and back of which were somehow covered with burs. (Did he live in a thicket?) The breeze was having its way with his thinning black hair and his teeth were in predictably dire condition, but he had a tough, trustworthy face. "Okay," he said.

His name was Achmed, and he had been born and raised in Jerusalem. For the first few minutes of our ride, Achmed referred to his fellow Palestinians as "they," until, finally, he tired of that game and turned around and asked us what we thought of the conflict. I did not share with Achmed the judgment of one of the characters in a Keith Gessen novel, with which I largely agreed, which was this: the basic problem was that Palestinians were idiots and Israelis were assholes. Nonetheless, Jay and I told him what we thought. Our answers seemed to satisfy Achmed, who now began to refer to the Palestinians as "we."

"You may not sense this," he said, "but, actually, I am a hopeless man. For the first time in this life, I have no more hope."

"No hope at all?" Jay asked.

"Life now is too bad," Achmed said. "The lack of services, the wall, all these . . . *crazy* settlers. We don't know how to negotiate; we never have. They use that against us."

Achmed's first attempts to find an unblocked road up to the Mount of Olives were not successful. At every turn, Israeli security forces turned us away. Standing guard at one checkpoint, however, was an Israeli soldier with whom Achmed claimed to have good relations. Achmed stopped, got out of the car, walked over to the lieutenant, and tried to lobby for our passage through his checkpoint. The young lieutenant greeted Achmed warmly but soon became a looped reel of gestural negation. When Achmed got back into the cab, he said, "I told him you were journalists. He told me that made you even less likely to get through."

I asked, "So what now? Is that it?"

Achmed fiddled with his radio's volume knob, though the radio was not on. "There is another way. A longer way. Through our neighborhoods." This would involve circling Jerusalem almost entirely, whereupon we would come to a street we could see from where we idled but could not currently reach, for it was on the other side of the lieutenant's checkpoint. "You will visit some neighborhoods that not many tourists get to see," Achmed said. Jay and I agreed: the longer way it was.

Twenty minutes later, at least according to a sign, we passed beyond Jerusalem's city limits. Five minutes later, we passed back into Jerusalem, but through neighborhoods that seemed more desert villages than suburbs. All were poor, and a few appeared devastated. Some had raw sewage streaming down the streets. "They could fix it," Achmed said when I asked about the sewage, "but they don't. You will not see such conditions in Zion Square."

As we rolled through one neighborhood, the children looked up from their improvised toys—sticks, half-deflated soccer balls, broken kites—to eye us suspiciously. "Why aren't these roads blocked off by soldiers?" Jay asked.

"Israeli soldiers don't know these roads," Achmed said.

At this Jay was puzzled. "But we're in Jerusalem."

"Yes."

"They don't know streets *inside* the city limits?"

Achmed shrugged: the ignorance of Israeli soldiers was not his problem. The deeper into Palestinian Jerusalem we pushed, the more homemade truck-tire-piled Palestinian checkpoints we were beginning to encounter. I asked what they were for. Achmed explained that anyone wounded in the gunfire in the Old City would be brought to a Palestinian hospital, up here, rather than taken to an Israeli hospital, down there. Later in the day, Israeli security would drive up, visit all the Palestinian hospitals, and arrest anyone being treated for gunshot wounds. These truck-tire checkpoints would be lit on fire and abandoned as soon as any Israeli security forces approached. Which meant the security forces would have to clear the burning tires themselves. Make them do it enough times, Palestinian thinking went, and maybe they would give up and turn around.

Somewhere we had taken a wrong turn. We faced the wrong side of a dead end within a Palestinian neighborhood cleaved in two by Israeli settlers, or so Achmed claimed. (We got lost, I was sure, due to Achmed's insistence on pointing out every single settler's home and describing the damage they had done to the neighborhood.) As Achmed turned around, a dozen Palestinian children poured from the mouth of a nearby driveway and surrounded our car. All at once, they started to punch the windows and slam their small, rocklike fists down on the hood, shouting, "Yehudi! Yehudi!" Instantly, Achmed was outside the car, screaming at them. Every child scattered and fled through various door- and alleyways. When Achmed returned to his seat, his eyes were all wildness and fire.

"Why did they do that?" I asked.

Achmed turned and looked at me. "They thought you were Jews."

"What did you tell them?"

Achmed looked at me. "I told them you aren't Jewish."

"You haven't asked us if we are Jewish. Do you want to know?"

"In my cab," he said, "you are free to be what you are." With that, he turned off his meter, turned the car around, found the street he was looking for, and steered us up a series of steep, narrow paths that did not appear navigable at all. The neighborhoods were now a-prowl with packs of young men obviously looking for trouble. I realized why when Achmed switched on the radio, which was spectrum to spectrum with news of the troubles in the Old City.

Finally, near the base of the Mount of Olives, a dirty, unpromising alley spat us out onto a street a hundred yards *behind* the checkpoint manned by Achmed's lieutenant friend. And it had only taken an hour. I patted Achmed on the shoulder. "You're good."

"No one can close everything," he said. "Not even Israelis."

We stopped in the parking lot of the Seven Arches Hotel, the large, spacious patio of which provided panoramic views of the entire city. I asked Achmed if he would wait for us in the car while Jay and I had a look. "We are together now," Achmed said. "I will wait."

"Actually," Jay said, "do you want to come with us?"

Achmed answered by plucking his keys from the ignition.

We arranged ourselves along the farthest edge of the Seven Arches Hotel's patio and looked down. The first thing we saw:

the Jewish tombstones that covered much of the mount's slopes. Some Jews believe that the Messiah will appear on the Mount of Olives, after which the dead will be raised. Those Jews had paid what Achmed estimated as around sixty thousand dollars for the privilege to be buried near the Messiah's arrival point. They were, in other words, avoiding an uphill walk on a day in which all known physical laws would be negated. Beyond the tombstones were the golden onion domes of Magdalene Church, the Garden of Gethsemane, a highway, and, just past that, near the Lions' Gate, three light-flashing Palestinian ambulances waiting for more wounded. Around the corner from the ambulances, half a dozen Israeli soldiers were maneuvering along the city walls. This was why the Israelis did not want people coming up here, Achmed told us. From this vantage point, anyone with a cell phone could tell the Palestinians barricaded inside their redoubt where Israeli troops were and what they were doing. I looked around. A few feet from us were several Palestinian men with cell phones, into which they spoke quietly.

Elsewhere in the city, life, to coin a phrase, went on. Cars filled the highways. Tourists moved through Old City streets. In the distance: Israeli skyscrapers, Palestinian slums, the soft yellow desert and its hard brown rocks. A few feet away from us, to our right, Ben Wedeman, CNN International's reporter, went live. Wedeman told the camera that so far seventeen Palestinians and thirteen Israeli soldiers had been wounded. He was dressed in a pine-green sweater, a cell phone clipped to his waist. His cameraman was eating a falafel with one hand and keeping his camera steady with the other. On our left was a Russian reporter, who I gathered was delivering the same statistics. Above us a dirigible floated into view and circled the Aqsa Mosque.

Suddenly gunshots, many of them, from the Lions' Gate, where, yesterday, Jay and I had walked the Via Dolorosa. Another peal of automatic-weapons fire scared up a ribbon of birds, which poured so liquidly from the Aqsa Mosque it was as though the building had been turned upside down. There was real fighting down there now, the automatic-weapons fire punctuated by gas-grenade flashes. Someone was firing on an advancing column of Israeli soldiers from the second floor of what looked like an apartment building. Then the building's first floor ignited from within; smoke poured from every window. Achmed guessed that the Israelis were trying to gas out the building's inhabitants. Then I remembered: a school was on that corner.

Something exploded down the street from the besieged apartment building, though what was unclear; its boom took a surprisingly long time to reach us. A Japanese man next to me said, in English, "Oh wow. Oh my God *wow*." Another explosion, then, in the same place. These explosions were not the red-yellow, pyrotechnically enriched explosions of an action film. They were flat, dirty, white-yellow explosions. Clouds of tear gas and cordite blew through the Lions' Gate: a new Via Dolorosa atop the old. Then the call to prayer began.

"It's a war," Achmed said, as the muezzins sang. "It's really a war."

"Do you have any Israeli friends?" Jay asked him.

"Yes," Achmed said. "I do. Sometimes they drive me crazy."

The fighting had marooned a few tour buses up here, and what I guessed to be American Christians ventured out to have a look at the source of their inconvenience. Soon these Christian men and women were standing next to us, looking down from the Mount of Olives with their hands over their mouths.

What, really, was so shocking? Were we not standing atop the birthplace of a certain kind of religious nationalism? Zion lay all around us. See where the Prophet left this earth, where Christ rose from the dead, where the Messiah would, finally, appear. Which of us, in this war, was not Judas to someone?

BARTHOLOMEW

Saint Bartholomew on the Island: Rome, Italy

ALONG THE TIBER • ISOLA TIBERINA •
BARTHOLOMEW'S CENTRALITY • NATHANAEL OF
CANA • THE APOCRYPHA • WITHIN THE CHURCH •
ADALBERT • TRAVELS & DEATHS • MARTYRDOM
CULTS

I.

Early one morning, I walked along the calm, torpid Tiber
River, the sky above streaked with watermelon light. While
Rome's busiest streets were lined with anorexic sidewalks
unable to accommodate the girth of two stout tourists, the
banks of the Tiber were graced with walkways as spacious as
patio decks. As I walked, I came upon occasional islets located
just offshore. In the city's museums, I'd seen nineteenth-
century woodcuts that showed gentlemen picnicking with
ladies on these tiny riparian retreats. Today, Rome's homeless
had colonized much of the Tiber's walkways and many of its
islets. I passed several of their encampments: the cardboard-
box homes, the clotheslines hung with stained, once-white
clothing. The dogs—so many of Rome's homeless had dogs—
watched me with curious, liquid eyes as I passed, their owners
asleep beside them.

In the middle of the Tiber, there was one large, remarkable
island, Isola Tiberina (Tiber Island), which had been so incorporated into the surrounding city that newcomers usually had
to stare for several minutes before realizing it actually *was* an
island. Its diamond shape and rounded, streamlined edges made

it resemble a mothballed galleon miraculously run ashore in the middle of Rome. This was by design. During ancient times, the island was made to look like a trireme, the many-oared warship common to the Greco-Roman world. Sadly, the only remaining part of this ancient edifice was an eight-foot-long section of travertine marble prow on the island's southeastern edge. On the prow's facing, the erosion-smoothened shape of a snake-coiled staff could still be seen. Both serpent and prow were references to one of Tiber Island's many origin myths. In the third century BCE, supposedly, during a devastating plague, desperate Romans had requested the aid of healers from the great Peloponnesian shrine of the Greek god Asclepius, son of Apollo. Asclepius's ambassadors arrived in a trireme and had with them a snake, their god's symbol, which on sight of Tiber Island squirted free from its basket and swam for shore. A healing shrine was constructed on the island at the spot of the serpent's landing. The island had been honored for its restorative character ever since.

Fatebenefratelli Hospital now stood on a raised area at the island's western tip. Most of its windows' curtains were drawn, giving the hospital a sullen, bedridden look. Outside, on the hospital's back veranda, a few young doctors and nurses smoked in their pale orange hospital fatigues. A white travertine apron girdled the island, where, on sunny summer days, many teenagers lounged, sunbathed, and awaited phosphorescence. Beyond the island, the Tiber River turned rapid, spilling in hard white waterfalls over a series of small manufactured ledges, at the base of which swirled an eddy-entrapped polyethylene gumbo of soccer balls, raft-sized Styrofoam hunks, and plastic Coke bottles.

The two bridges that connected Tiber Island to Rome dated from the first century BCE. The more ancient of the two, Ponte Fabricio, was the city's oldest standing bridge. The Ponte Cestio, the younger bridge, led to a neighborhood known as Trastevere; Ponte Fabricio led to the Jewish Ghetto, home to Rome's largest synagogue, which was located directly across the river from the hospital. Trastevere was the Jewish quarter in the first and second centuries, and the ghetto was where, in the sixteenth century, Pope Paul IV ordered all Jews to remain after nightfall. These erstwhile ethnic bastions were today highly fashionable neighborhoods.

Large numbers of Jews had lived in Rome even before the Diaspora, arriving within the sometimes coerced, sometimes voluntary (Herod, for instance, educated his sons here), but largely constant traffic that began between imperial Rome and Palestine in 63 BCE, when Pompey conquered the region and terminated several decades of Jewish independence under the Hasmonaean monarchy. Many of Rome's first Jews were slaves or prisoners of war who received eventual emancipation and settled in Trastevere. Judaism likely brought Rome its first Christians as well: the founders of the Roman church are widely presumed to have been Jewish Christians.

For decades, few in Rome bothered to distinguish between the two faiths. Only when Christianity became more Hellenized, and its concerns more clearly delineated from those of the Jews, did most Romans parse the differences. The emperor Claudius ordered one of Rome's most famous Jewish expulsions from the city in the 40s. The historian Suetonius, writing eighty years after the fact, noted that Claudius's expulsion was the result of a Jewish riot led by one "Chrestus," whom Suetonius apparently misunderstood to be a Jew operating in Rome. Whatever the case, this "riot" suggests early tensions in Rome's synagogues between those who maintained some type of faith in Jesus and those who did not.

Claudius's expulsion order is mentioned in the Acts of the Apostles, during a sequence that finds Paul in Corinth. There Paul meets Aquila and Priscilla, who had "recently come from Italy . . . because Claudius had ordered all the Jews to leave Rome."* Although Aquila is a Jew, he and his wife are also believ-

---

* Actually, it is likely that Claudius banished only the agitating ringleaders of Rome's Jewish unrest—which is to say, its Jewish Christians. To ban "all the Jews," as Acts has it, would have been impossible. As Roman citizens, they would have had to be tried individually before banishment.

ers in Jesus, having already been baptized when Paul meets them. They wind up accompanying Paul on his travels to Ephesus. Although Aquila's appearance in Acts is brief, we are told his home region (Pontus, in modern-day Turkey), his wife's name (Priscilla), his occupation (like Paul, a tent maker), and the reason he is in Corinth. Aquila is the very definition of a minor New Testament figure, and yet we are privy to quite a bit more biographical information concerning him than, say, the apostle Bartholomew, whose resting place happened to be on Tiber Island.

II.

In all the canonical apostle lists, Bartholomew occupies a central spot among his brethren. This placement determined how he was viewed. As one early Christian wrote, "Bartholomew, at the center of the sacred number twelve, is in accord by his sermonizing with those preceding him and those following, as strings of the harp make harmony." Yet Bartholomew's name appears merely four times in the New Testament and never beyond the lists of the Twelve. He says nothing and is ascribed no action. His name (bar Tolmai) means "son of Tolmai." Jerome believed Bartholomew hailed from a noble family, deducing that Tolmai was a reference to 2 Samuel 3:3, where in a genealogical list we meet one "King Talmai of Geshur," whose daughter Maacah bore David's son Absalom. A later piece of Christian deduction links Tolmai to the name Ptolemy, making Bartholomew a scion of the Egyptian dynastic line. The contrasting tradition of Bartholomew's having been a simple farmer comes from the literal Hebrew meaning of *talmai,* "one abounding in furrows."

Matthew, Mark, and Luke—otherwise known as the synoptic ("seen together") gospels due to their similarities and Matthew's and Luke's seemingly clear reliance on Mark—all list the apostles Philip and Bartholomew together. Meanwhile, John, who does not mention Bartholomew, indicates a close friendship between Philip and Nathanael. Thus, Bartholomew has traditionally been understood as being the same person as Nathanael, which would make Bartholomew his patronymic and Nathanael (which means "God has given") his first name: Nathanael bar Tolmai.

John's Nathanael of Cana appears twice in the gospel. His first appearance involves Philip, who tells him he has found the one "about whom Moses in the law and also the prophets wrote." Nathanael is skeptical but goes to see Jesus anyway. On seeing Nathanael approach, Jesus proclaims him to be "an Israelite in whom there is no deceit!" Nathanael asks, "Where did you get to know me?" Jesus tells Nathanael that he saw him sitting under a fig tree, apparently during a vision, which impresses Nathanael greatly. He cries out, "You are the son of God!" Jesus, allowed one of his few moments of humor, says, "Do you believe because I told you that I saw you under the fig tree? You will see greater things than these."

Nathanael's other appearance is near the end of John, when several disciples are fishing in Galilee after Jesus's resurrection but before his ascension. Nathanael, in this scene, is given nothing to say, but his inclusion among important disciples such as Peter and Thomas is interesting, as is the relative priority John gives Nathanael in Jesus's calling of the apostles. From gospel to gospel, the order of the first group of apostles' calling is inconsistent, but tradition has worked out a more or less accepted order: Andrew, Peter, John, and James, followed by Philip and Nathanael. While the synoptic gospels contain Jesus's primary calling of the two pairs of brothers, they lack the calling of Philip or Nathanael. If John's fishing scene and his account of Nathanael's early calling is an echo of something even vaguely historical, Nathanael bar Tolmai—whose existence is already teetering on several presumptive pinheads—might then be reasonably viewed as one of Jesus's first and most important followers.

Yet Bartholomew is otherwise absent from Christian scripture. Early Christians set out to remedy this problem, resulting in an unusually colorful farrago of apostolic lore. The first five hundred years of Christianity are marked by an eruption of writings, now collectively called the Apocrypha—the word, which derives from Greek, means "hidden away"—that set out to explain what the gospels and epistles did not. While none of this work became part of the New Testament, a good deal of it intruded, in an almost viral way, into the greater body of Christianity.[*] The stories told within the Apocrypha were irresistible to many Christians, perhaps more so due to the stories' unofficial, unsanctioned status among church leaders. In many ways, exploring and adding to apocryphal stories was an early form of fan fiction: Tertullian writes of one unfortunate Christian presbyter who, having been identified as the author of the apocryphal *Acts of Paul,* was brought to trial, convicted, and stripped of his office. Yet without the Apocrypha, the Twelve Apostles would seem even more irrecoverably distant. It is within these strange works that we find most instances of apostolic quirk or personality.

Nearly every bit of apocryphal writing has its oddities: fish resurrected from the dead, sentient dogs, gouged-out eyes miraculously healed, unusually loquacious demons, and wonderfully dislocating sentences such as "Jesus went and sat at the rudder and piloted the craft." But the apocryphal literature involving Bartholomew is highly peculiar: one episode involves the apostle learning secret cosmic knowledge from Mary the mother of Jesus, despite her warning that to disclose this information will destroy the world; another work, attributed to Bartholomew, has Jesus battling the six serpent sons of Death; another, *The Acts of Philip,* in which Bartholomew co-stars, features the apostles coming across a talking baby goat and leopard, who adorably take Communion together; yet another appears to involve, of all things, a werewolf.

---

[*] Incredibly, the first raft of apocryphal Christian material was not available in any English translation until 1727, though certain popular legends inspired by the Apocrypha were widely familiar to Christians.

What might the resting place of Bartholomew resemble, given his adventures outside the literature of the New Testament? A sand castle guarded over by a chimera and gryphon? A glittering rocket ship? No. The church of San Bartolomeo all'Isola was small and somewhat plain. An equally modest police station had been built beside it. I sat for a while watching the police station until two chain-smoking carabinieri (Rome's military police) emerged and stood next to their boxy dark blue Jeep. Their uniforms—black, red-striped pants and tight Kevlar vests—were simultaneously splendid and silly. These men looked as prepared to enter into hostage-exchange negotiations as they did to punch a train ticket to Assisi.

Within an hour or so, the church piazza began to fill with people, many of them enjoying the next-door café and nursing tiny cups of coffee. A few seekers wandered through the piazza, including a steady stream of small, portly nuns in the habits of their preference or order: the nursing orders in white, the Franciscans often in brown, the French Little Sisters of the Lamb in blue, the Filipina sisters in black. The few tourists who bothered to stop did so only to consult their maps. It was easy to see why. Compared with many Roman places of worship, Saint Bartholomew on the Island seemed the product of an almost pathological degree of architectural restraint. Pitched roof, simple wood mullions in its windows, plain columns. While the foundation of this church was more than one thousand years old, the building itself would not have looked terribly out of place in an otherwise humble town square in 1904 Nebraska. At the spot where the "mast" of the island's simulated trireme had once stood was a statue of Bartholomew himself. Bearded and curly-haired, he was holding the curved flensing knife with which he was, according to legend, skinned by Armenian heathens. Other legends have Bartholomew being crucified and then skinned. Other legends have him being skinned, crucified, and then beheaded.

The day before, I'd gone to the Sistine Chapel to see another

Bartholomew. In the lower right-hand corner of Michelangelo's *The Last Judgment,* you can find a bald, muscular, nearly naked Bartholomew holding his own earthly hide while he gazes up at a beardless Jesus. The skull-less, floppy face dangling from Bartholomew's hide is a cunning self-portrait of the artist himself. Michelangelo began work on *The Last Judgment* decades after he painted the ceiling of the Sistine Chapel, an undertaking he had to be coaxed into accepting. During both Sistine projects, the conditions under which Michelangelo labored were horrid. He constructed his own scaffolds because he suspected the first scaffold built for his use had been designed to kill him. Some of this perceived abuse must have moved Michelangelo to powerfully identify with Bartholomew, whose gruesome traditions mark him as the most hideously tormented of all the apostles.

Inside Saint Bartholomew on the Island, I was met by an assortment of soft, peaceful darknesses. All the wooden pews and kneelers were freestanding, movable. The nave, lined with a dozen columns, was tiny. Up near the chancel, I could see small candlelit chapels on either side of the altar. High windows tinted lilac on one side and pink on the other created a pollinated-seeming glow in the eaves above. These were not stained-glass windows (the creation of which necessitated an elaborate and costly process that had fallen in and out of favor in church construction over the centuries) but rather simple colored glass.

I walked along the church's right aisle and found a large black metal bowl hanging on the wall. The church's custodian, a young Italian woman wearing faded red jeans, Puma sneakers, and a tight gray sweater, approached. Her hair was straight, black, and flat, her skin as nearly white as the strip of scalp revealed by her severe part. She was smiling, big-eyed, eager to talk. Quite obviously, I was her first visitor of the day.

"It was stolen once, in 1981," she said, when I asked about the large black metal bowl. "But then returned in 1985. No one knows why it was stolen. Relics like this are often stolen in Rome. And usually they're returned. Such a theft is too difficult for many thieves to live with."

"So the bowl's an official relic?" I asked.

She nodded. "This is the bowl in which the remains of Bartholomew were first brought here. Until then, our church was devoted to Alberto." Or, as he was also known, Saint Adalbert, who in the late tenth century resigned his bishopric in Prague due to frustration with the stubborn pagan leanings of his converts and came to Rome to live as a monk. In Rome, he befriended Otto III, who later dispatched him back to his homeland, where he was martyred by an ax-wielding pagan. At some point in the late tenth century, Otto built this church in honor of him. Or such were the legends.

An ancient legend preserved by Jacobus de Voragine mentions Bartholomew's remains being held in Mesopotamia as of the sixth century. Another of Jacobus's legends describes how, after Bartholomew's flaying, the "pagans" in Armenia, "profoundly" displeased by the miracles that attended Bartholomew's body, put the bones into "a leaden coffin" and threw it into the sea. By "God's will" Bartholomew's storm-tossed remains reached the island of Lipari, near Sicily. This would have required God's will, or at least a flatbed semi, seeing that the Caspian Sea, from whose shores the Armenians supposedly pushed Bartholomew's coffin, has no connection to the Mediterranean. When Bartholomew's body reached Lipari, a local volcano, "which did harm to those who lived nearby," drew back in reverence at "a distance of a mile or more."

In the early ninth century, Saracens invaded Sicily, sacked Lipari, and supposedly looted Bartholomew's tomb. In a legend known to Jacobus, Bartholomew appears to a surviving monk and demands that his scattered bones be collected. The monk angrily asks why he should do anything at all for Bartholomew, "since you allowed us to be overrun and did nothing to help us." Bartholomew explains that he attempted to protect the people of Lipari, but their sins had grown so brazen he "could no longer obtain pardon for them." Duly chastised by this questionable theodicy, the monk wonders how he can ever hope to find Bartholomew's bones amid the greater carnage. Bartholomew promises that if the monk looks for them at night, he will find bones "that shine like fire" among the less blessed ribs and scapulae. The monk does as Bartholomew asks and puts the bones on a ship bound for Benevento, a town in southeastern Italy.

The greater portion of Bartholomew's remains did not stay long in Benevento, for in the tenth century Otto requested the bones be sent to Rome, apparently for safekeeping. Eventually, they found their way into Adalbert's church. The bishop of Benevento seems to have kept some of Bartholomew's body, for in the eleventh century he raffled Bartholomew's arm to England's Edward the Confessor, who, in turn, handed it over to Canterbury Cathedral.* None of this bone trade is particularly unusual, and almost all of the apostles exist in fragments, sometimes even in churches devoted to them, where different body parts are scattered around church grounds. Still, the fact that the skinned, tortured Bartholomew of tradition was so frequently dismembered after his death says something about the lucklessness with which he has been perceived through Christian time. Given his gruesome fate, it is probably fitting that today Bartholomew is largely known for his feast day's connection to a bloody Paris night in 1572, when thousands of Protestant French Huguenots were dragged from their beds and slaughtered in the street by French Catholics, which is known as the Saint Bartholomew's Day Massacre.

The custodian walked over to the altar, where Bartholomew's remains were kept in a massive, tub-shaped, lion-head-adorned sarcophagus of porphyry granite. A slightly oversized slab lay atop Bartholomew's sarcophagus, beside which a batch of fresh sunflowers had been left. These flowers were courtesy of a "pilgrim," the custodian told me. She went on to explain that Bartholomew had been martyred in Turkey and was considered the patron saint of Spain. This was interesting—which is to say,

---

* This accounts for the apostle's unusually strong veneration in England, where many dozens of churches, and one of its best hospitals, are devoted to him.

entirely new—information to me, given that tradition generally holds that Bartholomew was martyred in Armenia and James son of Zebedee is widely acknowledged as Spain's patron saint. Before I could challenge her, a gaggle of Spanish-speaking tourists, led by an amply chinned, fast-talking guide, entered the church. The custodian and I loitered politely in the church's wings while the guide gathered his group around the altar. "Besides Spaniards," the custodian said to me quietly, "we have many tour groups from Lipari, where Bartholomew's remains were first kept. It is all part of a famous Italian pilgrimage route."

The Spanish guide gestured and talked. "I think James is the patron saint of Spain," I whispered to her.

"Okay," she said.

The Spanish tour guide pointed up at the ceiling and at the walls, all of which were covered with paintings of monks beneath opened heavens, Rembrandtishly dark crucifixions, popes healing lepers, oriental heathens astounded by placid Christian interlopers' miracles, and one strange painting of an adult Jesus holding himself as an infant. When, finally, the Spaniards left, the custodian pointed out the short, wastepaper-basket-sized chunk of an old Roman column found in front of the altar. An image of a man had been carved onto it. Bartholomew? "No," she said. "Alberto. It's from the tenth century." I asked her if it seemed strange that Adalbert, a martyr with historical ties to Rome, had been usurped by an apostle about whom so little is known. "There are many churches dedicated to Bartholomew," she said. "It's a very ancient devotion. He has many visitors, as you just saw." She stared at his sarcophagus for a moment. Then she shrugged. "But in the end, yes, it's also a tourist attraction."

III.

At some point in the third or fourth century, a myth emerged among Christians that Bartholomew had traveled to India in the first century and evangelized its people. Ambrose, the fearsome fourth-century bishop of Milan, wrote of "the winged feet" with which Bartholomew reached the fabled land. Eusebius knew of the same legend, which involved the Christian scholar Pantaenus, who was supposedly the first known head of a Christian academy in Alexandria. According to Eusebius, Pantaenus "found that Matthew's gospel had arrived [in India] before him and was in the hands of some there who had come to know Christ. Bartholomew, one of the apostles, had preached to them and had left behind Matthew's account in the actual Hebrew characters."

The tradition that Bartholomew traveled to India is an old one, at least among Western Christians. In *The Golden Legend,* Jacobus de Voragine collated several such legends, describing both Bartholomew's mission to and supposed death in India. One Jacobus source provides the most elaborate physical description of an apostle found in ancient Christian writings:

> He has black, curly hair, white skin, large eyes, straight nose, his hair covers his ears, his beard long and grizzled, middle height. He wears a white robe with a purple stripe, and a white cloak with four purple gems at the corners. For twenty-six years he has worn these, and they never grow old. His shoes have lasted twenty-six years. He prays a hundred times a day and a hundred times a night. His voice is like a trumpet; angels wait upon him; he is always cheerful, and knows all languages.

Although this is clearly a description of a lunatic, Bartholomew's evocation here would guide many later physical representations of him.

Some scholars view the legends of Bartholomew's travels in India as a result of a geographical misunderstanding common in ancient times. In this view, "India" was used as shorthand for any distant place, much as "Timbuktu" is used today. Other scholars point out that India was not necessarily so fantastical a clime for early Christians to imagine. Alexander the Great traveled through India as early as the fourth century BCE, as any educated writer at the time would have known, and in *The Jewish War* one of Josephus's fanatical Zealot leaders says, "If we do need the testimony of foreigners, let us look to those Indians who profess to practice philosophy."

The land to which Bartholomew has been most frequently linked is Armenia, the first nation to make Christianity its official creed, though, once again, the evidence of his travels there is obviously legendary. According to one fancifully exact account, Thaddaeus preached in Armenia for twenty-three years and was joined by Bartholomew around 60 CE. Bartholomew was martyred, according to this traditional chronology, around 68, a few years after Peter and Paul.

It may be that the early Armenian Church claimed its apostolic connection to Bartholomew for purely tactical reasons, which was a common gambit for many communities whose beliefs ran counter to a hardening Christian orthodoxy. In the case of the Armenian Church, those beliefs concerned what is now called Monophysite Christianity, which holds that Jesus's humanity and divinity were not separate but united in one cohesive nature. The Western church, which regarded Jesus's humanity and divinity as entirely separate, rejected Monophysite beliefs as anathema, even though its thinkers took their own sweet time in discerning the precise nature of the internal coexistence of Jesus's humanity and divinity. Monophysitism became the official stance of Armenian Christianity in the middle of the fifth century, after the Council of Chalcedon, which granted equal stature to Jesus's human and divine selves. Religious historians, however, would be well advised to thank their lucky stars for the Armenian Church, which translated and preserved an impressive amount of early theological work, written by the giants of first- and second-century Christianity and later destroyed by the forces of orthodoxy. Several of these texts, important works by Irenaeus among them, today survive only in Armenian.

IV.

On the Tiber island, Bartholomew's young custodian was eager to discuss an easel-propped painting that stood behind the sarcophagus. The painting, a recent commission, had been done in the floating, allegorical Byzantine style and depicted rows and rows of Christian martyrs. Above the angels hovered Bartholomew and Adalbert carrying a banner that read, in Latin, "We are all one thing," which is to say, Christian. As though to illustrate this point, the martyrs depicted in the painting came in every age and gender and size and color. All wore white robes and all carried palm fronds, the traditional symbol of the martyr. I asked the custodian what was the big deal about this fascinatingly unremarkable painting. "Important things are happening in our church," she said. In the jubilee year of 2000, for example, Pope John Paul II announced that Bartholomew on the Island would from now on devote itself to celebrating the martyrs of every branch of Christianity, with a keen focus on newer martyrs, such as the Catholic priests who died in the Holocaust, the Russian Orthodox priests who died in the gulag, and even "Protestant martyrs," she said, like Martin Luther King Jr.

Behind the martyr painting was a much larger painting that depicted Bartholomew's martyrdom. It was a nasty piece of work, showing the apostle, tied to a tree, being circled by fearsomely mustached, knife-wielding, dark-skinned men in turbans. Amazingly, this was not even the most offensive image I had seen of Bartholomew's martyrdom. The most offensive image I had seen was painted by Nicolò Circignani—a sixteenth-century analogue to the torture-horror filmmaker Eli Roth—which is found in Rome's Chiesa dei Santi Nereo e Achilleo. The image depicted pagans in the bloodily nightmarish middle stages of tearing off

Bartholomew's skin, with one pagan bracing himself against a tree for better pulling leverage. Circignani's work savored the spectacle of bloody apostolic martyrdom, and I was hardly the only one troubled by it. On a visit to Rome, Charles Dickens was so disgusted by Circignani's visions of apostolic murder he could hardly stand to look at them.

The custodian checked her cell phone for incoming text messages. It was getting close to lunchtime, Italy's three-hour midday bacchanal of triumphant do-nothingism, and she was meeting a friend. But I had another question for her. With Christianity triumphant, and Christians able to worship freely in Rome for many centuries, why this fixation on martyrdom? Had this fixation not done enough damage to the faith already? Why continue to roll in the entrails of the martyred?

Several early Christians attempted to warn their fellow believers about valorizing martyrdom. Origen, whose father was a martyr, was ambivalent, concerned that consciously seeking out death from oppressors was a form of suicide. Clement of Alexandria disliked martyrdom, because it required another man to sin. Slowly, and then definitively, these views lost out. Consider a letter written by the disciples of the famously martyred early Christian leader Polycarp, which was written in the first half of the second century. This letter—the first recorded description of Christian martyrdom—proclaims their martyred leader's bones to be "more precious than stones of great price, more splendid than gold." Or consider Ignatius, who wrote the following to the Christians of Rome in the early second century while on his own way to martyrdom: "Let me be food for the wild beasts, through whom I can reach God." The only Christian who would dare come between him and death, Ignatius wrote, was one who "hated" him. Or consider Tertullian, writing around the turn of the third century: "Does God covet man's blood? . . . I might venture to affirm that he does." Tertullian went on to refer to martyrdom as "a second new birth" and, sounding more than a little Islamist, cautioned the pagan magistrates of Carthage that the "oftener we are mown down by you, the more in number we grow; the blood of Christians is seed."

Those who die for their faith will always be admired by their co-religionists. But in a culture in which faith is normative rather than embattled, fascination with those who die for their faith quickly loses its devotional aspects. As far back as the second century, Marcus Aurelius made this point in his *Meditations,* criticizing Christians for their "obstinacy," the undignified and "tragic show" they put on, in their lust for martyrdom. While some Christians were martyred for their faith, and even thrown to lions, the earliest Christian accounts of martyrdom fail to make clear one interesting wrinkle: killing men and women for perceived apostasy was highly uncommon among pagans, and most ancient-world authorities were inclined to be *lenient* toward Christians, many of whom, like Ignatius, *demanded* death. Martyrdom, then, is a difference-obliterating mind-set that leaves death as the only thing to venerate. Dying in Buchenwald, assassination by South American death squads, starving in the gulag, suffering the bullet of a racist Memphis sniper—did these fates have anything measurably in common with the supposed martyrdoms of Bartholomew, Adalbert, and Polycarp? If not, why did this church want to pretend that they did?

The custodian would hear none of this. "Roman Christianity *is* the story of martyrdom," she said, clearly irritated by my questions. "This church's goal is to remind the world that martyrdom is still going on. Seventy million Christians have been killed for their faith, and more than half of them died in the last one hundred years." She took me to the small shrines along the church's western wing and stopped at the reliquary of a Salvadoran priest who was shot in the head by Communists in the 1980s. On display was a photograph of him at his desk, slumped over a book, the bullet wound behind his ear hauntingly small. The book he was reading when he was assassinated was on display here, as was his stole. She then bid me to follow her to the church's most recently installed reliquary, which was dedicated to some Anglican priests murdered by Malaysian guerrillas in 2001. Inside the display case was a blood-spotted cloth belt and a walking stick. "You see?" the custodian said, clearly convinced that these modern relics proved her point. Without martyrs, there would be no relics, and without relics we would not be standing here.

A platter of candles was nearby, half of which were lit. As the candles wept wax tears, their stubborn little flames quivered in a draft I could not quite feel.

HISTORESAI: ON PAUL

GALATIANS • AGAINST CEPHAS • PAUL & THE PILLARS
• THE GENTILE QUESTION • PAUL'S AUDACITY • THE
FATE OF THE JERUSALEM CHURCH • THE WAY •
EBION • A CURIOUS DISTINCTION • "YOUR LAW"

I.

From a purely historical perspective, Paul's letter to the Galatians—which argues to a confused, apparently skeptical audience that Christians were no longer bound by Jewish ritualistic thinking—might be the most significant work of the New Testament. Among other things, it enshrines for all history significant tensions between two of Christianity's first and most prominent figures: Paul, the Pharisee turned Christian who preached in the name of Jesus across a wide swath of the Mediterranean world; and Cephas/Peter, the supposed leader of the Twelve Apostles. Because of this, Galatians has proved, for many believers, a disquieting document indeed.

According to the scholar J. Louis Martyn, reading Galatians is "like coming in on a play as the curtain is rising on the third or fourth act," for "what has already occurred has involved a number of persons in addition to Paul and the Galatians." Among the players are Paul, Cephas/Peter, James the brother of Jesus, and missionaries the Jerusalem church has dispatched in an apparent attempt to keep watch on Paul.

The letter—written sometime in the later 50s, before any gospel we know of had been composed—is addressed to the "churches of Galatia," which suggests that the epistle-triggering crisis was not centered on any one church but rather spread evenly throughout the region, which today would be much of south-central Turkey. The Galatian Christians were Hellenized Gentiles who, until Paul's missionary outreach, had probably been pagans; it is unlikely that their community contained many Jews. Ethnically speaking, they were probably Celts (the Latin word for "Celt" is *Gallus*) who had gradually migrated eastward from their homeland in the European heartland's Danube basin. Celts moving in the opposite direction had also claimed the British Isles and Gaul, which, like Galatia, was named for them.

Most scholars place Paul in Greece or Macedonia when he received news of his Galatian converts' upset. What happened was this: Some time after Paul left the Galatians, they were visited by Christians who still maintained Jewish ceremonial rites such as circumcision. These visitors, in turn, demanded that the Galatians obey the same rites. Paul disagreed, believing Gentile Christians coming into the faith were not required to obey aspects of Jewish Law such as circumcision. Paul's letter was intended to be read aloud to every Galatian church; Paul himself was probably mindful that his circumcision-favoring opponents would still be among the Galatians as the letter was read, which adds an extra talon or two to its already sharp tone. The writing of Galatians was apparently such a personally upsetting occasion for Paul that near the end of the short letter he pushes his scribe out of the way and takes from him his pen: "See what large letters I make when I am writing in my own hand!" The conflict between Paul and these rival missionaries had obviously been boiling for some time. That the Galatian churches were now affected by it was, for Paul, the last straw.

Paul first came to Jerusalem from his native Tarsus (in modern-day southern Turkey) to study in one of Jerusalem's four hundred synagogues. Although Paul might have begun his Pharisaic career in Greek-speaking Hellenist synagogues, his teacher, at least according to Acts, was Gamaliel, one of the most respected instructors of his day. As a Pharisee, Paul lived the

Law, promulgated the Law, and menaced those who broke it. This history was evidently part of Paul's baggage, as even the author of Acts, Paul's most enthusiastic biographer, writes of the man barging into the homes of Christian believers, serving as accuser during their various trials, and approving of their stoning.

It has often been argued that Paul seems to know little about Jesus's earthly life. He rarely refers to his sayings, teachings, or biographical details. But all one can say definitively is Paul did not often find the occasion to write extensively about these things. He was not, after all, writing his letters to convince any one of Jesus's existence. Paul probably had a clear idea about the broader details of Jesus's life, seeing that he was an enthusiastic opponent of the faith for its first three years and was bound to have heard the stories. When it came to Jesus, Paul had no written gospel or record of events. What we know he did have was a visionary experience on the road to Damascus, during which he claimed to have encountered, in some manner, a deity he often calls "Christ Jesus." (The notion of Paul's being knocked from his horse during that vision is extra-scriptural and was probably first added to Christian legend by Renaissance-era painters such as Caravaggio.) Paul believed this revelation, received no more than three years after the crucifixion, was an occasion of both personal and global significance. He is insistent in his letter to the Galatians that his personal experience of Jesus was not taught to him as a tradition but rather actively experienced—so much so he makes sure to stress his *lack* of connection to the Jerusalem church and the original followers of Jesus. After Jesus "called me through grace," he writes, "I did not confer with any human being, nor did I go up to Jerusalem to those who were already apostles before me." This is Paul's first indication in the letter that he and the Jerusalem church are not necessarily interested in the same thing.

He then tells the Galatians a story. Three years after his visionary experience of seeing Jesus, and after spending time in Arabia and Damascus (the purpose of which is undisclosed, though we can assume they were missions), he finally went to

Jerusalem "to visit Cephas." The verb he uses to describe his meeting with Peter, the infinitive form of which is *historesai* and from which we derive the word "history," can mean either "get information from" or "become acquainted with." Whether Paul was seeking information or acquaintance, he stayed with Peter for fifteen days—a short visit, given the rigors of travel in ancient times—and he is careful to note that he "did not see any other apostle except James the Lord's brother," the leader of Jerusalem Christianity.

Paul follows this story with a studied portrayal of himself as a loner away from Jerusalem for fourteen years. Then, "in response to a revelation," he returned to Jerusalem with Barnabas and Titus sometime around the year 50. Barnabas was a Jewish Christian closely connected to the Jerusalem church—according to Acts, he introduced Paul to the Jerusalem leadership—with an interest in preaching to Gentiles that was as fervent as Paul's. Titus was a Gentile Greek. Paul, "though only in a private meeting," conferred with the Jerusalem church's "acknowledged leaders": James, Cephas, and John, whose identities he feels no obligation to explain, which suggests they were familiar figures among the Galatian Christians. What was discussed on this long-delayed return to Jerusalem, Paul writes, was circumcision and whether his self-understood mission as apostle to the Gentiles, which he had now been pursuing for a decade and a half, was "in vain."

Paul had problems in Jerusalem. At his private meeting with Cephas, John, and James, a group he calls the "false brothers" wished to circumcise his Greek companion Titus, who was, no doubt, resistant to the idea. As for the Jerusalem church's leaders, Paul writes of them so irritably that he resorts to the unhappy rhetorical turn known as an anacoluthon: "And from those who were supposed to be acknowledged leaders (what they actually were makes no difference to me; God shows no partiality)—those leaders contributed nothing to me." Nonetheless, Paul writes that the Jerusalem church's leaders "recognized the grace that had been given me" and extended "to Barnabas and me the right hand of fellowship, agreeing that we should go to the Gentiles and they to the circumcised." In other words, Paul is telling the Galatians that he has already settled with the leadership of the Jerusalem church issues of Jewish observance such as circumcision; his teachings are thus free from moral or religious error. Obviously, the traveling missionaries shadowing Paul around Gentile Christian communities disagreed.

The gospels portray Jesus instructing the Twelve Apostles to "go therefore and make disciples of all nations," and the legends of the Twelve most often find them preaching in comfortably foreskinned lands. But other passages in the gospels line up with Paul's portrayal of the Jerusalem Christians, which is to say men who remained resistant to allowing non-Law-abiding Gentiles to join them. Matthew, for instance, has Jesus telling the Twelve during his ministry, "Go nowhere among the Gentiles, and enter no town of the Samaritans, but go rather to the lost sheep of the house of Israel." While John depicts Jesus conversing amiably with a Samaritan woman, the Jesus of the synoptic gospels, Matthew and Luke especially, shows only a few ecumenical leanings prior to his resurrection.* Nevertheless, Matthew's gospel famously concludes with Jesus's command that the remaining members of the Twelve "make disciples of all nations." (Mark's Jesus makes a similar statement, but during his earthly ministry.) Almost certainly, Matthew's final scene reflects the missionary imperative of a very different church from that which existed in the 50s. A decade and a half after Jesus's death, the Jerusalem church, led by two apostles and one of Jesus's brothers, was at the very least hesitant to open the faith to non-Law-abiding Gentiles.

What Paul describes as "a private meeting" with the Jerusalem leadership in Galatians later becomes, in Acts, a plenary gathering in which all the important figures in the Jerusalem church take part. Included among the participants in Acts' ver-

---

* A notable exception occurs in the gospels of Matthew and Mark, when Jesus wanders into the non-Jewish territory of Tyre and heals the deranged daughter of a "Syrophoenician" woman whose cutting sense of humor evidently pleases Jesus.

sion of events are "believers who belonged to the sect of the Pharisees," which is to say Jewish Christian scribes who insisted that Gentile believers "be circumcised and ordered to keep the law of Moses." But after listening to Paul and Barnabas describe "all the signs and wonders that God had done through them," James the brother of Jesus announces, "I have reached the decision that we should not trouble those Gentiles who are turning to God." The two meetings, as described by Paul and Acts, cannot be reconciled. In Galatians, Paul meets with a small group and his mission is accepted without qualification. In Acts, it is a community-wide meeting that ends with a hugely significant doctrinal readjustment.

After James's decision, according to Acts, a new missionary letter addressed to various Christian communities, which outlines community expectations about the Law, is drawn up, in which Paul is mentioned and sanctioned as an accepted messenger. The letter also censures "certain persons who have gone out from us, though with no instructions from us," persons who have "said things to disturb you and have unsettled your minds," which sounds very much like the types of missionaries who are damaging Paul's reputation in Galatia. One of the bearers of the Jerusalem church's letter is sent to tell Gentile Christian communities that the Jerusalem Christians will not further burden them with any rules other than "essentials" such as abstaining from meat sacrificed to idols, drinking blood, and fornicating. In his letters, Paul never mentions any such decree, and a number of his teachings confound its suggested ground rules; many scholars thus suspect Luke created Acts' Jerusalem conference episode to smoothen the intra-Christian bumps revealed by Galatians, a letter Luke might or might not have been aware of when writing about Paul several decades later.* Nevertheless, the point is

---

* How familiar was Luke with Paul's letters? Amazingly, this has never been adequately determined. Plausible scholarly arguments have been mounted that Luke (a) knew the letters intimately, (b) did not know them at all, and (c) knew a handful of those familiar to us and possibly some that have been lost.

clear: James the brother of Jesus, the leader of the world's first Christian community, still had *to come to a decision* to allow non-Law-abiding Gentiles into the faith.

"The strategy of two distinct missions with independent ground rules," the scholar John Painter writes, "might have been an attempt to find a diplomatic solution to a difficult problem. . . . Had it been possible for the two missions to remain separate and distinct . . . the solution might have worked." But what Paul set into historical motion with his Gentile mission was too overwhelming for a theological two-state solution.

II.

"Pillars" (*styloi* in Greek), the word Paul uses in Galatians to describe the Jerusalem leaders, was probably a term used by the Jerusalem church itself, though it does not occur in scripture before or after Galatians. Going by its Temple imagery, we can assume the term was conceptually Jewish. As Paul relayed to the so-called Pillars his desire to continue his mission to the Gentiles, he must have been keenly aware of their enduring connection to Judaism.

Soon after Paul's meeting with the Pillars, which, again, was around 50 CE (at least half a decade before Galatians was written), Peter visited Paul at Antioch (in modern-day Turkey), the former capital of the Seleucid Empire and the wealthiest, most important city of the Roman Empire's eastern provinces. Antioch was home to Paul's first major congregation—it was also where the term "Christian" was first coined by outsiders to describe the movement—and its Christian community contained an admixture of Gentile and Diaspora Jewish believers in Jesus. Shortly behind Peter, though, came "certain people from James," who, in Paul's account to the Galatians, shamed or intimidated Peter into abandoning the table he shared with Gentiles at the common meal. Until the arrival of James's people, the Jewish Christians of Antioch shared their meals with Gentiles, apparently unconcerned about any questions of doctrinal purity.

While Peter might have been personally fond of this openness—there is evidence throughout the New Testament that Peter was remembered as having shown interest in Gentile Christians—he could not bring himself to flout the Law before the vicarious eyes of James the brother of Jesus, his fellow Pillar of the Jerusalem church.

After Peter abandoned the Gentile table, Paul writes he "opposed him to his face"—a ploy that might have backfired, for "the other Jews joined [Peter] in his hypocrisy," including Barnabas, who had hitherto been one of Paul's closest associates. Let us say that the account in Acts of the Jerusalem conference is accurate; James still dispatched brothers to monitor Paul in Antioch. Whatever the case, we know from Paul himself that he, at least, believed he had come to an "agreement" with James and the Pillars about his Gentile mission, but this agreement was rather more tenuous than Paul understood. So who were these "false brothers," this "circumcision faction," sent to spy on Paul? Paul does not name them and implies they were a cabal within the Jerusalem church. What is clear is that they had authority, and it is not a speculative leap to imagine they represented the interests of James the brother of Jesus.

While the row at Antioch concerned dietary law, it was the circumcision debate that resurfaced in Paul's Galatian churches. The fact that the Galatians' visitors made a bunch of Gentiles contemplate undergoing the supremely unappealing ritual of circumcision goes some way toward establishing the respect with which the Galatians greeted their visitors and the fear these visitors inspired in them. While the Galatians' visitors were what we today would broadly understand as Christians, they were Jewish Christians who believed the only way into their faith was through circumcision and other Judaic rituals—Christians in the apparent way James the brother of Jesus, if not Peter himself, was a Christian.

It is a near historical certainty that a few of Jesus's earliest followers—and, going by Paul's first letter to the Corinthians, perhaps even members of Jesus's family—were involved in some type of missionary effort within Judaea and a few select points beyond, the initial focus of which appears to have been Jews and other Semitic peoples but which gradually opened itself up, in some way, to Gentiles. This mission was apparently overseen by, and in close contact with, the Jerusalem mother church.* It is a historical certainty that Paul was involved in a wider, more diffusely governed, and better understood missionary effort, the focus of which was Gentile communities and which did not prescribe obedience to Jewish Law. These two missions sometimes cooperated but, not surprisingly, came into at least occasional conflict over matters of observance and doctrinal emphasis.

As one of many Christian messengers, Paul began at a disadvantage. Most Greeks and Jews knew nothing of the life or teachings of the obscure Galilean healer Paul was championing as God resurrected, and it is quite clear from Paul's own epistles that many regarded his message as something between nonsense and insanity: the words of a man who traveled too much, thought too much, and spent far too much time alone. Many who did show interest in Paul's preaching later encountered other Christian missionaries, whereupon they discovered that a number of Paul's views were different from those held by people who, like Peter, personally knew Jesus. Paul had no hierarchical structure beneath him, whereas Jesus's original followers, many still living in or working out of Jerusalem, appear to have enjoyed a large

---

* The word translated in the New Testament as "church," *ekklesia,* means "assembly." Drawn from secular Greek political vocabulary—it was used to indicate a democratic town meeting during the high point of Athenian democracy—the word appears in the gospels only twice, both times in Matthew. It is thus with great caution that scholars speak of a "Jerusalem church," which creates in the minds of modern readers a number of associations that are semantically untenable and historically misleading. Here it is used to describe nothing more than a community of more or less like-minded believers who share some form of ritual observance. Closer to the end of the first century, there definitely was something that could be described as the Palestinian church, emphasis on *church,* and it likely descended from Jesus's original followers in Jerusalem.

and (at least initially) well-run organizational foundation. After
a decade of missionary work, Paul could claim no more than
five hundred followers around the Gentile Mediterranean. At
the same time, the Jerusalem church claimed thousands of followers throughout Palestine. In addition, Paul was circumspect
about many of the most charismatic aspects of early Christianity, such as speaking in tongues and channeling visions, largely
because he feared it made Christians look foolish to outsiders.
Paul's mission, furthermore, was sometimes sabotaged: in his
second letter to the Thessalonians, he has to argue against a letter the church has received that claimed to be from him. (The
fact that Paul's second letter to the Thessalonians was probably
not written by Paul brings the impersonation wonderfully full
circle.) Paul's greatest disadvantage, however, was his perceived
authority as he competed with missionaries from the Jerusalem
church whose claim to represent the message and meaning of
Jesus was, on its surface, unassailable.

Over time, the Twelve Apostles became something quite
different from what the New Testament's glancing accounts of
Jesus's original followers suggests. Their trajectory within and
without the New Testament is awesomely complicated and tied
to innumerable and often untrackable developments within
Christian theology but basically goes like this: they begin as a
Jewish eschatological idea (Twelve Apostles to judge the twelve
tribes of Israel), expand into devout missionaries spreading
the word to Gentiles, mature as pastoral leaders of many early
churches, expire as glorified martyrs, and finally fossilize into
the foundation on which orthodox beliefs were built. Paul's ideas
about Jesus ultimately won out, and his victory was no small part
of the long, strange process by which the Twelve transformed
from Jewish judges into Christian cornerstones.

III.

If one reads between the lines in Galatians, several things
become clear. Those who lived in the middle of the first century

and believed in the messianic fulfillment of Jesus had become a prominent movement not only in Jerusalem but beyond. Many Gentiles were attracted to this movement. Attempts were being made to work out the differences between those who wished the faith to remain predominantly Jewish in its character and those who wished to enter into some uncharted spiritual territory. Those who knew Jesus personally still possessed a corona of authority. Galatians suggests that when Paul opposed Cephas/Peter "to his face" at Antioch, he might have undergone a personal revolution in his faith. In this way, Christianity can be said to have begun not when Jesus was born, or when he was crucified, but rather during a debate about who should sit with whom during dinner.

Given the events in Jerusalem and Antioch that preceded Paul's arrival in Galatia, far from the reach of the Jerusalem church, it is likely that his message had begun to change and become (to the Christians of Jerusalem at least) radicalized: it was Jesus's death and resurrection that marked this new faith, not any observance of ancient laws. To the entirely Gentile Galatians, this must have seemed a thrilling prospect. Many Greek-speaking pagans admired the Jews, but found themselves closed off from Judaism by a series of alien cultural requirements.

In the minds of many within the Jerusalem church, conversely, Paul might have been perceived as having traversed a bridge too far. Its leader James probably came to realize that in agreeing to Paul's suggestion that Gentiles not undergo circumcision, he had, in effect, given Paul the perceived right to shape and alter the Jewish faith's other, more visible rituals and rules, thereby endangering the Jewish identity and the nature of early Christianity. Paul was probably also feared by the Jerusalem Christians because of his rhetorical brilliance and the gale force of his liberating message. Of the apostles, Eusebius wrote, "Those inspired and wonderful men, Christ's apostles, had completely purified their lives and cultivated every spiritual virtue, but their speech was that of every day.... [H]aving neither the ability nor the desire to present the teachings of the Master with rhetorical subtlety or literary skill, they relied only on demonstrating the divine Spirit working with them, and on the miraculous power of Christ fully operative in them." Paul, on the other hand, "surpassed all others in the marshalling of his arguments and in the abundance of his ideas." While this is not historical information, its psychological canniness feels roughly convincing.

By the time of the Galatian crisis, at some point in the early 50s, Paul's churches were spotted throughout modern-day Greece, Macedonia, and Turkey. Some were in small towns, such as Philippi, and some were in cities, such as Corinth and Ephesus. Most were centers of trade, predominantly Greek speaking, and connected by magnificent Roman roads. Paul's Law-less, entirely Christ-based gospel was spreading, and the worried, confused leaders of the Jerusalem church clearly felt they had to do something to bring it into line. Thus the delegation to Galatia was dispatched, at James's order, to revisit with Paul basic cultic issues that had been addressed so imperfectly in Jerusalem, and which visit Paul later represented to his Galatian converts as sabotage.

IV.

To Roman Catholics, Peter is the foundation of the Roman church, which was and is Paul's church, formed and driven by Paul's ideas. Yet Peter, according to Paul's ancient witness, understood himself as the apostle to the circumcised.* Protestants, on the other hand, reject the idea that Jesus intended Peter to begin a papal line to forever hold sway over the Christian world and instead claim Paul's visionary, personal experience of Jesus as the true crystallization of Christian faith. Yet Paul himself was suspicious of visions. His own experience led him to appreciate visions but with the secondary recognition

---

* This is one of the most historically important admissions Paul made. Throughout his letters, Paul claims there is but one gospel. But in calling Peter the apostle to the circumcised, Paul is acknowledging the existence of another gospel.

that they could be abused. In his letter to the Colossians, he writes, "Do not let anyone disqualify you, insisting on . . . worship of angels, dwelling on visions, puffed up without cause." Paul's work within young and necessarily unstable churches had convinced him that visions could be employed to justify any new thing that the visionary had seen, and apparently the Colossians were having visions that Paul was leading them astray. (Later, the Gospel According to John would be even more strident on this issue: Jesus calls anyone who claims to have seen Heaven during a vision a liar.) Historically speaking, then, it is possible that both Catholics and Protestants have claimed for themselves inappropriate apostolic guarantors.

For those who do not hold to the tenets of any Christian orthodoxy, Paul is among the more maligned figures in early Christianity. Nietzsche, for instance, referred to him as a "morbid crank" guilty of "the falsification of true Christianity." Not often appreciated are the cultural force fields into which Paul routinely crashed. Let us imagine the man having some success with pagan Gentiles. For these people, becoming a member of a self-identified Christian group was unlike any other association in the ancient world. Paul is never more likable in his letters than when he discusses the transfiguring power of his faith and the lives he has seen it change. Much of Paul's epistolary warmth comes from his faith in the inclusiveness and egalitarianism of early Christianity. The official titles that distinguished important members in other cultic groups are absent from Paul's letters.* Two words Paul regularly employs are "brother" and "sister," which is one of the ways scholars have separated Paul's genuine letters from those written in his name by his followers. The undisputed Pauline letters use "brother" or "sister" almost five dozen times, the disputed letters fewer than ten times.

Enter Paul's opponents, who swooped in on these delicate

---

* The titles he does use, such as *diakonos*, are disputed, and there is little scholarly agreement about what those who held these titles were expected to do.

communities to make unbending demands such as circumcision, keeping the Sabbath holy by refusing to work, and refusing
to purchase meat from pagan butchers. The average Jerusalem
Christian might have had little frame of reference for the com-
plications early Gentile believers in Jesus faced in non-Jewish
milieus. In predominantly Jewish communities like Jerusalem,
such exclusivity and separateness could be indulged, but in his
slow, painstaking work of winning pagan hearts, Paul could not
realistically ask Gentiles to avoid pagan butchers: at the time,
almost all butchers were priests of one stripe or another.* He
could not ask Gentiles to keep the Sabbath holy: virtually all
of them would have worked for pagan employers and quickly
lost their jobs. This issue came up in the Roman church, and
Paul sensibly addresses it in his letter to the Romans by saying, "Some judge one day to be better than another, while others
judge all days to be alike. Let all be fully convinced in their own
minds." (In Mark, a Paul-like Jesus tells the Pharisees, "The Sabbath was made for humankind, and not humankind for the Sabbath.") The group against whom the thoroughly pragmatic Paul
stands in opposition is, again, almost certainly a delegation from
the Jerusalem church, which is led by at least two apostles and
the brother of Jesus. The peculiar dialectic of the first Christian
leaders unable to agree on such seemingly fundamental issues
would probably strike the average Christian of today as utterly
inexplicable.† Most would probably want to know whose views

---

* The omnipresent importance of this issue can be seen by how often it comes up in
early Christian literature. In his first letter to the Corinthians, Paul ties himself into
a rhetorical square knot trying to find a reasonable position. He says to "flee from
the worship of idols" (that is, do not eat pagan meat), because "pagans sacrifice . . .
to demons and not to God." He then announces, seemingly definitively, "You cannot
partake of the table of the Lord and the table of demons." Backpedaling mightily,
he then says, "If an unbeliever invites you to a meal and you are disposed to go,
eat whatever is set before you without raising any question on the ground of conscience." Paul, for all his gifts, must have been a triumphantly confusing teacher.
† Ancient Christians had an equally difficult time grappling with the implications of
this divide. In an obvious attempt to sidestep the issue, Clement of Alexandria and

are closer to those of Jesus. Despite writing in closer historical proximity to Jesus than the gospel writers, Paul is unable to make even one explicit citation of Jesus's words to support his positions. Yet the writers of the gospels later use Jesus's words to buttress many of Paul's positions. The chicken thus contemplates its egg.

A venerable view of the conflict contained within Galatians, eloquently defended today by the scholar Michael Goulder, puts forth Paul as the missionary enemy of Peter and James the brother of Jesus. But this may be too simple a postulation to adequately capture the nature of early Christian confusion. The scholar John Painter proposes a complicated, more nuanced view of the likely scenario faced by Paul and the Jerusalem church. Painter identifies no fewer than six factions within the Jerusalem church and Gentile Christian movement. The first faction, comprising men like the Christian Pharisees mentioned in Acts and referred to by Paul in Galatians as "false brothers," were Law absolutists fiercely opposed to Paul's mission to the Gentiles. The second faction was made up of those who, in Painter's words, "recognized the validity of the two missions but were themselves

---

Origen argued that the Cephas with whom Paul crossed swords in Galatians was not the apostle Peter at all. While Jerome believed Cephas and Peter were the same person, he agreed with one aspect of Origen's argument: the debate between Peter and Paul was simulated to smoke out those Christians still ritualistically inclined toward Judaism. The explanation horrified Augustine, who politely but sharply requested that Jerome "provide us with some rules for discerning when lying is expedient and when it is not." When Augustine's letter finally reached him (one or more intervening letters between the men have been lost; their epistolary debate seems to have lasted many years), Jerome somewhat breezily admitted he had "dictated to my amanuensis sometimes what was borrowed from other writers, sometimes what was my own, without distinctly remembering the method, or the words, or the opinions which belonged to each." More lost and delayed letters passed between the two—the contents of which were often made public, to Jerome's anger and Augustine's sincere embarrassment—but Jerome, with more than a teaspoon of sophistry, held to his position on Galatians. While he and Augustine closed the matter on fairly good terms, most scholars give the argument to Augustine on merits.

committed to the mission of and to the circumcision"; the leader of this faction, Painter proposes, was James the brother of Jesus. The third faction, led by Peter, also accepted the two missions but with a greater conceptual openness to Gentiles; from Paul's letter to the Galatians, it seems clear Peter accepted that the two missions had different ground rules, even if the lines between them sometimes blurred, and that Gentiles were theoretically free from aspects of Judaic ritual but Jews were not. The fourth faction, which counted among its leaders Paul's friend Barnabas, had a more open-minded philosophy on the Law; as Painter writes, "Their policy was that home rules applied when the missions intersected." The fifth faction, led by Paul, believed in a gospel that obliterated the distinction between Jew and Gentile. The sixth faction, which comes glimpsingly into view within some of Paul's letters, "advocated an absolutely law-free mission recognizing no constraints whatsoever, ritual or moral"; Paul's problems with the first three factions might have stemmed from his being unfairly linked to this last and most radical Gentile Christian faction. Painter's vision of early Christianity coheres not only with internal New Testament evidence but with the laws of human nature. In any elaborate human undertaking—and here the early Christian mission qualifies marvelously—factionalism of this kind is the rule. There is an argument to be made that the gospels themselves are products of similar factionalization.

The discrepancy between what Paul presumed to know about Jesus and who Jesus actually was became only one of the arrows in the rhetorical quiver his opponents emptied against him. In the third-century corpus known as the Pseudo-Clementine literature, an author writing under the name of Clement of Rome attributes to Peter the following statement: "Observe the greatest caution, that you believe no teacher unless he brings the testimonial of James the Lord's brother from Jerusalem, or whomever comes after him. Under no circumstances, receive anyone or consider him a worthy and faithful teacher for preaching the word of Christ, unless he has gone up there, been approved, and, as I say, brings a testimonial from there."

Despite the Pseudo-Clementine corpus's pseudepigraphical authorship, such sentiment may reflect an accurate historical memory, for here is Paul, who might have lacked such recommendation, in his second letter to the Corinthians: "Are we beginning to commend ourselves again? Surely we do not need, as some do, letters of recommendation to you or from you, do we?" Later in this letter, we see evidence of the relentless whisper campaign used against Paul reducing him to his wit's end: "Are they Hebrews? So am I. Are they Israelites? So am I. Are they descendents of Abraham? So am I. Are they ministers of Christ? I am talking like a madman—I am a better one." Paul engaged elsewhere in similarly reckless rhetoric, even going so far as to claim that the Law came to an end in Jesus, with whom Paul, as he wrote to the Galatians, had been co-crucified. This mystical self-confidence allowed Paul to claim, among other things, that he knew Jesus better than Jesus's own brother.

Paul's letter to the Galatians makes any number of similarly astounding claims; its third chapter is a virtual thesaurus of Jewish blasphemy. In 3:8, Paul writes, "The scripture, foreseeing that God would justify the Gentiles by faith, declared the gospel beforehand to Abraham, saying, 'All the Gentiles shall be blessed before you.'" Because, in the Jewish tradition, Gentiles did not have the Law, they were viewed by some as sinners living outside the parameters of divine sanction and forgiveness.* Paul nevertheless uses the proto-Jewish ancestor to show how Gentiles fit into the Judaic tradition. Hearing this read aloud, the Galatians' visitors probably could not believe Paul's audacity. In 3:19, Paul makes an equally bizarre claim: namely, that the Law "was added because of our transgression." In other words, the Law was intended to *provoke* disobedience to God so that he

---

* Some scholars have challenged the notion that most first-century Jews automatically regarded Gentiles as ritually impure. As in most mixed societies, the demands of religious mandate were erratically chipped away by the niceties of individual experience. Several books of the Hebrew Bible, in fact, incorporate Gentiles into their apocalyptic scenarios, sometimes subjugating them to Israel but sometimes deigning to include them within God's salvific plan.

would have no other choice but to send "the offspring," Jesus, to rectify the matter.

According to Michael Goulder, Paul's dilemma was "impossible" because he "believed two contradictory things." The Law was God's, yes, and as such the moral benchmark for Gentiles, but parts of it were no longer necessary. Paul often quoted the Hebrew Bible when he needed something to support his views but also believed that Jesus had rendered important parts of it obsolete. This was—and remains—a difficult argument to sustain. (The second-century philosopher Celsus was more than happy to point out the religious difficulty here: "Well, who is to be disbelieved—Moses or Jesus?") Even Goulder, who is sympathetic to Paul, has unkind things to say about Paul's reasoning in the third chapter of Galatians, which "is not a happy chapter. It is written by a man with his back to the wall. . . . Even if Paul were justified in his claim that *salvation* is based on *faith,* the plain sense of scripture is that you should keep the Law as well." The final third of Galatians finds him arguing that "the circumcised do not themselves obey the law," a charge clearly launched out of desperation.

Anyone who has written or received a poison pen letter can chart the stages of Paul's emotional journey throughout Galatians: factual appeal, attempted outreach, growing anger, and finally a barrage of insult. It ends with his attempting to clean the slate of the entire issue: "For neither circumcision nor uncircumcision is anything."

V.

Later Paul would take another run at the Law. The result was his letter to the Romans, probably his most brilliant and sustained intellectual statement, not to mention one of Western civilization's central documents; Martin Luther considered it the "chief part of the New Testament" and "the purest gospel." Romans is also, significantly, the one letter Paul wrote to a

Christian community with which he had no direct experience. That personal distance is used to great rhetorical benefit.

One conclusion Paul comes to in Romans is this: "Do we then overthrow the law by this faith? By no means! On the contrary, we uphold the law." This is hardly what we would expect the author of Galatians to argue. Some scholars have wondered if Paul, when informed of his Galatian letter's unfavorable reception, was forced to reevaluate his beliefs. We can be virtually certain that the borderline heresies of Galatians would have been shared with the Jerusalem church, to which Paul later pledged financial support from his wealthier Gentile converts. While Acts shows Paul, on his third and final visit to "the brothers" in Jerusalem at some point in the early 60s, being "warmly" welcomed, "the Jews from Asia" (who these shadowy figures might be is not explained) are not so forgiving. "This is the man," the Asian Jews proclaim, "who is teaching everywhere against our people, our law, and this place." They then "seized Paul and dragged him out of the Temple," but while "they were trying to kill him," Paul is said by Luke to have been rescued not by the brothers of the Jerusalem church, as one might expect, but by a Roman tribune and some soldiers, who put him into protective custody. From there, Paul is sent to Rome and, according to tradition, executed, an event unrecorded by the New Testament.

Yet, from a modern perspective, the disagreement between Paul and his opponents was not that profound. Paul accepted that those who were observant of the Law before coming to a belief in Jesus could remain under the Law. But what about those who were *not* under the Law before coming to a belief in Jesus? Did the Law apply to them at all? Belief in Jesus meant some abandonment of strict Judaic observance, but how much and to what degree? As far as we can tell, Jesus went only so far in the minds of many Jerusalem Christians, and the place at which their Jesus stopped was the Law. Their Jesus was in some way godly, their Jesus was resurrected (Paul grants his opponents belief in the resurrection), but he did not override the Law. He was, instead, a divine sacrifice made by God in order to forgive Israel its sins and welcome Gentiles into an amended pact. Paul's Jesus was something more powerful yet: a cosmic reboot who annihilated all earthly difference.* As Paul wrote to the Galatians, "There is no longer Jew or Greek, there is no longer slave or free, there is no longer male and female; for all of you are one in Christ Jesus."

We know what happened to Paul's church, the spires and domes of which fill the cities of the Christian world.† The fate of the Jewish Christians of the Jerusalem church is more difficult to locate, though like a dying star their influence continued to pulse for centuries. Roughly four decades after Paul's martyrdom (traditionally thought to have occurred around 65 CE), Ignatius, the bishop of Antioch, while on his way to his own Roman martyrdom, wrote to his fellow Christians in the city of Philadelphia. Foremost on Ignatius's otherwise occupied mind was this: "But if anyone expounds Judaism to you, do not listen to him. For it is better to hear about Christianity from a man who is circumcised than about Judaism from one who is not." In other words, seven decades after the death of Jesus, Christianity's apparently subordinate relationship to Judaism was still being debated, and the agitators, as we can see from Ignatius's letter, were not always Jewish themselves but *Gentiles* convinced by the arguments of Paul's opponents.

Remnant communities filled with the intellectual inheritors of Paul's opponents developed their own body of (mostly vanished) literature throughout the second century and in many cases used Peter and James the brother of Jesus as their mouth-

---

* The historian Diarmaid MacCulloch notes that Paul's belief in the universality of Jesus's deliverance might have been fed by the fact that Paul was a citizen of the Roman Empire, a civilization whose "sense of racial exclusiveness" was uniquely lax. How Paul became a Roman citizen is yet another of the New Testament's mysteries, though many suspect that his citizenship derived, in some way, from his father, who might have been a slave who achieved manumission.

† As for Paul's remains, they are today purportedly held within a Roman basilica called Saint Paul Outside-the-Walls.

pieces. *The Epistle of Peter to James* (a pseudepigraphic epistle), for instance, attacks any Law-less gospel as false. "For some from among the Gentiles have rejected my legal preaching," "Peter" writes, "attaching themselves to certain lawless and trifling preaching of the man who is my enemy"—a clear reference to Paul. In a now-lost second-century apocryphal work known as *The Ascent of James,* a figure probably intended to be Paul attacks and badly wounds James on the steps of the Temple. The story, while clearly legendary and ahistorical, further establishes the toxicity of later Jewish Christian feelings toward Paul. Other, angrier Jewish Christians apparently went so far as to question whether Paul was a Jew at all. There may be something to this. If Paul, as he claimed, underwent rabbinical training as a Pharisee, why is the Jewish scripture with which he appears familiar the Greek Septuagint rather than the Hebrew original? Would not his professed trade of tent making—which would have presumably brought him into frequent contact with forbidden tanned leathers—have been an odd occupation for a once-devout Jew to pursue? An especially spectacular example of the Jewish disownment of Paul, deemed heresy by the fourth-century Christian bishop Epiphanius, in whose work the charge survives, claims Paul was a Greek who converted to Judaism only to win the heart of a young woman from Jerusalem. She was said to have spurned Paul, thus poisoning him against the faith.

VI.

As for the Jerusalem and Palestinian churches, what happened to their members cannot be reduced to any one event. One problem, it seems, was money. Acts describes Barnabas selling his Cypriot farm and giving the money to the Jerusalem church, which was apparently in keen need of funds. How seriously money was regarded by the early church can be seen from Acts' sad story of Ananias and Sapphira, who sell their property but do not donate all the money to the church. The

Holy Spirit quickly strikes them dead, one after the other, for withholding.

It would appear that many in the Jerusalem and Palestinian churches believed the end of the world was near, Jesus's return was imminent, and money would no longer have any value. This profligate, fatalism-born charity attracted many followers, perhaps as many as three thousand, a number of whom were no doubt hungry, desperate people in search of a free meal. Within years, though, the tithes ran out, and the world had not ended; the Jerusalem church's worries about money, and supporting its increasingly embattled community, became dire. This is one explanation for why, fifteen years later, the Pillars asked Paul to use his wealthy Gentile converts to help them financially, which, Paul claimed, "was actually what I was eager to do."* Paul's last, disastrous visit to Jerusalem, which ended with him in Roman chains, was supposed to see him deliver to the Jerusalem Christians these promised tithes. The New Testament is strangely silent as to whether the money was ever received.

By the mid-60s, several hammers had fallen on the Jerusalem church. James the brother of Jesus, the Jerusalem church's leader, was killed by Temple authorities around 62. The Jewish revolt against Rome began four years later, and Jerusalem itself was largely destroyed in 70. According to Eusebius, "after the martyrdom of James and the capture of Jerusalem which instantly [sic] followed," the surviving members of Jesus's original circle of fol-

---

* Paul might have reasoned that a fine way to stay on the Jerusalem church's good side was to keep the tithes coming. Paul's agreeableness here resulted in his and the Jerusalem church's actively working together. One of its representatives, Silas, traveled with him to Greece; at Philippi, according to Acts, they were publicly beaten by local magistrates. Unfortunately, during their travels, Silas apparently encouraged the same careless, end-of-days communalism that had landed the Jerusalem church in such woebegone straits. Later, Paul patiently tries to instruct the Thessalonians out of this mess, urging them with his stolid tent-maker logic "to work with your hands, so that you may ... be dependent on no one." This was his first letter to the church. Apparently, it did little to solve the problem, for the second letter to the Thessalonians is much blunter: "Anyone unwilling to work should not eat."

lowers, including his brothers, fled across the river Jordan "and settle[d] in a town in Peraea [Jordan] called Pella." The historicity of the Pella flight is disputed, but it is known that many Jewish Christians took refuge in various cities and towns within Jordan and Syria following the Jewish revolt against Rome. Some Jewish Christians evidently remained there after Simon, according to tradition, led the church back to Jerusalem in the mid- to late 70s.

The first Christians, all of whom were Jews, did not refer to themselves as Christians. They were apparently known to outsiders as Nazarenes and initially referred to themselves as "followers of the Way." The phrase appears many times in Acts ("so that if he found any who belonged to the Way"; "He had been instructed in the Way of the Lord"; "some stubbornly refused to believe and spoke evil of the Way") and may be related to certain sayings of Jesus's that stressed the importance of traveling through narrow gates rather than wide ones: "For the gate is narrow and the road is hard that leads to life; and there are few who find it" (Matthew 9:14).

The astonishing speed with which "Nazarene" or "Nazorean" vanished from Christian use is puzzling, though its Semitic roots were never fully extirpated: even today, the word for "Christian" in Arabic is *Nasrani*. Yet for those Christians living only a few hundred years after Jesus, "Nazarene" had become a confusing, vaguely threatening term. The fourth-century bishop Epiphanius, for instance, related the story of the Jerusalem church's flight to Pella after the Roman destruction of Jerusalem and described the descendants of those Christians as belonging to a sect he called *Nazoraioi,* or "Nazarenes," all of whom he regarded as apostates, despite his admission that "all Christians were called Nazarenes once." In other words, incredibly, the Christians Epiphanius recognized as having clear historical ties to the original followers of Jesus were condemned by him as heretics. Not every church father was as unkind to the Nazarenes as Epiphanius, and some, such as Jerome, showed measured interest in the sect. The great historical irony is that the Nazarenes, as best as can be reconstructed, were, aside from their continued observance of Mosaic Law, proto-orthodox Christians and, according to Jerome, did not regard the Pauline mission as a mistake, even though many other—indeed, probably most other—Jewish Christians did.

What likely poisoned the Nazarenes' reputation were various schismatic developments within Jewish Christianity itself. In time, there would arise in Jordan and Syria—where the Nazarenes had fled and taken root—Christians known as Ebionim or Ebionites, which means "the poor." This was a term used in Psalms for the persecuted; it was also an apparently accurate descriptor of these Christians' perceived liquidity. According to Epiphanius, the Ebionites had become impoverished by money-sharing practices similar to those depicted in Acts. Epiphanius did not believe any of this and, like Tertullian before him, attributed their beliefs to their teacher, a man named Ebion, who, unfortunately for this thesis, did not exist.

While Christians calling themselves Ebionites held varying beliefs, a large group of them appear to have used a gospel known by multiple names in antiquity, from *The Gospel of the Ebionites* to *The Gospel According to the Twelve Apostles,* which was narrated by the apostles themselves and of which no complete copy survives. These Ebionites appear to have denied the virgin birth and been largely vegetarian, going so far as to eliminate "locusts" from the canonical gospels' itemization of John the Baptist's diet by changing the Greek word's first letter, thus turning "locusts" into "honey cakes." These were the most anti-Paul and radical Jewish Christians, and eventually their beliefs drifted into something that barely resembled Christianity at all.

Unfortunately for the Nazarenes, "Ebionite" appears to have become the accepted designation for any Jewish Christian after the second century—"a catch-all," in the words of the scholar Ray A. Pritz, "for Law-keeping Christians of Jewish background." Somehow, these direct inheritors of Jesus's message managed to become, by the fourth century, proclaimed enemies of the

Christian church—and not only the Christian church. According to Epiphanius, even Jewish children hated the Nazarenes: "The people also stand up in the morning, at noon, and in the evening, three times a day[,] and they pronounce curses and maledictions over them. . . . Three times a day they say: 'May God curse the Nazarenes.'"

The New Testament thus achieves a curious distinction. It chiefly describes the growth and consolidation of a Jewish sect whose original name was forgotten, confused, and finally traduced, its descendants brushed aside as heretics. The Law itself became a powerful taboo for Gentile Christians, thus proving the worst fears James the brother of Jesus held about Paul's mission.

There are indications of this patently bizarre trajectory found within the New Testament itself. The Gospels According to Mark and John frequently attack any vestigial loyalty to Jewish Law. John's relatively late composition date—probably the late 80s, possibly the early second century—can be seen by how remote the struggle over the Law now seems to its author. John's Jesus speaks of "the law of Moses" and, more strangely, "your law." Perhaps the most telling moment in John's gospel occurs when Jesus confronts "the Jews who had believed in him." Jesus tells them, "If you continue in my word, you are truly my disciples. . . . I know that you are descendants of Abraham; yet you look for an opportunity to kill me, because there is no place in you for my word." On hearing this, the Jews who once believed in Jesus try to stone him, because Jesus has just claimed he existed before Abraham and, thus, the Law itself. This could easily have been interpreted as blasphemy, the penalty for which was, often, stoning. The "Jews" John attacks in his gospel are *believers* in Jesus. But by the time of John's final stage of composition, all of those who knew Jesus were dead, and the warmth or tolerance that Christians of different understandings were once willing to show one another was no more.

PHILIP &
JAMES SON OF ALPHAEUS

The Church of the Holy Apostles: Rome, Italy

THE CAPITOLINE • SANTI APOSTOLI • FATHER
DARIO • THE LITTLE • MANY JAMESES • LOVER OF
HORSES • WAITING TABLES • INSIDE THE CHURCH
OF THE HOLY APOSTLES • THE LETTER OF JAMES •
THE ACTS OF PHILIP • THE WELL OF THE MARTYRS •
A TENNESSEAN

I.

A fine vantage point to see Rome, I was told, was from atop
the highest stair of the Victor Emmanuel Monument on
the Capitoline Hill. One afternoon, on my way to the Church of
the Holy Apostles, I headed up there. Soon spread out before
me was a pine-splashed stonescape of dune-brown and sodium-
white buildings squatly penitent among the higher domes and
cross-topped steeples. Deep rivers of shade filled the narrow
streets.

At the base of the Capitoline Hill was the Piazza Venezia's
forbidding roundabout. Tourists scrambled across the zebra-
striped crosswalks, half the cars not bothering to slow down. Via
del Corso, one of Rome's most storied streets, was just beyond
the Palazzo Venezia, at the piazza's northern edge. Down the
Corso I went, looking for a cross street called Via Santi Apostoli. I
knifed through the quickly forming, quickly closing holes in the
crowds, past the tourists licking their gelati into little globes as
small and cold and colorful as outer-rim planets and around the

Italian businessmen in their fine suits and flowery ties swinging their briefcases like battering rams. The hard right turn I finally took onto Via Santi Apostoli was not unlike stepping from a storm into a cave: the street was silent and empty. On the right, past the café, was a health club and something called the Time Elevator Roma, an Epcot-esque motion-simulated roller-coaster ride through various Roman epochs. The door to Time Elevator Roma was affixed with a bizarre sign, at least by Roman standards: OPEN EVERY DAY.

The small and cobbled Via Santi Apostoli ended at the Piazza dei Santi Apostoli, a long, narrow municipal rectangle bordered by mostly characterless buildings. Santi Apostoli, or the Church of the Holy Apostles, stretched along the piazza's eastern edge. It was one of Rome's older churches, founded perhaps as early as the sixth century, but its various reconstructions and restorations had diminished its ecclesiastical appearance. It looked, more than anything, like some minor baronial residence. Behind the roof's marble balustrade stood statues of the Holy Apostles themselves, but the marble had gone pitted and soot colored, ceding the apostles the tragic look of partially melted snowmen.

The exterior of this handsomely dull basilica suggested little of its impressive pedigree. The great Italian sculptor Antonio Canova had one important early work inside the church and another outside on its portico; Michelangelo had for a time rested here in state before his body's transfer to Santa Croce in Florence. The original sixth-century church was destroyed by an earthquake in the mid-fourteenth century and abandoned until 1417, when Pope Martin V set out to rebuild Santi Apostoli. Clement XI ordered the church's next reconstruction in the early eighteenth century. The basilica's ground-floor arcade featured nine gated arches, all presently closed.

A pink-plastered three-story building next to the church contained both a convent and the offices of Rome's Franciscan order, whose headquarters the Church of the Holy Apostles provided. The door was open, though the front office was empty and dark.

The air was thick with retirement-community smells of intimate negligence: candle wax, plastic flowers, ash. A thin, unsmiling English-speaking nun appeared and asked what I wanted. I told her I had an appointment with Father Dario. What, she asked, was the purpose of my visit? I told her I wished to learn more about the church and its apostolic inhabitants, Philip and James son of Alphaeus, to whom this church had been jointly dedicated fourteen centuries ago. "Are you a historian?" she asked.

"No," I said.

"Good," she said. "Usually the historians get their information from us." With that, she went to summon Father Dario.

It was midwinter, but the church courtyard felt unseasonably warm. An obviously homeless woman seeking charity sat on one of the courtyard's marble benches. Her thin white socks, having long lost their elasticity, were collapsed little bundles atop her cheap tennis shoes. Then Father Dario appeared, greeting the homeless woman and me in turn. He was a short pugnacious man in a black V-neck sweater with a black collared shirt beneath it. Violent slashes of black hair marked the backs of his hands and knuckles.

He led me away from the courtyard and into a dark side office distinguished by a wheeled garment rack and a large stained-glass window. The sun passed through the window's metal-edged panels in diffuse amalgams of color, leaving overlapping quadrangles of red, blue, and orange light on the floor. The sun did not travel far into this room, the rest of which was shadowy until Father Dario turned on his desk lamp.

Father Dario was surprised, he said, when he learned that an American student—I didn't bother to correct this—had come here to talk to him about Philip and James son of Alphaeus. In fact, he went on, no one had *ever* come here to discuss the apostles with him.

"Never?" I said.

"No," he said. "Not once in my six years of service." With some pride he noted that Philip's and James's bodies had been at the Church of the Holy Apostles since 560. "The remains of their bodies," he quickly clarified. "Minus the liquids."

He sat at his desk and proceeded to search through its drawers, finally setting out on its tabletop three books, all of which were available for purchase in the gift store: *La Basilica dei Santi XII Apostoli, Filippo e Giacomo, Iscrizioni Della Basilica e Convento dei Santi Dodici Apostoli in Roma.* They were thin, more like samizdat pamphlets than books.

I paged dumbly through these offerings for a while. Then I looked up and asked Father Dario how exactly Philip and James were venerated today.

Father Dario nodded. "The third of May is their feast day."

This was not quite my question. "How," I asked, "were Philip and James different from the other apostles? What specifically marked their cult?"

Father Dario smiled impatiently. He was about to speak when there came a soft, barely discernible knock on his office door. Father Dario rose to answer it. An impressively pregnant woman, smiling apologetically and wearing coveralls and a winter coat, walked into the room. Her son, no older than ten and wearing a ragged red jacket that he was in the process of unzipping, followed her in. Both were black-haired and cola colored— South American, possibly. Father Dario welcomed the pair with enthusiasm, after which they stood next to me. "This is my son," the woman said to me, in Spanish-accented English. "Hello," the boy said. She was carrying a white grocery bag stretched tight around a long submarine of bread. Two things seemed clear: she was poor, and she was here for something.

"One moment," Father Dario said to me. I threw up my hands obligingly. He then turned to the woman and spoke in Italian, which she answered in a series of halting *sìs* and *nos*.

When they finished talking, the woman and her son did not leave. Father Dario nevertheless returned his attention to me. "I am disappointed," he said, "in the devotion of the following of these saints here. There is not a great following for them. This is a general Catholic crisis. It has happened to the cults of the saints in general. All of them." He frowned. "Saints today, I think, are in movies and politics. Beautiful men for beautiful women. Those are our saints now."

The boy walked past Father Dario's desk and stopped at the wheeled garment rack, from which a dozen priestly vestments hung. The boy reverently touched them, as though pondering a possible priestly future for himself. The woman looked at Father Dario for his reaction. Father Dario's impassive face had a morbid cheddar hue in the light of his desk lamp. No one said anything for several seconds.

"Which of the two apostles is more celebrated here?" I asked Father Dario at last.

Father Dario debuted a new, beetle-browed expression. It said, *I have more pressing work to do than this.* "I'm sorry. What is your question?"

I repeated it.

"Philip is more known," he said. "It was Philip who assisted Christ during the miracle of the loaves and fishes and Philip who said, 'Show us the Father.' Saint James is the author of the Letter of James. Have you read it?"

"Yes," I said. "Of course."

"Then you know its most famous quote: 'Faith without works is dead.'" Now his face softened, as though nothing more needed to be said of Philip and James. The woman, aware that some rare and valuable point had been made, grinned and nodded. The boy was still gently touching Father Dario's vestments.

II.

Philip and James son of Alphaeus are unusually elusive figures in early Christianity. The former might or might not have been the first apostle to make a non-Semitic Christian convert, while the latter might or might not have been the brother of Jesus. Yet both slip like sand through the fingers of identification.

This can, in part, be blamed on the Acts of the Apostles, a book that obscures so many questions, from the precise nature of the forces that drove apart the first community of Christians to why James son of Zebedee was executed to why exactly Paul was accosted in Jerusalem and apprehended by the Romans. The years Acts attempts to cover—roughly, 33 to 60—were momentous ones for the region, the faiths the region birthed, the rulers who held it subject, and the people who called it home. One would hardly gather this from the text of Acts. Using Acts to determine certain events in early Christian history, one scholar has written, is "the path to bewilderment."

For instance, Aretas IV, the king of the Nabataeans, crushed the forces of Herod Antipas, the tetrarch* of Galilee, in 36 CE. Pontius Pilate quashed a prophet-led Samaritan uprising in 37 CE, which ultimately led to his dismissal and return to Rome. The same year saw Caiaphas, the Jewish high priest at the time of Jesus's execution, lose his long-held office, and Tiberius, emperor of Rome since 14 CE, die of natural causes, only to be replaced by the mad Gaius Caligula, whose move to build a statue of himself in Jerusalem set off some of the most determined opposition the Romans had yet encountered in Judaea. In 39, the floundering Herod Antipas, who had beheaded John the Baptist and (according to Luke) mocked Jesus at his trial, was deposed by Gaius and exiled to Gaul. Incredibly, these years were relatively *calm* ones for the region.

By the mid-40s, however, Roman Palestine had been brought to a boil. A mysterious Jewish prophet named Theudas stepped forth around 45 CE to attract several thousand followers, to whom he promised he would part the Jordan River. While en route to the Jordan, Theudas was captured by Roman horsemen and swiftly beheaded. During one of the first Passovers of Ven-

---

* "Tetrarch" literally means "ruler of a fourth part," which is to say, king of one-fourth of Herod the Great's kingdom, which his sons and grandsons variously ruled, always with Roman approval, in the years after his death in 4 BCE.

tidius Cumanus's procuratorship of Judaea (which lasted from 48 to 52), a Roman soldier, according to Josephus, "pulled up his garment and bent over indecently, turning his backside toward the Jews and making a noise as indecent as his attitude." This act—maybe the most politically significant mooning in human history—led to a demonstration and, later, a riot in which hundreds, if not thousands, of Jews were trampled to death. (Josephus tells us thirty thousand Jews died in the riot. As with virtually all of Josephus's numbers—as when he overestimates the height of Mount Tabor by a factor of twenty—this is probably a gross exaggeration.) Shortly thereafter, Jewish bandits robbed a Roman slave in the countryside outside Jerusalem; Cumanus ordered his troops, again according to Josephus, to arrest the inhabitants of all neighboring villages and bring them to his headquarters. In one village, "a soldier found a copy of the sacred Law, tore it in two, and threw it on to the fire" in full view of many hostile Jews. A second large-scale demonstration resulted, during which Cumanus showed some restraint. This was followed by a Jewish-Samaritan guerrilla war in which Cumanus openly sided with the Samaritans, a misadventure that led to Cumanus's recall to Rome and, after some high-level intrigue, banishment. Finally, in 59, the seventy-eight-year-long renovation of the Second Temple, begun under Herod the Great, was completed. The Temple was instantly regarded as one of the most glorious buildings in the world.

Most of these historical events do not find their way into Acts. While Acts does mention Theudas ("Theudas rose up, claiming to be somebody, and a number of men, about four thousand, joined him; but he was killed"), it is an extremely awkward passage, because the author of Acts seems to regard Theudas as someone who lived long ago. A famine that left greater Judaea devastated merits a single mention, and an Egyptian prophet who persuaded several thousand Jerusalemites to follow him to the Mount of Olives is obliquely mentioned when Paul is confused for him.

From this we can see that secular and Christian histories of New Testament times are incomplete mirrors in which occasional glints of one appear in the other. What has been lost within these incomplete reflections has distinct bearing on the problematical identities of both Philip and James son of Alphaeus.

III.

James son of Alphaeus appears in the apostle lists of Mark, Matthew, Luke, and Acts. Mark 15:40, however, also contains a reference to a man literally called "James the little." While nothing in Mark suggests James the little is the same person as James son of Alphaeus, much less an apostle, Christian tradition has long identified James the little as James son of Alphaeus. Because most translations render Mark's "the little" as "the less," "the lesser," or "the younger," ancient and modern interpreters alike have understood Mark's diminutive as a way to distinguish James son of Alphaeus from the more prominent apostle James son of Zebedee, the brother of the apostle John, traditionally known as James the Greater.

Mark tells us James the little had a mother named Mary and a brother named Joses. Jesus, as well, had a mother named Mary and, according to Matthew 13:56 and Mark 6:3, brothers named James, Joses, Simon, and Judas. During the crucifixion of Jesus, Mark 15:40, Matthew 27:55, and John 19:25 place a number of women at the scene, several of whom are named Mary. In Mark and Matthew, the women are "looking on from a distance," while in John they are "near the cross of Jesus." Mark mentions as present any number of women, among them "Mary Magdalene, and Mary the mother of James the [little] and of Joses, and Salome." In Mark's account, then, there is no stated presence of Mary the mother of Jesus. Matthew, on the other hand, names among the women "Mary Magdalene, and Mary the mother of James and Joseph, and the mother of the sons of Zebedee." Again, no explicit mention of Mary the mother of Jesus. In John, they are

"[Jesus's] mother"—John never names this woman as Mary—
"and his mother's sister, Mary the wife of Clopas, and Mary Magdalene." John does not appear to know Jesus's mother's name,
for if he did, he probably would not have reported her sister's
name as Mary.* Traditionally, "Mary the wife of Clopas" has been
identified as the mother of James son of Alphaeus, the logic
being that Clopas and Alphaeus are different transliterations
of the Hebrew name Halphai or Chalpai. Today, however, most
scholars reject this potential solution to James son of Alphaeus's
supremely confusing, highly speculative identity.

In three of the four gospels, we are told Jesus had a mother
named Mary. We are told a certain James had a mother named
Mary. We are told Jesus had a brother named Joses. We are told
a certain James had a brother named Joses. We are told Jesus had
a brother named James. In New Testament times, a relatively
small number of names were in cultural circulation, and these
were all common ones. It is nevertheless odd that virtually every
time this James is mentioned in the gospels, a flock of Marys and
Joseses swoops in on him—so odd that some scholars regard
"James son of Alphaeus" as the composite result of a complicated
editorial (and doctrinal) process by which James the brother of
Jesus, whose prominence in early Christian history is indisput-
able, was overwritten and replaced by an apostle notable only
for his obscurity.

Confusion between James son of Alphaeus and James the
brother of Jesus is almost as old as Christianity itself. That James
the brother of Jesus was the leader of the Jerusalem church—
and, thus, early Christianity itself—there can be no doubt. Paul's
letter to the Galatians and the Acts of the Apostles both attest to
this fact, though obliquely, as do numerous early extra-scriptural
traditions, in which James the brother of Jesus is usually referred
to as James the Just or James the Righteous. Despite this, the

---

* Luke characteristically avoids the confusion by noting only "the women who had
followed [Jesus] from Galilee"; he neglects to provide their names.

New Testament withholds from James the brother of Jesus any formal recognition of leadership.

Many of the earliest church fathers, however they regarded James's identity, did not question the idea that Jesus had brothers. The gospels mention them, as does Paul in his first letter to the Corinthians. Tertullian, too, assumed the "brothers of the Lord" were his blood siblings. But other church fathers saw things differently. Ignatius of Antioch, writing around the turn of the first century, was among the first to argue for Mary's perpetual virginity. By the late second century, the notion that Jesus had blood brothers declined as asceticism and celibacy gained importance in the early church. By the fourth century, it was doomed outright when Mary's perpetual virginity—which denied her having ever enjoyed sexual relations—grew closer to becoming actual Christian doctrine, despite clear biblical evidence against it: Matthew notes that Joseph "had no marital relations with [Mary] until she had borne a son." Modern Christians theologically committed to the concept of Mary's virginity explain this passage away by debating the types of intentionality in orbit around the word "until." But as the scholar John Painter points out, this passage surely would not have been written in such a way by any writer "who wished to maintain that Mary remained a virgin even after the birth of Jesus."

A second-century apocryphal work known since the sixteenth century as the *Protoevangelium of James,* which is a kind of conflation of Matthew and Luke's nativity stories with several eccentric additions (such as a midwife personally inspecting Mary's hymen), made an influentially early case that Mary was forever ignorant of matters of the flesh. Its purported author, who presents himself as Jesus's stepbrother James, argues that Joseph was an elderly widower when he met Mary and that his sons, James included, were the children of his dead wife.

The *Protoevangelium* exists today in over a hundred Greek manuscripts. That so many manuscripts survived helps establish its ancient popularity, which was bolstered by the fourth-century bishop Epiphanius, who championed the "stepbrother solution" to explain the presence of James and the rest of Jesus's brothers in the gospel tradition. The stepbrother solution today remains the predominant Eastern Orthodox position on the issue of Jesus's kin. Yet the *Protoevangelium* fell out of favor in the Western church when Jerome, later in the fourth century, argued that Mary the mother of Jesus had a sister named, yes, Mary, who had a son, James, and that Jesus's brothers were in fact his cousins. Not a single aspect of Jerome's deduction had a scriptural or traditional basis.

Thanks to Jerome, the stepbrother solution provided by the *Protoevangelium* was no longer needed in the Western church. All were cousins, and from there many in the Catholic and, later, Armenian Churches accepted that James son of Alphaeus, "James the little," and James the brother of Jesus were the same person, which is to say the cousin of Jesus. After this was established, as John Painter writes, "James ceased to be a point of focus or concern in any Western tradition." Today many Catholics distinguish James son of Alphaeus from James the brother of Jesus, but not very stridently: the available evidence is confusing enough to baffle the most dogged New Testament detective.

In his first letter to the Corinthians, Paul mentions James the brother of Jesus, noting that the risen Jesus "appeared to James, then to all the apostles." That Paul knew of a tradition in which Jesus graced James with a postresurrection appearance means this tradition ranks among the earliest elements of Jesus's resurrection story. While the New Testament contains no Jesus appearance to James, various other early Christian texts dramatized the scene. Jerome cited one such passage from a now-lost work known as *The Gospel of the Hebrews*. Other traditions appear to have tried to negate Jesus's appearance to James, including John's gospel, which tells us, "For not even [Jesus's] brothers believed in him." (Yet the author of John's gospel also mentions something, on two occasions, that no other evangelist does, which is that Jesus's brothers occasionally traveled with him and the disciples.)

James the brother of Jesus was the central figure of Jerusa-

lem Christianity and one of the central figures in all of Christianity for the first three decades of the faith's existence—and
the only member of Jesus's circle to make an appearance in any
contemporaneous extra-biblical literature. Yet James's role in the
early church was "almost obliterated from the consciousness" of
Christianity, in the words of John Painter. This diminishment
would have real consequences for how the later Gentile Christian church would come to understand its history and relationship to Judaism.

Hegesippus, an apparent Jewish Christian who wrote around
170 CE and whose multiple works are lost but for some scattered citations, noted "there were many Jameses" among the first
group of Christians, but he singled out James the brother of Jesus
as "holy from his birth." In Hegesippus's account, James never
drank wine, never shaved, was a vegetarian, and wore exclusively linen garments. James was supposedly allowed access to
the Temple after the death of Jesus, meaning he was still in the
graces of the religious authorities. Moreover, both Eusebius and
Clement of Alexandria were familiar with traditions that honored James as Jerusalem's first bishop, and later strains of Jewish
Christian thinking, contained in apocryphal works such as *The
Gospel of Thomas, The Gospel of the Hebrews, The First Apocalypse of James,* and the Pseudo-Clementine literature, would all
remember James's leadership of the Jerusalem church.

Now, if the fraternal successor to Jesus pursued Jewish rather
than Gentile Christianity, and did so because he believed it was
what his brother would have wanted, Gentile Christianity could
reasonably be viewed as anything from an accident to a mistake.
Supporting this view is the fact that Christianity began Jewish
and remained predominantly Jewish for several years following
the death of Jesus. While the first Jewish Christians might not
have been beloved by their fellow Jews, the evidence, contained
within Acts and elsewhere, suggests they were initially tolerated
by them, if occasionally chastised. (Not until the early second
century is there definitive evidence that Jews looked upon all

Jewish Christians as apostates.) James, however, presents a different case. Not only did the Jews of Jerusalem tolerate James, but the evidence indicates that many accepted and venerated him—for decades.

From the perspective of Gentile Christianity, obscuring James's prominence and the existence of Jesus's brothers eventually became emotionally necessary, as any acknowledgment of Jewish Christianity's legitimacy seriously compromised Gentile Christianity's assumed preeminence. To illustrate this, we need look no further than Melito, the mid-second-century bishop of Sardis, who referred to Jesus as "him whom the Gentiles worshipped and uncircumcised men admired," which was certainly not the case during Jesus's lifetime. In the third century, Hippolytus of Rome could transmit details about James son of Alphaeus's life and death without having any idea he was possibly discussing James the brother of Jesus. By the fourth century, Eusebius was arguing that Jesus had not "received physical chrism from the Jews," and thus was not Jewish.

Modern scholars of faith are more polite than Eusebius, but many are no more willing to contemplate the ramifications of James's relationship to Jesus, Christianity, and Judaism. The believing scholar Paul Barnett, in discussing Acts, notes that by 49 "James is clearly the leader . . . as he remains when we see him again in the late 50s." However, "there is no reason to believe that he shaped the understanding of the earliest Jerusalem disciples. According to the book of Acts, the teaching of Peter was critical in this regard." But how could James have led the Jerusalem church for decades and *not* shaped the religious understanding of that community? One wonders if conservative scholars fear answering this question precisely because of *how* the historical James might have shaped the first community of Christians.

Those writing in the closest time to James—which provides, of course, no guarantee of historical accuracy—note that he was famous for his asceticism and devotion to the Temple. As Paul's letter to the Galatians establishes, he was in the habit of send-

ing out envoys to other Christian communities to make sure
proper Jewish ritual was being followed. He appears to have had
friendly relations with the Pharisees of Jerusalem (in the gospels,
Jesus's frequent sparring partners) and, according to Hegesippus, not only wore priestly (that is, Jewish) robes but prayed in
the Temple's Court of the Priests, where unauthorized intrusion
was punishable by death. Contrast this with Paul, who is shown
in Acts to undergo ablutions when he entered the Temple, only
to be seized by an angry Jewish mob shortly thereafter. At one
point in Acts, the Sanhedrin seize and stone to death a Greek-
speaking Jewish Christian named Stephen, but afterward its
members decide to leave James and the apostles alone. Whether
the Stephen story has any factual basis is debatable, but many
scholars believe the story accurately reflects tensions within
early Christianity. If the Sanhedrin really did decide not to act
against Christians under James's guidance, it could mean a few
things. Among the most interesting: they were not perceived as
having broken covenant with the Law.

IV.

The identity of Philip is less contentious than that of James,
and its ramifications are not nearly as seismic; as a question,
however, it is no more settled. Philip was one of only four apostles who came to Jesus with a Greek name.* This was not that
unusual: by the time Philip would have been alive, Hellenism
had been woven into Palestine's cultural fabric for more than
350 years. Greek culture entered Palestine thanks to Alexander
the Great, who defeated the forces of Persia's Darius III in 333
BCE. According to the scholar Martin Hengel, Alexander's many
but impermanent military victories in the Near East were the
beginning of what we now know as "Hellenism," a coinage of
nineteenth-century classical scholarship. Building on Alexan-

---

* The others are Peter, Andrew, and Thaddaeus. Peter's given name has both a Greek
(Simon) and a Hebrew (Simeon) form.

der's victories, agents of classical Greek culture helped create "a common Greek cultural consciousness," which especially flowered in Greek-conquered lands rife with ethno-tribalism. Rudely introduced to the wider world and shown that their own cultures were comparatively weak, many subjugated Greek subjects were eager to discover this new way of being and thinking. Nevertheless, the arrival of Hellenism in Palestine was viewed as traumatic by many Jews, who had been content with Persian rule for centuries. The Persians had, among other things, allowed the Jews to return home after their exile under the Babylonians, the hated destroyers of the Davidic dynasty.

After Alexander died in 323 BCE, his squabbling generals battled one another for control of the massive empire they had helped bring to heel. Over two chaotic decades, Palestine was marched on or occupied at least half a dozen times by hostile armies, most of them Hellenist in character. In 301 BCE, Palestine fell under the rule of the Ptolemies, a Hellenist dynasty founded by a Macedonian who reinvented himself as a pharaoh and ruled out of Egypt. The Ptolemies would turn out to be some of the least meddlesome rulers Palestine's people would ever have, though their taxes were exploitatively high. Under Ptolemaic rule, the Torah was first translated into Greek, and many Jews came into familiarity with Greek ways of learning and thinking. Greek became Palestine's lingua franca, at least in trade, and its means of accounting the world's weights and distances were quickly standardized.

Ptolemaic rule depended on a Hellenized Jewish intelligentsia, whose appreciation for a more secular, inclusionist worldview had hitherto been unknown in a land of prevailing monotheism.* Schools, organizations, and academies promulgating Hellenism rose up all around the eastern Mediterranean.

---

* Among Greek intellectuals, monotheism was a fairly common belief, but this was typically a syncretizing monotheism philosophically at odds with the exclusionist monotheism of the Jews.

This cultural blending was not mandated or forced by the Ptolemies; Palestine was important to them only because it supplied a buffer from their enemies in Syria. In any case, as wares and merchants from the Mediterranean world began to trickle into a region long isolated by geography and tribalism, many Jews were intrigued and fascinated by what they found. Those who took up Hellenism most fervently were upper-class and aristocratic Jews, and many viewed Hellenism's cosmopolitan challenges as the best path for the closed, hermetic, Temple-state world of Judaism to take.

In 200 BCE, the Ptolemies withdrew from Palestine due to pressure from the Seleucid monarchy, which, like the Ptolemaic monarchy, had its roots in Alexander the Great's military command structure. The Seleucids saw Hellenism as the answer to Palestine's tribal backwardness. Jerusalem would be no longer a religious city-state but a Greek polis. For the first time, thanks to the obtuse Seleucid tyrant Antiochus IV Epiphanes, Greek culture was forcibly imposed on Palestine's Jews under the name of "reform." At one point, the Seleucids effectively outlawed strictly interpreted Judaism. Some Jews were force-fed pork, others attempted to hide their circumcision markings, and the Temple itself was briefly, and disastrously, consecrated in the name of Zeus and Baal, the god of the Philistines. The Seleucids underestimated the intensity with which average Jews would respond to all this. In every other land in which Hellenism had taken root, divinities were fluidly subject to cross-cultural trade, substitution, and augmentation. Judaism was the first religion Hellenism had encountered that insisted on proclaiming its truth as antagonistic to all others and which sometimes punished its apostates with death.

In 168 BCE, a group of Jewish revolutionaries led by Judah Maccabee succeeded in winning autonomy from the Seleucids, leading to eight decades of Jewish independence. In 63 BCE, the Romans conquered Palestine and ended Seleucid rule, but the prolonged, mutually fascinated, and often unhappy contact between Jewish and Greek culture had left a deep mark on both: not for nothing is *synagogue* a Greek rather than a Hebrew word.

In some ways, Jesus himself was a reflection of, and a response to, Hellenism. The recently opened world of Jewish thought gave his followers a new vocabulary, one that allowed them to imagine him as God; this, in turn, led an entrenched and newly radical Jewish conservatism to reject him along the same lines. The historical irony is that Jesus himself was, probably, a culturally conservative Jew. The Seleucids and the Maccabees and Jesus all arrived at the fault line between Hellenism and Judaism from different directions—and, one way or another, all were destroyed by it.

V.

By the first century CE, even Palestinian Jews outside the intelligentsia had begun to bestow upon their children Greek names. The apparent popularity of the name Philip, which means "lover of horses," might be traced to Alexander the Great's father, Philip of Macedon.

The traditional view of Philip the apostle is that he was a Hellenist, which is to say a Greek-speaking Jewish believer. Philip was also one of two apostles, along with Peter, specifically noted by early Christians to have enjoyed a wife and children. In the Gospel According to John, we are told Philip is from Bethsaida, "the city of Andrew and Peter." Philip's occupation is never mentioned by John, but tradition has generally assumed that Philip was a fisherman like Peter and Andrew. Given the modest soil in which most sects (and cults) have initially grown, it would make sense, sociologically speaking, that many of Jesus's first followers were friends from the same area and employed in the same line of work.

John is the only gospel to depict Philip's calling—to provide Philip, in fact, with any activity at all. The day after meeting Peter, John writes, "Jesus decided to go to Galilee. He found Philip and said to him, 'Follow me.'" Philip immediately chases down his friend Nathanael of Cana, whom he tells, "We have found him about whom Moses in the Law and also the prophets wrote, Jesus son of Joseph from Nazareth." Who, many commentators have wondered, is "we"? And why was Philip looking for "him about whom Moses in the Law and also the prophets wrote"? One traditional argument holds that Philip might initially have been a disciple of John the Baptist's and was in search of the charismatic leader the Baptist supposedly promised was near.

Philip does not appear again until John's sixth chapter, shortly after Jesus has gone to Jerusalem and angered the Temple authorities by healing a lame man on the Sabbath. The act causes enough commotion that Jesus is dogged on his return to Galilee by a "large crowd." Jesus asks Philip where they can buy enough bread to feed these enthusiasts. Philip replies they do not have nearly enough food to feed the crowd. Andrew quickly points out a little boy with five loaves of barley bread and two fish, which Jesus proceeds to multiply "as much as they wanted."

In the twelfth chapter of John, we find one of the gospel's more interesting and mysterious interludes. The time is Passover. Jesus has just raised Lazarus from the dead and ridden into Jerusalem on the back of a young donkey to the exultant "shouting" of Jerusalem's citizens. The Pharisees, watching Jesus, tell one another, "Look, the world has gone after him!" Others have turned up at the Passover festival, including those to whom John refers as "some Greeks." These men approach Philip and tell him they wish to see Jesus. Philip consults with Andrew, and after that the Greeks are taken to meet him.

It is unclear whether these Greeks are God-fearing Gentiles (pagans who have taken a hedged-bets interest in the god of the Jews) or actual converts to Judaism.* Gentiles were not allowed

---

* Many Greeks admired the Jews, for their antiquity if nothing else. One of Aristotle's pupils wrote of his master's being out-wisdomed by a Jew; a later pagan writer asked, "What is Plato but Moses speaking Greek?" Not until after the Maccabaean revolt did Greek views of the Jews correspondingly dim.

into the Temple any deeper than its outer court, where women and Jews employed in professions that left them perpetually "unclean" (tanners, for instance) were also relegated. Nothing in Jewish scripture recommended the exclusion of Gentiles from the Temple; it was, rather, indicative of priestly suspicion of the wider world. The rituals and ablutions required for entrance into the Temple would not have surprised Greek God fearers, who had likely cleansed and purified themselves in any number of pagan temples, but the ethnic nature of their exclusion would have come as a great, and unfamiliar, shock.

Whatever the precise religious beliefs of John's Greeks, they regard Jesus's intermediary as Philip, a nonentity in the synoptic gospels. Are we to suppose they have approached Philip because of his Greek name? Do they know him from some previous encounter? Or is the author of John making a theological point by allowing Jesus to react welcomingly to some curious Greeks, thereby showing that Jesus is not for Jews alone?

The last time Philip figures in John's gospel is during the Last Supper, when Jesus announces, "I am the way, and the truth, and the life. No one comes to the Father except through me." This statement has since become one of the bases of Evangelical Christianity: only through Jesus is salvation possible. Another explanation for this sentiment—which has echoes in Matthew, Luke, and especially Acts, though its framing is less severe—is that John is putting into Jesus's mouth harsh, polemical statements traceable to the particular situation out of which John's gospel was written. When Philip tells Jesus, "Lord, show us the Father, and it is sufficient for us," Jesus instantly chastises him: "Have I been with you all this time, Philip, and you still do not know me? If you know me, you will know my Father also." Philip appears to speak for those in the gospel's intended community who do not yet understand what faith in Jesus means.

In Acts, a certain Philip, traditionally called Philip the Evangelist, plays an important role in the growth of the church. This Philip comes to prominence shortly after the apostles are flogged in the Temple, at a time when "the disciples were increasing in number" and two groups of Christians are attacking each other "because their widows were being neglected in the distribution of food." The Twelve, whom Acts pointedly neglects to align with either faction, deal with the food distribution crisis by agreeing that there is too much work and too few people to do it. After noting, somewhat imperiously, "It is not right that we should neglect the word of God in order to wait on tables," the Twelve instruct their fellow Christians to pick "seven men of good standing" to deal with the food crisis; one of the men selected is Philip. Now, is this Philip the apostle Philip, one of the Twelve? Many early Christian writers (Eusebius, Irenaeus, Tertullian, Polycarp) believed Philip the Evangelist and Philip the apostle were one and the same; today, however, most Christians have abandoned this belief and regard the Philips as different men. The question is whether Luke, the author of Acts, believed they were the same person. Given that he does nothing to differentiate them, it appears Luke believed they were. Whatever the case, Philip the Evangelist travels to Samaria to preach, where he has an encounter with "a certain man named Simon" whose use of magic has previously "amazed" the Samaritans. Simon Magus—as he has come to be known, though Acts never refers to him in this way—accepts Jesus, after which Philip baptizes him. When news of the Samaritans' acceptance of Philip's ministry reaches Jerusalem, Peter and John make the seventy-mile journey to visit Philip. As the two apostles are laying their hands on the people, Simon Magus offers Peter and John money for the same ability.*

---

* Thus the crime of *simony*, whereby one purchases favor or influence within the church. While later commentators would argue that Simon Magus faked his faith in Jesus, Acts specifically notes, "Even Simon himself believed." Based on the text of Acts, it seems as though Simon is guilty of nothing more than catastrophically poor judgment. Simon would go on to have a colorful career in Christian Apocrypha, and church fathers like Irenaeus would claim that the gospels were written to counter Simon's false teachings. By the fourth century, Simon was the subject of intense hatred; on him all deviations from orthodoxy were blamed. Eusebius referred to

Philip moves on, at angelic order, to Gaza. On the way, he encounters a treasury minister, and eunuch, from Ethiopia, whom he swiftly baptizes—the first recorded Christian ministry to a non-Semite. Philip is "snatched away" by the Lord and eventually ends up in Caesarea, where Paul later visits him and his daughters. Philip does not appear again in Acts. According to legend, he left Caesarea shortly after Paul's visit and moved to Hierapolis with his prophetess daughters, who would themselves go on to play a role in later Christian legends, often as virgins martyred to preserve their chastity.

VI.

Inside the Church of the Holy Apostles, a cylindrically hefty priest was mopping the floor. That the church's own priests engaged in janitorial duty was a surprise to me. The priest himself did not seem very taken with the idea either: his frown deepened as he wrung out the mop, gathered up his bucket, and headed for another quadrant of shoe-print-clouded marble.

The church's nave was large even by the impossible standards of other storied Roman churches. The pillars dividing the nave from its two aisles (almost as wide as the nave itself) were the size of small buildings. Three chapels, each with its own suite of wooden pews, lined both aisles, with two more chapels stashed away elsewhere. The light inside the church had a moon-gray heaviness.

The ceiling's central vault fresco was by Giovanni Battista Gaulli, a friend of Bernini's more commonly known by his Genoese nickname: Il Baciccia. According to the art books, he was

---

Simon as "a great opponent of great men, our Saviour's inspired apostles"—Moriarty to the Twelve's collective Holmes—and noted how "astonishing" it was that Simon's purportedly feigned acceptance of Jesus "is still the practice of belief in those who to the present day belong to his disgusting sect," which means Simonian Christianity endured into the fourth century.

regarded as a master of the technically demanding vault painting. *The Triumph of the Franciscan Order,* the vault painting I
now looked up at, was completed two years before Gaulli died
in 1709 but was apparently regarded by specialists as a minor
work. The vault painting above the high altar addressed a theme
not often seen in such proximity to a church's most consecrated
site: the expulsion of the rebellious from Heaven. This painting,
Fallen Angels, by the fifteenth-century painter Giovanni Odazzi,
was ambitious and wizardly. Odazzi's angels were literally falling out of the painting, producing behind them the optical illusion of a painted "shadow."

The colossal painting behind the high altar, *The Martyrdom
of Saint Philip and Saint James,* was completed in the early eighteenth century to replace a moisture-damaged fresco. The artist,
Domenico Maria Muratori, painted very little after this, and little
wonder: *The Martyrdom of Saint Philip and Saint James* was, at
forty-five feet high and twenty-one feet across, reputedly the single largest painting in Rome. In the upper left of the painting, a
kneeling, youthful James, wearing blue and pink robes, looks to
the heavens while a savage, shirtless Hebrew prepares to brain
him with a club. In the painting's lower right, an old, loincloth-
wearing Philip is being pulley lifted into position while a rabble
jeers him from the base of his cross. From above, an angel rushes
down to place the crown of martyrdom on Philip's head. Adrift
around both doomed apostles is the usual swarm of portly cherubs, while behind them looms an opened porthole into Heaven
itself—a swirling maw of pink light.

When I had asked Father Dario about some of the discrepancies concerning the identities of Philip and James, he brushed
them aside: "There is only one Philip. He died by the cross. And
there were only two Jameses: the brother of John and the cousin
of Jesus. One died by the sword. One died by the stick." Reliably
Catholic positions, as was Father Dario's citation of the verse of
the Letter of James that held that "faith by itself, if it has no
works, is dead." James's words have long lent Roman Catholics

comfort against Protestant opprobrium. The letter, which identifies its author only as "James, a servant of God and of Lord Jesus
Christ," has its difficulties from both a historical and a spiritual
perspective. Its concerns are overwhelmingly ethical rather than
spiritual; Jesus is mentioned only twice. It contains what one
scholar describes as "among the best" Greek in the New Testament; at the same time, it is considered the most overtly Jewish
Christian work within the New Testament. "For whoever keeps
the whole law but fails in one point," James writes, "has become
accountable for all of it." The passage is in direct opposition to
an important part of Paul's message ("For we hold that a person
is justified by faith apart from works prescribed by the law"),
though we need not assume the author of James had read Paul's
letter to the Romans or was attempting to counter him directly.*
James's letter is stridently on the side of the poor, the orphan,
the widow, the suffering: "Are any among you sick? They should
call for the elders of the church and have them pray over them,
anointing them with oil in the name of the Lord. The prayer
of faith will save the sick, and the Lord will raise them up; and
anyone who has committed sins will be forgiven." Its occasionally harsh tone ("Even the demons believe—and shudder") is
matched by its moments of forgiving understanding ("For all of
us make many mistakes"). Even though James anticipates the
end-time to a degree greater than most New Testament works,
there is a calm at the core of the text that indicates a certain
kind of Jewish Christian understanding. James is a dignified letter about a church succumbing to a marginalized, undignified
fate—and awaiting its righteous deliverer.

There can be little doubt the letter wends back to James
the brother of Jesus traditionally, whether as something James
wrote himself or something written in his name by a follower.
The latter is almost certainly the case, as James 5:6 ("You have

---

* Hilariously, Paul and James refer to the same passage from Genesis to make their
respective points.

condemned and murdered the righteous one, who does not resist you") seems to contain an allusion to James the brother of Jesus's death. No scholar can be sure of its date of composition. Although Irenaeus quoted it around 180, it was not actually mentioned by name until the third century, by Origen.

Philip has no New Testament texts attributed to him, but his adventures in the Apocrypha are a highly entertaining mix of torture, magic, seismology, and interspecies encounter. *The Acts of Philip*, written sometime between the fourth and the sixth centuries, belongs to a group of writings that seem based on vague historical traditions enriched by forceful portrayals of the apostles as unparalleled thaumaturges. *Acts* such as Philip's owe as much to Christian doctrine, which they try to endorse, as they do to the raw material of Eastern and Mediterranean mythology, which they shamelessly exploit.

Philip's *Acts* does not exist in any complete edition and seems cobbled together from at least three separate bundles of Philip material. Much of it appears to have been inspired by other noncanonical *Acts* (it contains a prayer also found in *The Acts of John,* for instance), but it establishes the basic chronology of Philip's traditional story: leaving Galilee for Athens, journeying in the "land of the Parthians," healing various people, meeting a leopard and a baby goat with Bartholomew, and finally arriving in Hierapolis. In due course, Philip and Bartholomew meet Nicanora, the Jewish wife of the local governor. When they pray for her, "her tyrant husband came" and "dragged her by the hair and threatened to kill her." Philip and Bartholomew are then "arrested, scourged, and dragged to the temple."

Philip wonders aloud if he should call down fire from Heaven to destroy their torturers, but Jesus appears and rebukes his apostle, calling Philip "unforgiving and wrathful" and promising that he "shall indeed die in glory and be taken by angels to paradise." Jesus then proceeds to rescue the seven thousand pagan souls Philip had earlier exterminated in a fit of pique. A remorseful Philip, still hanging by his pierced ankles, instructs his friends to build "a church in the place where I die, and let the leopard and the baby goat be there."

Philip gets truncated treatment in Jacobus de Voragine's *Golden Legend,* though Jacobus does argue, using Jerome as his evidence, that Philip the apostle and Philip the Evangelist were different men. Working off his usual assortment of ancient sources and traditions, Jacobus writes that the apostle Philip preached "through Scythia" for two decades, before doing battle with some pagans' dragon god. Philip commands the dragon "to a desert place" before raising from the dead all the dragon's victims. Philip then travels "to the city of Hierapolis in Asia," where he "put down the heresy of the Ebionites, who taught that the body assumed by Christ was only a phantom." With him in Hierapolis, Jacobus writes, are two daughters, "dedicated virgins both of them."

The bishop of Ephesus, Polycrates, writing around 185, noted that in "Asia great luminaries sleep . . . such as Philip, one of the twelve apostles, who sleeps in Hierapolis with two of his daughters, who remained unmarried to the end of their days, while his other daughter lived in the Holy Spirit and rests in Ephesus." Philip's original Hierapolitan tomb, now a ruin in modern-day Turkey, is today fully excavated. An ancient-world healing spa known for its Niagaracally massive waterfall, Hierapolis was ruled by Romans but culturally Greek. Ephesus was within easy traveling distance of Hierapolis, and there the apostle John is supposed to have established a Christian enclave similar to that which Philip founded in Hierapolis. Because the Gospel According to John mentions Philip so prominently, the notion that these two old friends were close to each other was apparently so appealing that many of the church fathers later expanded on it. In other words, the traditions associated with Philip are the likely result of sentiment braided together with some dimly recalled history. Hierapolis was supposedly home to an active snake cult, for example, and this may explain Philip's apocryphally widespread encounters with dragons.

VII.

The death of James the brother of Jesus is different from that of Philip. For one, his existence is a near historical certainty. For two, the tradition of where and when he died is roughly reliable. Beyond these two facts lies a rain forest teeming with postulation.

The earliest mention of James the brother of Jesus outside Paul's letters comes from the first-century historian Josephus's *Jewish Antiquities,* in which James is described as "the brother of Jesus, who was called Christ." An earlier mention of Jesus by Josephus claims "he was a doer of wonderful works" and that he "appeared" to his disciples "alive again [on] the third day." Most scholars consider these Josephus passages about Jesus the product of later Christian interpolations. (The earliest copy we have of Josephus's *Antiquities* is from the eleventh century, giving Christians nearly a thousand years to alter the text beyond the parameters of scholarly detection.) No Christian apologist cited the passage until the fourth century, and when Origen, in the mid-third century, discussed Josephus, he noted that Josephus "did not believe in Jesus as Christ." Then again, "Christ," to someone of Josephus's time and placement, would have had nothing in common with the version of the word used even a few decades later. If the passage is genuine, it could merely indicate that Josephus regarded Jesus as an anointed one favored by God.

Josephus's mention of James the brother of Jesus is less controversial, and most scholars believe that much of the passage is genuinely Josephus's. In it, Josephus writes of Ananus ben Ananus, the Temple high priest and Sadducee whose brief rule in 62 was marked by one fateful decision. While the new Roman procurator was on his way to Jerusalem from Alexandria to report for duty, Ananus "thought he had now a proper opportunity" to display his authority. He thus "assembled the Sanhedrin of judges, and brought before them the brother of Christ, whose name was James, and some others; and when he had formed an accusation against them as breakers of the law, he delivered

them to be stoned." In other words, something transpired among
the Temple authorities, dramatically affecting their view of Jewish Christians and James the brother of Jesus. Unfortunately,
Josephus does not tell us why James was suddenly regarded as a
breaker of the Law or reveal the names or religious affiliation of
the "others" executed alongside him. After James's death, "those
who were considered most . . . strict in their observance of the
Law"—almost certainly a reference to the Pharisees—"were
most indignant."*

Later writers would depart considerably from the portrait
of James's death as drawn by Josephus, though they were clearly
aware of it. According to Eusebius, after Paul's arrest by the
Romans (which Acts describes) the Jews "turned their attention
to James the Lord's brother." Eusebius mentioned Clement of
Alexandria's brief account of James's murder ("the Righteous
One . . . was cast down from the Pinnacle of the Temple and
beaten to death with a laundryman's club") but quoted at length
"the most detailed account," provided by Hegesippus. In this version, it is Passover, an annual source of unrest and administrative headaches for the Temple as well as the Roman authorities.
Among the Jews, Hegesippus noted, were a number of sects with
differing views of Jesus, as well as an anti-Christian "uproar"
among the "Scribes and Pharisees." To lower tensions in the city,
the Temple authorities sought the assistance of a most unlikely
candidate: James the brother of Jesus.

James, Hegesippus tells us, obeyed the scribes and Pharisees

---

* Christians unaware of James's reported fraternity with the Pharisees will no doubt
find it somewhat startling. Surprisingly little is actually known about the Pharisees
of Jesus's lifetime. They were, most basically, a small group of lay Torah interpreters
devoted to observance of Jewish purity rules. Some estimates indicate they made up
no more than 1 percent of the population. The Pharisees first emerged during the
Jewish Maccabaean revolt (166–160 BCE) against the Seleucids. Pharisee influence
waxed and waned in the intervening decades, but the gospels inaccurately portray
the Pharisees of Jesus's time enjoying a historically nonexistent consensus of belief
and maintaining their organizational power at a moment when Pharisee influence
was, in fact, weakest.

and assumed his perch on the Temple parapet. The authorities publicly assembled to ask the man they addressed as the "Righteous one" what was meant "by the 'door of Jesus.'" James replied, "Why do you question me about the Son of Man? I tell you, He is sitting in heaven at the right hand of the Great Power, and He will come on the clouds of heaven." This was obviously not what the authorities were expecting. As the crowd shouted hosannas, the scribes and the Pharisees conferred. Their conclusion? "We have made a bad mistake." They threw James from the parapet, thus fulfilling, at least in Hegesippus's mind, a prophecy found in Isaiah. Then they began to stone James. While some in the crowd cried out in distress at the sight of the Righteous one's bloody stoning, "a fuller"—that is, one of many laundrymen who used blunt wooden clubs to beat garments clean, and whose vats have been located by archaeologists as being not far from where the James of legend would have landed—"took the club which he used to beat out the clothes, and brought it down on the head of the Righteous one."

One does not need much knowledge of the history of these times to recognize the patently bizarre notion that the Temple authorities would seek out the brother of Jesus to dampen Jerusalemites' enthusiasm for him. In Josephus's earlier and more straightforward account, James's death came about due to some presumably intra-Jewish schism; Hegesippus's version seems to be a Christianized retelling and might have derived from the Jewish Christian devotion to preserving tales of James's unparalleled righteousness.

Eusebius, in his retelling of James's death, indicated that the "more intelligent Jews" of his acquaintance accepted the Roman destruction of the Temple a few years later as an act of divine vengeance for its people's treatment of James, which view he also attributed to Josephus; Origen twice made a similar attribution, though his own view was that the destruction of Jerusalem "was on account of Jesus the Christ of God." Yet the relevant passages are lacking from all extant copies of Josephus. These passages might have been the result of Christian editorial meddling that was later abandoned as James receded from prominence in early Christian history. Needless to say, the death of James was obviously never going to be widely accepted by Christians as an explanation for the destruction of Jerusalem. What that would implicitly suggest about the relative importance of Jesus and James was simply too confounding for Christians to contemplate.

James the brother of Jesus was once important enough to have caused some to wonder whether a city was destroyed by God to avenge him. By the time the New Testament had achieved literary fixity, he was both diminished to Jesus's cousin and linked, humiliatingly, to a man called "the little."

VIII.

A marble whirlpool of stairs in front of the altar of the Church of the Holy Apostles led down into the *confessio,* also known as the Well of the Martyrs. The sign above the stairs read, TOMBA DEI SANTI APOSTOLI FILIPPO E GIACOMO.

According to one legend, Pope John III (561–574) requested Philip's remains from the Christians of Hierapolis. This conflicts with one tradition that indicates Philip's and James's remains were already in Rome as of 560, the supposed date of the Church of the Holy Apostles' dedication, and another that places them in Constantinople as of 572. Further complicating matters, the Armenian Church in Jerusalem has never relinquished what it claims to be its relics of James. These can be found today in the Cathedral of Saint James on Mount Zion. According to the Armenian tradition, James's initial resting place was in a tomb on the Mount of Olives that James had purchased and constructed for himself. When this tomb was destroyed in the fourth century, Armenian priests ferried James's body to Mount Zion, where James was believed to have lived, and a cathedral was built up around the ruins of his ancient home. According to Armenians, the relics they today venerate are the arm and the finger of James the Lesser, whom they regard as James son of Alphaeus and the cousin of Jesus. They also claim to possess the "throne" of James, mentioned by Eusebius, but it was obviously built much later than the first century. To make already extremely confusing matters more confusing, next to the altar is the resting place of what the Armenians claim to be the head of James son of Zebedee, who was supposedly beheaded in Jerusalem in the early 40s. When I politely asked the Armenian brothers of the Cathedral of Saint James—whose namesake they know as Surp Hagop—for clarification on these matters, all I received were some vividly incurious stares.

In 2002, an ossuary dating from the first century surfaced in Israel. It bore the inscription YAKOV BAR YOSEF AHUI D'YESHUA, "James son of Joseph, brother of Jesus." While a number of scholars initially vouchsafed the ossuary's authenticity, in 2003 the Israel Antiquities Authority issued a report that claimed the ossuary was genuine but its inscription was not. The IAA has declined to provide specific reasons for its decision, and scholars who maintain their belief in its authenticity are equal in number to those who doubt it. It is unlikely the matter will be satisfactorily resolved.

The Roman crypt Philip and James today quietly occupy was refurbished between 1869 and 1871, shortly after a renovation of the church uncovered the original *confessio*. While their remains had long been believed to be beneath the church, various reconstructions had blocked off access to the crypt. And so, in the second half of the nineteenth century, the supposed remains of Philip and James were gazed upon by Christians for the first time in four hundred years. During the restoration of the Well of the Martyrs, much of the foundation of the original sixth-century church had been preserved, and artisans were brought in to cover the well's walls with tempera-paint images that resembled the ancient Christian art found in Rome's outlying catacombs of Calixtus and Domitilla.

After walking down handsome Renaissance-era stairs into a hive-like simulation of premodern Christianity, I marveled at how faithfully approximated these motifs were. The images (peacocks, fish, palms, scenes of unadorned human figures enjoying table fellowship) were bold in their primitivism, the colors (red, blue, a little yellow, some brown) starkly limited, the interstitial design elements (clean straight lines, grape bundles, chalices) unobtrusive and sparse. The well was arranged in a circular, twist-about fashion, lined with small tomb niches for other, less celebrated martyrs. At the base of the stairs was the tomb of Philip and James, both men of contested identity, one of whom might have prayed in the Jewish Temple for years after the death of Jesus and one of whom might have spread the faith beyond its Jewish rootstock. Given what we know about the debates of early Christianity, and where the traditions associated with Philip and James would have placed them in those debates, it may well be that the traditional versions of these two men would have had little to say to each other at civilized decibels. Two thousand years later, that did not matter. They were together now in undying apostleship.

A young man sat in one of two plastic-backed chairs before the tomb. He was reading his Bible. At the sound of my approaching footfalls, he half turned to me but quickly resumed his reading. He was one of those young men you could not imagine having ever been a boy. His thinning hair was some indeterminate color between brown and blond. His jeans were the bright clean blue of open ocean, and his spotless white shirt was buttoned up to his Adam's apple. He was reading the King James: Acts of the Apostles. He did not stir as I sat down next to him.

There was no door into the tomb of Philip and James. I could look inside only through a small grate's iron lattice. On either side of the grate were faded tempera paintings labeled JACOBUS and PHILIPPUS, the former carrying a homely sack and the latter holding what looked to be a basket of fish. Below the grate was a small kneeler cushioned by two red pillows. The area behind the grate was spacious, though the sarcophagus that held the apostles' remains was as small as a love seat and cruder than I had been expecting. Chiseled into the sarcophagus were equally crude images of Philip and James helping Jesus feed the five thousand, both gesturing in amazement at the baskets of bread and fish while Jesus stands between them.

Although the young man's lips moved as he read his Bible (the effect was meditative rather than remedial), he made no sound. He had obviously come here to pray and reflect. I had not. I found here only sawhorses on which to prop this man's faith and skeptically saw away. To me, a miracle was nothing more than a storytelling enhancement of the sort that naturally occurred within all oral traditions. And yet the feeding of the five thousand was such a seductive miracle. Many of the New Testament's other miracles—raisings of the dead, demons thrown from men to swine, healed paralytics—spoke of imaginations as limited by superstition as they were defined by it. But in the feeding of the five thousand, without a doubt my favorite Christian miracle, something else could be detected.

"Make the people sit down," Jesus tells Andrew in the Gospel According to John. There was, John's author tells us, "a great deal of grass in the place for people to sit." This is an unusually tactile detail, as are the words John uses for the food Jesus miraculously multiplies. Mark, for instance, refers merely to "five loaves" and "two fish." John, however, mentions that the bread was "barley loaves," and the word he uses for "fish" is, in Greek, "smoked fish." While the other gospels tell the story in passed-on, seemingly secondhand terms, John's description of the feeding of the five thousand contains seemingly unmistakable reported details.

I could imagine a hot day. I could imagine a number of curious people spontaneously following a young man of great wisdom, a young man rumored to wield power over the mysterious afflictions they saw every day in their villages. They are not sure where they are going, and once the young man stops to speak, they find themselves on the other side of the Sea of Galilee, the nearest town now very far away. Many are feeling hunger pangs, uncertain of why they have come so far. What will they do? One of the young man's friends arrives, unexpectedly bearing food. The people are happy and relieved, and among them talk circulates of the surprising tenderness with which the wise young man hands out victuals to the people, few of whom he knows well.

Eventually, the story is written down. Years go by, then decades, and in this time the crowd increases from fifty to five hundred to five thousand. The unexpected arrival of the follower bearing food vanishes from the telling. An event experienced by its participants in miraculous terms is transformed into a miraculous story. The core of the story remains the same: the hungry were fed when they were not expecting to be, and the young man who fed them did so of his own volition. You could base a code of ethics on a single act of unexpected munificence and perhaps even fashion from it a crude if supple morality, but you would not have a cosmology, or anything close to one, and cosmologies were what most people craved.

The young man stood, apparently confused as to how best to take his leave of Philip and James. After a moment of silent consideration, he bowed, awkwardly. I sat there for a few moments by myself before thinking, *I want to talk to him.* I tracked him down outside, around the corner from the piazza, as he was walking toward the Palazzo Venezia, which was today hosting a Julian Schnabel show. The sky, surrendering the deep, breathing blue of mid-afternoon, was slowly giving way to the jaundice of dusk.

The young man seemed startled, at first, to be approached by me but warmed considerably when I told him why I wanted to talk. He agreed to have a drink on the patio of a small café on the corner of Via del Corso. When the waiter brought two large, astronomically expensive bottles of Peroni and presented the bill, the young man started digging into his pocket. He was relieved when I told him it was my treat.

His name was Glenn. He was from Tennessee and in Rome on an Evangelical Bible tour. He told me he was "sick to death" of being guided around, and while he was uncomfortable with Catholicism, he had read about the Church of the Holy Apostles in his guidebook and decided he wanted to pay his respects to Philip and James. "Why?" I asked him, given the Evangelical antagonism to the cult of the saints.

"Because," he said, "they were my Savior's friends and they died for him. They deserve our respect and our love, whatever my position on how Catholics choose to revere them." And how did he feel about the possibility that James son of Alphaeus might have been the brother of Jesus? Glenn shrugged. "That wouldn't shock me. I know it's a possibility. I accept Matthew 1:25—that Mary had normal relations of the body with her husband. There's nothing in Christian doctrine that forbids normal relations between a man and a wife. Do you know what Paul says? Paul says it's a 'doctrine of demons' to deny a man sexual expression with a woman within the confines of marriage." He drank from his beer, squinting as though tasting a much harsher spirit. "The apostles were just men. Great men, but men. Yes, they performed miracles, but only through the power of the Holy Spirit, which is available to all of us. To suggest that they had the same power as Jesus is blasphemous. And it's why we oppose Catholicism."

Nevertheless, I said, he came to see Philip and James. "I went to Saint Peter's, too," he said quickly. "The apostles aren't important to me. I think about their example—and it's not always a great example, by the way—but as a Christian I don't find any *spiritual* nourishment there. As someone who reads the Bible and studies what it says, I find the fact that I just looked at Philip and James's tomb interesting. As a *person,* as someone who finds the history interesting. But not as a Christian."

Soon more beers were ordered, and our discussion gathered in a number of orbital matters regarding his faith. With a now-reddened face, Glenn leaned forward, his finger thrust out in a combatively friendly way. "If the Bible says Paul and Peter argued, that's not a shock. They were both men. They were not divine. When they wrote their letters, they were under divine guidance, but in how they behaved, of course they sinned, of course they showed vanity, but the writing of their letters is different. That's God doing the talking. They were his vessel."

I met this line of reasoning with an equally out-thrust finger: Okay, but what of the rest of the process? Did the same underwriter of divine veracity oversee every other area of biblical transmission? The writers of the New Testament were working under divine guidance. Fine. But what of those who selected the books of the New Testament? What of the copyists? The translators? The printers? The interpreters? All of these were sinners besides. Or did God step in at every one of the thousand places where the possibility for human error and frailty and misunderstanding intersected with scripture's earthly manifestation?

Again, Glenn laughed, showing his small, hard Chiclet teeth. "I know what you're getting at. But I believe the Bible is without the errors of man. I believe that. I have somewhat of an idea that there's controversies concerning translation, but this is the book Christians turn to, and have turned to, and it has nothing to do with apostles or translators."

We sat there awhile longer, mostly silent, while Glenn finished his beer. No one had ever had this argument before and felt as if he won, just as no one had ever had this argument before and felt as if he lost. Before going, Glenn wished me luck on what he called my "journey." And so I wished Glenn luck on his.

PETER

Saint Peter's Basilica: Vatican City

THE WORLD'S SMALLEST COUNTRY • THE PIAZZA
OF SAINT PETER • GAIUS'S MONUMENT • THE
FOUNDER OF THE ROMAN CHURCH • GROTTOES •
THE CONFESSION • "FEED MY LAMBS" • *THE ACTS
OF PETER* • THE RED WALL • THE MOST EGREGIOUS
BLUNDER • HOLY MOUSE

I.

One-third of the world's smallest country is a garden.
Roughly eight hundred citizens call it home. It has its
own currency, postal service, army (Stalin famously wondered
how many divisions its leader could field; the answer was
more than he suspected), and one adult bookstore. From 1870
to 1929, the rulers of the world's smallest country regarded the
nation that surrounds it as an apostate land worthy of divine
condemnation. Yet the location of the world's smallest country,
to say nothing of the authority of its principal citizen, is not
founded on a site of civic declaration. It is not the victory plain
of an ancient battle. It was not placed in recognition of some
ethno-tribal border. The only reason the world's smallest country exists is due to a modest, two-thousand-year-old grave site,
the location and contents of which are evidenced by findings
best described as interpretive.

During the time of Jesus, not many Romans traveled beyond
their city's walls to the hill-hemmed drainage marsh known,
even then, as the Vatican field. Tacitus called it a "notoriously
pestilential neighborhood," and others likened the wine made
from Vatican grapes to poison. Fittingly, the Roman emperor

Nero showed a malignant fondness for the Vatican field and on its grounds oversaw a series of brutal executions, one of which might have laid the metaphysical cornerstone of the blue-gray marble colossus known as Saint Peter's Basilica.

The rain, falling from a wet-newspaper-colored sky, struck the marble piazza with aeroballistic force. The sound was like that of a thousand spankings, and the piazza's two fountains enthusiastically overflowed. Several nuns huddled under the protection of one of the piazza's two colonnades and stared out at the rain with tamp-mouthed resignation. Vatican police go-carts, also keeping under the colonnade, rolled past the nuns. The piloting officers' matching white sashes, belts, and pistol holsters brought to mind lightly armed hall monitors.

The piazza of Saint Peter's Basilica was the last portion of the Vatican complex to be completed. Work on it did not begin until 1656, thirty years after the basilica itself was consecrated. The man responsible for the piazza, Gian Lorenzo Bernini—who in order to finish his commission passed up a chance to design the Louvre—laid the two curved colonnades that hug the ovular piazza like parentheses. One hundred and sixty-four twelve-foot-tall statues were perched atop these colonnades: Bernini called them his "cloud of witnesses." Every statue required about two months' work for the master and his workshop students. An entire limestone quarry was leased, and nearly exhausted, to provide Bernini with the requisite stone. Bernini's last "witness" was not mounted until a century after the pope who commissioned the piazza had died. Seen through curtains of unending rain, Bernini's witnesses looked as imperturbable as idols.

Whether one was an agnostic or an Evangelical, a bishop or a mullah, a Scientologist or a Jain, the basilica's gargantuan, overriding reality could not help but psychologically validate the legend on which it had been founded. The basilica built in the name of a Galilean fisherman once known as Simon son of John was commissioned by a hated pope (Julius II), constructed on what was then the holiest site in Europe (Constantine's Basilica, where nearly two hundred popes were consecrated), initially designed by a then-minor homosexual architect (Donato Bramante), enhanced by several geniuses (Michelangelo among them), despised by Martin Luther (who called it "a very minor thing"), admired by George Eliot (who claimed standing before it was like entering "some millennial Jerusalem"), begun in one era (the Renaissance), and finished in another (the Baroque). The construction of Saint Peter's Basilica required the passing of thirty papacies. Nothing like it had ever been attempted before. Saint Peter's Basilica was not a church. It was a self-contained world.

Jesus died knowing no land, apparently, but Palestine. That was his self-contained world. Europe, however, claimed his most prominent early follower, from whose grave spawned the entirety of Western Christianity, first in Catholic adulation, then in Protestant flight.

II.

He has been called the Prince of the Apostles, even though the last thing he needs is another sobriquet. No fewer than six names are used for him in the New Testament: Simon, Simon Peter, Simeon, Simeon Peter, Peter, and Cephas. His given name, Simon, is among the New Testament's most popular. Seven discernible Simons make an appearance in the gospels: Simon Peter, the apostle Simon the Cananaean (also known as Simon the Zealot), Jesus's brother Simon, Judas's father Simon, Simon the leper (who in the Gospel According to Matthew hosts Jesus), Simon the Pharisee (who in the Gospel According to Luke wonders why Jesus lets a sinful woman wash his feet), and Simon the Cyrene (who in the Gospel According to Matthew is "compelled" to carry Jesus's cross when Jesus, apparently, weakens). If we add to this tally the Acts of the Apostles, we have yet more Simons, including the spell-casting wizard of Samaria.

The uses of his many names are difficult to unravel. The first gospel to be written, Mark, simply tells us that Simon is the one "to whom [Jesus] gave the name Peter." Early in the Gospel According to Matthew, we meet "Simon, who is called Peter," but later the gospel's author chooses to elaborate on this tradition when he has Jesus say, "And I tell you, you are Peter [*Petros*], and on this rock [*petra*] I will build my church." Among Aramaic-speaking Jews, Peter would have been known as Simeon; among Greek-speaking Jews and Gentiles, Simon. Following Jesus's renaming, he would have been known among Aramaic-speaking Jews as Cephas (from *kepha,* or "rock"); among Greek-speaking Jews and Gentiles, Petros (from *petra,* also "rock"). Neither of Peter's names is a direct translation from "rock"; they are more akin to neologisms. Greek is a gendered language, and the Greek word for "rock" is feminine. In written Aramaic, which, like Hebrew, does not use vowels, the Latin-alphabet equivalent of Cephas is indicated in this way: *kp'.* The word is infrequent in ancient Aramaic literature and almost never appears as a proper name. There is even less evidence for *Petros* being used as a proper name prior to Peter's rechristening. According to the scholar Pheme Perkins, "The term may well have been created to provide a Greek translation for the Aramaic 'Cephas.'" Because neither name means "rock," exactly, the most equivalent English name would be something like Rocky. Only Matthew attempts to explain why Jesus called Peter Rocky, and it appears to have something to do with how Jesus would build his church. What Jesus actually intended has been the subject of thermonuclear Christian debate.

With the wildly myriad tradition of his name, actions, and intended position in the faith so contested, it is little wonder that believing Christians have long struggled with Peter's portrayal in the New Testament. During Jesus's trial, Peter is singled out by every gospel writer as having denied knowing Jesus; Paul's letter to the Galatians calls Peter a hypocrite. While Jesus addresses Peter more frequently than any other apostle, Peter is also condemned more harshly than any other apostle. Peter is finally the only apostle within scripture audacious enough to rebuke Jesus to his face. In some sense, the New Testament can be read as an account of the spectacular failings of a not particularly bright man named Simon Peter. But the gospels contain another, equally unmistakable tradition that stresses Peter's prominence. No other New Testament figure, save for Jesus himself, can be so richly interpreted.

Early Christian history can be divided into three stages of development: (1) the era of the historical Jesus; (2) the era of a Palestinian church centered on Jerusalem; (3) the era of the later, larger Gentile church. The three most important figures in early Christianity, aside from Jesus, are Paul, James the brother of Jesus, and Peter. Paul is absent from the first stage, occupies an ambiguous place in the second, and is prominent in the third. James has an ambiguous place in the first, is prominent in the second, and is absent from the third. Peter, and Peter alone, is the only one of Jesus's early followers to have a place of prominence in all three stages of Christian development.

When we speak of the historical Peter, all that can be determined is this: He was probably one of the first called disciples of Jesus. He was considered among a wide swath of Christians around the Mediterranean world to be the most famous disciple of Jesus. He was known by multiple names. He had what other Christians understood as an early encounter with the risen Jesus. He took part in a form of missionary activity. He served as some kind of mediator between Paul and James. Beyond this: only legend. Atop this: a massive basilica named in his honor.

III.

Pietro Zander is a Vatican archaeologist tasked with preserving excavations in the areas beneath Saint Peter's Basilica known as the grottoes and the necropolis, around which he would serve as my guide. Very few non-Catholics receive the opportunity to see the necropolis, and even Catholics have their difficulties. For many, the wait to descend into the necropolis was months. To be deemed worthy of seeing the necropolis, one often had to be, or at least claim to be, undertaking some sort of religious pilgrimage. This being the case, the vast majority of those selected by the Vatican to visit the necropolis were nuns, priests, or active Catholic laypeople.

Like many archaeologists, Zander appeared to possess a mind in which childlike excitement had been made recombinant with a cooler, more adult desire for precision. I met him in his office in the Fabbrica, one of the Dijon-colored buildings that surround the Vatican complex and which controlled the Vatican's day-to-day operations. (Through the Fabbrica, we would be entering the grottoes.) Zander's impressive coif was the color of pencil lead. His fine blue suit had almost certainly never seen a department-store clothes hanger. Virtually every man who worked in the Fabbrica was dressed as exquisitely as an Italian mogul. Standing in the hallway outside Zander's office, with cologned functionaries striding by, was like being downwind from a cosmetics laboratory.

Just beyond the grottoes' receiving area, Zander stopped at a small diorama model that he used to explain how the belief came to be that Peter was buried on the Vatican hillside. "Peter was buried in a small ditch," Zander said, "probably covered by two terra-cotta tables, which were used to make a pitched roof, and which was then covered. Fifty years after his death, other tombs, family tombs, small mausoleums, were built there, not because Peter was there—these weren't Christians—but because the dead had to be buried outside the city walls, according to Roman law, and this was the closest tomb area outside the city walls."

The first person known to mention this memorial atop Peter's burial site was Gaius, a Roman Christian about whom almost nothing is known, though Eusebius called him "a man of the greatest learning." His *Dialogue Against Proclus,* a (probably) imagined debate between a Christian and a pagan composed around 200, is no longer extant, but Eusebius cited it as proof that Peter and Paul had been buried in Rome: "I can point out the monuments of the victorious apostles. If you will go as far as the Vatican or the Ostian Way, you will find the monuments of those who founded the church." While Gaius did not specify where on the Vatican Hill Peter's monument was, 125 years later Constantine built on the hillside his basilica, then one of the largest in the world, and placed its apse directly over a small roofed structure, known in architectural terms as an aedicule, that earlier Roman Christians had built atop what they believed was Peter's grave. There is little doubt that Gaius and Constantine were working off the same tradition. The aedicule, quite modest, amounted to a doubly pillared portico built into a red wall, with a trapdoor allowing access to the subjacent grave. The diorama Zander now lingered before was that of this original aedicule.

Constantine built his basilica two decades after the 313 Edict of Milan, in which Constantine (along with his co-signer, and temporary ally, Licinius Augustus) gave "Christians and others full authority to observe that religion which each preferred." Constantine was not overly involved with his basilica's construction, as most of his attention was being commanded by various building projects in his new capital of Constantinople. The emperor did, however, break ground with the papal shovel, fill twelve bags with soil—one for each apostle—and carry them to the basilica's first work site.

In building this basilica, Constantine eradicated the existing cemetery in which Peter had purportedly been buried more than 250 years earlier. By Constantine's time, this cemetery contained the bodies of many honored Christians; building over it meant leveling an entire hillside. It is estimated that a million cubic feet of soil was removed from the Vatican, all of which was done with tools scarcely more elaborate than buckets.

Zander walked through a spare white room that displayed

funereal stones and cinerary urns unearthed from the original Vatican cemetery. He stopped at another small diorama that showed the evolution, still imperfectly understood, of Peter's burial site. How, I asked Zander, are the Vatican's archaeologists able to know what Constantine's original memorial to Peter looked like? Having anticipated this question, Zander opened a book he was carrying. Inside was a picture of a fifth-century ivory chest found in Dalmatia, onto which was carved a depiction of Peter's Constantinian memorial.

Constantine's decision to build was widely viewed as a double-barreled sacrilege at the time. Burial matters in Rome were taken very seriously. Violations concerning "sepulture" were sometimes capital offenses. Christianity was not yet Rome's prevailing faith (paganism was not formally banned until 391), and in violating so many graves, Christian and pagan alike, Constantine risked his entire rule. "Constantine was convinced," Zander told me, "that this was Peter's tomb. Otherwise, why do this?" What it all amounted to, he went on, was "two thousand years of documented devotion."

By the time Saint Peter's Basilica was complete in 1626, accessing Peter's grave was no longer possible. In 1939, after the death of Pope Pius XI, the Vatican began to excavate the grottoes, which were found directly beneath and extended slightly beyond the basilica's four-hundred-foot-long nave. These grottoes were a remnant of Constantine's Basilica; for centuries, the Vatican had used them as a storage area. In seeking to expand and remake the grottoes into a subterranean chapel, the Vatican decided to lower the grottoes' floor. The Vatican's diggers immediately began to uncover bodies, most of them modestly interred. This was no surprise: the tradition that the Vatican was used as a cemetery was well documented. Three months into the dig, however, came quite a surprise: the uncovered top portion of a wall.

A Vatican archaeologist was summoned, and picks and shovels were abandoned for baskets and brushes. After they

had removed six thousand cubic feet of earth, the workers were
startled to find themselves standing in the middle of a tomb
replete with Venus paintings, stucco friezes of birds, and a few
intact cinerary urns. These were pagan tombs, clearly, and most
likely dated from before the third century, when Roman paganism began to drift away from cremation, possibly due to a growing pagan belief in some form of an afterlife. Another tomb was
found, with a Latin epitaph that suggested it had belonged to a
Christian. As digging continued, and fill earth was cleared from
yet more roofless tomb structures, the diggers realized they were
uncovering nothing less than a largely intact portion of the original Vatican Hill cemetery. Again, this was a surprise but not
quite a shock. In the seventeenth century, a marble sarcophagus
had been discovered during repairs near the basilica's high altar.
Its sensible—but to Christian eyes, scandalous—inscription
("Mix the wine, drink deep, and do not refuse the pretty girls
the sweets of love") so alarmed the Vatican authorities that they
destroyed the sarcophagus and threw its pieces into the Tiber.

The most recent excavation, begun in Fascist times, occurred
at a difficult moment for Italy. "Before that," Zander said, "no one
dared dig below the altar. It was a matter of respect. You didn't
want to disturb the sleep of the first popes." A few of these early
"popes," it was believed, had been buried near Peter. Some within
the Vatican urged Pius XII to authorize a search for the remains
of Peter. Pius was not initially supportive of the idea, because a
long-honored tradition held that the grave's sanctity had to be
preserved, but the digging continued. More tombs were uncovered, one of which dated to the middle of the second century
and belonged to a family known as Valerius. Here, scrawled in a
small niche beneath a charcoal drawing of a face, the excavators
found their first mention of Peter. The words ("Peter pray Christ
Jesus for the holy . . .") were only partially legible and in Latin. As
the evidence amassed that the excavation was heading directly
toward Peter's grave, Pius granted his permission to excavate the
apostle's burial area. He asked only that no word of what the

Vatican was doing reach the public until an official report was ready for release. The excavators would work quietly for the next decade.

"Pius wanted the dig to happen," Zander said. "He pushed it. He wanted the area excavated because he wanted to confirm the tradition of Saint Peter's tomb. He also wanted to give a scientific answer to growing Protestant questions about whether Saint Peter was martyred and buried in Rome. It was political, yes. Papal primacy is founded on this spot, and it is founded here because this is where Peter was buried."

The methods the initial excavation used were, Zander allowed, deeply regrettable. "Unfortunately, the excavation was carried out in very difficult circumstances, which led to the loss of certain information that would have helped us better understand the situation. They used too much haste." The Vatican's diggers were forced to work so quickly, he went on, because their excavation had compromised the basilica's structural integrity.

With that, Zander waved his large, courteous hand toward the entrance of the grottoes.

                                    IV.

Catholic tradition holds that Peter brought the faith to Rome. Today, the Vatican's view of this long-battered, almost certainly inaccurate belief is highly qualified. The actual founder of Roman Christianity is not known. The scholar Peter Lampe, in his groundbreaking work on the origins of Roman Christianity, used multiple sources—ancient pagan history, scripture, archaeological studies—to determine beyond all reasonable doubt that Roman Christianity began as a number of Jewish cells in some of the poorest Roman neighborhoods, particularly the crowded, stinking, and destitute harbor quarter and brick-making neighborhood of Trastevere. Once established, Christian believers gathered in homes across the city and worshipped according to their own understandings, with no centralized authority. There was evident friction between these new Christians and the city's Jews, one cause of which might have been the Christians' successful efforts to win non-Jewish God fearers* away from the synagogue. The synagogues fought back in some manner dramatic enough to have moved the emperor Claudius to take action. In the late 40s, Claudius banned a large number of "Jews" (early Christians, almost certainly) from Rome. This expulsion marks Roman Christianity's first historical appearance.

Despite its eventual destruction of Jerusalem, Rome was not a fierce enemy of the Jews. In fact, Diaspora Jews frequently sought out Rome's protection, and Rome (Claudius's expulsion edict notwithstanding) usually provided it. Josephus, the great first-century Jewish philosopher Philo, and others suggest that, among Diaspora communities at least, elite Jews could find favor among the Roman authorities. Even during the Jewish War against Rome, Jews did not suffer unusual maltreatment in Rome, provided they did nothing to support the insurrection.

The first Christians in Rome might have anticipated equal benevolence: as immigrant slaves, many of them occupied a position of similar social ambiguity. In fact, Christianity likely infiltrated Rome via slavery, as a number of Jewish (and, thus, Jewish Christian) slaves were sold to Roman aristocrats by members of the Herodian dynasty. Later, many Roman Christians voluntarily sold *themselves* into slavery, the proceeds of which they apparently used to feed the poor in their communities.

The break between Gentile God fearers and Roman Jews did not happen instantly. In all likelihood, a theologically immature form of Christianity reached Rome by the late 30s or early 40s. A decade would go by before Claudius's expulsion edict. During this time, early Roman Christians, many of them former God fearers, most likely periodically attended the synagogues of their

---

* Again, pagans who took an interest in the god of the Jews, attended synagogue, or maintained some of Judaism's behavioral requirements.

choice, and most of the Jews of these synagogues, however grum-
blingly, tolerated them. One result of Claudius's expulsion was to
permanently separate Christians from Rome's synagogues. Less
than twenty years later, during the anti-Christian terror of Nero,
Jews and Christians were viewed as distinct groups of people.

Well into the third century, not a single Roman church
was anything other than a private home. (The world "basilica"
does not occur in the Roman tradition until the fourth century.)
This lack of a public place of worship made early Christianity
much unlike Judaism or paganism; meetings between pagan
groups often occurred in private homes, but to worship there
was unusual. Yet Roman Christianity as a whole apparently had
access to quite a bit of money. Various scattered references allow
us to infer that by the middle of the second century Roman
Christianity was the richest of all the world's Christian communities and had been for some time. Roman support was a
good thing for the Christians of the Mediterranean world, but
it caused unease among the Christians of Rome, who feared the
corruption of the faith as it moved deeper down the corridors
of power. *The Shepherd of Hermas,* a product of early Roman
Christianity that dates from the beginning of the second century, contains a devastating portrait of rich, hypocritical Roman
Christians.

Just as there were no churches in early Roman Christianity, there were no "popes." There were, perhaps, presbyters or
bishop-like figures but no single recognizable leader of the faith.
Paul mentions no leader in his letter to the Romans, and neither
does Ignatius in his letter to the city, written roughly fifty years
later. The first titles of identifiable ecclesiastic authority do not
occur before the middle of the third century.

For Catholics, then, it would seem that the only salvageable
part of Peter's foundation of the Roman church was the idea that
Peter came to Rome and ultimately died there. And now, in the
grottoes, Zander and I were getting close to his supposed tomb.

He encouraged me to explore, but much of the area was a

red-velvet-rope-lined maze used to corral those not fortunate
enough to have Zander guiding them. There were two grottoes:
the Old Grottoes (the part contiguous to Saint Peter's nave) and
the New Grottoes (a U-shaped gallery beneath the basilica's central crossing), which are older than the Old Grottoes but were
opened to visitors later. Hulkingly squat columns divided the
Old Grottoes into three aisles festooned with the doorless crypts
of several popes and esteemed Catholics, including John Paul I;
Queen Christina of Sweden; and Adrian IV, the lone Englishman
in the history of the papacy, who had been entombed beneath a
Medusa-headed sarcophagus for reasons unknown even to Zander. Also here was Pius XI, whose death had instigated the grottoes' refurbishment.

Hundreds of people were moving through the grottoes'
velvet-rope maze in herd-animal silence. Many of them were
priests and nuns. No cameras flashed, and no guidebooks were
consulted. A good number of the grottoes' visitors seemed in a
state of reverently subdued grief. Zander suggested we abscond
to the part of the grottoes found directly beneath the basilica's
confessio and directly above the site of Peter's purported grave.

Above the archway leading into this space was a carved marble scroll sculpture, on which was written SEPULCRUM SANCTI
PETRI APOSTOLI. On either side of the archway, a stone lion lay
with its paws forward. Mounted nearby was a pair of angel statues salvaged from Constantine's Basilica. The archway itself was
roped off. Zander seemed genuinely pained he could provide
no escort closer than this to the "tomb," which seemed to glow
within a soft ocher light that had no immediately discernible
source, other than, possibly, God.

The anti-Christian emperor Julian the Apostate once rather
cunningly condemned the Christian practice of revered burial:
"You have filled the whole world with tombs and sepulchers, and
yet in your scriptures it is nowhere said that you must grovel
among tombs and pay them honor." There was a time, however,
when Christians venerated the dead by drinking half a bottle

of wine with a few like-minded friends beside small memorials; when secrecy governed all ritual; when proofs of faith were more personal if no less strongly felt. A few scattered leavings of this abandoned form of Christian devotion could be found in the necropolis, toward which Zander and I now headed.

V.

In all the gospels, Peter is called by Jesus to join him, yet these accounts are so disparate that many writers seeking to harmonize Peter's call are reduced to circumlocutions such as "It was sometime later. . . ." Simply put, the accounts of Peter's calling cannot be harmonized without severe temporal corner cutting. In Mark, Peter "immediately" abandons his nets to follow Jesus when called. This is followed by an episode in which Jesus heals Peter's sick mother-in-law. Mark places Peter's call after the arrest of John the Baptist, but Matthew locates the call as occurring some time before the arrest. Luke abandons this sequence and depicts Jesus, without the stated presence of Peter, going to Capernaum's synagogue and driving out "an unclean demon" from one of its worshippers. He then walks into Peter's house and heals his mother-in-law, even though in Luke's chronology he has not yet explicitly met Peter.

Another tradition entirely is at work in John's gospel. Peter's brother Andrew, a disciple of John the Baptist's, witnesses his master commend a walking-by Jesus as "the Lamb of God." Andrew and another, unnamed disciple of John the Baptist's spend the day with Jesus. On what is apparently the following day, Andrew finds Peter and brings him to Jesus. Jesus looks Peter over and says, "You are Simon son of John. You are to be called Cephas." Unlike Andrew, Philip, and Nathanael, all of whom are bid to follow, the Jesus of John's gospel does not explicitly call Peter. All he does is meet and rename him.

All of this is to say that markedly different early Christian attitudes about Peter can be detected in the gospels. The Gos-

pel According to Mark, for instance, was most likely addressed
to a predominantly Gentile Christian community uneasy with
Judaism and uncomfortable with the Twelve Apostles generally
and Peter specifically. Yet the church father Papias provided later
Christians with the belief (one that persisted until the nineteenth
century) that Mark, in writing his gospel, relied on Peter's eyewitness. Papias's testimony on the relationship between Mark
and Peter is attributed to an unnamed "presbyter." The work in
which Papias laid out these third-party claims no longer survives,
but Eusebius quoted from it: "Mark, who had been Peter's inter-
preter [in Rome], wrote down carefully, but not in order, all that
he remembered of the Lord's sayings and doings. For he had not
heard the Lord or been one of his followers. . . . Mark was quite
justified in writing down some things just as he remembered
them. For he had one purpose only—to leave out nothing that
he had heard, and to make no misstatement about it." The gospel
was not believed to have been in order? And what does "just as
he remembered them" actually mean? The mention of Mark's
being "quite justified" and that his "purpose" was "to make no
misstatement" suggests that the legitimacy of Mark's gospel was,
at the time of Papias's writing, suffering attacks. Today virtually no scholar accepts Papias's belief that Mark relied on the
historical Peter,* though the theory did lead to Peter's tormented
portrayal throughout Christian history. One early Christian fabu-
list had Peter waking up every morning only to burst into tears
at the sound of a crowing cock. No wonder, when the gospel he
supposedly dictated portrays him as being so inept.

The Gospel According to Matthew was most likely addressed
to a predominantly Jewish Christian community struggling
with its mandate toward Gentile believers. In Mark, "the disciples" are often said to ask something of Jesus. In Matthew, it is
usually Peter who does the asking. Peter's role as the spokes-

---

* Many scholars doubt that Papias is even referring to Mark's gospel, but rather to
some early "sayings" text attributed to Mark.

man of the Twelve, while somewhat apparent in Mark, is owed largely to Matthew's redactions of Mark. This is only one aspect of Matthew's many small but telling departures from Mark. In Mark's gospel, for instance, we are given a scene in which Jesus tells the disciples to sail forth across the Sea of Galilee to Bethsaida, while Jesus "went up on the mountain to pray." By nightfall, Jesus, "alone on the land," notices his disciples struggling "against an adverse wind." In the morning, Jesus walks on the water out to his disciples, which terrifies them. After telling the disciples, "Take heart," Jesus calms the wind. Yet Mark notes that the disciples, still puzzled by his parable of the loaves from the previous day, saw their hearts "hardened" toward Jesus, which is by any measure an emotionally mystifying turn of events. Matthew, for his part, apparently found this scene interesting enough to include but frustrating enough to reshape. When Matthew's Jesus approaches the boat on the water, the disciples once again fear him. Peter, however, volunteers to walk out to meet Jesus. Peter does not get far. At the gust of a "strong wind," he begins to falter and sink. Jesus "reached out his hand and caught him, saying to him, 'You of little faith, why did you doubt?'" Matthew provides Peter with no answer, though "those in the boat" proclaim, "Truly you are the Son of God." Reading through the gospel as a whole, one is left with the clear sense that Matthew's Peter is somehow *closer* to Jesus than he is in the other gospels.

The Gospel According to Luke was most likely addressed to a predominantly Gentile Christian community at greater ease with its Jewish Christian forebears. At numerous points, Luke makes more changes to Mark's portrayal of Peter than Matthew; indeed, his Peter is arguably even more sympathetic. Luke goes out of his way to explain Peter's behavior. One example is how Mark and Luke portray Peter while Jesus prays at Gethsemane shortly before his arrest. In Mark, Peter and the other disciples cannot stay awake, yet it is Peter whom Mark's Jesus confronts: "Simon, are you asleep? Could you not keep awake one hour?" In Luke's version of this scene, Peter is not named, and Jesus's response is much kinder: "Why are you sleeping?" Mark's Peter falls asleep because he is tired; Luke's disciples fall asleep "because of grief." In Mark (and Matthew), Peter swears "an oath" during Jesus's trial that he does not know Jesus, but in Luke Peter's denial is far less severe. Luke is also alone in noting that Jesus, having overheard Peter's denial, "turned and looked" at his friend, which in some strange, subliminal way renders Peter all the more sad and vulnerable. This may be the most humanly heartbreaking moment in the gospels; one historian describes Jesus's wordless confrontation of Peter as among "the most eloquent quiet stares in human history." But then Luke *needs* Peter to be sympathetic, for in the Acts of the Apostles he has him leading the reassembled Twelve.

The Gospel According to John was most likely addressed to a singular community that understood itself as having been founded by an eyewitness to the events of Jesus's life. Within the gospel proper, this character is called the Beloved Disciple, who is frequently paired with Peter, often in an undercutting way. The Beloved Disciple's first explicit appearance in the gospel is during the Last Supper, when Jesus announces that one of the disciples is a traitor. The Beloved Disciple is sitting next to Jesus, apparently athwart Peter: "Simon Peter therefore motioned to him to ask Jesus of whom he was speaking." The point is a pointed one indeed: Peter cannot talk to Jesus about the traitor's identity without using the Beloved Disciple as an intermediary.* John additionally makes Peter the disciple who cuts off the ear of the high priest's servant during Jesus's capture, when, in the other gospels, this aggressor apostle remains anonymous. While the Beloved Disciple stands bravely at the foot of the cross during Jesus's crucifixion, Peter is nowhere to be found. Later the Beloved Disciple beats Peter to Jesus's tomb in a literal race.

---

* Augustine would later argue that Peter wanted to know the traitor's identity because he sought to make a preprandial assault on him.

VI.

Peter's confession to Jesus that he, Jesus, is the Messiah is one of the most important moments in the gospel tradition. In Mark, Jesus suddenly asks the disciples, "Who do people say that I am?" The disciples respond by saying that there is talk of Jesus's being many people: John the Baptist, Elijah, one of the other prophets. Jesus then asks them, "But who do you say that I am?" Mark's Peter steps forth to answer, "You are the Messiah." After ordering his disciples to keep this secret, Jesus "quite openly" discusses how the Son of Man "must undergo great suffering ... be killed, and on the third day rise again." Peter, however, "took him aside and began to rebuke him." Jesus, "turning and looking at his disciples," unloads on Peter a public counter-rebuke: "Get behind me, Satan! For you are setting your mind not on divine things but on human things."

In Matthew, Jesus also asks who the people say that he is, but it is Peter who answers: "You are the Messiah, the Son of the Living God." Matthew's Jesus is so moved by Peter's answer that he makes the *Petros-petra* pun. When Matthew's Jesus promises he must undergo great suffering, he does not frame it in Mark's "Son of Man" terms. Peter's response is also different. While Matthew notes that Peter "began to rebuke him," his words themselves are pillowy with concern: "God forbid it, Lord! This must never happen to you." Jesus's response is similar to that of Mark but contains a critical additional phrase: "Get behind me, Satan! You are a stumbling block to me; for you are setting your mind not on divine things but on human things." Mark's Jesus is angry; Matthew's Jesus is befuddled. Mark's Peter is doltishly prone to misunderstanding; Matthew's Peter is full of misplaced love.

Luke's rendering of Peter's confession is the shortest. Here, Jesus is praying alone alongside the disciples, with none of Mark's "crowd" about, and the roundelay begins. Peter's eventual confession holds that Jesus is "the Messiah of God," which, within a first-century context, may be a kind of Christological middle ground between Mark's "Messiah" and Matthew's "Son of the Living God." While Luke's Jesus expounds on his eventual suffering, Peter does not rebuke him, and he does not liken Peter to Satan. In Luke's hands, the whole confession sequence has a rushed-through air about it, as if it were something the author recognized as touchy.

In the twenty-first (and last) chapter of John, Peter has returned home to Galilee. He announces to Thomas, Nathanael, the sons of Zebedee, and two others, "I am going fishing." The other disciples come along but, despite fishing through the night, catch nothing. By daybreak, "Jesus stood on the beach; but the disciples did not know that it was Jesus." Jesus asks if they have caught anything, and they tell him no. "Cast the net to the right side of the boat," Jesus tells them, "and you will find some." Soon their nets are so full "they were not able to haul it in because there were so many." With that, the Beloved Disciple recognizes Jesus ("It is the Lord!"), which forces Peter to dress quickly ("for he was naked"), jump into the sea, and swim to Jesus. Once Peter is ashore, Jesus tells him, "Come and have breakfast." As they finish eating, Jesus says, "Simon son of John, do you love me more than these?" Peter replies, "Yes, Lord; you know that I love you." Jesus responds, "Feed my lambs." Jesus then asks Peter a second time if he loves him, and Peter responds positively again. "Tend my sheep," Jesus says. When Jesus asks Peter if he loves him a third time, Peter's heartbreak and torment are achingly apparent: "Lord, you know everything; you know that I love you." Jesus then tells Peter, "Feed my sheep."

Part of what makes this scene so affecting, and its sensibility so strangely modern, is that one is not sure to whom one's sympathy is supposed to drift. Is Jesus behaving cruelly by forcing Peter to repeat his love, or is he extracting from Peter a reasonable emotional debit? This is a most rare type of ambiguity for the New Testament—that of a seemingly intentional emotional ambiguity. It is also imaginative in a way few other gospel scenes can claim to be. Imaginative writing succeeds primarily by giving readers just enough information to assemble the particulars of the physical world in which a scene takes place. Oftentimes, gospel stories are distinguished by the vital information they *withhold,* typically during scenes in which pronouns such as "he" and "they" are bandied about with unclear referents. John 21 is imaginative writing of a very high order. Somehow one can sense Peter looking down, perhaps into the dying fire over which he cooks his fish, while he answers Jesus's questions.

The other dynamic being played out here concerns the tradition of leadership in the early church. Due to the "feed my sheep" sequence's rough resemblance to the scene in Matthew in which Jesus presents Peter with the keys of the Kingdom of Heaven, scholars believe the tradition of Peter's intended leadership role, at least within the Twelve, was widely familiar to early Christians. Quite possibly, it has some historical basis.

In Acts, after Jesus's ascension to Heaven, it is Peter who stands "up among the believers" and announces what it is they must do. Their first duty, interestingly, is to restore the Twelve. Peter is the agent of that restoration. The available evidence suggests that Peter played a central role in the years immediately following Jesus's death.* After his visionary experience with Jesus, Paul, by his own admission, traveled to Jerusalem to speak to one person: Cephas. If Peter had not had the foresight to revive and reinvigorate the memories of Jesus among those who first

---

* One interesting aspect of Acts is the pains it takes to turn Peter into a surrogate Jesus. In one example, Peter is summoned to Joppa, where a woman named Tabitha has recently died. After praying beside her body, Peter says, "Tabitha, get up." In Mark, Jesus heals an unnamed little girl with the words, "Talitha cum," an Aramaic phrase that translates as "Little girl, get up!" (*Tabitha,* in Aramaic, means "gazelle.") Earlier in Acts, Peter's healing of a lame beggar on the steps of the Temple first draws the Jewish authorities' notice, just as, in the gospels, Jesus's miracles spook the authorities into acting against him. Peter (with John) argues before the Sanhedrin just as Jesus debates the Pharisees. Peter, too, undergoes a highly familiar persecution, suffering arrest (during Passover) and a resultant confrontation with the authorities (indeed, with Herod).

followed him, some have claimed, then Jesus's legacy might well have suffered the same neglect as any number of ambitious Galilean prophets and agitators.

One way to understand the Acts of the Apostles is as Luke's attempt to show how Christianity, after a decisively early abandonment of its sectarian Jewish origins, open-armedly greeted the larger Mediterranean world, as represented by the Roman centurion Cornelius, "a devout man who feared God with all his household." Cornelius is visited by an angel, who tells him that he must send for "a certain Simon who is called Peter." This man, Cornelius learns, is currently lodged in Joppa. Once Cornelius has sent out his messengers, Peter has a vision in which it is revealed to him that what "God has made clean, you must not call profane." While Peter's vision is literally about dietary law, it is figuratively about Gentiles. When Peter meets Cornelius the next day, he tells him, "I truly understand that God shows no partiality, but in every nation anyone who fears him and does what is right is acceptable to him."

This appears to present an open-and-shut case that Peter was understood by early Christians as having been interested in expanding the faith to Gentiles. But Acts also notes that Cornelius was not a typical Gentile but a man already observant of a few Jewish rituals or rites. This is of course nothing like Paul's later missionary efforts among Gentiles, many of whom had little frame of reference for the God of the Jews and his many alarming requirements. Nevertheless, it is surely significant that Acts shows Paul reaching out to Gentiles only *after* Peter has baptized Cornelius. Raymond E. Brown argues that the Cornelius episode may be "a creation of Lukan *theology*. According to Luke's conception such a major step as the mission to the Gentiles had to be the work of the Twelve; and so, one of the Twelve, indeed the most prominent, is described converting a Gentile under divine guidance." A Roman Gentile, at that. This is also crucial, because by the end of Acts, Jerusalem is all but replaced by Rome as Christianity's desired epicenter.

VII.

According to Acts, the Christians in Jerusalem began to be hounded by the Jewish authorities around 41 CE. After the execution of James son of Zebedee, Peter is arrested by Herod. With angelic assistance, Peter escapes from prison; following that, Acts tells us only that Peter "went to another place." Presumably, this means that Peter left Jerusalem. Peter briefly reappears in Acts during what is known as the Jerusalem Council, where, seventeen years after the death of Jesus, it was decided, at Paul's instigation, that Gentiles did not have to undergo circumcision to enter fully into the faith. Peter argues on behalf of Gentiles, compelling James the brother of Jesus, the evident leader of Jerusalem Christianity, to relent. There is no reliable record of where Peter was during the long period between his disappearance and his reappearance in Acts, though his movements can be cautiously summarized: Antioch (which we know thanks to Paul's testimony), Corinth,* and "Babylon,"† which may or may not be code for Rome. Later legends locate

---

* Paul, in his first letter to the Corinthians, mentions a faction among the Corinthians devoted to Cephas, but what exactly this signifies is not clear. The context in which Peter comes up concerns Paul's wish that the quarreling Corinthians "be in agreement and that there be no divisions among you, but that you are united in the same mind and the same purpose." Later in the letter he cautions, "Let no one boast about human leaders. For all things are yours, whether Paul or Apollos or Cephas or the world or life or death or the present or the future—all belong to you, and you belong to Christ, and Christ belongs to God." That the Corinthian party that claimed to "belong to Cephas" was the result of Peter's missionary work is certainly possible. It is equally possible that those Corinthians who claimed allegiance to Cephas were attempting to distinguish themselves from the followers of the two most prominent local leaders of the Corinthian community: Paul and Apollos. Possibly, these Corinthians were high-mindedly attempting to appeal to Cephas as a less partisan figure.
† Supposedly written by Peter himself, 1 Peter claims to have been composed in "Babylon." It also mentions two figures familiar to us from Paul's letters: Silvanus (probably Silas, the Jewish Christian minder assigned to Paul by the Jerusalem church) and Mark (whom Paul, according to Acts, refused to take on a journey for fear of being abandoned by him but whom the author of 1 Peter refers to as "my son").

Peter in Gaul, Britain (where Peter is supposed to have had a vision at the spot where the Abbey of Saint Peter, Westminster, today stands), and Mesopotamia, among other places. Eusebius connected Peter to the regions of Pontus, Cappadocia, Bithynia, and Galatia, all in Asia Minor, but only because 1 Peter, whose authenticity Eusebius accepted, was addressed to these communities. Nonetheless, Antioch, Corinth, and "Babylon" are the only places to which Peter is linked by the New Testament itself. Of these, only the Antioch linkage is conclusive.

The traditions that place Peter explicitly in Rome emerge no earlier than the late first century. Legends of Peter's *dying* in Rome are to be distinguished from those of Peter's *preaching* in Rome, however, almost all of which are of far later vintage. An early mention of Peter's death comes in *1 Clement,* which was almost certainly written by the prominent Roman Christian of the same name, a man sometimes referred to as an early pope and who was probably a Jewish Christian: "Peter, who, because of unrighteous jealousy, endured not one or two but many trials, and thus having given his testimony went to his appointed place of glory." Although Rome is not mentioned, Clement was likely alluding to a Roman death, because he was writing from Rome and furthermore referred to Peter as belonging "to our own generation." Clement wrote these words around the turn of the first century, allowing for the possibility that Clement knew Peter or someone who did. Ignatius, in his letter to the Romans, noted, "I do not give you orders like Peter and Paul." Ignatius, who died around 110, also seems to indicate that Peter was in some way active in Rome, though some have argued that Ignatius is referring to a now-lost letter to the Roman church that purported to be from Peter. Yet Ignatius mentions nothing of Peter's death having transpired in Rome.

But for Ignatius's enigmatic mention of Peter's somehow issuing "orders" to the Romans, every notion that Peter preached in Rome dates from the second half of the second century, close to a hundred years after Peter's supposed death. The church father Irenaeus, for instance, argued that Peter had not only died in Rome but spent considerable time there, often in the company of Paul. Bishop Dionysius of Corinth, writing around 170, noted "the seed which Peter and Paul sowed in Romans and Corinthians alike. For both of them sowed in our Corinth and taught us jointly: in Italy too they taught jointly in the same city, and were martyred at the same time."

By the fourth century, Peter had become an integral part of the Christian foundation stories of Rome, Jerusalem, Antioch, and Corinth. It is likely that the Roman portion of these foundation stories has its origin in 1 Peter's mention of "Babylon." Few scholars, however, regard the letter as having been written by Peter. Its Greek, for one, is too skillfully employed.* The letter is addressed to the communities of Asia Minor, whose members might have been only hazily aware of when Peter was martyred. Exhorting the Christians of Asia Minor to behave themselves amid unspecified "trials," 1 Peter asks that its recipients "set all your hope on the grace that Jesus Christ will bring you when he is revealed," an event the author assures his audience "is near; therefore be serious and discipline yourselves for the sake of your prayers." First Peter also demands that its audience submit to "the authority of every human institution"; commands slaves to obey "your masters with all deference," even "those who are harsh"; and asks women to "accept the authority of your husbands." While the style may be Pauline, the rhetoric is less so. Paul asks his audience to emulate him, or try to. First Peter asks for obedience, so that the "chosen" of Asia Minor can be "sprinkled" with their Messiah's blood.

* Traditionalists point out the letter's citation as having been written "through Silvanus," a native Greek speaker, as getting around this small pertinence. But language is as much conceptual as it is grammatical, and very little of 1 Peter has the feel of a Galilean fisherman's mind. These are subjective matters, certainly, but not entirely subjective. The Peter of the gospels rings far truer to his purported background, even during spasms of the miraculous, and Paul is such a living, breathing presence in his authentic letters that he practically leaps from the page.

If 1 Peter is probably pseudonymous, 2 Peter is absolutely pseudonymous. Even some in the early church cast doubt on its authorship. Second Peter's composition probably postdates 1 Peter by anywhere from two to five decades. In all likelihood, 2 Peter was the last work of the New Testament to have been written, and it clearly portrays what one scholar describes as "a defensive, institutionalized church." It is also one of the most colorless epistles, full of warnings of "false prophets," eager to recount its putative eyewitness of the transfiguration, and weary with its author's knowledge that "my death will come soon, as indeed our Lord Jesus Christ has made clear to me." Among its few points of interest is what it obliquely reveals about the under-fire position assumed by mid-second-century Christianity. That Jesus had not returned as promised was obviously a source of genuine Christian embarrassment: "For we did not follow cleverly devised myths when we made known to you the power and coming of our Lord Jesus Christ, but we had been eyewitnesses of his majesty." Obviously, the author of 2 Peter is responding to pagan and Jewish critics of Christianity who were accusing it of being little more than "cleverly devised myths." The author of 2 Peter, going for broke as "Peter," puts himself forward as one uniquely able to correct those who do not understand Paul's letters, which the author acknowledges have "some things in them that are hard to understand, which the ignorant and unstable twist to their own destruction." In all likelihood, this is another giveaway to 2 Peter's later date of composition, for in the middle of the second century Paul fell out of favor with many Roman Christians due to the heterodox Christian Marcion's use of his work. Second Peter's defense of "our beloved brother" Paul likely formed the basis of the later legends of Peter and Paul having preached in Rome together. The letter's most distinctive accomplishment is to equate Paul's letters with "the other scriptures," making it the first and only New Testament text to grant Paul the same authority as the Hebrew Bible.

With 2 Peter, a most peculiar New Testament journey is

complete. Peter enters the stories of the first Christians as a man of radiational ambiguity, suffers the public scorn of Paul, eventually grows into Jesus's promised role of earthly shepherd, key keeper, and rock, and bids his flock farewell with the acknowledgment that scripture can be hard to understand. It is as if the author of 2 Peter is describing not Paul's letters but the complicated representational predicament faced by the Prince of the Apostles himself.

VIII.

Early Christians were as fascinated as we are by the questions surrounding Peter's travels and beliefs. In some apocryphal traditions, he is firmly identified with Jewish Christianity. In other traditions, the Gentile Christianity of Rome confidently claims him. In other, more heterodox traditions, Peter is sometimes put forth as representative of a superior, secret understanding of Jesus's message and other times dismissed as having missed the point of Jesus entirely. Peter is the subject of such frequent apocryphal treatment because he was apparently the only apostle sufficiently well known to warrant the attention of seemingly every Christian understanding.

The Preaching of Peter, or the Kerygma Petrou, dates from the first half of the second century and is known to us only through citation by the church fathers. It appears to have been an entirely distinct piece of Petrine literature and, from what scholars can tell, argues strongly on behalf of Christian monotheism. A later strand of the Peter tradition is contained in what is known as the Pseudo-Clementine works, which were purportedly written by Clement of Rome and addressed to James the brother of Jesus. In actuality, the Pseudo-Clementine literature is pseudonymous, dates to no earlier than the third century, and probably originated in Syria. Notable for their depiction of Peter's battle with Simon Magus in Caesarea, the Pseudo-Clementine works portray a Jewish Christian Peter opposed to Pauline arguments, even though Paul himself is never directly named. (In the text, Simon Magus is insinuated to be Paul.)

Another prominent "Peter" text, *The Gospel of Peter* is mentioned by several ancient authorities, none of whom regarded it as anything but unorthodox; Eusebius owlishly noted its "lies." Despite this, *The Gospel of Peter* was apparently quite popular and circulated among monks and copyists in private. Serapion of Antioch, in the year 200, permitted a nearby village church to use it during the liturgy but recanted when he actually read the work, even though he allowed that "most of it is indeed in accordance with the true teaching of the savior." Not until the late nineteenth century was a lengthy fragment of *The Gospel of Peter* found by a French archaeologist in a monastery in the northern Egyptian city of Akhmim.

The Acts of Peter was one of the earliest documents to gather together various Peter traditions in written form. Composed in either Rome or Asia Minor sometime between 160 and 200, it was popular among many kinds of Christians but in time became the subject of wide condemnation. No complete Greek version of the manuscript exists—scholars estimate that a little over half the total manuscript has survived—and the only wholly extant Greek portion of *Acts* is its account of Peter's martyrdom, which was apparently circulated independently. Nonetheless, much of what we know about Peter traditionally comes from this work, including the notion that he was crucified upside down.

Its story begins in Caesarea, where Jesus appears to Peter and demands that he go to Rome to do battle with the hated magician Simon Magus, a figure now widely represented in second- and third-century Christian storytelling as evil's embodiment on earth. Knowing he must confront Simon, Peter is on the next ship out. When Peter arrives in Italy, an innkeeper named Ariston takes Peter aside to tell him that Simon has made many converts in Rome. In the city itself, Peter stays with a presbyter named Narcissus; Simon Magus, meanwhile, is staying at the home of a Roman senator named Marcellus. Once a holy, giving

Christian, Marcellus now refuses to give his money to the poor and beats any beggar he happens upon. Soon Peter is marching, with supporters in tow, to Marcellus's front door.

Peter finds there a doorman too afraid to act against Simon Magus, whom he calls "the liege of Satan." Peter grants a nearby dog the ability to speak and sends the beast inside to persuade Simon Magus to come out and fight like a man. Simon Magus, when confronted, begs the talkative hound to tell Peter he is not home. Rather like a child sensing it is losing an adult's attention, the *Acts of Peter*'s author has Peter restore life to a smoked fish hanging in a nearby window. The stunned crowd proclaims its belief in Peter. Marcellus commands Simon Magus to leave his house, which, finally, he does, only to have buckets of human waste emptied on his head.

The account of Peter's martyrdom in *The Acts of Peter* is quite different from the traditional story of his death. In this version, Peter has made inroads with many wealthy Christians. Among his converts are the concubines of the local ruler, from whom Peter persuades the concubines to withhold sex. Then, alerted to a plot against him, Peter leaves Rome in disguise, but before he can get beyond the city, Jesus appears to him and asks Peter where he is going, because he, Jesus, is on his way to Rome to be crucified again. Peter heads back to Rome to meet his fate.

Tradition most often places Peter's death around 64 CE; Eusebius names the fateful year as 67. What is known is that on July 19, 64, a fire broke out in Rome that destroyed thirteen of the city's seventeen regions and incinerated as many as two thousand souls. The Roman historian Tacitus noted that the fire "in its fury ran first through the level portions of the city, then rising to the hills, while it again devastated every place below them." Even the imperial palace was consumed. One of the only parts of Rome to have been wholly spared the fire was the heavily Christian neighborhood of Trastevere, which was protected by the Tiber River.

Although viciously hostile to the rebellious Jews of Roman

Palestine, Nero is thought to have viewed Roman Jews with a modicum of sympathy. His wife, Poppaea Sabina (whom Nero later kicked to death), was, according to Josephus, a God fearer (in his words, "a religious woman"), and Nero's favorite actor, Aliturus, was a Jew from Judaea.* Some scholars have proposed that Rome's Jews, still smarting from having so many God fearers lured away from their synagogues, might have fed Nero information that the arsonists responsible for the blaze were Christian. Whatever the case, Nero began to look for scapegoats on whom to blame the devastating fire.

Tacitus wrote that "an arrest was first made of all who pleaded guilty; then, upon their information, an immense multitude was convicted, not so much of the crime of firing the city, as of hatred against mankind." (Tacitus believed arsonists working at Nero's order had set the fire.) While he had no use for Christians, Tacitus was appalled by the way they were treated. Christians were covered "with the skins of beasts, they were torn by dogs and perished, or were nailed to crosses, or were doomed to the flame and burnt, to serve as a nightly illumination, when daylight had expired." None of these punishments were out of line in the Roman world. Many were common. The punishment for arson, in fact, was public immolation. The total number of Nero's Christian victims is not known, but it could easily have stretched into the thousands.

According to tradition, Peter was arrested by Nero and held for close to a year in Mamertine Prison, which is today a small devotional structure next to the ruins of the Forum. Later traditions hold that while ensconced there, Peter converted nearly four dozen of his jailers and shouted to his imprisoned wife, "Remember the Lord!" as she was led away to her death.

As the Christian imagination matured, the martyrdoms of

---

* Aliturus (which was likely a pseudonym) befriended Josephus while he visited Rome as a young man, and Poppaea helped Josephus secure the release of the Jewish priests he had traveled to the city to rescue. (See page 376.)

Peter and Paul were claimed to have occurred in Rome at the same instant—which, probably not coincidentally, happened to fall on the very day of Rome's founding. An influential fifth- or sixth-century Christian mystic who wrote under the name Dionysius later described "the mob of pagans and Jews . . . spitting in [Peter's and Paul's] faces" while they were led to their execution sites. According to other legends, the early Roman Christian bishop Anacletus was, within twenty years of Peter's death, hosting memorial services next to a shrine that had been raised atop what he and his co-religionists believed was the historical Peter's grave.

Again, none of these legends are contemporaneous, and most emerge a hundred years or more after the fact. When one considers the comprehensive silence about where Peter's death had taken place among early Christians, the unreliable conduits through which such information was eventually passed on, and the superhuman sobriety required of early Roman believers to question the alluring possibility that the most famous apostle was buried in their city, maybe the most astounding thing about Peter's grave is the fact that it *cannot* be dismissed out of hand.

IX.

Zander walked down a narrow, winding, altogether unpromising staircase and came to a thick glass door that had no knob or handle. On the opposite side of this space-age portal was the ancient necropolis. Adjacent to the door was an enemy-stronghold numeric keypad, into which Zander quickly tapped his pass code. With a whoosh the glass door opened, releasing a burst of cool, chlorine air. Zander explained that the door was hermetically sealed as a preventative measure: for many years, the necropolis had suffered from seeping microbial moisture. Since 1998, a carefully maintained "microclimate" has been used to facilitate its preservation. Once inside the necropolis, Zander and I stood in the middle of a narrow street, between two largely continuous rows of mausoleums. Around us fell a thin shower of avocado light, the sources of which were covered with greenish filters to combat microorganism growth.

Two tour groups were currently visiting the necropolis. One group was exclusively made up of nuns; the other was 90 percent priests. The necropolis's coal-colored street, which had the smooth pulverous appearance of a cooled lava flow, was almost two thousand years old. Once a major thoroughfare that led out of the city, this road had probably been laid when the necropolis's first tombs began to go up in the second century. Zander motioned around at the bordering and largely roofless sepulchral buildings. "This was once a beautiful, panoramic area," he said. In other words, everything around us had once stood in the open air. That seemed as incredible a thing to ponder as Peter rising from the dead and shaking my hand.

For twelve centuries, nearly every part of the necropolis remained unchanged from when Constantine's workers finished filling the sepulchral structures with dirt and had their last, unknowable thoughts before sealing the area off from human reach. Walking here, I felt a spidery shiver of the uncanny, much in the way a certain type of dream can be simultaneously bizarre and familiar. The bricks of the necropolis gave off a kind of low subterranean hum. To say this place felt holy, somehow, was, to my shock, not an overstatement.

This was only a small piece of the original necropolis, much of which Constantine's workers probably destroyed. Nineteen necropolis tombs in total had been excavated. They were arranged in the manner of rooms in two facing railroad apartments. Twelve tombs made up one row, seven the other. Many of their doors and windows had been covered with glass for preservation purposes. Zander walked downhill along the road that divided the mausoleum rows toward one of the smaller tombs. The majority of those buried here, he again emphasized, were not Christian. Additionally, many of the necropolis's dead appear to have enjoyed a measure of wealth, whether as freedmen—

former slaves who had achieved citizenship through the manumission of their owners or by magistrate ruling—or merchants. Some had been buried with their own slaves. In a few of these tombs, however, there was some Christian evidence. This supported the theory that Roman Christianity was, for many years, widely practiced among slaves and that some of these slaves succeeded in partially or wholly converting their masters. (Rich Romans were nothing if not religion faddists.)

Zander told me the necropolis had been in constant use almost to the day that Constantine began building his basilica. Thus, he went on with a sigh, there were likely more nearby tombs and mausoleums waiting to be uncovered, but digging for them could not be essayed without seriously endangering the foundation of Saint Peter's Basilica. The other hindrance was more prosaic. Any further dig would have to be launched from the grottoes and the necropolis, and given how many tourists came through both areas, and the amount of time needed to survey the surrounding area properly, another large-scale excavation might well be impossible.

Zander stopped at a mausoleum that had belonged to the Aelii family and been dated, he said, to the reign of Antoninus Pius (so-named for his senatorial edict that deified his predecessor Hadrian), which began in 138. This was one of the necropolis's plainer mausoleums, with none of the elegant travertine lintel work that marked the doorjambs of other tombs. (It is assumed Constantine's workers stripped this tomb of its lintel.) Zander invited me to look into the mule-gray space and note the small stairway that led to a veranda used for postmortem celebration. Zander explained how families often gathered on such verandas to partake in what he called "banquets with the dead," which were typically held on the first and last days of the mourning period and on the birthday of the deceased. Roman pagans believed that the dead continued to consume food and drink from the afterlife, and their urns and tombs were outfitted with holes and "libation wells," into which their relatives poured wine and food.

I asked why many of these tombs had been rather brusquely sheared off at the top. Zander looked up, squinting. "Constantine's architects did that, to avoid the top of the mausoleums from sticking up through his basilica's floor."

A few of the necropolis's nineteen surviving tombs were still undergoing work. The exterior brickwork of those that had been subject to restoration had a bright, almost festive red-brown glow; the ones that had not been restored looked as though they had survived three winters' worth of salt blizzards. Zander stopped at one tomb to point out one of the necropolis's few unambiguously Christian symbols.*

Zander led me to the tomb's far wall. It appeared that one of Constantine's workmen picked up a piece of sharpened coal shortly before sealing off the necropolis and used it to sketch a smeared portrait of Peter. This charcoal Peter portrait was not nearly as strange as a restored third-century ceiling mosaic Zander soon pointed out in another mausoleum, this one belonging to the Iulii family, which was the only entirely Christian mausoleum in the necropolis.

The Iulii mausoleum's ceiling mosaic has been called the most conclusively important discovery made during the Vatican's excavation of the necropolis, and it came within an eyelash length of being lost forever. When the Vatican's excavators broke into this small, eight-foot-long tomb and began clearing away its fill dirt, they noticed on its facing walls apparently Christian images: on the left, the Good Shepherd; on the right,

---

* What appeared in some tombs to be Christian imagery did not make it so. Other tombs' mosaic images of shepherds, meal taking, and scroll-holding women are sometimes indicative of, for instance, Orpheus worship. Bucolic scenes depicting shepherds, after all, were Christian symbols only to other Christians. For many years in early Christianity, the Egyptian ankh was used to symbolize Jesus.

Jonah falling off a boat and being swallowed by a sea-monstery beast while two gawking fishermen stood above him on the boat's prow. Pressed into the wall mosaic around these images were thousands of tiny tiles made of green-and-gold glass paste, arranged to resemble a complicated network of vines. The Iulii tomb was one of the few in the necropolis to have had a vaulted roof, and it was through this roof that the excavators had gained entrance. When the excavators had at last cleared the tomb's fill dirt, they looked up to see a stunning mosaic they were horrified to realize they had partially destroyed.

Employing a more elaborate use of the walls' viny, glass-tile backdrop, the mosaic depicted its beardless Jesus as a white-robed sun god riding two equally white horses across a golden sky within a burst of thick planks of light. It became known as Christ Helios and today stands as the only known occurrence of such mongrelized devotional imagery. Almost unimaginably beautiful, the Christ Helios mosaic—the earliest known Christian mosaic—suggests how intertwined pre-Constantine Christian iconography had been with Roman paganism. It illuminated the difficult psychic breakthrough Jesus truly represented. In trying to understand their god, Rome's first Christians were still subject to familiar pagan ideas.

Zander took me to some of the necropolis's earliest tombs, many of them found in the vicinity of Peter's monument sculpture mentioned by the Roman Christian Gaius. A few of these tombs had been briefly looked into in the seventeenth century, when the placement of the high altar's baldachino—the bronze Bernini sculpture whose weight was estimated at more than 100,000 pounds—necessitated emergency basilica foundation work. The earliest of the necropolis's mausoleums, Zander said, dated from about six decades after Peter's traditional date of martyrdom. This was a long time in a society subject to Rome's socioeconomic expansions and reversals. Those buried closest to Peter were evidently poor, and many of their bodies had been laid in unlined, unprotected shallow ruts. The farther one trav-

eled from Peter's grave, the richer those buried in the necropolis became. Not until the third century did any major Christian
figure see burial in its soil, which was likely due to the Vatican
hillside's unsavory association with the poor immigrant population of Trastevere. Gradually, though, the necropolis became a
popular burial site. Christians were following Peter; pagans were
following fashion.

Not everyone agreed with Zander's early dating of some of
these tombs. The scholar Peter Lampe writes that the earliest
tombs of the necropolis are from no earlier than the middle of
the second century, a little shy of a century after Peter's traditional martyrdom. Nevertheless, Lampe believes that the burial
sites closest to Peter's grave—many of which are angled in such
a way as to suggest an ongoing attempt at proximity in increasingly limited space—were probably crypto-Christian, seeing that
"it was not desirable, at least in the first two centuries, for the
average Christian to advertise his or her Christianity openly, let
alone engrave it on stone." He also believes there were likely earlier Christian burials near Peter but virtually all of them have
been lost to time. It was easy to forget, while wandering the
necropolis beneath dozens of feet of earth and marble, that all of
its burials were carried out in broad daylight and became subject
to the intrusions and caprices of the outside world in a way that
catacomb-buried Christians were not.

As Zander led the way up a landing flanked by columns
once part of the twelfth-century altar of Calixtus, behind which
stood the one surviving column of the monument sculpture
mentioned by Gaius, I asked him how anyone could be sure that
Peter's grave was here. Zander cited the church's official position
on the matter. "The remains," he said, "are believed to be those of
the blessed apostle Peter."

To say the least, the Catholic Church's position on this matter
was an embattled one. On the lower rim of the cupola beneath
the glorious dome of Saint Peter's Basilica is this Latin rendering of Jesus's words to Peter in the Gospel According to Mat-

thew: *"Tu es Petrus et super hanc petram aedificabo ecclesiam meam et tibi dabo regna caelorum."** Catholics also point to the last chapter of the Gospel According to John ("Feed my sheep") as other evidence that Jesus bequeathed administrative power to Peter, who in the Catholic mind serves as the single best diviner of what his earthly ministry meant and what his heavenly rule intends—a kind of subaltern Messiah.

Unfortunately for Catholicism, Peter's authority was never a settled matter in early Christianity. The notion that Jesus's keys to the Kingdom of Heaven gave Peter special duties—and, later, lent the Roman church its authority—was resisted by a number of early Christians. No one appealed to the crucial passage of Matthew until 256, during a debate between a Roman and a Carthaginian bishop. Many church fathers—including Origen, Eusebius, and John Chrysostom—understood the *Petros-petra* passage in Matthew to mean that Jesus would build on Peter's *confession* to Jesus rather than Peter the man. After all, the powers granted to Peter were given to the other apostles as well, at least according to the synoptic gospels and Acts. Not until the fifth century, with the pontificate of Leo the Great, who called himself the "unworthy heir" of Peter, was the doctrine of "Petrine supremacy" put forth to all Western churches with the full wind-tunnel authority of the papacy behind it. (Leo's naked power play had roots in his outrage that Constantinople had been granted equal stature with Rome.) That doctrine would endure for a thousand years before questions about what Peter's authority actually meant—and whether it allowed a string of whore-mongering and busily procreative popes—eventually tore Western Christianity in two.

One Protestant response to the Catholic understanding of Matthew points to Paul's first letter to the Corinthians: "For no

_____

* "You are Peter and upon this rock I will build my church and I will give to you the keys of the kingdom of heaven."

one can lay any foundation other than the one that has been laid; that foundation is Jesus Christ." Some Protestants also point to 1 Peter, where "Peter" writes that Christians should let themselves "be built into a spiritual house," which they interpret as Peter's own warning against ceding inappropriate authority to earthly institutions. The Roman Catholic side of this debate was not helped by the document that putatively entrusted secular authority over Rome and the whole western half of the Roman Empire. Known as the Donation of Constantine, it purports to be a fourth-century agreement between Constantine and Pope Sylvester I and was supposedly drafted shortly after Constantine abandoned Rome for Constantinople in 326 but was in fact an eighth-century forgery.

In light of this and much, much else, it is tempting to regard Roman Catholicism as an ancient, power-grabbing conspiracy, but that would not be accurate. Papal authority, whatever horrors it eventually proved capable of, evolved gradually and (insofar as the word can be used for a man-made institution) naturally. Lampe cites the "theological pluralism" of Roman Christianity deep into the second century. The city was home to not only proto-orthodox Christians but also Marcionites, Valentinians, Carpocratians, Montanists, Jewish Christians, and Quartodecimans. Almost all of these Christian understandings were imported into the city from other lands, meaning that none could claim the advantage of having originated in Rome. Lampe also notes the basic tolerance that existed between these groups. Because few Christians had much of an idea of what went on in Rome's other Christian churches, they probably viewed one another as being "in spiritual fellowship" and "united by common bonds." Only near the end of the second century, during the bishopric of Victor I—the first African-born bishop of Rome, a furious proponent of the use of Latin, and an avid excommunicator—did threats of exclusion from the greater body of Christianity occur.

Irenaeus, as quoted by Eusebius, noted that during the late

second century Christians of different understandings were able to part "company in peace" and remain "in communion." There were teachings regarded as "false," certainly, but few denunciations. It became gradually clear, however, that disagreements on smaller issues—such as the preferred date for Easter—were often tips of much larger doctrinal icebergs. After what Lampe describes as "faint-hearted attempts" by the Roman bishops Eleutherius (ca. 175–189), Soter (ca. 166–175), and Anicetus (ca. 155–166) to establish a more centralized Roman authority, Victor I became the first Roman Christian to put himself forward as undisputed leader of the city's faithful. From this came what Lampe calls "the development of a monarchical episcopacy in the city." It then became a simple matter of justifying this development by working intellectually backward.

Prior to Victor's rule, Irenaeus had cataloged twelve Roman figures, beginning with Linus and ending with Eleutherius, all of whom he imagined serving in clear succession. The apostolic ring of twelve Roman Christian leaders who traced their lineage to Peter was obviously intentional. Lampe argues that this list did not originate with Irenaeus. The twelve names were not invented but rather pulled from the miasma of Roman Christian history. Most crucially, this development came about almost entirely due to what Lampe calls "social-historical factors": duties such as overseeing aid shipments to other Christian communities around the Mediterranean and coordinating the Roman Christian treasury inadvertently strengthened the hand of the Roman bishop. Men such as Eleutherius were forced to further communication among various Christian cells around Rome, write letters, maintain some basic theological consistencies, and receive visitors from other Christian delegations. Gradually, a larger sense of authority adhered to the bishopric, and the papacy was born.

To its credit, the modern Catholic Church has proved responsive to the findings of modern science and textual biblical criticism.* The church has retreated from many previous bulwarks, and serious Catholic scholars acknowledge the historical weakness of the belief that Peter founded the church, just as they acknowledge the third-century origins of the papacy. But Peter's grave was one of its last firewalls, a historical area into which doubt could not be allowed to spread.

The writer John Evangelist Walsh, whose credulous account of the Vatican's excavation of Peter's bones is well matched by his middle name, imagines that the first visitors to Peter's grave "must have been some sons and daughters, certainly some of the grandchildren or other descendants, of those Roman Christians who had actually watched Peter being led to crucifixion, who had stood witness as his wracked and lifeless body was lowered into the earth. These first visitors, possessing a very recent and personal tradition about Peter, could hardly have been misled as to the location of his grave."

There is, of course, absolutely no reason why this must be the case. One need only look around the world, ancient and modern, to find any number of fervent beliefs that developed *despite* any evidence to support them. Consider American tragedies such as the Kennedy assassination or the attacks of September 11. Within only a few years of both events, hundreds were claiming to have been present for events they did not see, and tens of thousands professed knowledge of divergent secret histories—this, in an age of widely available information, photographic records of what had happened, and universal literacy. Remove these empirical mufflers, and what sorts of beliefs might come into being?

History, in many ways, comes into being as a contrast

---

* The Catholic position on biblical inerrancy is particularly refreshing. According to the Biblical Commission Instruction of 1964, readers are not to understand that the gospels report everything literally or that the events described in them necessarily took place in the manner depicted.

between interested and disinterested witnesses. Early Christian history is marked by its comprehensive absence of disinterested witnesses.

I was thinking of this as Zander and I stopped in a small circular chapel found directly beneath the basilica's high altar, the heavily illustrated walls and ceiling of which appeared to contain the complete narrative contents of both the Christian and the Jewish testaments in gold relief. Once, Zander explained, this space had served as the crypt of Constantine's Basilica. Prior to Constantine, Christians had celebrated an early form of Mass here. Zander then walked me through the curved hallway that ringed the chapel and corresponded to the apse of Constantine's Basilica. Evenly spaced along the ellipsoid wall were paintings of the twelve "popes" who supposedly followed Peter in doctrinally unbroken succession. All held palm fronds, the traditional symbol of the martyr, even though almost nothing is known about most of them, including whether or not they were martyred. After this, Zander returned to the area near the surviving column of the Peter monument mentioned by Gaius and directed my attention to the no-longer-evident breach point through which the Vatican's excavators had plunged in their search for Peter's grave.

Zander pointed out that when Pius finally overcame his personal reservations and approved the attempt to locate Peter, no one had any idea what they might find. In some ways, Pius placed the historical foundation of Roman Catholicism in serious peril. What if they found nothing? The Vatican's initial discoveries of uniformly pagan inscriptions and graves were not promising. Adjacent to one pagan tomb, however, they found what appeared to be a graveyard that comprised seven plain graves, many of them arranged at angles that seemed to point to a central, honored grave. One of these seven graves, moreover, contained tiny remnants of gold thread. A simple grave, angled toward another, containing precious metal: all suggested that this grave belonged to one of the early "popes" that tradition claimed had been buried near Peter.

Finding Peter's grave was not easy. Digging straight down into the suspected gravesite was out of the question. (The lesson of the Christ Helios mosaic's discovery had been fully absorbed.) Instead, the excavators were forced to crack open distant necropolis sectors and, from there, tunnel sideways toward the area they suspected contained Peter's grave. Even so, the excavators were serially impeded, first by part of the Constantinian Basilica's sixth-century altar, which was itself surrounded by Pope Calixtus's twelfth-century altar. There was no way around either without damaging both. During a resultant archaeological flanking maneuver, they discovered two walls. The first was quickly dubbed "the red wall" due to its faded but distinct painted red plaster. The second was dubbed "the graffiti wall" due to the numerous, often illegible scratchings made on it. The bricks of the red wall were embossed with stamps that conclusively dated the bricks, if not the wall itself, between 146 and 161—long before the construction of Constantine's Basilica. The red wall was, in any case, substantial: eight feet high, seven feet wide, and two feet thick.

The graffiti wall was estimated to date from around 250. On it, a number of names and apparently non-Christian inscriptions were identified—as was the so-called chi-rho symbol, wherein the first two Greek alphabet letters of "Christ" are written in overlap and which early Christians used as a secret reference to Jesus. The graffiti wall, the Vatican eventually deduced, had originally been built to shore up the red wall at a place where its foundation had cracked. Its plenitude of Christian scratchings was apparently what had saved this homely stopgap structure from being razed later.

At the foot of the red wall, the excavators found their first skeletal remains, which dated from the fourth century. From here out, tools were forbidden. Using their hands, the excavators dug a foot deeper and came across another grave they suspected (and which later study verified) dated from the first century. Pope Pius was summoned. While the excavators gathered together the grave's scattered bones, the thin, beak-nosed pontiff silently observed them from a large chair. Most of the 250 bones and fragments the excavators found were small: toe and finger pha-langes, vertebrae bits, rib splinters, but also a few larger, intact femurs and tibias, all of which were sent off for study.

In the summer of 1968, Pope Paul VI made the "happy announcement" that "the relics of Peter have been identified in a manner which we believe convincing." The "very patient and accurate" methods used by the Vatican, Paul claimed, all pointed to "a result which we believe positive." What was not immedi-ately clear in Paul's proclamation was the fact that the "relics" in question had been found nearly three decades previous. The long pause between their discovery, study, and affirmation was due to what has been described as "perhaps the most regrettable and egregious blunder in archaeological history."

"When they found Peter's grave," Zander explained, "it was the central grave. It was more like a ditch. And the other graves radiated out from it. It was also an active, much-cared-for, and restored tomb. They found bones down here, many bones, but there were problems. It was a confusing situation."

Part of what made it so confusing was the excavators' igno-rance of what it was they had discovered. Believing the red wall was the Gaius monument and expressly built for Peter, they could not understand why it appeared to have been built directly over Peter's grave. Indeed, its construction succeeded in cutting Peter's grave in two—and not even handsomely, as it intersected the grave at an awkward hundred-degree angle. Yet the early, modest aedicule that memorialized Peter had clearly been built into this oddly placed red wall.

No wonder the excavators were confused. Early Roman Christians had apparently opted to honor Peter by ruining the sacred concinnity of his grave. Peter Lampe, in a thrilling piece of historical detection, argues the following: The red wall was built before the aedicule and, initially, had nothing to do with Peter. Another Roman had decided to build his—in all likelihood, quite grand—mausoleum, and these plans happened to cut the venerated, still secretly attended grave of Peter in half. The Christians could not prevent this, because those who built the red wall were not Christian but pagan, and the Christians themselves were poor. At some later point, when the social situation had changed enough to allow for a more public acknowledgment of Peter's grave, the aedicule was built into the red wall. Evidence for Lampe's theory can be found in the form of a nearby graffito. The graffito in question, a fish scratching, might not have been the product of spontaneous devotion but was rather a way for Christians to give other Christians a sense of how to reach their now-obstructed place of veneration. As convincing as Lampe makes all this sound, there were still a number of uncertainties and imponderables, and the difficult scholarly work (a sample: "$F_{10} = : \gamma \approx \theta$. When θ was first built, its upper ridge lay either close under or right at the original surface") continues. It will always continue.

The study of the bones the excavators found in the soil at the foot of the red wall was led by the pope's personal physician, which probably ensured something less than impartial inquiry. The Vatican said nothing publicly of its excavation or exhuming work, and for several years World War II interrupted its efforts. Of the exhumed bones themselves, however, it was quickly determined that among them were *three* fibulas and *four* tibias. The conclusion, however disappointing, was clear: if these were Peter's bones, others had been mixed in with them. One of the bones had come, moreover, from a woman. Another blow quickly followed: a fourth of the bones found were of cow, horse, sheep, and goat origin.

When the excavation resumed, faded markings were found on the red wall in an area that the graffiti wall had previously obscured. These were the first four Greek letters of Peter's name (the rest was broken off) and, beneath them, three Greek letters: *ENI*. At long last, the Vatican's excavators had definitive proof that this burial site was linked with Peter. They judged that the inscription had been made around 250, shortly before the graffiti wall was built. On the graffiti wall itself, meanwhile, many of the individual graffiti had faded since excavation had begun a decade earlier, due to the necropolis's punishing humidity. An appropriately trained archaeologist, Margherita Guarducci, was finally brought in to look at the graffiti wall. Guarducci was able to translate a few phrases that had hitherto eluded the excavators. "Christian men buried near your body," read one barely legible scratching, which she estimated as having been written around 300.

In 1963, five years after Pius XII died deeply disappointed that Peter's bones had not been definitively identified and shortly after his successor, John XXIII, also passed away, Guarducci asked an innocent question about what else had been found in the tomb. She was told of the first bone harvest and then, to her astonishment, of bones that, in the early 1940s, had been found in a small, camouflaged hole in the graffiti wall and that were then secreted away in the papal apartment by Monsignor Ludwig Kaas. This occurred during a low point in Kaas's relations with the excavators. Kaas, who was in charge of the excavation, was not an archaeologist, and his suggestions often rankled those beneath him. Kaas had made the chance discovery one night after the excavators had gone home, as was his wont, because he believed that the excavators too often left human bone fragments lying amid other rubble. Inside the graffiti wall, Kaas found two corroded coins, several bone fragments (some quite large), a few bits of cloth, and some threading. Kaas, inexplicably, never informed the other excavators of his discovery. The bones, Guarducci learned, were still sitting in the papal apartment in a mislabeled box. Guarducci came to believe these bones had been hidden away in the graffiti wall, probably at the order of Constantine himself, and were, in fact, Peter's. When

Guarducci presented her argument on behalf of the bones' provenance before the pope in 1962, they were, at long last, studied.

Because the graffiti wall's bones did not amount to anything near a complete skeleton, the type of information their study stood to reveal was limited. Determining matters such as sex and height and body type was possible but difficult. Discovering any information related to cause of death was impossible. The examiner soon determined that to the best of his knowledge the graffiti wall bones represented the remains of one man and one nearly complete mouse.* Of the human fragments, the most intact were all leg bones. The panoply of skull fragments and finger bones led the examiner to conclude that the collective remains had been transferred into the wall within some type of bag or receptacle, because any manual transport was liable to have shed such tiny bones. The examiner's final findings held that the bones were those of an older man of stout build. Two of his most suggestive findings hinged on the bones' interaction with their surrounding environment. Unlike the clean white mouse bones, the graffiti wall bones were caked with ancient, hardened bits of earth, which suggested that they had been interred for some time in loose dirt—much like the dirt you might find in a shallow rut into which an executed and hastily buried criminal would be heaved. A number of the bones were, moreover, stained a dark red, possibly from dye, which suggested that after the bones had been disinterred they had been wrapped in purple, gold-threaded fabric.

By all available evidence, the bones had been buried, removed from the earth, wrapped in cloth, and hidden in the graffiti wall. All of this happened in uncertain order, at unknowable times. Guarducci, after pondering these findings, remembered the PETROS ENI graffito. She reinvestigated the phrase that

---

* The mouse bones had apparently never been exposed to soil, which suggested that the creature had worked its way into the graffiti wall hiding place, become trapped, and died.

had initially mystified her and learned that in some types of ancient Greek, "eni" had occasionally been used as a contracted form of a verb that meant "to be within." According to this reading of the inscription, the graffito scanned differently: "Peter is within."

Soon after she formulated her theory, she went to the new pope, Paul VI, who happened to be a family friend, to share its particulars. After hearing her out, the pope asked for new analyses to determine whether the soil on the bones matched that of the soil at the base of the red wall (it did) and whether the tiny filaments of fabric found among the bones were in fact pure gold (they were). Given the clumsiness of the bones' discovery and mishandling and the Vatican's niggardly release of certain information, these findings left holes large enough for the moon to pass through. Why could the bones not have been those of another prominent early Christian? If they were Peter's, why were they hidden so inexpertly? Exactly how old were the bones? Carbon dating would provide a two-hundred-year window for the bones to fit into temporally, which is not nearly precise enough to answer the question.

There is, moreover, another twentieth-century discovery that could place Peter's tomb in Jerusalem, in a Franciscan monastery known as Dominus Flevit. In 1952, a digging monk accidentally broke into a crypt that contained sarcophagi belonging to one Mary, one Martha, one Lazarus, and one Simon bar Jonah. Mary, Martha, and Lazarus were the names of prominent early followers of Jesus, but they had never before been so closely linked to Peter. The belief that this Simon bar Jonah sarcophagus holds the remains of the historical Peter has never escaped fringe-theory orbit, most wonderfully exemplified by F. Paul Peterson's 1960 anti-Catholic tract *Peter's Tomb Recently Discovered in Jerusalem!* (From its pages one learns, among many other digressions, that "Abraham Lincoln was assassinated by a Roman Catholic and that all those in that terrible conspiracy were either Catholic or Catholic taught.") Yet a few Franciscans to whom I spoke

in Jerusalem appeared willing to entertain the possibility that
Peter's tomb was not in Rome. I asked one Franciscan what such
an upheaval of Roman Catholic tradition would mean for him.
"Nothing," he said.

X.

Again I followed Zander as he approached Peter's tomb. The
imperial Roman splendor of the necropolis now gave way to
the harder, antiseptic stylings of modern architecture. The dirt
courtyard through which the Vatican's excavators had once
pawed was now covered by a softly lit platform of metal grat-
ing, the central part of which was a checkerboard that allowed
visitors to look down upon several broken chunks of marble
that dated from the second and third centuries.

While Zander and I walked into this area, I asked him about
the lingering questions surrounding Peter's bones. "This," he
said, looking around, "is Peter's tomb. Whose bones? *This* is
Peter's tomb. We don't stake our reputation on whether these
are the actual bones of Peter. The important thing for us is that
the *place* has been identified so absolutely." He looked over his
shoulder. "And there they are."

Behind a bronze gate, once again in the graffiti wall crack
from which Monsignor Kaas had sixty years before unsuspect-
ingly rescued them, and wrapped in purple fabric, the bones
the Vatican believed to be Peter's were kept in nineteen rubber-
padded Plexiglas boxes, all of which bore the papal seal. The
bones were boxed in accordance with the part of the body from
which they derived. The largest box, and the most visible, contained the best-preserved bone—the left tibia. Another, smaller
box contained the mouse skeleton, making it the holiest *Mus
musculus domesticus* in all of Christendom. These bones had
been here since 1968, after a brief ceremony presided over by
Paul VI that restored them to their ancient hiding place.

The history traceable to these flakes of calcium and fragile marrowless tubes was as difficult to quantify as all the places reached by star-emitted light. The restored complex within which they rested was only slightly less unreal. First largely pagan, eventually wholly Christian, built over not once but twice, lost, and rediscovered. It was a near-perfect analogy for Christianity itself: its origins seemingly clear but in fact profoundly opaque, its message apparently obvious but in fact deeply mysterious, its contemporary influence outwardly secure but in fact seriously compromised.

Before any mighty basilica stood in their city, Roman Christians had one thing: their experience within a tradition. They, like all people of all faiths, processed their experience by what attended it, the details that surrounded it, but also from the inferences, the *sensations,* they drew from it. Their religion, like all religions, was an experience-decryption device: belief necessarily precedes any story that it intends to explain. The first Christians did not abandon Judaism because they saw the man they knew as Jesus risen in Jerusalem; every account of the resurrection is secondhand, and everything known about the women and men, such as Peter, who first followed Jesus suggests that their break from Judaism was prolonged, difficult, and often resisted. The first Christians who knew neither Jesus nor Judaism believed because others came to them with stories that intended to explain the confusion of their world and ease the painful placement of all individuals within it. One of the most consistent figures in these stories was, of course, the hardheaded, stubborn, frequently mistaken believer they knew as Peter.

I wondered if Zander might speak for himself and not the Vatican. "What," I asked him, "do you believe?"

He thought about this, looked away, pondered it more, and drew in a short, decisive breath. "Speaking archaeologically, I think these are probably the bones of Saint Peter."

Christianity begins with a missing body. Today one of its oldest and most federal expressions bases its legitimacy on the remains of an existing one. Whether that was progress or a regression, I could not say. Zander and I returned aboveground, and I walked home across the piazza of Saint Peter's Basilica. It had not stopped raining. The witnesses of Bernini looked sightlessly on.

ANDREW

Saint Andrew's Church: Patras, Greece

CORINTHIAN CHRISTIANS · MANLY ANDREW ·
THE PRESS SECRETARY OF THE TWELVE · SAINT
ANDREW'S CHURCH · ANDREW'S TRAVELS · FATHER
SPIRIDON · CHRIST PANTOKRATOR · *THE ACTS OF
ANDREW* · YEHOHANAN BEN HAGKOL · FRIENDS

I.

Many journeys around Greece are beset by twisty, chaotic itineraries involving half a dozen trains, but traveling from Athens to Patras was a straight shot on splendid new rails built for the 2004 Athens Olympics. The ride itself was almost entirely coastal, crossing over a slender isthmus before entering the Peloponnese Peninsula. After passing through yet another hideously enchanting Greek town, I turned to Arman, a young opera scholar from Chicago, and said I could not imagine living in such a beautiful place. It would drive me insane.

"For what it's worth," Arman told me, "Camus said roughly the same thing."

Arman and I had been living in Italy for four months—two of several dozen recipients of a bizarrely extravagant prize given every year by the American Academy in Rome, which puts up writers, artists, and scholars in a mansion and feeds them and otherwise lets them be for an entire year. To our mutual frustration, Arman and I were getting almost nothing done in our hilltop Roman mansion. When I mentioned my trip to Greece, Arman volunteered to join me.

When our train briefly stopped at Corinth, I removed from

my bag my New Revised Standard Version and reread Paul's two letters to the Corinthians. Southern Greece comprised the Roman province of Achaea, and first-century Corinth was its sleepy capital, primarily known for its crafts. It was also the southernmost point of Paul's known mission. The beliefs of its church, and the difficulties it faced, are today the most confidently reconstructed of early Christian communities, thanks to the sheer amount of detail Paul provides in his letters to the believers there.

Paul wrote 1 Corinthians after a months-long stopover, though it was apparently his second letter to the community. He eventually came to Corinth again but was gravely insulted during his visit. He wrote another letter, now lost and referred to as the Letter of Tears, that is conjectured to contain Paul's reaction to his shabby treatment. Paul eventually calmed down and wrote 2 Corinthians, which is thus his fourth letter to the community.[*] What prompted Paul's first—technically second—letter to the Corinthians was a request from his local supporters for guidance on several issues.

There were serious divisions in the Corinthian church, with some Christians claiming allegiance to Paul and some Christians claiming allegiance to others. A few of the Christians claiming allegiance to Paul claimed to have been baptized by him, which Paul, high-mindedly attempting to make peace, says is not possible, given that he baptized "none of you except Crispus and Gaius." The pro-Paul Corinthian faction also informed Paul that there was "sexual immorality" within the community, including one man "living with his father's wife." In the letter, Paul reminds the Corinthians that he has previously asked them to avoid "sexually immoral persons." One Corinthian faction, how-

---

[*] It should be said the actual sequence of events and epistles is highly debatable and not at all apparent from scripture. Also, an epistle known as 3 Corinthians, rejected as pseudonymous by the early church, is accepted as canon by the Armenian Church.

ever, was claiming that sex itself was immoral. Paul argues that this is simply not the case, though he does note that "he who refrains from marriage will do better" than he who seeks marriage. A few Corinthians, it seems, were using the Eucharistic meal as an excuse to get drunk. Paul: "What! Do you not have homes to eat and drink in?" During these Eucharistic meals, rich Corinthians were apparently unable to abide eating alongside their socioeconomic lessers. Yes, at the very origin of the religion itself, we find Christians humiliating other Christians during the Lord's Supper for the high crime of being poor, but this should come as no shock: citizens of the Roman Empire belonged to one of the most economically stratified and class-conscious societies the world has ever known. Even so, Paul's temper reaches its breaking point: "What should I say to you? Should I commend you? In this matter I do not commend you!" Finally, the use of prophetic visions and tongues had apparently gotten so out of hand that one Corinthian, while in a visionary state, cursed Jesus himself, which resulted in Paul's long, carefully worded harangue against the abuse of visions and tongues, which he claims render the mind "unproductive." Perhaps the most amusing portion of the entire Pauline corpus is the ground rules he sets down governing the use of tongues: "If anyone speaks in a tongue, let there be only two or at most three, and each in turn."

In 2 Corinthians, Paul was again forced to address the fact that many Corinthians remained unimpressed by him. Paul quotes one of his opponents—"His letters are weighty and strong, but his bodily presence is weak, and his speech is contemptible"—and reminds his audience that while other, more physically impressive and pedigreed teachers might have spent time with the Corinthians, Paul, unlike these otiant men, "did not burden anyone" with a need for free food and shelter, even though Paul believed he had an evangelist's right to both. These other visitors, moreover, preached a different gospel from

Paul's, which moves Paul to compare them to Satan, who "disguises himself as an angel of light." While Paul admits he "may be untrained in speech," he goes on to note all that he has suffered during his mission, from "imprisonments" to "countless floggings" to having been "shipwrecked." On top of all that, Paul says, "I am under daily pressure because of my anxiety for all the churches." He promises a third visit, during which, he says, he "will not be lenient—since you desire proof that Christ is speaking in me."

These letters are remarkable not only for their wealth of information about the Corinthian community's confusions and struggles but also for how revealing they are of Paul's sugar-and-salt personality. When they are read not as scripture but as the loving, sometimes aggrieved words of a man addressing the accusations and concerns of a specific historical audience, they reverberate with the privileged energies of an intercepted missive—which is, in fact, what both texts are. I could, for a moment, see and hear both the Corinthian Christians and Paul himself. In leaving Corinth for Patras, and in closing my Bible, I was stepping from the floodlights of actual Christian history and through the drowsily velvet curtains of Christian legend. According to tradition, Andrew, the apostle whose obscurity was the least historically explicable, was martyred in Patras.

II.

Arman and I arrived in Patras too late to do much more than drink. We ended our night in a barren, hauntingly joyless club called the Disco Room. When, at 3:00 a.m., we staggered out of the Disco Room and looked down toward the end of Patras's major thoroughfare, Agios Andreou, we saw a glowing X-shaped cross that distinguished the square of Patras's flagship church, also named Agios Andreou. Arman, after carefully contemplating the X-shaped cross, asked if I saw it, too. Arman, who was Jewish, seemed noticeably relieved when I said that I did.

The X-shaped cross is known in heraldic terms as a saltire, though it is more commonly called Saint Andrew's cross. As such, it is found on any number of flags, many from lands that claim a connection to the supposed mission of Andrew. The flag of Scotland is emblazoned with Andrew's cross, as is the Union Jack, as is the flag of the Russian navy. Andrew himself is the patron saint of Romania, Luxembourg, Ukraine, Russia, Scotland, and, of course, Greece, where he is most fervently honored. In Greek, *andreas* means something akin to "masculine," "manly," or "brave." One scholar calls the name "very rare" among Jews, and many have wondered whether Andrew, like his brother Simon Peter, had a Jewish name the gospels do not record.

According to John's gospel, Andrew was the first called member of the Twelve, after which he brought into Jesus's circle Peter, who would become the most famous of all the apostles. According to Mark, Andrew is with Jesus as he begins his public career in Capernaum, after which he enters "the house of Peter and Andrew" and heals Peter's ailing mother-in-law. Later in Mark, when Jesus goes to raise from the dead the daughter of Jairus, "one of the leaders of the synagogue," he specifically forbids everyone to follow him "except Peter, James, and John"— apostles who have all received special nicknames from Jesus and who will later be the only witnesses to the signal demonstrations of his power: the raising of Jairus's daughter, the transfiguration, the teaching on the Mount of Olives (wherein Jesus prophesies the destruction of the Temple), and Jesus's pre-arrest agony at Gethsemane. Despite being Peter's brother, Andrew is denied access to this "inner three" circle of disciples.

Matthew, for his part, mentions Andrew only once outside his list of the Twelve, and Luke mentions Andrew only within his list of the Twelve. Why Andrew all but disappears from the synoptic gospel story as it developed from Mark is one of the New Testament's many narrative mysteries. For unknown reasons, John's gospel contains a relatively large portion of unique Andrew material. The gospel first places him in Bethany, some eighty miles away from Capernaum—a walking journey of several days—where he is an apparent member of the group surrounding John the Baptist. After the Baptist hails a walking-by Jesus as the "Lamb of God," John tells us, two of the Baptist's disciples immediately begin to follow Jesus; one of these young men is Andrew.

After spending a day with Jesus, Andrew seeks out his brother Peter and tells him, "We have found the Messiah," and brings him before Jesus. Following this, Andrew is narratively absent from John until Jesus's feeding of the five thousand, when he is said to point out the nearby "boy who has five barley loaves and two fish," which Jesus proceeds to use as miraculous raw material. The next time Andrew appears in John's gospel is when "some Greeks" (citizens, probably not coincidentally, of Andrew's future spiritual protectorate) approach Philip and proclaim their interest in meeting Jesus. John's dogged narration of what happens next ("Philip went and told Andrew; then Andrew and Philip went and told Jesus") is the last of Andrew's gospel appearances.

One popular Christian writer imagines Peter and Andrew as placidly accepting their assigned roles—one glorious and honored, the other obscure and sidelined—in the gospel tradition. "To be fair to both," he writes, "let us say that Peter became the fisherman of men en masse and Andrew was a fisher for individuals." Yet Andrew's few gospel appearances *do* seem to mark him as a mediating figure. Andrew introduces Peter to Jesus, points out the boy with the loaves and fishes, and handles Jesus's Greek well-wishers on behalf of Philip. To indulge in the dutiful anachronisms of modern popular Christianity, the Andrew of the gospels comes off as the Twelve's press secretary: invisible but for when Jesus needs him to step forth and make his talents known.

III.

Arman and I spent a good portion of our first morning in Patras emetically acquainting ourselves with the various porcelain basins of our hotel room's lavatory. After these horrors subsided, the only thing I could keep down was grapefruit. Eventually, I asked Arman if he wanted to join me for a walk down Agios Andreou to Saint Andrew's Church. His answer was a complicatedly silent stare. I set off alone.

Agios Andreou was a street of abrupt and decisive phases. Near the port of Patras's landing area, for instance, there was an overabundance of banks. These gave way to the bars and cafés Arman and I had crawled the night before. This gave way to furniture stores and gas stations and solar-panel depots and other motley concerns. A gigantic cruise ship—a nine-story neighborhood set afloat—was leaving port and, as I walked, almost kept pace with me; it seemed, comically, as though this ship were following me. In the bright sunlight, the ship's shiny metal was as hard to look at as a huge white sun. (At night, these ships looked like astonishingly massive light sculptures floating through the interstellar silence of space.) Once the ship pulled ahead, I had a clear view of the Bay of Patras, home to many large pointy islets and islands that, from a distance, resembled Matterhorns of forested rock.

Much of Patras was closed because of a recently concluded festival that involved three days of celebration and a week of recovery; an air of postcoital exhaustion hovered low over everything. One old man stopped to ask me what I thought of Greece. When I told him that I already liked it much better than Italy, he laughed, shook my hand, and then began talking about his daughter. There was "not so much good jobs," in Greece, he told me, especially for "the young Greek woman." (It would get worse.) He asked, "In America has good jobs for the young Greek woman?"

Saint Andrew's square was big and empty enough to presently host two games of pickup soccer. The church complex comprised three buildings: the old Saint Andrew's Church, a low yellow-white building with a red-tile roof and few windows; a small, slender four-story structure next to the old Saint Andrew's, which faced the ocean and appeared to have once been some kind of sea-monitoring lookout tower; and the new Saint Andrew's, a large, forcefully symmetrical anthology of domes, towers, and right angles. If one only glanced at its large central blue dome and the eleven smaller blue domes that surrounded it and the busily designed latticework that distinguished its eight full towers, one could not be blamed for mistaking Saint Andrew's Church for a mosque.*

I approached the church's ocean-facing entrance, which was typically used by parishioners, and passed through the shade of a few sharp-leafed palms planted along the square's perimeter. Only one tree marked the square proper, in the shade of which a Romany woman sat and begged.

In the early twentieth century, according to the official church guidebook, Patras announced "an international competition for the elaboration of the architectural design" for a new church. The new Saint Andrew's Church, as it stands, adhered to the cross-in-square design commonly employed by the architects of Byzantine churches and still often used today. The architect of Saint Andrew's Church, however, was a Frenchman. The church guidebook admits that the Frenchman's original design led to "a violent criticism," seeing that this "imaginative and indeed

---

* The architectural use of domes enters Islam *through* Christianity, funnily enough. After Muslims conquered Constantinople in 1453 and Islamized Hagia Sophia, the city's largest and most grandly domed church, Muslim devotional architecture moved away from courtyard-based structures and toward domed ones.

imposing design" did not meet "the requirements of the Orthodox Byzantine style. Besides, it was obvious that the French
architect . . . was influenced by the Western architectural style."
Today, however, the people of Patras are justifiably proud of
Saint Andrew's Church. Able to accommodate seven thousand
worshippers, it is the largest church in Greece.

The sign that greeted me as I entered read, THANK YOU
FOR ENTERING THE CHURCH PROPERLY DRESSED. Greek Orthodox
beliefs were often extremely conservative; I hoped no strictures
had been placed on denim and T-shirts. In the church's shallow
narthex, a perturbed man wearing a mustard-colored sweater,
green slacks, and a belt as high as his rib cage approached me,
his hand demandingly extended. "Money," he said.

As I reached into my pocket for the entrance fee, I looked
down at the floor mosaic, noting among the otherwise impecca-
bly Christian symbols and designs two highly unusual animals.
The first was a rabbit, historically avoided in most churches
because of the Latinate similarity of *cuniculus* (rabbit) and *cun-
nus* (cunt). The rabbit, in Christian allegory, became a symbol
of sexual prolixity, which is evident today in our phrase "breed-
ing like rabbits." The second unusual animal was an octopus, for
which many months of scouring dictionaries and encyclopedias
of Christian art would fail to exhume a single exegetical mention.

IV.

The official guide to Saint Andrew's Church claims that its
namesake's missionary travels were a "herculean undertaking,
even by modern standards." According to the church guide,
Andrew began in Bithynia (in modern-day Turkey) and then
moved on to the cities Sinope, Amisus, and Trapezus. From
here, he journeyed less comfortably to Scythia and into the
Caucasus regions, before ending up in Ukraine, where he
supposedly planted a cross at the site of a Kiev church today
devoted to him. After this, he backtracked to Byzantium, where

he founded its first Christian see, allowing Constantinople its later status as the patriarchate of the Eastern Orthodox faith.[*] His next stops were Thrace, Macedonia, and Thessaly, before, finally, he returned to Greece. "The coming of Andrew to our city," the official Patras guide says, "is evidenced by absolutely authentic old Christian sources."

Yet many early Andrew traditions place him exclusively in Scythia. According to Eusebius, writing in the fourth century and working off information he received from Origen (the first of the church fathers to mention Andrew), "Thomas . . . was chosen for Parthia, Andrew for Scythia, John for Asia, where he remained till his death at Ephesus." Scythia might have served as a kind of ultima Thule of anti-Christian hostility and as absolute rhetorical proof of the apostles' devotion. At the height of its influence several hundred years before the birth of Jesus, Scythia encompassed part of Kazakhstan, Turkmenistan, Iran, Russia, and even Poland. By the first and second centuries CE, however, Scythian-controlled territory had shrunk to a fraction of its former size; the Scythians themselves had become a subject people severed from their marauder-nomad origins. The writers of apocryphal Christian literature involving Andrew, which Origen and Eusebius were clearly familiar with, persisted in portraying the Scythians as the same beastly tribe that had once terrified Herodotus.[†]

The traditions of Andrew's having founded the mother churches of the Russian Orthodox and Byzantine faith developed too late, and out of a too-obvious need for fast-tracked authority, to be taken seriously. According to *Butler's Lives of the Saints,* the tradition of Andrew's founding the Byzantine patriarchate (which does not appear before the fourth century) was

---

[*] This almost certainly legendary tradition allowed the Eastern Church to claim for itself an apostolicity intended to rival that of Rome.

[†] The Scythians are mentioned once in the New Testament, in Paul's letter to the Colossians, in which they are used as a metaphorical yardstick for ethnic wildness.

deeply "connected with the prestige attached to his claimed relics," which the Christians of Constantinople believed they held. Andrew's connection to Kiev (which does not appear before the ninth century) is likely due to its church's desire to imagine for itself venerable Byzantine heritage. Andrew's obscure prominence (or prominent obscurity) as the little-discussed brother of the most famous apostle made him the perfect founder for a certain kind of early Christian community, particularly those, like Kiev's, that were less affected by the theological debates and leadership crises that marked the development of Western Christianity.

In time, however, a small, struggling group of westerly Christians in the British Isles staked its claim to Andrew. There were Christians in Britain as early as the fourth century, but Andrew was not imagined as having evangelized that land until many centuries later. An early fourteenth-century declaration of the Scottish faith cited Andrew, "the first to be an apostle," as its church's founder and spiritual father. Roman Catholicism, of course, claimed Peter. As tensions between the Scottish and the Roman Catholic churches grew (they would break relations entirely in 1560), Andrew, as Peter's brother, expanded in mythic prominence among his Scottish claimants.

When the official guide to Saint Andrew's Church speaks of Andrew's death in Patras as having been confirmed by "absolutely authentic old Christian sources," it is speaking primarily of *The Acts of Andrew,* an apocryphal work many early Christians resisted due to its unsavory championing in heterodox circles. Despite that, Saint Andrew's Church was decorated with numerous scenes drawn from this strange work. As I looked about the narthex, I noticed a man clad in black from ankle to Adam's apple—unbuttoned black sport coat over a black undershirt, bell-bottomishly roomy black pantaloons—emerge from a side room and wander behind the desk of the ticket-taking area. He was either a Greek Orthodox priest or the Prince of Darkness's personal assistant. He began to obsessively straighten the book

and pamphlet shelves behind the ticket-taking partition. Here
was a man who had made the church's tiniest matters of upkeep
a personal concern. "Father," I said, moving toward him. "Excuse
me?"

The priest turned to me. He was a young man with a beard
that made him seem decades older. I had seen other Greek Orthodox priests, and they, too, had sported large beards, but his was
a transcendent achievement in hirsutism. The longer I looked at
his beard, the less beard-like it seemed. Thick and frizzy, it was
more apron than beard.

I asked the father if he was available to provide a tour of the
church.

My request seemed to surprise him. "Where are you from?"
he asked.

As I told him, he raised his hand and admitted with a quick
laugh that he did not understand English well. I slowly explained
that I was a writer from the United States interested in Andrew.
The father leaned forward and tilted his ear toward me while
keeping his eyes fixed on the marble floor. His face was distinguished by a concerning number of dark brown moles; a milky,
ripe pimple graced the center of his forehead.

"Andreas," he said, once I had finished talking. "Yes. Andreas
here. Come. Church first, then Andreas."

Father Spiridon began our tour by asking me if I thought
his church was beautiful. I told him that it was among the most
beautiful churches I had seen. We stopped beneath the wooden
chandelier hung from the impressively high dome on equally
impressively long chains. With only a dozen feet between it and
the church floor, this chandelier resembled a piece of lowered
theatrical scenery. The decorative focus was a two-headed eagle
that sat perched atop the chandelier. (Patriarchs of the Eastern
Church often wore similar two-headed eagles in necklace form.)
This eagle, Father Spiridon told me, represented two things:
"People and God. One. One people, one God, one Jesus."

That sounded like three things, I decided not to say. Instead, I waved my hand across the church's many freestanding chairs, all of which lacked kneelers. I knew that in many Eastern Orthodox churches men and women are separated during the service. I asked Father Spiridon if that was the case here. He shrugged and made an equivocating hand gesture. "No," he said, "because now the church a little . . . free. More free than before."

"You support that change?"

He shook his head, not understanding my question.

"Yes to change?" I asked, my thumb up.

He nodded. "Change good," he said, putting up his own thumb. "Yes." As for the freestanding chairs, Father Spiridon explained it this way: "No chair in Orthodox Church in Russia, Ukraine, Serbia. But in Greece chair." With that potential sticking point past us, he directed my attention to the church's dome. "Look now."

Gazing omnipotently down at us from the dome was the Byzantine Jesus. His great brown bun of hair was parted smartly down the middle. He wore majestic white robes, held a book, and was encircled by rings of angels and saints. Far beneath him, along the dome's edge, was a smaller figure of Andrew on an X-shaped cross. What stayed with you, when looking up at the Byzantine Jesus, was the face. The expression of the typical Byzantine Jesus ranged from blank to disappointed to blankly disappointed. It was, almost always, a face devoid of love or concern.

"Pantokrator," Father Spiridon said.

According to the precepts of Eastern Orthodox church design, the dome must always be occupied by an image of the so-called Christ Pantokrator, and Christ Pantokrator must always be represented in a certain way: on his heavenly throne, surrounded by carefully arranged angels, iconographically unchallenged by the local figure (in this case, Andrew) to whom the church was devoted, holding the Law, and exuding the general air of being, in the words of one writer, "more emperor than friend." An apt

if inexact Greek-to-English translation of *Pantokrator:* Christ the
Everything Ruler. Christ the Everything Ruler was certainly not
the Jesus of the gospels. He was, instead, a calculatedly imperial
warrior Jesus as imagined by the heirs of Constantine.

Father Spiridon directed my attention to the semi-
hemispherical dome of the apse above the church sanctuary.
"Maria," he said. Just as the Pantokrator had to be in the dome,
the apse of most Eastern Orthodox churches had to be occupied
by Mary, and, below her, the Twelve. In many traditions, Mary's
head had to be covered by the maphorion, a veil native to Greek
rather than first-century Palestinian culture. This church's apsidal Mary was depicted as stretching her arms protectively over
a modern Patras and its coastal waters, on the cursive waves of
which bobbed (rather incongruously) a tiny white cruise ship.
Thanks to an ovular cutaway, the fetal Jesus—probably the most
upsetting Jesus I had ever laid eyes on—could be seen within
Mary's egg-shaped womb. Fetuses do not typically have hair; this
fetal Jesus not only had hair but a widow's peak. Most fetuses do
not wear clothes; this fetal Jesus wore several layers of robes.
This was another convention of Eastern representation. While
the art of Western Christianity evolved to allow for fully and
fragilely human representations of the infant Jesus, the art of
Eastern Christianity did not. Its infant and fetal Jesus was almost
always depicted as a miniaturized and rather freakish mini-man.
The one exception to this was the so-called Glykophilousa Virgin, in which Mary holds the baby Jesus to her cheek, which
became allowable in the East only due to the image's heartstring-
pulling popularity.

"Theotokos," Father Spiridon said, pointing at Mary. "English
word same as Greek? Many word Greek, English—many word
same." He pointed at a nearby chair. "Thronos. Throne. Same
word. Understand?"

As with Pantokrator, Theotokos was less a word than a theological festoon. Literally, it means "God bearer" and emerged

from the fourth-century debates over Mary's role in carrying Jesus to term. At issue was the nature of his divinity. A group of Christians popularly known as Nestorians—their name coming from Nestorius, the powerful patriarch of Constantinople—held that Mary was merely the *Christotokos,* or "Christ bearer." This meant a Jesus whose divinity did not predate his conception. Of course, the position of what ultimately became Christian orthodoxy held that Jesus was preexistently divine—that his birth gave him form but did not create him. In 431, at the Council of Ephesus, Theotokos became Mary's official title, which led to the so-called Nestorian schism and relocation of many of Nestorianism's adherents to Persia, India, and beyond.

Spiridon pressed me: "Theotokos. Maria. Baby. Understand?"

"I understand," I said. "Yes."

Father Spiridon pointed at the pendentive arches that supported the church's dome, which were decorated with scenes from the life of Jesus, as was almost always the case in Byzantine-style churches. These pendentives were used to illustrate key motifs of Eastern Orthodox iconography: *Genesis* (or Nativity), the *Metamorphosis* (or Transfiguration), the *Stavrosis* (or Crucifixion), and the *Anastasis* (or Resurrection). Father Spiridon showed me the mosaics on the olive-green-tinged columns beneath the pendentive arches. All held images of the gospel writers. "Lukas," he said, pointing. "Mattheus. Ioannes. Markus." He approached the nearest pillar—that of John—put his hands around the pillar's edges, and attempted to shake it. The pillar, obviously, did not budge. "They," he said, lightly touching the polished tesserae arranged to represent John. "This," he said, grasping the pillar again. "Understand?"

"The evangelists support the church."

He bowed with obvious tutorial pride. "Yes. Very good."

Father Spiridon's delight at my understanding him in turn delighted me. I then realized we were almost twenty minutes into our tour and had moved less than eight feet.

V.

In the largest and, consequently, least accurate sense, "Eastern Church," "Eastern Christianity," and "Eastern Orthodoxy" refer to several theologically distinct forms of Christianity that share cultural roots with the Byzantine Church as created by Constantine when he moved the Roman Empire's capital from Rome to the city state of Byzantium—supposedly founded by Andrew—in 330, seventeen years after the Edict of Milan allowed Christianity equal standing with the empire's other religions. Modern Eastern Orthodox churches include the Greek Orthodox Church, the Russian Orthodox Church, the Albanian Orthodox Church, and the Macedonian Orthodox Church.*

"Eastern Orthodoxy" is mostly useful as a negative description: Christianity as it developed outside western Europe. The final, definitive split between Eastern and Western Christianity did not take place until the eleventh century—the traditional date of 1054 may be too precise for such a long, protracted, and immensely complicated process—but speaking in the neat terms of a "split" between East and West does not do justice to the variations and differing theological emphases within Eastern Orthodoxy itself.

Eastern Orthodoxy is more mystical than Western Christianity, but also more rigid. Its churches are arguably more beautiful, but its decorative art is far more torpid. Its conception of Jesus is more distant, but its theology is more attractively complicated. It is additionally more mindful of its traditions, for which there are historical reasons. Four of the five ancient patriarch-

---

* Eastern Orthodoxy should not be confused with Oriental Orthodoxy, whose ancient, still-existing churches include those of Ethiopia, Eritrea, Syria, and Armenia. These churches broke off from the Byzantine Church in the fifth century, unable to abide the doctrinal fine tunings of the Council of Chalcedon in 451. Despite their shared rejection of Chalcedon, these churches are today independent and have their own hierarchies and theological peculiarities.

ates of Eastern Orthodoxy—Jerusalem, Antioch, Alexandria, and Constantinople—were all, at various times, seedbeds of Christian heterodoxy.

The surviving forms of Eastern Orthodoxy are all that remains of a roundly defeated faith. In 1453, when sixty thousand troops answering to a twenty-one-year-old sultan named Mehmet II surrounded Constantinople, the city's Christians prayed against hope that their eight thousand soldiers would be able to hold off the invaders, among whom were several thousand Christian mercenaries. Their prayers were not answered. The emperor Constantine XI Palaeologus, the guardian of Byzantine Christianity, died (supposedly) on the ramparts of Constantinople, slashing away at its Ottoman invaders. The eleven-hundred-year-old church founded by Constantine formally terminates with this last Byzantine emperor's straw-stuffed head (again, supposedly) going on a victory tour of the cities of the Muslim world. All Eastern Christian missionary activity ended. A great faith became a captive faith. Many of Eastern Orthodoxy's founding sees are today located in non-Christian lands. An exception to this is the Russian Orthodox Church, which is particularly assiduous in tracing its roots back to Byzantium and which rose to great heights indeed,* especially when, after 1453, Moscow became the principal seat of Eastern Orthodoxy not controlled by Muslims.

Working out God's calculus with regard to his Eastern subjects was a particularly difficult task for the Greek Orthodox Church, which conducts its services in the very language in which its scriptures are written. An interesting emotional dissimilarity between Western and Eastern Christianity can be seen in how both view the book of Revelation. In the Western tradi-

---

* According to a legend that might actually be true, Russia drifted into the orbit of Eastern Orthodoxy because Yaroslav of Kiev, an eleventh-century Russian prince hunting for a state religion who greatly disliked the German devotional architecture he had seen, was told that Constantinople's churches were beautiful.

tion, it is avidly scoured; in the apocalypse-clobbered Eastern tradition, Revelation was old news.

Devotional Byzantine art began to cohere into a self-conscious style around the fifth century. Compared with the devotional art of Western Christianity, Byzantine art is less "realistic" (allowing for the fact that "realism," strictly speaking, did not exist until hundreds of years after the Byzantine style codified), and its repertoire of motifs is more limited, owing to a generally more oppressive orthodoxy. As we walked on, I realized that for all of Eastern Orthodoxy's deco-doctrinal rigidity and the practiced emptiness at the core of Byzantine art, none of that really mattered. I had not lied to Father Spiridon: This *was* one of the most beautiful churches I had ever seen. The entwined and purposefully abstract patterns, floral imagery, and peacock pennae used as edging all over the church were inventive, subtle, and arresting—one of the more benign examples of Islam's influence on Byzantine Christianity. The atmosphere of the church, embodied by a man willing to drop everything to take a curious stranger on an impromptu tour, was also more welcoming than any I had visited. And from time to time, a breeze from the sea blew in through the open front doors, causing me to turn, and there, gloriously, was the Mediterranean, blaringly blue and roiling with distant whitecaps. To look out from the middle of a church and see the ocean was pleasurable in a way I had no name for.

Father Spiridon squired me around with no discernible method. After patiently describing some aspect of an object in one corner of the church, he walked me to the directly opposite church corner. Eventually, we wound up in the apse area, from which Father Spiridon shooed an injured pigeon—an awkwardly hopping rotundity—from our path.

Behind the apse area was what is called the sanctuary. It was blocked off from the rest of the church by a white marble wall known as an iconostasis (which means "stand for images"). The iconostasis began as columns that divided the sanctuary area from the rest of the church; this can still be seen in Western churches, but in the Eastern tradition it evolved into a large opaque screen or outright wall whose door-shaped enclosures usually contained a number of tiered icons, the displayed order and subject matter of which was predictably subject to tight doctrinal control. One attained access to the sanctuary via one of the iconostasis's three doors. Only one door, the Beautiful Gate, was frontal, and from it the church patriarch emerged during the liturgy.

The crenellated iconostasis of Saint Andrew's Church was quite grand. I followed Father Spiridon around to one of its two remaining gold-painted side doors, which were used when the liturgy was not under way. He opened the door and walked into the sanctuary. Inside the small room was an altar and, on it, several burning candles that filled the space with a low, wavy auburn light. Father Spiridon was in the process of kissing the altar when I walked in. I did not get a chance to see much else. When Father Spiridon noticed me entering, he crossed himself and rushed toward me and pushed me out the door. "Only Orthodox! Only Orthodox man here! Only Orthodox man!" While I apologized, the cleaning lady of Saint Andrew's Church approached. She spoke for a moment in a language best described as Greeklish, pointed at a nearby icon of the baby Jesus and at Father Spiridon. "Jesus good," she said, "Father Spiridon good. Both good." Father Spiridon laughed, thanked her, clapped his hands together, and announced, "Now icons."

Most icons are small paintings, often in panel form, of Jesus, Mary, John the Baptist, an apostle, saint, or, sometimes, in particularly large icons, a combination of some or all of the above. Icons are extremely ancient. Eusebius, in the fourth century, mentioned seeing icons of Peter and Paul and, in Edessa, an icon of Jesus that Eusebius believed had been painted from a living likeness. The Greek love of icons gave rise to a period known as Iconoclasm (the word literally means "image breaking"), which lasted from 726 to 843. Iconoclasm was an imperial response to repeated collisions between the conquistadors of Islam and Byzantine Christianity, whose forces saw their first defeat by a Muslim Arab army as early as 636. In 721, Islam formally forbade representative art—technically, anything "with breath"—in religious settings. Iconoclasm might thus have been intended to shore up citizens of the Byzantine Empire against what its leaders feared as the Muslims' fiercer, more refined faith. Other scholars have argued that Iconoclasm had nothing to do with Islamic iconophobia. They point out that various strains of iconoclastic belief existed within Christianity since the fourth century. The fanatical fourth-century Christian bishop Epiphanius, for instance, once tore to pieces a portrait of Jesus in a church in Bethel. Jews have often been iconophobic themselves,* which suggests a revulsion to representative art that may be a by-product of Middle Eastern culture generally. But Iconoclasm, in any event, was a miserable failure, due to both the irregularity with which it was enforced and the emotional currents against which it ran. All Iconoclasm really did was drive representative devotional art underground, especially within monastic communities, which became clandestine icon factories. After Iconoclasm, Eastern Orthodoxy reasserted its artistic controls with flourish-crushing severity.

While iconic subject matter was open to choice, the icon's formal presentation was not. The rules binding the aspiring iconist were (and remain) bewilderingly myriad: The subject must be displayed frontally. The subject's name must be displayed via inscription. Subjects must wear certain types of cloth-

---

* The prohibition against worshipping "graven images" is the second of the Ten Commandments, after all, which Eastern Christians have stepped around by arguing that icons are not graven, which is to say, not sculpted. Western Christians, incredibly, led by the argument of Augustine, stepped around the forbidding of graven images by renumbering the Ten Commandments. This involved, in one scholar's words, "tucking the graven image prohibition inside Commandment One, rather than making it a free-standing Commandment Two."

ing, and these must be colored in certain ways. Any subject of divine stature must be larger than a subject of non-divine stature. The subject's hands must be displayed in certain ways (one hand position often found in Eastern Orthodox art comes from a pagan tradition that has to do with the physical expression of the philosopher's right to teach).

Saint Andrew's Church, like most Eastern Orthodox churches, contained numerous icons. They were displayed everywhere, from the walls to the bays to the sanctuary to the portable examples near the entrance to the iconostasis itself. Interestingly, Eastern Orthodox churches are given some decorative latitude when it comes to icons. Individual churches are allowed to choose which saints to display in icon form, though this typically boils down to preferences that have more to do with region, history, and culture than with strict matters of faith.

One of the most interesting beliefs attendant to icons—one eventually codified by Eastern Orthodoxy itself—holds that iconic images *themselves* were divine transmitters. The potential for pandemic religious derangement here is clear and obvious and allows one to understand why Iconoclasm occurred. The Greek devotion to icons remained nonpareil—though beleaguered Russian Christians have certainly done their best to challenge it—and the Greek Orthodox Church still annually celebrates the ninth-century day on which the empress Theodora restored the veneration of icons as the Triumph of Orthodoxy, during which what purports to be a copy of the document that reversed Iconoclastic policy is read out loud.

Father Spiridon began our icon tour along the church's eastern wall—one saintly figure on a molten gold background after another. "Here Spiridon," Father Spiridon said, pausing at one icon.

"Your namesake?" I asked.

"My name," he said. "Spiridon. Corfu. Four hundred years old."

"Spiridon was martyred four hundred years ago on Corfu?"

He shook his head. In a few moments, we had worked it out (I think): the icon was four hundred years old and had been painted on Corfu, where Spiridon's relics were still kept.

"Here Zecharias," he said, a moment later, and waved a finger over the palm leaf Zecharias held. "Martyr. Understand?"

"The martyr holds the palm leaf. Yes. I understand."

"Eight martyrs of Patras," he said. "He one of eight."

"Got it."

"Here Gregorius. *Episcopo*. Understand?"

"*Episcopo?* Bishop?"

"Yes! Bishop. Martyr. Nyssa."

"He was martyred in Nicaea?"

He took hold of my wrist, gently but firmly. "No. Nyssa. He *theologios*."

"Oh. Gregory of Nyssa!"

"Yes!"

The Gregory icon was one of four handsome icons devoted to the Doctors (in the theological sense) of the Greek Church: Gregory, Basil, John Chrysostom, and Athanasius. All wore the omophorion, a wide, cross-embroidered stole. Now Father Spiridon pointed at an icon of a very young man in a nightgown-like garment, holding a book and an oil lamp. Father Spiridon said, "Protomartyr," and looked at me, as though daring me to guess his identity.

"Stephen?" I said. "The first martyr?"

"Yes! Stefanus. First died. First martyr."

Father Spiridon's cell phone sounded, the ring tone set to the tune of *The Nutcracker*. As he turned away to answer, I thought of how odd it was that a man who clearly knew the history of his church exceedingly well, and spoke Greek and Latin, was forced by my ignorance of Greek (and Latin) to have a conversation that resembled the colloquy of two toddlers precociously fascinated by religious history. How might some of the earliest Christian missionaries have explained Jesus to, say, the Scythians? "Big

man. Jesus. He come from sky. He die for all good. He dead, but
no. He alive again. Save you. Save me."

   More icons followed, several of which I correctly identified,
after which Father Spiridon grabbed my wrist and smiled. "You,"
he said, "theologian!" Wanting to keep pleasing him, I began
responding to icons by throwing out a saintly name and waiting
for Father Spiridon's affirmative wrist touch. When I was wrong,
and I was often wrong, I compounded the error by quickly recit-
ing every name from Christian history I could recall in the hopes
of eventually getting it right. This method proved most spectacularly ineffective when we came to a section of icons devoted to
saints local to the traditions of Greek Orthodoxy, an inordinate
number of whom seemed to have been banished to islands. My
icon batting average crept back above .350 when we came to one
of Jerome that showed him wearing a hood and holding a small
scroll. Next to Jerome were two icons of armored sword-wielding
angels with *Mona Lisa*–ishly ungendered faces. "Who?" Father
Spiridon asked me of these.

   "Jerome, Gabriel, and Michael," I said, ashamed these were
so easy.

   "Yes!" Father Spiridon took my wrist again, but with some
softer, more intimate urgency. Apparently, he wanted to share
something with me. "My mother," he said. "America. Fairfax, Virginia. Six months old. Lived in Fairfax, Virginia. Hospital. My
mother. Small problem."

   Six months old? His mother was six months old and living
in Fairfax, Virginia?

   "No."

   Father Spiridon was born in Fairfax, Virginia, but there was
a problem, and his mother returned to Greece with him when he
was six months old?

   "No." After a few more volleys, it was established that Father
Spiridon's mother had needed heart surgery in Fairfax, Virginia,
and was hospitalized there for six months. Much of that time
Father Spiridon was with her, which is how he learned English.

VI.

The Acts of Andrew is one of five "major" apocryphal acts. The others are *The Acts of Paul, The Acts of Peter, The Acts of John,* and *The Acts of Thomas,* none of which was available in a single collated edition until, amazingly, 1898. According to a now-abandoned tradition, their supposed author, Leucius, a fierce advocate of chastity and asceticism and an opponent of marriage, had been a traveling companion of the apostle John. Their genuineness was contested harshly by the church fathers. Eusebius: "To none of these has any churchman of any genera-tion ever seen fit to refer in his writings. Again, nothing could be farther from apostolic usage than the type of phraseology employed, while the ideas and implications of their contents are so irreconcilable with true orthodoxy.... [T]hey must be thrown out as impious and beyond the pale."

All five *Acts* were, in some manner, canonized by the Manichaeans, a faith instituted by one Mani (216–276 CE), the Babylon-born son of Jewish Christian or Ebionite parents who frequently referred to himself as an "Apostle of Jesus Christ." It is believed the Manichaeans used the noncanonical acts in lieu of the canonical Acts of the Apostles. This is significant because few Near Eastern religions proved more infuriating to the Chris-tians of the third and fourth and fifth and sixth *and* seventh centuries than Manichaeism, a theological stitch-up of various Christian, Jewish, Buddhist, and Zoroastrian tropes. Eusebius judged the faith a "demon-inspired heresy" and "deadly poison" that was "brought from Persia" and "infected our own world." The *Acts'* damning association with Manichaeism provides one explanation for Eusebius's ferocious condemnation.

The stories these works contained were nevertheless impor-tant to many church fathers, because they were virtually the only information they had as to what the apostles were up to after Jesus's ascension. Most scholars believe the original versions of the apocryphal *Acts* were written in the second and third centu-

ries, with later additions to the texts cropping up in the intervening centuries.

No complete *Acts of Andrew* exists. The sixth-century bishop
Gregory of Tours found an apparently complete Latin translation of it, which he deemed "excessive" in its prolixity. "And of
this," he wrote, "I thought good to extract and set out the 'virtues' only, omitting all that bred weariness." What he expunged
included several of its miracle stories, which Gregory deemed
too fantastical,* along with passages that praised celibacy and
denounced military service, which necessitated sacrifices to
pagan gods. In *The Acts of Andrew,* the hero's death requires
many pages to transpire; Gregory deals with Andrew's passing
in three fleet paragraphs. This gloss of what Gregory called "a
book of miracles of the holy apostle Andrew" is today the guide
scholars use to reassemble various other extant fragments of the
work, which survive in Greek, Latin, Coptic, and Armenian.

An important part of *The Acts of Andrew,* that of its hero's
martyrdom, has no fewer than eight distinct versions, the most
important of which is Armenian. It floated around the ancient
Christian world independent of the *Acts* of which it was once
part, though some scholars have argued that Andrew's *Acts* and
martyrdom were joined later in the development of the Andrew
tradition. Another work that has a clear but uncertain relation
to *The Acts of Andrew* is *The Acts of Andrew and Matthias in
the City of the Cannibals.* Dennis Ronald MacDonald, who has
closely studied the texts, believes they were once the same work.
This, he argues, explains much of the confusion surrounding
the church fathers' apparent confusion as to where Andrew was
active as a missionary.

The unknown author of *The Acts of Andrew* was apparently
influenced by the earlier *Acts of Peter,* which survives in a single
fragment. Both open with one apostle (in *Peter,* Paul; in *Andrew,*

---

* Anyone who has read the miracles that Gregory himself reported at immense
length in his other writings will find this reticence duly astounding.

the Judas-replacing apostle Matthias) before suddenly refocusing on the apostle for whom the texts are named. In *Peter,* its namesake receives the shipboard aid of one captain Theon; in *Andrew,* its namesake receives the shipboard aid of a bona fide captain Theon, which is to say Jesus himself in disguise. In *The Acts of Peter,* Peter converts many of his jailers to Christianity; in *The Acts of Andrew,* Andrew does the same. Both Peter and Andrew, finally, request in their respective *Acts* to be crucified in a manner different from that of Jesus.

VII.

It was time to see the chapel area that contained the supposed relics of Andrew, perhaps the most traveled relics of any of the Twelve. One tradition, recorded by Jerome, has the relics being removed from Patras and taken to Constantinople's Church of the Holy Apostles, which was consecrated in 356, as a way to compete with the Roman church and its collection of Peter relics. Some of Andrew's relics were, in turn, removed from Constantinople in the fifth century by the legendary saint Regulus, a former resident of Patras and the first bishop of the Scottish church. Regulus was told by an angel to carry Andrew's remains to "the ends of the earth." After being shipwrecked off the coast of Scotland, he buried his share of Andrew relics at what is now St. Andrew's, thereby altering the fate of golf forever. Supposedly, in the early thirteenth century, Andrew's relics were removed from Constantinople, possibly by Catholic crusaders, and sent to Amalfi, Italy. In 1461, a Byzantine tyrant sent Andrew's skull to Pope Pius II in Rome, and a painting of Pius receiving the skull can still be found in the chapel beside Peter's tomb in the Vatican. The skull would eventually take an honored spot atop one of the four gargantuan pillar reliquaries placed around the high altar of Saint Peter's. Another Roman church, Sant' Andrea al Quirinale, designed by Bernini and containing Guillaume Courtois's seventeenth-century painting of Andrew's martyrdom—perhaps the most beautiful painting of its kind—once claimed to have had a few of Andrew's relics, though my visit there turned up nothing. In 1964, Pope Paul VI returned the Vatican's collection of Andrew relics (a finger, a cranial fragment, and small bits of the cross to which Andrew was supposedly tied) to the patriarch of Constantinople, who restored them to their rightful place of adoration in Patras. Paul's gesture was intended to repair relations between Roman Catholicism and the Eastern Orthodox Church, and it probably came as startling news to the Christians of Amalfi, as its duomo—which, like Amalfi itself, is dedicated to Andrew—holds in its crypt its own purported Andrew skull.

Although Father Spiridon had not yet been born when Andrew's relics were returned to Patras, I asked him if people here still talked about it. "Many priest still talk about that day," he said—one of his infrequent bursts of nearly perfect conversational English. The local guidebook to Patras puts it this way: "The relics were restored again to our city during an official celebration which occurred in the presence of 31 archbishops and a high-rank mission from the Vatican . . . 502 years following the delivery of the Saint's skull to Pope Pius I." Moreover, the guidebook claimed, the relics of Andrew served as a force that "shields, protects and preserves our city as well as the Greek Nation against all perils and situations." The Greeks' adoration of relics was, among the nations of western Europe, the watermark of a certain kind of religious credulity. They were much more credulous about their relics than, say, German and French Christians and slightly less credulous than, say, Italian and Spanish Christians. I wondered, unkindly, if this did not go some distance in accounting for the relative modernity of these nations.

The guidebook also referred to some unspecified "damage" done to the original reliquary—which was made of gold, shaped like a human face, and several hundred years old—in which Andrew's remains had arrived from Rome. One of Patras's less stable citizens was not able to tolerate the head-shaped reliquary and, shortly after its arrival, seized the object, removed its contents, and dashed it against the floor. In this action, the deranged man had his reasons: Greek Orthodox doctrine has on the books an ancient forbiddance of three-dimensional representations of the human face. Thus did Patras, in living memory, experience a one-man revival of Iconoclasm. When I asked Father Spiridon about the smashed reliquary, his mouth and eyes and nostrils all identically widened and, just as quickly, contracted. Suddenly he looked very tired. I dropped it.

There was a lengthy queue of people waiting their turn to seek Andrew's blessing. Father Spiridon and I walked around them by traversing the reliquary's parclose. As we looked upon the pride of his church, Father Spiridon offered no tour guidery. The reliquary was enclosed by low white marble walls, with two narrow gaps to allow in visitors, and surrounded by silver candelabras. Above the reliquary, held up by several thick green columns, was the Canopy of Martyrdom, its bottom decorative edge so precisely carved and delicately perforated that it resembled the work of some nanomachine sculptor.

At the center of the reliquary itself was a keg-shaped stand, on it a glass case of bank-teller-window density. Behind the glass was a silver canister shaped not like a human face but like Saint Andrew's Church itself. This replacement vessel was engraved with traditional scenes of Andrew's life. For several minutes, Father Spiridon and I watched Andrew's visitors approach the relics. Many of them scribbled out a message on a slip of church-provided paper, folded it, and stuffed it into a slot beneath the case. One old man in a suit and tie wrote a long message and left immediately, while an old peasant woman wearing multiple shawls wrote no message but kissed the glass. A man who had what appeared to be leprosy—his hair falling out in clumps, his nose peeled, a good portion of his cheek reduced to open red sore—prayed before the relics for the longest time, not surprisingly. A pair of teenage girls earnestly wrote out their prayers and hurried away.

When the line thinned, Father Spiridon kissed the glass, crossed himself, and gestured for me to join him. We stood there looking at the silver canister for at least half a minute. The only thought that occurred to me was why "gentle Andrew," as Patras's guidebook calls him, had served throughout Christian history as one of the most martial apostles. Crusades-era chronicles include frequent mentions of him, sometimes turning up as an apparition to lead lost crusaders to safety, sometimes materializing in the middle of battle to enthusiastically massacre Muslims. Scottish Christianity, too, is filled with warlike Andrew omens. One legend claims that on the eve of a decisive eighth-century battle against the English a Scottish king named Hungus was visited in a dream by Andrew, who promised him victory. During the battle itself, an X-shaped cross appeared in the sky.

When I told Father Spiridon I was finished, he guided me around the Canopy of Martyrdom to a large bronze case bolted to the church wall. It contained pieces of the cross to which Andrew had supposedly been tied and was, naturally, X shaped. The case's glass panels allowed an interior view of plush maroon padding and chunks of what appeared to be driftwood. The best I could say about these relics—which arrived in 1979 from Marseille, where they had been stored since the thirteenth century— was that they did not appear to have endured two thousand (or one thousand, or two hundred) years of disintegrating wear. I asked Father Spiridon about this, and for the first and only time that day he shrugged in a way that indicated that even he had his doubts about their authenticity.

We had two final stops to make. The first was, in Father Spiridon's words, "old church Andreas." The local guidebook claims that the church had been built on "the exact place" where Andrew had been crucified. According to legend, it had also been the site of a temple built in honor of Demeter. A nearby wellspring was part of this temple's oracle, a wellspring now called the Well of Saint Andrew.

We walked inside Old Saint Andrew's through a doorway

draped with carpets that bore the image of the apostle crucified. The air had a crowded, librarial mustiness, which was heightened by the sight of several Greek Orthodox priests in their black habits and strange hats walking silently about on the thickly carpeted floor. The church's murals looked somehow submerged and faded, and the ceiling was cracked in several places. The one area in which Old Saint Andrew's surpassed New Saint Andrew's was its frankly impossible number of icons, which a number of old Greek women were visiting, and kissing, one by one.

Everyone within the church turned to greet Father Spiridon lovingly, and he was intercepted for a blessing half a dozen times. During one such blessing, I wandered away and found Andrew's sub-reliquary near the church sanctuary, behind a wooden throne. This smaller reliquary was, like its big brother next door, silver and surrounded by a marble shrine. A plaque read, EX DIGITO. The finger of Andrew. Father Spiridon soon rejoined me and explained that the finger had once been kept at the monastery on Mount Athos, a semiautonomous monastic republic given to a Christianity harsh enough to forbid anything female—animals included—to set foot anywhere near it.

"You look Athos?" Father Spiridon asked me.

By now, I had come to speak fairly good Greeklish and understood that he was asking me if I had ever been to Mount Athos. "No," I said.

"Come," he said, and led me to what I gathered was his favorite icon: Mary and Jesus, their bodies cast in effulgent silver. Father Spiridon directed my attention to the blood coming out of Mary's cheek. "This Athos," he said. "Very beautiful. Go to Athos and look. Athos have this. Original. Long ago Turkey people, bad people, Mussulman people—"

Father Spiridon, no!

"—they take original. Look blood? They do to Maria." He made a stabbing motion. My best reconstruction: bad Turkey Mussulmen attacked Athos, stabbed the original icon, after which it bled. This was a replica of that mugged icon.

We went outside for our final stop: the Well of Andrew. It was surrounded by a black gate and covered by a wooden canopy. Father Spiridon explained that an open, pleasant area next to the well was where Andrew had actually been crucified. Before we descended into the well, I asked if I could stand at the spot of Andrew's crucifixion. Father Spiridon sighed and extended his hand, as if to say, *Go ahead, weirdo.*

There were, I supposed, worse places to have been crucified than this wind-strafed, seaside pulpit. The view was not quite panoramic, but I could see a good portion of the sea and up into the hills above Patras's lower quadrant. Of all the apostolic crucifixions, Andrew's is among the least historically preposterous, in that the earliest crucifixions for which we have evidence took place in Athens in the seventh century BCE. Rome apparently first learned of crucifixion from the Carthaginians during the Punic Wars.

Crucifixion seems to have begun as a way to humiliate the already dead; the Romans were the first to make it punishment in and of itself. Its punitive aspects were a by-product of crucifixion's actual intention, which was to psychologically terrorize the families and friends and allies of the crucified. In the Roman world, crucifixion was mostly applied to the lower classes (an obscure reference to the socio-economics of crucifixion can be found in Tacitus, where he speaks of a man being "executed as slaves usually are") or political offenders or both. The first record we have of Jews practicing crucifixion comes from Josephus, in which he writes of the Hasmonaean ruler Alexander Jannaeus, who ordered eight hundred captive rebels to be crucified in the middle of Jerusalem, after which he "butchered their wives and children before their eyes." Josephus lamented the "brutality" and "impiety" of crucifixion, as it was not a Jewish form of punishment, and even the New Testament (Hebrews 12:2) speaks of crucifixion's obvious "shame." The second-century anti-Christian writer Celsus referred to "the disgraceful circumstances" in which Jesus died, and one apparently popular pagan form of

anti-Christian mockery was a bit of graffito that depicted a crucified donkey.

Near the end of the Jewish War, the Romans were crucify-
ing so many Jews, as many as five hundred a day, that the entire
region ran out of wood. For all of this, the archaeological evidence supporting the practice of crucifixion is astonishingly
weak. Only one body, out of the thousands that have been recovered, shows clear evidence of having been crucified in Roman
Palestine. The remains were found in 1968, in a tomb just outside
Jerusalem proper, the victim's heel bone driven straight through
with a nail. His name: Yehohanan ben Hagkol. It is estimated
that he was executed sometime between 50 and 70 CE, when he
was in his twenties.

"At any period of history," the scholar Raymond E. Brown
writes, "those who practice torture are not overly communica-
tive about the details." Which means it is not at all unusual that
the details that would allow us to understand crucifixion in the
ancient world remain so sketchy. Among the many things we do
not know about Jesus's crucifixion is the shape of the implement
on which he was crucified. Early depictions of a traditional cross
in relation to Jesus are few and far between. The oldest example
is from the second century and shows a tiny, weirdly contorted,
nude Jesus carved into a gem. This may be a Sethian Christian
artifact of religious derision directed at rival Christians who, the
Sethians believed, overemphasized the crucifixion. The gospels
say surprisingly little about the nature of Jesus's crucifixion. In
Mark and Luke, it is covered in a single sentence. John takes
two sentences. In Matthew, it is a clausal aside: "And when they
had crucified him . . ." We do not have the faintest idea if nails
were actually used to crucify Jesus. Of the synoptic gospels, Matthew and Mark are silent on nails, and Luke merely suggests that
nails were used when his resurrected Jesus asks the disciples to
look at his hands and feet. John's gospel is less ambiguous about
the use of nails, with Thomas's proclaiming that only when he's

touched "the mark of the nails in his hands" will he believe in Jesus's resurrection. The only other early Christian documents to say explicitly that nails were used to crucify Jesus are *The Gospel of Peter* and Ignatius's letter to Smyrna, neither of which is canonical.

Incredibly, historians cannot even be sure that a cross was involved. (Several early Jewish Talmudic references to Jesus's execution seemed to indicate that he was, of all things, stoned.) While the Jesus tradition came to involve a crossbeam crucifixion, one very early depiction of his crucifixion—found in Saint Sabina, in Rome, from the 430s—shows a kind of shared scaffold against which Jesus and the two executed alongside him are tied or nailed. From this, we can see it was not always assumed that Jesus and the bandits were individually crucified. If a stake with a crossbeam *was* involved in the crucifixion of Jesus, how was it attached? Again, we have no idea. The *crux immissa* (the Latin name for our familiar cross) is only one of several options. It might have been, for instance, V shaped. It might have been an upright stake. The author of *The Epistle of Barnabas* and Justin Martyr both believed Jesus had been crucified on a T-shaped cross. Andrew's X-shaped cross was known in antiquity as the *crux decussata* and is as likely as any other to have been used against the historical Jesus. How would an X-shaped cross have changed our understanding of him? Splayed in such a way, would he be even more vulnerable, even more humiliated?

I told Father Spiridon I was ready to follow him into the Well of Andrew. Ten rather graceless steps later, we stood in a dark enclosure of rough, uneven walls. Before me was a white marble basin and a rusty faucet. If you drink from the Well of Andrew, one legend holds, you will return to Patras.

"Old years water for gods," Father Spiridon said as I drank.

"What?"

"Old years. Water. For gods."

"Gods."

He began listing them off on his nail-bitten fingers. "Zeus. Apollos. Poseidonus."

"The old gods!"

"Yes! *Historia!* Understand? Old time?"

"I understand. Old time. History."

Finally—and, considering how much time we had spent together, oddly—Father Spiridon asked me my name.

"Thomas," I said.

He demanded that I follow him back into the old church Andreas. Soon enough, we were standing before a startlingly pretty icon of Thomas, in which he was depicted touching the wounds of Jesus. Father Spiridon pointed at me. "Thoma." He pointed at the icon. "Thoma."

"Didymus," I said, using Thomas's Greek name.

Father Spiridon looked over his shoulder. "Yes," he said. "Thoma. Didymus. Same." He then asked me if I would like to stay for the late-afternoon Mass. Although I had not attended a religious service since I was a teenager—I had, in fact, made it a point not to—I agreed.

The Greek Orthodox service, I soon learned, was a ritual of commendable impracticality, performed as it was by at least half a dozen priests, none of whom talked to the parishioners or made any attempt to connect with them. For the vast majority of the service, the priests remained turned away from the parishioners. The actual Mass was performed in the sanctuary, unseen. Throughout the service, the priests walked in and out. There was endless chanting and singing and recitation: everything in the Greek liturgy, save for the sermons, was sung, and never, in contrast to the Western tradition, alongside instruments. At one point, I had incense whisked at me from a distance of twenty feet.

Two and a half hours later, the service concluded. Father Spiridon asked if I enjoyed it. I told him I had. I meant it, too. What I had just seen was among the more enjoyably incomprehensible human gatherings to which I had ever been party. But, I said, I needed to return to my hotel, where I had a friend who, for all I knew, had maybe died of alcohol poisoning. Father Spiridon extended his hand, but I pushed it away. We were friends, and friends embraced.

JOHN

The Ruins of Saint John's Basilica: Selçuk, Turkey

SAINT BLUE JEAN • EPHESUS • "TEACHER, WE SAW
SOMEONE CASTING OUT DEMONS IN YOUR NAME" •
SONS OF THUNDER • JOHN & PETER • THE DISCIPLE
WHOM JESUS LOVED • THE TEST BENEDICTION •
"BARBAROUS IDIOMS" • GODOFREDO • ISOBEL &
ARTHUR • THE GOSPEL OF ARTEMIS

I.

The Roman province of Asia, today called western Turkey, exerted on Christianity an influence comparable to that of Rome or Jerusalem. Paul, as his letters demonstrate, worked frequently within—and struggled almost as frequently against—the churches of Roman Asia. The Gospel According to John, the most spiritually rebarbative gospel, was probably written in Roman Asia, as were the embattled epistles attributed to John. Revelation was addressed to "the seven churches" of Roman Asia, one of which the text's author laments for having "abandoned the love you had at first" and, in the next breath, commends for its hatred of a rival sect. Montanism, an early and audacious form of heterodox Christianity that challenged the authority of the apostles themselves, had a Roman Asian provenance. Around 112 CE, a proconsul in Roman Asia named Pliny wrote to the emperor Trajan about the problems he was having with the local Christians, who were being denounced by their enemies anonymously. At a time when Christians throughout the Roman Empire dared to mark their graves only with coded scribbles, the reckless Christians of Roman Asia were erecting obviously Christian tombstones for themselves.

A province noted for its relative wealth and sophistication and home to numerous pagan mystery cults, Roman Asia became an accidental colander of early Christian beliefs. By the second century, it was Christianity's foremost intellectual battleground. By the fifth century, a number of orthodox Christianity's major theological positions were being settled by councils convened within its cities—many of which were chosen as council sites precisely because of how prevalent strands of heterodox beliefs were within Roman Asia's famously argumentative churches.

The originally Central Asian people who gave Turkey its name did not cross Turkey's modern-day borders until the eleventh century. Prior to this great migration, Turkey was home to some of the most important Christian communities in the world. Unlike most Muslim-majority nations, modern Turkey is constitutionally forbidden to endorse any state religion. Even so, 98 percent of its seventy-one million citizens are Muslim. The percentage of Turkish citizens who self-identify as Christian can be generously rounded up to 0.0000011 percent. Istanbul provides the patriarch of Eastern Orthodoxy with an official seat and palace, yet Turkey does not contain a single Christian seminary.

Imagine a twenty-fourth-century Syria overrun by Mormons. The near-total extinguishment of Christianity from Roman Asia once seemed as unlikely.

II.

I went to Selçuk with my friend Suzy, who had been living in Istanbul thanks to a journalism grant. We arrived at noon and spent our first hour exploring. This was followed by a tactical retreat to our air-conditioned hotel room. Later in the afternoon, when the sun seemed less punitive, we headed to the ruins of Saint John's Basilica, the way to which carried us along a wide thoroughfare named in honor of Mustafa Kemal Atatürk, the father of modern Turkey and the direct object of one of modern history's more benign personality cults. All along Atatürk were bakeries, tractor-part shops, and cafés, their amply shaded patios filled with Turkish men playing dominoes and drinking hot apple tea and smoking cigarettes. Quite a few of these men were arguing. I asked Suzy if she could tell what they were arguing about. She directed my attention to the man who was thrusting his finger down on a copy of that day's *Hür-riyet,* the front-page photograph of which I had already seen at the airport. This photograph had been taken during the previous day's session of parliament, where it was being debated whether the Turkish constitution should be amended to include more "direct democratic involvement" (code for allowing the continued erosion of Turkish secularism) in the election of the president. What the *Hürriyet* front-page photograph showed was two deputies from rival political parties debating that issue with their fists. (It would get worse.)

One of the local guidebooks I had picked up made much of Turkey's religious equanimity and cited as evidence the last century or so during which the Christian sites of Selçuk had been protected. Not mentioned was the longer period during which the Christian sites of Selçuk were systematically ignored. A century ago, there was little certainty as to where Saint John's Basilica had been located. No Christian church of comparable significance had been lost for as long. The apostle John, meanwhile, is the only member of the Twelve whose supposed remains are unaccounted for. Muslims were able to venerate many Christian sites at no cost to their beliefs; any site or relic with any importance to Muslims, on the other hand, was necessarily abhorrent to Christians. While Islam recognized and admired Jesus, he rated nothing more than a silver medal. Jesus's disciples, meanwhile, had little significance to Muslims, though they do turn up within the Qur'an, in which they refer to themselves as "helpers of Allah" and "submitting ones."

By now we were close enough to the basilica ruins to come across signs pointing our way toward "St. Jean," which was also the name of the street along which the ruins were found. The initial thing one noticed about the ruins was how little one initially noticed them. Instead, one's eye was pulled upward, along an adjacent hillside's green luxuriance, to the top of Ayasoluk Hill and Selçuk Fortress. Thanks to its placement atop one of the highest hills in town, the fortress ranked among Selçuk's most commanding examples of period architecture. It was also one of the least distinguished, amounting to a weathered slab of gray ramparts that only partially enclosed the open hilltop. A redundant number of Turkish flags dangled from the fortress walls, as did a two-story-tall silk-screen portrait of Kemal Atatürk, his face undulating in the breeze as though it were an image projected onto water.

Behind the walls of Selçuk Fortress not many buildings remained standing—a cistern, a bath, a small mosque—even though, once, the entire area had been ruled from Ayasoluk Hill, first by Byzantines, then by Turkish Seljuks, then by Turkish Ottomans. According to one archaeologist, the hilltop cistern was once the "apsidal part of a Byzantine basilica," which was devoted to John and predated the larger basilica at the base of the hill. One legend holds that John wrote the Fourth Gospel while living on Ayasoluk Hill. ("Ayasoluk" is a Turkish-inflected derivation from the Greek *hagios theologos,* or "holy divine.")

The most conspicuous vehicle on the streets of midsummer Selçuk was the tour bus, and down St. Jean Street they came, space-shuttle white, astronomically heavy, bottoming out at the ponderous upward turn into the basilica parking lot, their engines cutting off with a whomp, their passengers emerging from soda-machine-cool interiors. Suzy and I climbed up the hill after the buses, at the top of which was the parking lot and something called the St. Jean Souvenir Shop and Bookstore. Its sign promised, THE OFFICIAL BOOK ABOUT SAINT JEAN IS HERE. This caught my attention, as did the man who was standing beneath the sign and waving at us. We walked over to him.

"I know people think this sign is a very funny mistake," he said, by way of greeting. "Ha-ha. Saint Jean. Saint Blue Jean. But I like this sign. I made this sign. And I have the only official book about Saint Jean. But you should know that we Turks call him Yahya. Yahya same as Jean. Isa same as Jesus. Musa same as Moses. We have many of the same beloved."

The man, whose name was Mehmet, invited us to peruse the soft drinks within his Coca-Cola-brand cooler, his racks of post-cards, his rolled-up carpets, his piles of books, all of it amusingly overpriced. His "Saint Blue Jean" patter had drawn us in, though, as he knew it would.

While I consulted the only official book on Saint Jean, priced to move at only thirty euros, Mehmet moved in on Suzy. "You," he said to her, "are the most beautiful angel I have ever seen. You cannot be American. I refuse to believe this. American women, I say to you, are *huge*. You are a European woman, I think." He looked over at me with insistent, salesman eyes that would not take an answer for an answer. "A finer woman I do not remember seeing. If she is your wife or girlfriend, please say so, and I will drop this matter. If not, I will take her to dinner tonight."

Suzy and I had dated once, literally, as in we had a single date. Our smokiest physical encounter involved some awkward handholding. With Mehmet's dinner invitation alarmingly imminent, Suzy took hold of the arm I looped around her as though it were a flotation device. "She's my girlfriend," I said.

Mehmet bowed at the waist. "Then you are the luckiest man in Turkey. She is the angel from Heaven."

"Thank you," I said.

"No, do not thank me. This is the truth." To Suzy: "Your red hair—this is God's present to you! Tell me, what do you call the beautiful marks on your face?"

"Freckles?"

"They are the sunshine. Another gift from God!"

I asked Mehmet if he had ever visited the empty tomb of Saint Jean. "I have seen the tomb, yes," he said, his hands assuming oath-swearing positions. "A famous Italian priest once came to Selçuk, and I joined him in his journey beneath the earth to Saint Jean. This was ten years ago, and on that day I became a lucky man. If you would like me to help get you down into the earth of Saint Blue Jean, I will call my friend. If old manager is working, no problem, but sometimes the new manager makes a scandal. We will see." Mehmet speed dialed and put his back to us. A few seconds later, his big head tipped forward. Today the new manager was making scandals.

Over in the basilica's parking lot, one tour bus made room for another, like whales in an overcrowded pod. "How many people visit the basilica a day?" Suzy asked, demonstrating why she was living in Istanbul on a journalism grant and I was not.

"Sometimes fifty or sixty buses a day come here," Mehmet said. "Let me say that two thousand people visit Saint Blue Jean each day. Of course, we Muslims also favor Saint Jean. He is one of the four persons who wrote the original Bible. We are believing the original Bible. We are believing the four books. The four books"—he began to count them off on his fingers—"are the Talmud, the Bible, the Qur'an . . ." The final book evaded Mehmet's fingertip summons.

Suzy said, "The Hadith?"

"Yes! The Hadith. I must ask you, are you Muslim? If this is so, I will marry you today."

III.

Before the Turkish conquest of Anatolia, Selçuk was known as Ephesus, a city whose pagan and Christian histories are equally remarkable. A traditional Christian view holds that Paul founded the Ephesian church, and at some later point the apostle John, with the mother of Jesus in tow, took up residence in the city and thereafter led its Christian community.

Another traditional Christian view holds that John founded the Ephesian church, to which Paul (or, as most scholars believe, a follower of Paul's) later wrote his epistle. Both views are somewhat challenged by the fact that Paul, in his letters, never mentions John being present in or connected to Ephesus; nor does the author (or authors) of the New Testament's Johannine literature (traditionally thought to be John) mention Paul. According to Eusebius, Paul made his traveling companion (and forced circumcisee) Timothy the first bishop of Ephesus; in this tradition, Timothy is honored as the first martyr of Ephesus. Other traditions hand down the news that the first bishop of Ephesus was not Timothy but John. But which John? The apostle John or, perhaps, John the Elder, who was mentioned in the second century by Papias? Or were these Johns the same person?

Suzy and I walked up a cacti-edged path of broken marble slabs to the basilica's entrance, stepping over a dried-out, ant-swarmed turtle corpse, its pale green shell cracked in two. The marble used to line this path had been scavenged by Christians from the ruins of Ephesus, an hour's walk across town. "Ephesus," however, was something of a geo-historical catchall. Several cities called themselves Ephesus, and not all were located in the same place. The chronologically and culturally distinct ruins of Ephesus—only 10 percent of which, it is believed, have been excavated—are spread across six locations within an approximately ten-mile radius. Archaeologists suspect that the Aegean Sea's coastline, which has shifted considerably over the last few thousand years, accounts for the city's refusal to stay put.

Ephesus's most famous ruins—the ones raided by Christians and plastered on postcards—belonged to Greco-Roman Ephesus, which was attractively located between two large hills. They contained a commercial area (where one could walk past an amazing gallery of restored Roman buildings, homes, temples, latrines, at least one restaurant, and a sewer system) and an administrative area (home to the Library of Celsus, one of the most awe-inducing ruins in the world, and Ephesus's theater, a great stone clamshell capable of seating twenty-five thousand people). A third portion of Greco-Roman Ephesus's ruins, known as the Harbor District, had almost nothing left to it. The walk to the Harbor District, which brought visitors down the Arcadian Way, a long straight street once lined with columns and lit at night by oil-burning lamps, was nevertheless one of Selçuk's most enjoyable tourist activities. Many of Ephesus's celebrated visitors, including Paul, had walked that very street.

Another thing the Christians of Ephesus built with their absconded haul of pagan marble was the entrance arch of Saint John's Basilica, called, somewhat unwelcomingly, the Gate of Persecution. Suzy and I passed through it now. The gate's name came from a frieze that was no longer extant but might have depicted the persecution of Paul, who according to the Acts of the Apostles enjoyed a decidedly unhappy experience in Ephesus. The courtyard just past the Gate of Persecution was angled in such a way as to direct visitors toward what had once been the basilica's altar, beneath which was John's tomb. This was a reminder that Saint John's Basilica was, above all else, a pilgrimage church, its choke points intended to guide and accommodate large numbers of people. The courtyard also served as what a local guidebook described as the area "that would customarily serve as the last stand, if the fortress was overrun."

That was no idle fear. At various points in its history, Saint John's Basilica was more fortress than church. Ephesus, as a city, had two things going for it: its land was fertile, and its landscape was beautiful. The harbor brought in money and outside-world contact of all types and ambitions. The irregular, crumbling ring of fort walls that run along the base of Ayasoluk Hill—not uncovered and reconstructed until the 1970s—was built in the eighth or ninth century to keep out invading Arab raiding fleets during the incessant sea war between the Byzantine Empire and its Muslim enemies.

In the first century BCE, Augustus granted Ephesus the status of Roman Asia's capital city, and soon its population swelled to twenty thousand citizens. Greco-Roman Ephesus was more Roman than Greco, largely because Augustus was forced to rebuild the city after a dreadful first-century BCE earthquake brought much of it to the ground. In the fourth century, no fewer than three earthquakes devastated Ephesus. The city's once-large population, getting the message, began to dwindle, and its harbor, abandoned by the Aegean, silted up. By the fifth century, Christianity was ascendant in Ephesus, and the city was still regarded as important enough to host two major Christian councils, visitors to which complained about the heat, disease, and swampy malarial air. When Ephesus fell prey to a string of attacks perpetrated by marauders in the eighth century, most of its population was reduced to hiding behind the walls of Saint John's Basilica. In the twelfth century, Turks won lasting control of the weakened city, which they renamed Ayasoluk. In the fourteenth century, Ayasoluk was visited by the English knight and traveler John Mandeville,* who called it "a fair city, near to the sea. And there Saint John died, and was buried behind the altar in a tomb. And there is a fine church; for Christian men used to possess the city. But now it is occupied by Turks." So it was. So it is.

It took both Suzy and me a moment to realize that once we had passed through the courtyard, climbed more stairs, and followed a short path, we were, in effect, standing inside Saint John's Basilica. A surprising number of the columns that lined the basilica's now-phantom nave had been recovered and set upright on their pedestals, but this was, nevertheless, a ruined graveyard world. Other than the columns, almost no part of the basilica that had been restored reached higher than my shoulders.

We were two of many tourists. A thin, crew-cut American man who wore his large silver crucifix on the outside of his Massachusetts sailboat dealership T-shirt walked around aggressively chewing his gum. Several Asian women wore welding-mask-like Burberry sun visors that covered their whole faces, giving them the effect of extraterrestrials here to take a surface sample before heading back to the mother ship.

Near one of the basilica's side entrances, Suzy noticed that a crowd had gathered, which she suggested we investigate. It turned out our fellow tourists had decided that some storks living in messy, grass-padded nests atop the walls that surrounded the basilica were more interesting than the basilica itself. Sud-

---

* The accuracy of Mandeville's account of his journeys, like the existence of Mandeville himself, is disputed, though most scholars believe it has some factual basis.

denly, as though to prove this, two of the great birds took off, their wings' downdraft scattering the nests. After a few brisk, powerful flaps, the storks glided with immense, ultralight silence down Ayasoluk Hill. The storks came to rest atop the minaret of a nearby mosque, as though providing us all with a very nearly literal demonstration of the way in which Turkish winds blow.

IV.

In the popular Christian imagination, Peter is always gruff, tempestuous Peter; Thomas is always remote, questioning Thomas. Yet the tradition of how John has come to be seen and understood contains a number of severe conceptual breaks.

According to the gospels, John wants to immolate Samaritans and demands that Jesus put a stop to the work of an unauthorized exorcist. He is also the beardless boy apostle who lovingly reclines on his master's breast during the Last Supper. To some, he is a devoted disciple standing steadfastly at the foot of his master's cross, embodying everything Christianity can be, and to others he is a wizened seer sitting on the crags of Patmos, embodying everything Christianity can know. The flame-thrower mystic of Revelation is also the arch theologian of the Fourth Gospel. Meanwhile, in extra-biblical legend, John is a crinkly-eyed, lovable centenarian—and lifelong virgin—telling his disciples to always love one another. While these are not necessarily mutually exclusive identities, they are highly textured when compared with the simpler, more consistent images the New Testament and its legendary outgrowths allow us to form of the other apostles. Despite his changefulness, John is, for many Christians, perhaps the Twelve's most notionally familiar member. This is the enigma of John, one that his body's disappearance from its tomb on the Ayasoluk Hill has only deepened.

"John" derives from the common theophoric Hebrew name Yohanan or Yehochanan, means "God has been gracious," and appears in all four of the New Testament's Twelve Apostle lists. In Mark, John is listed third, after his brother James; in Matthew and Luke, he is listed fourth, once again after James. In Acts, though, John is listed second, which may have something to do with that book's depiction of John as Peter's traveling partner and ally. (Two important second-century apocryphal works, *The Epistle of the Apostles** and *The Gospel According to the Ebionites,* contain lists of the Twelve in which John, unusually, is listed first.) The Gospel According to John contains no explicit mention of John or his brother James; the book's final and most likely added twenty-first chapter does, however, refer to "the sons of Zebedee."

In the synoptic tradition, James and John are called to follow Jesus moments after he calls Peter and Andrew. As Mark has it (and Matthew closely follows him), Jesus goes "a little farther" along the seashore of the Sea of Galilee, where he sees the brothers "mending the nets" in a boat. Like Peter and Andrew, James and John are said to "immediately" follow Jesus. Unlike Peter and Andrew, they leave several people behind, including their father, Zebedee, and what Mark calls "hired men." Luke, however, tells us that the Zebedee brothers were "partners" with Peter and Andrew.

Scholars have done much to reconstruct the complicated social world of the first-century Galilean fisherman. Galilee was subject to Herodian rule, and the Herods continued many of the regional administration practices put into effect by previous dynasties. One such practice, it is believed, was the selling of fishing rights to individual fishermen. These permits were likely not cheap, which placed those who possessed them at the top of an occupational pyramid. Beneath the permit holder would

---

* Among the most fascinating pieces of Christian Apocrypha, *The Epistle of the Apostles* was considered sacred scripture by many early Christians, and it eventually fell out of favor largely because the date it audaciously pegged to Jesus's eventual return came and went. Most scholars regard the *Epistle* as an "anti-Gnostic" text, but sneakily so, in that it attempts to mimic the tone and structure of the so-called Gnostic texts with which the *Epistle*'s author was obviously familiar. The *Epistle* also appears to make the argument that Paul should be regarded as less authoritative than the Twelve.

have been various other workers and servants who did everything from piloting the boats to maintaining their nets to rifling
through the day's catch and tossing back into the sea any and
all catfish, which, due to their lack of scales, are not regarded as
kosher. Mark's account seems to indicate that James and John
work for a presumably permit-holding father; Luke's suggests
that they are a part of some shared-permit collective. An early
tradition, credited to Origen, identifies the Zebedee brothers as
"sailors," meaning they helmed their assigned boat rather than
fished from it.

In Mark and Matthew, whenever John and James are mentioned, James usually comes first, which is probably reflective
of the authors' understanding of their ages. However, as the
scholar R. Alan Culpepper notes, Luke, on four occasions spread
throughout his gospel and Acts, mentions John first—a sign,
possibly, that "Luke knew that John was the more famous of the
two brothers." Thanks to Christian attempts to harmonize the
gospels' accounts of which women were present at the cross during Jesus's execution, James and John's mother, Salome, has been
traditionally identified as the sister of Mary, the mother of Jesus,
though one would be hard-pressed to find this information in
the gospels themselves. According to the common Christian
understanding that sprang from this harmonization, James and
John were eventually imagined to be cousins not only of Jesus
but of John the Baptist as well.

Only once in the gospels are John and Jesus shown to have
a private interaction. The scene is included in both Mark and
Luke, though Luke's rendering of it is a third as long. In Mark's
account, John approaches Jesus and says, "Teacher, we saw someone casting out demons in your name, and we tried to stop him,
because he was not following us." Jesus's response is notable
both for its liberalism and for its hard-nosed realpolitik: "Do not
stop him. . . . Whoever is not against us is for us."

Culpepper believes that the nature of Jesus's response somewhat confounds the belief, held by some scholars, that the scene

was created by the early church in order to provide guidance as to how to deal with fringe figures who used Jesus as the stated source of their power. If the young church had created the scene as a response to later pastoral developments, what purpose would Jesus's accepting conclusion have served?

Thanks to Mark, and Mark alone, we learn that the Zebedee brothers were called by Jesus "Boanerges, that is, Sons of Thunder." Etymological explanations for this strange phrase range from "sons of earthquake" to "loud-voiced" to "shout-workers," but Culpepper regards Mark's "Sons of Thunder" as a more or less accurate translation of an Aramaic phrase Mark incorrectly transliterated.* This can be seen in later Syriac Christian traditions, which are generally believed to have preserved more authentic Aramaisms than the Greek of the gospels. In Syriac Christian texts, we find John and James referred to as *benay regesh,* or "sons of noise."

The traditional explanation for why Jesus called the brothers the Sons of Thunder has to do with their intemperate nature. Yet most of the evidence used to support this tradition comes from Luke, who does not record the nickname. One such scene occurs shortly before "the days drew near for [Jesus] to be taken up." Jesus, determined to meet his fate in Jerusalem, sends messengers ahead of him. These messengers pass through a Samaritan village and are in some way rebuffed. James and John somehow witness this Samaritan cold shoulder and approach Jesus. Quite shockingly, they ask him, "Lord, do you want us to command fire down from heaven and consume them?" Why the brothers believe they can wield such heavenly napalm is unclear. Jesus rebukes them all the same.

* "Boanerges" has some cross-cultural resonance: Castor and Pollux, the sons of Zeus, were both believed to sit at their father's side, where they wielded control over thunder and lightning. This may shed some interesting light on a later scene in Mark, when the Sons of Thunder ask Jesus, "Grant us to sit, one at your right hand and one at your left, in your glory." In other words, Jesus's nickname may be an example of a pagan religious belief interestingly breaching the hull of Christianity.

This is one of two rebukes the Zebedee brothers receive in the synoptic tradition, the other resulting from their awkward request to sit at Jesus's side in Heaven, which is contained in Matthew as well as Mark, though Matthew, perhaps to shield James and John from criticism, has their mother do the asking for them. Jesus's rebuke of the brothers in this case is notable for several reasons. First, Jesus asks them if they will be "able to drink the cup that I drink." The brothers respond, "We are able." Jesus then tells them, "The cup that I drink you will drink." Jesus appears to be predicting that the Zebedee brothers will die as martyrs. Indeed, there is an early tradition, eventually eclipsed by later legends, that John, like his brother James, was martyred. The second-century bishop Papias, for instance, apparently believed that John the apostle was martyred, and the tradition survives in various forms of Eastern Christianity as well. Culpepper believes the tradition might have grown out of the apostle John's fate being conflated with that of John the Baptist.

John's most interesting relationship, at least as it developed through Christian tradition, is not with Jesus but rather with his fellow apostle Peter. Many of the scenes in which John and Peter are traditionally believed to interact stem from the Fourth Gospel's inclusion of "the disciple whom Jesus loved," otherwise known as the Beloved Disciple.

In Luke and Acts, John and Peter are shown several times to work together. The first and only example in Luke takes place during the Festival of Unleavened Bread, shortly before Passover, when Jesus tells John and Peter to go to Jerusalem and find "a man carrying a jar of water," who will take them to what Jesus calls an "already furnished" room for the Last Supper.* In Acts, Peter and John are shown to be on their way to the Temple to pray, and, at the Temple's "Beautiful Gate," they encounter a lame

---

* Mark also includes a version of this scene, but the disciples Jesus sends on the errand are not named. A funny thing about both Mark's and Luke's take on this scene is whether Jesus is performing a miracle or demonstrating his capacity to plan ahead.

man who begs for alms. The lame man expects a handout; what he receives is Peter's command to "stand up and walk." The man springs to his feet and clings to Peter and John. In short order, "much annoyed" Sadducees arrest Peter and John. The next day, they informally arraign them. The once-lame man turns up at this arraignment, during which the Sadducees are said to notice the "boldness" of the otherwise "uneducated and ordinary" Peter and John. The Sadducees demand that the pair stop preaching about Jesus; to this, Peter and John say thanks but no thanks. The Sadducees want to punish them, but "the people," who are apparently on the apostles' side, make that politically impossible.

Peter and John turn up together again during the story of Philip's adventures in Samaria. When the apostles learn of Philip's successful evangelizing there, they ask Peter and John to join him. In Luke's gospel, John voices a wish to destroy Samaritans. In Acts, also written by Luke (though we do not know how much time passed between the two works' composition), John lays his hands in blessing on the Samaritans. It is difficult to know exactly what dynamic (if any) is at work here in John's journey from anti-Samaritan rage to pro-Samaritan tending.

Tradition tells us the apostle John is the same person as the Fourth Gospel's "disciple whom Jesus loved," also known as the Beloved Disciple—the purest, most perfect follower of Jesus— who stands at the center of the New Testament's most intriguing identity crisis: Thomas, Andrew, Philip, Mary Magdalene, Matthias, Lazarus (the only other man in John's gospel that Jesus is specifically said to love), Judas the brother of Jesus, John Mark, and Paul were all put forth as the Beloved Disciple's alternative identity at some point during Christian history, but John the apostle eventually won out. One explanation for this confusion lies in how obdurately the Fourth Gospel obscures the Beloved Disciple's identity. The text is read as though it were written by the Beloved Disciple, but only in one late verse does it claim to be a first-person work wearing a third-person mask.

The Beloved Disciple first appears by name at a surpris-

ingly late point in the gospel. It is the Last Supper, and Jesus
has just announced, for the second time, that he is aware that
he will be betrayed. John: "One of the disciples—the one whom
Jesus loved—was reclining next to him.* Simon Peter therefore
motioned to him to ask Jesus of whom he was speaking." The
other passages that mention the Beloved Disciple occur when
Jesus is on the cross ("When Jesus saw his mother and the disciple whom he loved standing beside her"), when Mary Magdalene discovers Jesus's empty tomb ("So she ran and went to
Simon Peter and the other disciple, the one whom Jesus loved"),
and twice during Jesus's resurrection appearance in Galilee ("The
disciple whom Jesus loved said to Peter, 'It is the Lord!'"; "Peter
turned and saw the disciple whom Jesus loved following them").

One instantly notices a thematic pertinence: four of the
five mentions of the Beloved Disciple angle him, in some way,
against Peter. The first example has an air of pettiness about it:
Peter, despite his intimate place at the table with Jesus, is not
even able to speak to his teacher without the intercession of the
Beloved Disciple. The tomb sequence, on the other hand, seems
overtly polemical. After hearing from Mary Magdalene about
the empty tomb, Peter and the Beloved Disciple rush off to see
it for themselves. "The two were running together," John tells us,
"but the other disciple outran Peter and reached the tomb first."

---

* A note about the homoerotics of the Beloved Disciple's head resting in Jesus's lap
during the Last Supper: Christopher Marlowe is probably the most famous example
of someone who wound up being tried for blasphemy by suggesting that the Beloved
Disciple and Jesus were "bedfellows," and some modern Christians address the matter with held breath. But there is no escaping the fact that a beardless youth learning
from an older man would have made perfect Socratic sense to many in the ancient
world. That is almost certainly *not* what is going on in the mind of the author of
the Fourth Gospel, but there can be little doubt that images of the Beloved Disciple
reclining in the lap of Jesus, as Christianity spread throughout the Greco-Roman
world, had certain, inescapable redolence. Even Leonardo's *Last Supper* skates
awfully close to the forbidden line: while the painting's composition did not allow
for anyone's head to be placed in the lap of Jesus, Leonardo portrayed John, whom he
understood to be the Beloved Disciple, as the most beautiful woman who never was.

Once inside the tomb, the Beloved Disciple—and John makes sure to emphasize this—"saw and believed." Nothing is said of Peter's belief.

This leaves us with the risen Jesus's appearances in Galilee during John's twenty-first chapter, which scholars view as a later addition for several reasons. Its position on Peter and his authority appears more equitable than the preceding chapters; its language is different; its subtextual quandaries have less to do with Jesus than the situation likely faced by the community responsible for producing the gospel; and it has a clear linguistic relationship to Luke's account of the calling of Peter, which John 21 might have retrofitted.

John 21 is an extended scene—quite extended, by the truncated narrative standards of the gospels—followed by a highly unusual coda. It takes place in Galilee, specifically the Sea of Tiberias (as the Sea of Galilee was also known), and involves "Simon Peter, Thomas called the Twin, Nathanael of Cana in Galilee, the sons of Zebedee, and two others." Once again, John coyly resorts to strategic anonymity. We know that one of these disciples is the Beloved Disciple, and given the way in which he is referenced in the rest of the gospel, he would seem to be one of the "two others." While the disciples are fishing, Jesus appears on the shore and tells them to cast their nets in a new place, where there are more fish. They do as Jesus suggests, "and now they were not able to haul [the nets] in because there were so many fish." Immediately after the fish are pulled into the boat, the Beloved Disciple says, to Peter, "It is the Lord!" John: "When Simon Peter heard that it was the Lord, he . . . jumped into the sea." Once again, Peter does not initially believe it is the Lord; he has to *hear* it from the Beloved Disciple.

The chapter's next mention of the Beloved Disciple similarly seeks to qualify, but what is at stake looms far beyond the narrative's stated purview. Jesus asks Peter three times if he will feed his sheep, and three times Peter agrees he will. Jesus then predicts Peter's martyrdom, which the author of John apparently

regards as an accomplished fact, after which Peter turns to the
Beloved Disciple and says, "Lord, what about him?" What follows
is one of the most haunting passages of the New Testament:

> Jesus said to him, "If it is my will that he remain until
> I come, what is that to you? Follow me!" So the rumor
> spread in the community that this disciple would not
> die. Yet Jesus did not say to him that he would not
> die, but, "If it is my will that he remain until I come,
> what is that to you?"
>   This is the disciple who is testifying to these
> things and has written them, and we know that his
> testimony is true.

This is the only time in the gospel tradition that the author
turns to his audience and claims to be witness to the events
recorded.

It would seem that this passage was intended to address
a question being asked within the Johannine community; its
mention of "the rumor" makes much less sense otherwise. If the
community claimed as its lodestar someone with a special relationship to Jesus, and at least part of the community believed
that this person would live until Jesus's return, what would have
happened when that lodestar died? Obviously, the community
would have been forced to explain to itself what that meant. And
here we have the community's conspicuously underwhelming
explanation: it was a big misunderstanding.

The Beloved Disciple, whatever his identity, and whatever
his fate, was not intended to be the apostle John. Those who
believe otherwise are implored to consult the work of three
scholars who have done extensive work on Johannine Christianity: Raymond E. Brown, R. Alan Culpepper, and Richard Bauckham, all of whom were or are believing Christians and one of
whom, Bauckham, is an extremely conservative (and intelligent)
advocate of what has been called "elegant fundamentalism." All

reject a Beloved Disciple intended by the gospel's author to be understood as the apostle John.

The real question about the Beloved Disciple is not whether he was John but whether the writer of the gospel expected his audience to know his identity. The way in which the gospel refers to the Beloved Disciple ("the disciple whom Jesus loved") is a noticeably formulaic, even ritualistic, phrase and could easily have been inserted into existing traditions. More than that, the Beloved Disciple material exists in what several scholars categorize as "tension" between John's gospel and the synoptic gospels, *which contain not a single trace of John's Beloved Disciple material.*

To my mind, the most convincing possibility is that the Beloved Disciple is intended to stand in metaphorically for the Johannine community itself. The metaphors throughout the Fourth Gospel are heavily worked, starting with its opening lines: "In the beginning was the Word, and the Word was with God, and the Word was God." Surely, a community inclined to view Jesus as an abstraction of this magnitude would have no trouble projecting itself, communally, into the gospel story. John 21, then, may represent a later stage in the community's journey, in which the original, spiritual thrust of the Beloved Disciple metaphor was replaced by literal interpretation. As the community's lot worsened, its scribes might have taken the original metaphor of a communal relationship to Jesus and reified it through explicit dramatization.

V.

The prominent members of the Twelve were all subject to a process in which possibly historical memories were legendarily expanded, some of which legends achieved quasi-scriptural authority. John presents a unique apostolic problem, in that the majority of memories and legends associated with him are dependent upon his being the Beloved Disciple. What this means is that a legend not originally about John claimed him early.

The first identifiable writer known to link John to the Fourth Gospel was Theophilus of Antioch, who died sometime in the 180s. He counted John (whom he did not explicitly name as an apostle) among "the spirit-bearing men" and considered his work (which he did not call a gospel, though he clearly meant the gospel) "holy." The next prominent early Christian to connect John to the gospel was Clement of Alexandria, who seems to have been aware of an earlier tradition. After telling us how and why Mark was written, Clement—or rather Eusebius's later gloss on Clement, because the commentary in which Clement made these claims is lost—noted, "Last of all, aware that the physical facts had been recorded in the gospels by his pupils and irresistibly moved by the Spirit, John wrote a spiritual gospel." These modest, paraphrastic lines would frame the perception of John for generations.

The church fathers made the argument for John's authorship in good faith. Within the synoptic tradition and Acts, the factual basis of which the church fathers had no reason to doubt, Peter and John were linked. They read the Fourth Gospel with care, noted an unnamed disciple's serial involvement with Peter, and sensibly deduced that this disciple must be John. Additionally, they believed that the Beloved Disciple was necessarily a member of the Twelve, if only due to the Last Supper, the synoptic portrayal of which seems to exclusively involve the Twelve. Finally, the Zebedee brothers have such prominent roles in the synoptic gospels; it made no sense that the Fourth Gospel would ignore them. Thus, by the fourth century, the apostle John was widely accepted as the gospel's author, and the gospel was widely acknowledged to possess a different character from that of the synoptic gospels, which was, in turn, partially attributed to John's advanced age when he wrote it.

The scalpel of modern scholarship has by now sliced all this to ribbons. One scholar has written that the severity of John's differences is such that "we can only treat it as a secondary source." An exaggeration, surely, but not by much. One thing the reader of John immediately notices is how densely, even rhythmically, *literary* it is. As storytellers, Matthew, Mark, and Luke largely avoid scenic writing. Their preferred mode is that of the vignette. This is especially noticeable when the synoptic gospels shift from their knockabout accounts of Jesus's ministry and move into his Passion, which is a long, continuous, and dreadfully intense scene in all four gospels. This has to do with how the oral traditions about Jesus developed. While the events of his ministry were likely passed on in a scattered, nonlinear manner, the Passion tradition was always a complete, prepackaged storytelling unit.

As often as possible, John writes in scene: the miracle at the wedding in Cana, the nighttime visit to Jesus by the Pharisee Nicodemus, Jesus's conversation with the Samaritan woman by the well, Jesus's confrontation by the followers of the Baptist, the raising of Lazarus, Thomas's doubt—all stories that are unique to John. In those stories that John shares with the synoptic gospels, one often finds a decisive added detail: that the fish Jesus multiplies are smoked, for instance, or that the perfume the woman pours over Jesus's feet could be smelled throughout the house, or that the woman who did the pouring was named Mary, or that it was Peter who struck the slave during Jesus's arrest, or that the slave was named Malchus, or that Jesus dipped bread into a dish to identify his betrayer during the Last Supper.

Another example: Mark describes how Jesus, early in his ministry, healed a lame man in Capernaum. John gives us a similar story but places the healing in Jerusalem. Not only in Jerusalem, but "by the Sheep Gate." Not only by the Sheep Gate, but near "a pool." Not just any pool, but a pool called "Beth-zatha." Additionally, this pool has five porticoes,* and sprawled on these

---

* An archaeological dig confirmed the existence of these five porticoes, which were long regarded as the product of John's imagination.

porticoes are the sick. Not just the sick, but the "blind, lame, and paralyzed." Mark's Jesus heals the lame man of Capernaum, who says nothing to Jesus, but John's lame Jerusalemite speaks, to distinctly heartbreaking effect: "Sir, I have no one to put me into the pool when the water is stirred up; and while I am making my way, someone else steps down ahead of me." Mark sketches a vague miracle story. John creates a small, detailed world.

Many scholars have explored the ways in which the Johannine tradition departs narratively from the synoptic tradition by noting how often its departures lack any dialectical force behind them. As Raymond E. Brown writes, "Unless theological symbolism moves him otherwise, John respects plausibility, and that evangelist was much closer to what would seem plausible in the 1st cent than we are." In some cases, its departures feel like remembered details. This is a large part of what makes John so fascinating. The gospel with the clearest markers for having an authentic eyewitness at its core also has the most elevated view of Jesus's divinity.

Many scholars believe the Gospel According to John contains *details* and *memories* that are historical but a theology that is not. Conservative Christian scholars have pointed out the convenient agnosticism of this position. But if Mark's gospel were our only witness to Jesus's ministry, for instance, Jesus's supposed divinity would be an open question. Say that John's theology truly was received from the source rather than developed over time. This would mean Mark made the inexplicable decision to assay a *less* emphatic case for Jesus's divinity. It is far more likely that John's gospel contains historical information later reinforced by theological elaboration.

Brown argues that the synoptic version of the Jesus story, with its climactic arrival in Jerusalem, was more dramatically satisfying and probably quite a bit "easier to preach" than John's story, in which Jesus goes back and forth from Galilee to Jerusalem throughout. John's gospel does not appear to have been shaped by the demands of "narratological preachability." It is a story text, a proclaiming text, and offers evidence of a community in obvious pain. The author of John darkly and frequently lingers on the issue of Jewishness, for instance, mentioning "Jews" ten times more than any other gospel. This is, without any doubt, the Fourth Gospel's most regrettable and historically disastrous legacy, though it is important to remember that the Johannine community was probably composed mostly of Jews, at least initially; its gospel's attacks must be understood as emanating from within Judaism, not without. In contrast to the synoptic gospels, John's Jesus has several secret Jewish admirers—Nicodemus, Joseph of Arimathea—who occupy important positions within the Temple hierarchy. John goes so far as to note that "many" among the Temple "authorities" believed in Jesus. The most anti-Jewish gospel is also the gospel that is most fixated on Jewish *approval* of Jesus.

Jesus himself tells his disciples during the Last Supper, "They will put you out of the synagogues. Indeed, an hour is coming when those who kill you will think that by doing so they are offering worship to God." Yet there is absolutely no historical evidence that anyone who followed Jesus was expelled from his or her synagogue or killed by the Jewish authorities during or in the immediate years after Jesus's ministry. (The Jewish authorities of Jesus's time were by and large not in the business of killing people over things they said.) The numerous passages of John in which synagogue expulsion is mentioned appear to refer to the Test Benediction, a daily synagogue prayer believed by some (but not all) scholars to have been formulated in the 80s by Gamaliel II, one of Judaism's most important leaders in the difficult period following the destruction of the Temple in 70. The apparent purpose of the Test Benediction was to exclude Jewish Christians and other perceived heretics from the synagogues. By taking events familiar to the Johannine community and placing them within the ministry of Jesus, John's author is presenting history as prophecy.

Aside from Paul, "John" is the New Testament's most prolific writer, with five books attributed to him: the gospel, three letters, and Revelation. Yet these attributions are far from certain. The Johannine epistles claim to have been written by a man who refers to himself as the "elder," and the author of Revelation says he is Jesus's "servant John." Tradition has generally regarded both figures as the apostle. If, however, the Beloved Disciple was not the apostle John, the connection between him and the "elder" of the Johannine epistles all but short-circuits. As for Revelation, several early Christians refused to identify its author as the apostle John—even though Revelation is the only piece of Johannine literature whose author identifies himself as John! Which John wrote the works attributed to him was a question several church fathers worked diligently to answer. Their efforts encased a single, merely perplexing question within a gnarl of combative confusions.

In the early second century, Papias wrote of two Johns, one of whom was obviously the apostle and one of whom he called an "elder" or "presbyter" named John. Papias appears to admit that he did not know the apostle but did know (or had heard) Elder John. This Elder John, according to Papias, had, apparently (possibly?), known (or had heard?) the apostle John. Suffice it to say that the passage in which Papias makes these claims is extremely confusing, and due to what one scholar describes as the passage's "flexible Greek," it may just as easily be that Papias was claiming a direct relationship not to either John but rather to people who knew them. That would put Papias at three stages of remove from the apostle and two stages of remove from the Elder.

Irenaeus, the second-century bishop and inexhaustible heresiologist, is the first Christian known to argue that the Fourth Gospel and the Johannine epistles were written by the apostle John, that the gospel was written while John "was residing in Ephesus," and that John lived up to the time of the Roman emperor Trajan, whose rule began in 98. The epistolary fragment in which Irenaeus divulged how he learned of this information presents a number of problems. According to Irenaeus, his source was Polycarp of Smyrna, who was martyred around 157. While "still a boy," Irenaeus wrote, and living in "Lower Asia," he met the celebrated Polycarp, who frequently talked about his "intercourse with John and with the others who had seen the Lord." Elsewhere Irenaeus wrote that Polycarp "was appointed by apostles to serve in Asia as Bishop of Smyrna." Yet no writer who lived before Irenaeus mentioned Polycarp's connection to John.

Irenaeus was familiar with the work of Papias, who he said "had listened to John and was later a companion of Polycarp." But which John did Irenaeus mean? Because Irenaeus never mentioned any Elder John, he must have meant the apostle. Papias, though, never clearly claimed to have known the apostle, as Eusebius was quick to point out a century after Irenaeus, writing that Papias himself "makes it clear that he [Papias] was never a hearer or an eyewitness to the holy apostles." Eusebius attributes Irenaeus's confusion to the fact that *two* Johns lived and were buried in Ephesus: the apostle John, who wrote the gospel; and another John, who wrote Revelation (a work Eusebius did not wholly approve of). It was the latter John, Eusebius argued, whom Papias was acquainted with. Yet the legend that grew up around John is largely based on Irenaeus's belief that Papias knew the apostle rather than the Elder.

Irenaeus had considerable motivation to interpret Papias's relationship to the apostle John in the way that he did, for he was determined to make a case for the apostolic origins of the Fourth Gospel. It would have done Irenaeus's argument no good to acknowledge the existence in Ephesus of Papias's other, non-apostolic John. In short order, he became the Fourth Gospel's most significant early supporter and worked hard to ensure its acceptance among proto-orthodox Christians.

The Fourth Gospel needed Irenaeus's campaign because many of the first Christian thinkers who found themselves attracted to it—and the figure of John himself—were heterodox.

One such figure was Montanus, who took up the Fourth Gospel's imperatives, as he understood them, at the very moment that Irenaeus was trying to argue on the gospel's behalf. The Christianity Montanus forged was apocalyptic and anticlerical. Moreover, it allowed women to participate in its rites and serve as its prophets. Montanist Christianity was also extremely popular, spreading throughout Roman Asia in the second half of the second century and eventually plucking from the ranks of proto-orthodox Christianity its first great Latin-speaking intellectual, Tertullian. The Fourth Gospel became so tainted by its association with various forms of heterodoxy that several early Christian writers and church fathers seemed reluctant even to mention it.

If the Gospel According to John is the voice of a Christian community in pain, the three Johannine epistles are the voice of a Christian community pelvis-deep in schismatic misery. Reading the epistles straight through may be the most unpleasant literary experience offered by the New Testament. For instance, 1 John 3:6 reads, "No one who abides in him sins; no one who sins has either seen him or known him." This is the ne plus ultra of Johannine thought and reveals its granite, uncompromising view of what it means to believe in Jesus. It also has no parallel in the New Testament, which frequently seeks to *console* those who sin.

Addressed to the "little children" of the author's community (which might have included other, nearby churches), 1 John[*] seems to be a desperate attempt to shore up, and protect, the faithful. The voice throughout the epistle is distinctly that of a desperate community leader attempting to inhabit an author-

---

[*] In a commentary written around 415, we find Augustine of Hippo mysteriously refer to 1 John as "the Epistle to the Parthians." Why Augustine knew the work under this name is not known, though the name probably did not originate with him. Whatever the case, "Epistle to the Parthians" stuck to 1 John for centuries and even sprouted legends that had John traveling to Parthia to evangelize.

ity that all within his troubled community had, at one point, accepted. After a brief note of congratulations, 2 John quickly gets around to warning all to keep away from anyone who "goes beyond" the teachings of Christ. That the writer of 2 John is addressing a broken and increasingly imperiled Christian community becomes more apparent in 3 John, which condemns the false teachings of a man named Diotrephes, apparently a community leader who broke away from the group and took others with him. Why the author or authors of the epistles never mention or appeal to the authority of the Fourth Gospel is a question without a good answer. If the epistles predate the gospel, which is possible but unlikely, it might be that the Johannine Christians' *lack* of a widely accepted documentary proclamation helped tear their community apart.

Revelation is the New Testament's most mongrel work. Thomas Jefferson memorably dismissed it as "the ravings of a maniac, no more worthy nor capable of explanation than the incoherences of our own nightly dreams." It contains a gospel in miniature, several specimens of epistolary counsel, fantasias, sprinklerheads of mysticism, and a prophetic, often violent unveiling of events soon to come (parts of which might derive from contemporaneous reactions to the eruption of Mount Vesuvius in 79 CE). Texts do not get bristlier than Revelation, yet it is astoundingly sketchy on explaining what specific transgressions have so angered its author. The offenses it does mention include fornication, eating meat sacrificed to idols, and tolerating false teaching, but that is about it. The rest of the New Testament frequently emphasizes that to be a Christian is to accept outside rule, but Revelation broils in confrontation and sedition, taunting both Rome and its emperor.

As with the Johannine epistles, a few early Christians rejected the apostle John as Revelation's author. Today near-universal agreement exists among modern scholars that Revelation was not written by a direct follower of Jesus. The author barely mentions the ministry of Jesus and speaks of the apostles—among whom he claims no seat—as a generation long past. Among the earliest, most notable, and farsightedly firm dissenters on this point was Dionysius, who began as a student of Origen's. While Dionysius admitted—tactically, it would appear—that he "would never dare to reject the book, of which many good Christians have a very high opinion," he was, all the same, "not prepared to admit that [the author] was the apostle, the son of Zebedee and brother of James." In a display of textual and linguistic sensitivity many hundreds of years ahead of his time, Dionysius based his rejection of Revelation's apostolic authorship on its use of Greek. The other Johannine works, he pointed out, "are written not only without any blunders in the use of Greek, but with remarkable skill." The author of Revelation, on the other hand, uses such "barbarous idioms" that its language is not "really Greek" at all. Later, when the Christian canon was beginning to take shape, Eusebius gave Revelation a place within the accepted *and* the disputed books of the New Testament. Without question, among all the works of the New Testament, Revelation had the hardest path into the Christian canon; the influence it has since had on bellicose and astrally pessimistic Christians, ancient and modern, makes it hard not to wish that doubters such as Dionysius had won the day.

VI.

While flying over Selçuk, I had noted how the ruins of Saint John's Basilica resembled a microchip, its tidy grids and patternless circuits enclosed by grass-green substrate. From the ground, the ruins were no less abstract. Suzy and I walked into two-walled rooms, through doorjambs framed by blue sky, across the shattered and grass-strangled flagstones of once-marble floors. The basilica's nave had been lined with several dozen sequoial columns of tinted rock. Of its five extant columns, only two had retained their capitals. On either side of the nave, there had been many chapels and a baptistery. The latter survived, its cracked stairs leading down into a pool partially filled with sand.

We entered what would have been the basilica's courtyard. Along its foot-worn zigzag pathways, a number of small, pretty purple flowers struggled to grow. We rested next to a squat little pile of restored redbrick foundation. Suzy swigged from her water bottle and passed it over to me. "Does anyone really know what this place looked like, or is all this restoration just guesswork?"

I told her that a fairly detailed description of Saint John's Basilica could be found in an apparently unfinished sixth-century work alternately known as *Buildings, On Buildings,* or *The Buildings of Justinian.* Its author was Procopius of Caesarea, who lived from approximately 500 to 565 and is generally regarded as one of the last secular scholars of the Greco-Roman world. Procopius's self-appointed task in *Buildings* was to visit, and write panegyrics about, as many structures commissioned by the emperor Justinian as possible. Of Saint John's Basilica, he wrote,

> On that site the natives had set up a church in early times to the Apostle John; this Apostle has been named "the Theologian," because the nature of God was described by him in a manner beyond the unaided power of man. This church, which was small and in a ruined condition because of its great age, the Emperor Justinian tore down to the ground and replaced by a church so large and beautiful that, to speak briefly, it resembles very closely in all respects, and is rival to, the shrine which he dedicated to all the Apostles in the imperial city.

Much of this was regarded by scholars as accurate. A small, wooden-roofed chapel, placed over what was believed to have been John's tomb, was built in Ephesus—though possibly not on Ayasoluk Hill—sometime in the second century. By the fourth century, the tradition that John and Mary were in Ephesus together had fully developed, and churches were built in honor of both of them,* probably during the reign of Theodosius I, the last man to rule over a united western and eastern Roman Empire.

As Procopius noted, the first substantive Ephesian church devoted to John was a relatively small structure. An intersecting series of vaults or catacombs were dug beneath this church, in which the supposed remains of its namesake apostle were interred. The remains were apparently much visited by Christians, but eventually the crypt was in some manner sealed off. In the fifth century, several Syrian bishops arrived in Ephesus and expressed their frustration at not being able to pay their respects to John's remains, though, according to one scholar, "whether this blockage was literal and architectural or bureaucratic and political is not known." In the sixth century, John's first church was destroyed at Justinian's order and replaced with a Latin-cross, triply naved, eleven-domed basilica three stories tall and more than 420 feet long. As Procopius indicated, Justinian's basilica was inspired by Constantine's Church of the Holy Apostles in Constantinople. Both churches stood as emblems of a faith suddenly free to draw on the financial succor of the Roman Empire. Within centuries, both had become emblems of Christian defeat. Today, a mosque stands on the foundation of Istanbul's Church of the Holy Apostles.

No consensus exists as to when Saint John's Basilica was destroyed. From the seventh century on, raiders hit Ephesus with increasing frequency. In the eighth century, Muslims briefly occupied Ephesus for the first time, after which the basilica's Gate of Persecution went up and walls were built around

---

* Saint Mary's Church is today a half-excavated ruin—an excavation that did not begin until the mid-1980s—but it was once considered important enough to have served as the site of the Council of Ephesus in 431, which formally condemned Nestorian Christians and, for the first time, endorsed the legend that Mary had once lived in Ephesus.

the hillside. As invading Turkish tribes—militarily and cultur-ally flourishing under the leadership of a family known as the Seljuks—consolidated their hold on Anatolia, the importance of Christian cities such as Ephesus began to fade among Byzan-tine strategists. The most decisive battle between Byzantine and Seljuk forces occurred at Manzikert (in modern-day eastern Tur-key) in 1071, which set the stage for the eventual Seljuk conquest of Anatolia. In the eleventh century, there are records of active monasteries in and around Ephesus and of improvements made to Saint John's Basilica, but in 1090 Seljuk conquerors installed themselves within the city. Seven years later, Christian crusaders wrested control of Ephesus away from the Seljuks and held the city for another two centuries. Some scholars believe that Saint John's Basilica was first destroyed during the Seljuk occupation of 1090–1097, but there is no way to be sure.

Whatever the case, Christian Ephesus was in ruins by the twelfth century. By the early fourteenth century, Ephesus had become, and would remain, a Turkish city. Yet its Christian com-munity did not immediately disappear, and there is a record of one of its bishops, Matthew of Ephesus, remaining in his seat well into the fourteenth century. At some point, the basilica was probably reconsecrated as a mosque. We do know, thanks to the eyewitness of a fourteenth-century German priest, that the basilica's grounds were at one point used as a bazaar. This same priest also noted that John's tomb was empty at the time of his visit and had been empty for some time. The last men-tion of a still-standing basilica—whether as a church, mosque, or bazaar—dates from the middle of the fourteenth century.

The Isa Bey Mosque, which is next door to the basilica ruins, was completed in 1375. This has led some to propose that Saint John's Basilica, after its Islamic reconsecration, was destroyed in an earthquake known to have occurred in Ephesus around 1361. Rather than rebuild the reconsecrated basilica, this theory goes, the Turks of Ephesus opted to build a new mosque in the same area. This may account for the frequency with which visiting

Christian pilgrims in later centuries mistook the Isa Bey Mosque
for the former Saint John's Basilica.

At the end of World War I, the Greek army occupied parts
of the Anatolian peninsula, and a handful of archaeologists took
the opportunity to exhume whatever remnants they could from
the Byzantine Christian era. Selçuk was among the most scoured
areas; the first pieces of Saint John's Basilica might have been
discovered at this time. However, the reconsolidated Turkish
army, now under Atatürk's leadership, succeeded in driving the
Greeks from what soon became the independent nation of Turkey.* The archaeological effort that began during the Greek occupation eventually continued, though now under the direction of
Turkish archaeologists encouraged by the policies of Atatürk to
study for the first time the Christian history of their people's
adopted peninsula. The ruins of Saint John's Basilica were confirmed as such in the early 1920s. In the 1950s, a restoration
effort was fully under way. In the late 1970s, the nave's surviving columns were reerected and the foundation fully revealed.
Although some work remained ongoing, the restoration as a
whole was declared complete in the mid-1990s. In all of this,
surely, Turkey deserves some credit. Not many Muslim nations
have tolerated, much less advanced the cause of, the unearthing
of a non-Muslim place of worship.

Suzy and I had yet to visit the basilica's bema and altar,
under which John's supposed remains had been kept until their
disappearance during the Middle Ages. A large English-speaking
tour group, at the urging of their guide, had begun to gather
around the bema. Suzy suggested we join them.

We assumed our places behind the tour group, and I sensed
what made visiting this tomb feel so different from those of

* And viciously at that. In 1922, the Turks burned the ancient city of Smyrna to the
ground and killed or expelled every one of its Christian citizens. Smyrna was the last
remaining bastion of Christianity left in Asia Minor, to which the faith first spread
two thousand years before.

John's fellow apostles. At every apostolic reliquary, you felt gusts of anxious longing. Apostolic resting sites were places that asked you to know what cannot be known, where the randomness of earthly remains arranged themselves into coordinates of cosmic faith. They were rationality's cease-fire zones. Here, though, beneath us, was a tomb of acknowledged emptiness.

Only one small section of the otherwise dirt-floored bema had been relaid with purple star-patterned marble. At the center of the bema was the altar—little more than a square burial marker, really—at every corner of which stood a thin white column. Nearby were two equally ugly grates. The smaller grate, found just off the altar's edge, was welded shut. The larger grate, located a few feet away from the altar, allowed access to the *confessio* below, provided you were able to persuade someone to remove its padlock. (It was through this passage that our friend Mehmet had visited John's tomb.) The *confessio* was said to contain four tombs arranged to resemble a cross, the largest of which was reserved for John. Although the *confessio* was first discovered in the 1920s, the tombs themselves remained unexcavated until the 1950s.

The tour guide—a short bald man with bowlegs and a silver goatee—now stood in the middle of the bema, next to the altar, his hand raised in indication that he was about to begin to speak. A large gold crucifix dangled from his neck. This crucifix, along with his dark skin, allowed me the brief excitement of imagining I had found that okapi rarity: an actual Turkish Christian! I then noticed the name tag pinned to his plaid button-down short-sleeve shirt: GODOFREDO. This was not a Turkish name.

"History proves us that John was the Beloved Disciple," Godofredo said in opening, "and today you are standing above his ancient tomb."

His audience comprised twenty gape-mouthed senior citizens, two childless couples, half a dozen families emitting a fascinating variety of ambient tension levels, and Suzy and me. Those of us who were not standing had turned some bricks piled along the bema's eastern edge into makeshift bleachers. I admired Godofredo's energy, if nothing else. All around him, several dozen miserably heat-weak human beings were sweatily headed toward dehydration comas, but perspiration beads streaked across his bald scalp like escape pods of excess vitality.

"John's tomb," Godofredo went on, "is now empty, and no one has known when his remains disappeared, or why they disappeared. However, history proves us that Turkish armies captured Ephesus in 1304. After that, beloved John's remains may be destroyed. There are the people believing that John's remains were hidden before the Turks arrived, but the one who hid John's remains I think forgot to tell anyone about this." Godofredo stopped and waited for the laugh his spiel had been timed to respond to. "Yes, I think he forgot to tell. Thank you. However, if the remains of beloved John were destroyed during the ancient times, we do not blame our friends in Turkey, who care so much to protect this basilica.

"After Lord Jesus Christ ascended to Heaven, history proves us that John and Peter worked together in Jerusalem. In that same city, John and the apostle Paul met each other and became great friends. But John understood he could not stay in Jerusalem and made his plan to leave. We know John owned a house in Jerusalem. We know the Virgin Mary, Mother of God, was living with John. So when John left Jerusalem, Mary was so happy to come with him, ah?

"He came to Ephesus to spread the new religion, like his brother apostles. The journey to Ephesus began around year 48, which is the last time John and Mary were living in Jerusalem, so you know. Between years 50 and 54, our beloved apostle John was founding the city's first church. Later, when Paul came to Ephesus, they journeyed through Asia together to teach the people about the Word of Lord Jesus Christ.

"History proves us that John and Paul were taken to Rome to face punishment. In Rome, John was almost killed two of the times. For the first time, he was given to drink a poison, but

John made his poison into the snake. The second time John was throwed into boiling oil, but thanks to our Lord Jesus he escaped. The Roman emperor Domitian, who hated the Christians, knew he could not hurt John, and so he exiled him to Patmos, the Greek island. And you know on Patmos beloved John wrote the Revelations. After the death of the emperor Domitian, John came back to his great church of Ephesus and as an old man wrote his gospel between years 95 and 100. According to the researchers, John's gospel tells about a different time in Jesus's life, and also many things about the divine love and the human love. Finally, beloved John, the only apostle to die naturally, was buried here, on the Ayasoluk Hill, according to his will."

Godofredo took several questions, his answers little anchors of precise simplicity. No one betrayed any skepticism of Godofredo's Life of John, but one person wanted to know how Godofredo was so certain that his dates were correct. Godofredo rather wishfully attributed his dates to the Council of Ephesus in 431 and Eusebius, after which his questioner's head pumped up and down in airtight satisfaction.

When the tour group left, I walked over to the grate and peered past the bars and into the darkness below, out of which emanated odors of animal-den pungency. Men—several hundred men, from the smell of it—had urinated through this grate and into the *confessio*.

Augustine records a legend that had John's tomb breathe in and out during certain times of the day, and during the Middle Ages the dust gathered from around John's tomb was thought to have healing properties; it had been sold as a tonic all over Mediterranean Europe. Now the dust around this still, unbreathing place was contaminated with inorganic salt and urea. A legend spawned from a second-century Christian polemicist's misunderstanding was strong enough to have saved the Fourth Gospel from oblivion and to enshrine it forever at the heart of Christian thought. Yet this same legend could not prevent its supposed author's tomb from becoming a public restroom.

VII.

If I had thought to ask Godofredo a question, it would have been about that poison-filled chalice from which John, as Godofredo said, was challenged to drink. In some versions of this legend, the high priest of Ephesus's Temple of Artemis gives John the poison; in others, the Roman emperor Domitian does. The John of legend transforms the poison into a serpent, which leaps (or, in some versions, sprouts tiny wings and flies) from the chalice. This legend—which possibly derives from Mark's tenth chapter, wherein Jesus tells the Zebedee brothers they must share the cup of martyrdom with him—eventually provided John with one of the more shocking symbols associated with any member of the Twelve: a snake.

John's most famous and enduring symbol is the eagle. Another of John's symbols: the cauldron. This was attributable to the other legend Godofredo had mentioned, which has John in Rome and being lowered into hot oil that miraculously fails to parboil him. Tertullian was an early promoter of this legend, which eventually led to a small, beautiful, and rather weird Roman chapel known as San Giovanni in Oleo (Saint John in Oil) being built on the spot where early Christians imagined John had been dunked.

A legend Godofredo did not mention has the apostle John standing as the groom at the wedding at Cana, which is described in the Gospel According to John's second chapter. John's bride in this legend is none other than Mary Magdalene. After witnessing Jesus transform water into wine for their wedding party, John and Mary decide to forgo marriage and devote themselves to the miraculous vintner himself.* While the Cana legend failed to create any symbols associated with John, it did brighten the aura of ascetic virginity that still traditionally clings to him.

---

* One can see an apparent representation of this shadow tradition in Paris's Notre Dame, where a mural of the Cana wedding scene features a groom wearing the type of halo normally reserved for an apostle.

Some of the most popular legends concerning John can be found within *The Acts of John,* portions that emerged, in all likelihood, from the unique Christian traditions of Alexandria. Many scholars judge *The Acts of John* to be one of the oldest pieces of surviving Apocrypha due to its erratic Christology and the fact that many other apocryphal *Acts* seem to be aware of it. Also telling is the text's failure to cite the New Testament, which indicates an author distant from nascent institutional Christianity and consequently driven more by pious imagination and what he could recall of whatever scripture he had heard. It was not formally condemned by the church until the Second Council of Nicaea in the late eighth century, though an earlier, less formal condemnation by the church judged it as something "to be consigned to the fire." Orthodox flame did, in fact, claim a goodly amount of *The Acts of John,* and the roughly 70 percent of the work that remains extant is in several languages and spread across numerous and often highly variant manuscript fragments.

To read any apocryphal work is to vacate a series of expectations. The first vacation is spiritual: However edifying these works purport or attempt to be, their noncanonical standing renders their message curiously distant from the expediencies of faith. For the nonreligious reader, the distance is similar to that which one feels in the presence of any religious work but with the added yardage of knowing that an apocryphal work is, in some faint but definite sense, a failed work. The second vacation is formal: The gospels, despite some considerable literary inadequacies (from a modern reader's viewpoint, at least), are commendable in many ways. They have structure, contrapuntal detail, rhythm, and style. This helps them remain grippingly relevant to millions of people, most of whom know nothing about life in first-century Palestine or the complicated manner in which Jewish and Greek thought enriched each other in the Roman world. Jesus's confrontation with Pilate, his frustration with his disciples, the agony of Judas, the miracles—all stand out, even for readers of no particular faith, as powerful stories about courage, fear, failure, love, and death. Apocryphal works are not like this. They are sloppy, repetitive, frequently boring, often obscure, usually ugly, bizarrely circuitous, and typically build to moments of dramatic import baffling to all but the most cross-eyed sectarian.

The apostolic heroes of the Apocrypha have precious few modes. They are stentorian moral teachers, wondrous miracle workers, tender-footed wanderers, and world-champion denunciators of Jews, pagan gods, marriage, sexuality, and most other forms of human pleasure. One can certainly become sick of reading the gospels, but one never really tires of them. The optimal reading of an apocryphal work, on the other hand, typically requires a morning cleared of any pressing commitments and a soundproofed room. Of all the apocryphal works, none is quite so wearying as *The Acts of John*.

It contains the usual apocryphal assortment of healings, rich men, demonically possessed wives, bugs controlled by apostolic telepathy, necrophilia, and self-castration. One famous passage describes John's effort to destroy Ephesus's Temple of Artemis, one of the Seven Wonders of the ancient world. By all evidence, the Temple of Artemis was the object of pathological hatred among early Christians. In the Acts of the Apostles, Paul visits Ephesus, criticizes those who worship at the temple, and is in short order driven out of the city. It is no surprise, then, that Christian fantasists would spend the next few hundred years imagining ways in which the temple was destroyed, most often by John, for *The Acts of John*'s account of its blessed demolition is one of several. It is probably the most appalling version of the story, though, if only for the moment when John tells Artemis's Ephesian followers, "I alone will call upon my God to kill you all because of your unbelief."

The temple was actually destroyed in the second half of the third century during a massive earthquake. A good deal of Ephesus was destroyed along with it—including, possibly, the first Ephesian chapel devoted to John. After the earthquake, Goth

plunderers looted what was left of the temple. Christians, however, remained angrily fascinated by the temple and its patron
goddess, which says something about the strength of Ephesus's
Artemis cult. In the early fifth century, John Chrysostom complained that Ephesus's Christians were too squishy-minded to
rid the city of Artemis and those who followed her. Sometimes
called the "Augustine of the East," Chrysostom was a relatively
unsophisticated thinker but a skilled public speaker. (Chrysostom comes from *chrysostomos,* "the golden-mouthed.") He was
also one of the first prominent Christian thinkers to view scripture literally, unlike earlier Christian intellectuals such as Clement of Alexandria and Origen. Around 405, Chrysostom might
have personally led the mob that destroyed the Temple of Artemis for the last time.

VIII.

Suzy decided to head back to our hotel to catch some Turkish
television news, which was her primary method of language
acquisition whenever she found herself away from Istanbul.
By 6:00 p.m., the ruins exhaled a half day's worth of absorbed
sunlight, and the heat began its laggard daily withdrawal.
Above, the sky was all lilac softness.

While I was walking back to our hotel to join Suzy for dinner, I saw two obviously Western tourists heading up St. Jean
Street to the ruins. I decided to follow them. Inside the ruins,
pale light fell on the toppled columns in the basilica courtyard,
across which the tourists walked in reverent silence. It was here
that I approached them. Their names were Isobel and Arthur,
mother and son from a place called Toe Head on the southern
coast of Ireland. Isobel wore a strapless orange tube top, her skin
boiled red but for where her bikini straps had been. Her face
was smooth and covered in a fine white down. Other than the
poached, sun-swollen bags under her eyes, she did not appear
nearly old enough to be Arthur's mother.

Arthur, meanwhile, looked as if he had stepped out of the New Testament and into a backpacker's hostel: long brown hair, crazy beard, big round irises of pimento-flecked hazel. His T-shirt featured a joint-toking, copyright-infringing Bart Simpson. I learned that Isobel's husband had passed away the year before; Turkey was one of his favorite places in the world. She had come to Selçuk with Arthur so they could enjoy one last family vacation together. Her husband was with them now. Or so it felt to her.

"So you've been to Saint John's ruins before?" I asked.

"No," Isobel said. "This is my first time here. I first saw the Virgin's House several years back, with my husband. We came back and saw it a second time, but for some reason we never made it here."

"Why not?"

"I'm not sure why, actually." Her eyes popped open a bit, and she looked away, as though fighting off a sudden, happy memory of her husband.

Her son, Arthur, sensed what was happening and took her hand. "We're glad we came," he said, while Isobel composed herself. "It's a moving site. It's extremely moving."

"I like it, too," I said.

Isobel, having recovered, said, "It's interesting for me to put it all in perspective. We know our religion but not our history."

"The history's very interesting," Arthur said.

"Have you been to the Virgin's House?" Isobel asked.

"I think tomorrow," I said. What I did not say was that I regarded Mary's House—previously known as Panaya Kapulu (the Chapel of the All Holy) and today known as Meryem Ana Evi (the House of Mary)—as one of the many sites around Selçuk whose purported connection to historical fact was even more specious than that of John's tomb. For instance, there was a tower in the administrative region of Roman Ephesus's ruins in which, it was said, Paul had been kept prisoner. Not too far away from the tower was a small funereal building that, it was once claimed, held the remains of the evangelist Luke.

The House of the Virgin Mary was found about five miles from Selçuk, on the slope of Mount Koressos. Popes Paul VI and John Paul II both visited the house—the latter celebrated Mass on its grounds*—and a million people visit it each year. It was "discovered" in 1891, though the local tradition behind it is apparently very old. The first official pilgrimage to the site took place at the turn of the twentieth century, but the government of Turkey did not officially recognize Mary's House as a legitimate, protected tourist site until the 1950s.

Many of the legendary accounts of Mary's death give the apostle John a prominent role. These legends, which begin to appear in the fourth century, were composed in virtually every major language used by early Christians, though from which Christian community the tradition first emerged is still debated. In any event, Christians—not to mention Muslims, whose Qur'an mentions Miriam, as Muslims know her, more frequently than the New Testament—were left with two traditions about the fate of the mother of Jesus. The traditions of Eastern Christianity and Islam generally hold that Mary died in Jerusalem and ascended to Heaven after three days in state, though many Eastern Christians accept that Mary lived in Ephesus at some point. The Western Christian tradition maintains that she was taken to Ephesus by John and later ascended to Heaven without death or burial. The former tradition is older. In fact, one can today visit Mary's tomb in Jerusalem's Kidron valley, which is a site jointly held by Greek Orthodox and Armenian Christians, though Muslims also pray there. (Until relatively recently, the tomb's custodians were Muslims.) Mary's Turkish house is also partially open to Muslim pilgrims, though Christians and Muslims pray to her in different rooms.

In the view of Raymond E. Brown, Mary as an individual "has no place in Johannine thought." Not only does she go unnamed in the gospel many Christians believe was written by the man

---

* The Catholic Church takes no official position on whether Mary ever lived in Mary's House.

who later cared for her, but she appears in the Fourth Gospel only twice. Her first appearance occurs during the Cana wedding scene, during which she notes that no one is serving wine. Jesus brusquely responds, "Woman, what concern is that to you and me? My hour has not yet come." Jesus's mother, as though goading her son, takes a few wedding servants aside and says, "Do whatever he tells you." Jesus, neither the first nor the last young Jewish man to find himself cornered by maternal ambition, dutifully transforms the wedding party's water supply into wine. (It is his first public miracle.) The second and final scene involving the mother of Jesus is the crucifixion, when Jesus commends her to the care of the Beloved Disciple. For the author of John's gospel, Jesus's mother appears to serve a symbolic purpose. Because one unnamed figure being entrusted to another unnamed figure cannot be history, it must be theology. The community that believed itself closest to Jesus thus used his mother to assume for itself a kind of vague dynastic authority.

"The Virgin's House is a very special place," Isobel said. "It's such a beautiful, simple site, and there's all this lovely greenery on the outside. When you go inside and see all the candles and carpets, you have this really quite amazing feeling. Every time you step inside, you feel it."

"What kind of feeling?" I asked.

"Oh, how can I describe it?" Isobel's face filled with joy, as though being asked to describe the feeling would be akin to reexperiencing it, which for all I knew it was. "First, of course, you feel something like grace. Real grace. Her grace. You feel the weight of all those Christians who've come before you."

"And Muslims," I said.

"Yes," Isobel said instantly, brightly. "They're there, too. And they're lovely, lovely people."

"We're going tomorrow," Arthur said. "I can't wait to see it."

Isobel smiled. "He's heard me talk about Our Lady's home for years now. All I can say is that it's a very special place."

"It's nice to actually find some Christians here to talk to," I said. "Most of the people I've met here don't seem to be at all interested in John or Mary or, really, anything."

"Are you here on mission?" Isobel asked.

"Oh, no. Nothing like that. I'm just here as a tourist."

Isobel allowed my admission to drift serenely past her. "Saint John looked after Our Lady, you know. He was the last person to be with her. So he means a lot to me. Quite a lot. Even if he hadn't written his gospel, he would still be important to me."

"He was loved by Jesus," Arthur said. "Of all the apostles, he was Jesus's favorite."

As though the interpersonal dynamics of the gospels could ever be that apparent. But to Arthur, and to many believers, the interpersonal dynamics of the gospels were precisely that apparent. As apparent as every miracle, as every word of Jesus. I knew that when Evangelical scholars put on their lab coats and took on the air of independent-minded detectives, the results were frequently ludicrous, as when Richard Swinburne writes that alternative hypotheses for Jesus's miracles "have always seemed to me to give far less satisfactory accounts of the historical evidence than does the traditional account." Dr. Swinburne, you don't say. Forget that this "historical evidence" was subject to the editorial control of people emotionally, spiritually, and intellectually committed to believing that everything in the gospels was true. Forget that the "historical evidence" the Evangelical scholar holds up alongside the work of Tacitus and Thucydides is of a completely different character. Even worse were the Evangelical scholars responsible for stuff like this: "Theologians working with a Humean definition of a miracle would look on the Easter resurrection of Jesus as a moment when God abrogated the existing laws of nature.... Underlying analogy is nomological universality. According to the principle of nomological universality, the same laws that govern the past and present will govern the future as well. This too needs critique." It was as though Michel Foucault emerged from fifty-eight semesters at Oral Roberts University.

But if you believed in the gospels, and you believed that John was the Beloved Disciple, he *was* Jesus's favorite, and quite obviously at that. And it felt good, suddenly, to be reminded by Arthur that not every Christian was an Evangelical scholar, that some things—indeed, most things—could be true and untrue at the same time, that the untrue could abide with the true as the believer abided with the unbeliever, and that a widow and son too young to lose his father did not need to choose anything right now but how best to honor the ghost they believed could look down upon them from the paradise of their understanding.

"I like the moment when John puts his head in the lap of Jesus during the Last Supper," I told Arthur. "It's such a beautiful, sad little detail."

"It's hard to believe," Arthur said, "that we're standing so close to his tomb."

With this Isobel swiftly agreed. "I was just saying, before you came up, that there are a few places in this world of ours that you simply must see, if you're a Christian. And I think this is one of them."

We walked to the edge of the basilica's courtyard, where we looked down the slopes of Ayasoluk Hill, over the old fort walls. Beyond the fort walls was the Isa Bey Mosque. Beyond the mosque were little squares of parceled farmland, out of which grew row upon row of grape bushes. Beyond the farmland was the only surviving pillar of the Temple of Artemis. And beyond it, the dim blue iridescence of the Aegean Sea. I described to Isobel and Arthur what they were seeing, a leapfrog view from Christianity to Islam to paganism, and said that all three westward-facing structures were clearly meant to replace one another.

"Which one was Artemis again?" Arthur asked.

"Fertility goddess," I said. "But not a Greek or Roman one." Artemis emerges from Anatolian myth as a mother goddess called Kybele, which, I went on, explained why her temple was so grand, even though it was built on top of a swamp. "She was a local girl, a virgin. Her cult spread everywhere—as far as Scandinavia. So it made some historical sense that the Ephesian Christians latched onto Mary as strongly as they did. You could say that Mary kind of replaced Artemis here."

"I'm not sure *I* would say that," Isobel said politely.

"No, of course," I said. "*One* could say. But when the Greeks got their hands on her, Artemis was reimagined as the daughter of Leto and Zeus, and it was said she was born near a spring. Today the House of the Virgin is near that spring. Guess what it's called now?"

"I don't know," Isobel said. "Mary's Spring?"

"Yep."

"That's very interesting," Isobel said, and laughed. "That's actually *very* interesting."

Arthur asked when the Temple of Artemis was destroyed. It had been destroyed a few times, I told him, and pieces of the ruins were not discovered until 1869, after a long and largely fruitless search by a British surveyor.

"I wonder," Arthur said, "where all of Artemis's people went after her temple was destroyed?"

It was a good question. After talking a little more, Isobel, Arthur, and I said farewell. We all hoped that we would see each other again, tomorrow, at the House of the Virgin, but we did not.

Later I wondered if perhaps the followers of Artemis ran away, but not too far away. Perhaps they gathered in a cave somewhere near the ruins of their goddess. Perhaps they were silent and much afraid. See them, looking at one another, huddled, trying to understand what had happened to them and why. Imagine the story that one of them, eventually, begins to tell.

THOMAS

Saint Thomas Basilica: Chennai, India

THOMAS CHRISTIANS • "JESUS IS VERY HINDU"
• THE TWIN • THE LOCKED ROOM • INCIDENT AT
PARANGI MALAI • THE NESTORIAN CHURCH • *THE
ACTS OF THOMAS* • KING GONDAPHORUS • "BE
PASSERSBY" • AROUND SANTHOME BASILICA •
EUTYCHUS OF TROAS • THE FLOOD

I.

For the last two thousand years, Christianity's distinguishing characteristic has been its remarkable ability to adapt to local cultural influences. It is simultaneously a Middle Eastern religion, an American religion, a European religion, an African religion, and an Asian religion, making it easily the most diverse form of monotheism on the planet. According to Plato, "To find the maker and father of this universe is difficult; but it is impossible, having found him, to proclaim him to all men." Christianity has come closer than any other faith to disproving this maxim.

India's Christians belong to one of the oldest, most deeply rooted Christian communities in the world. For centuries, they have existed in the bewildering matrix of the competing and, at times, hostile neighbor religions of Islam and Hinduism. While the Vedic religions we group under Hinduism are thousands of years old, Hinduism as a concept, religious identity, and tool of cultural organization arose partly in reaction to Indian Christianity in the late eighteenth century. Islam's relationship to Indian Christianity is just as striking. Ritual prostration, Ramadan, prayer mats, and even minarets have all been plausibly traced back to the ancient Syriac church that first brought Christianity into India.

Many Western visitors are surprised to learn of the antiquity and complicated cultural position of Christianity in India, but this historical obliviousness has a long pedigree. When Portuguese merchants landed in western India in 1498, they were astonished to discover brown-skinned believers in an entrenched, long-thought-vanquished form of Christianity many of them regarded as heretical.

Although Indian Christianity was shaped and affected by Western colonialism, it is crucially not a *product* of Western colonialism. To simplify greatly, there are three types of Indian Christians. The first are the Christians variously known as Orthodox, Syrian, or Thomas Christians, who trace their lineage back to the apostle Thomas and the Syriac church he supposedly founded. There are Roman Catholic Christians, many of whom, beginning in the sixteenth century, either were forced or tactically chose to gather under the protective umbrella of Rome. There are also Protestant Indian Christians, who constitute the subcontinent's most recently formed Christian community. As of 2010, there were anywhere from sixty to seventy million Christians living in India, giving it the seventh-largest Christian population on earth.

The first Thomas Christians were driven out of Syria and into Persia, Central Asia, and India by persecution, which was often fomented by their fellow Christians. Later, Zoroastrian persecution sent another wave of Thomas Christians to India. Muslim aggression led to yet another paroxysm, forcing Thomas Christians to variously disperse within India itself. Thomas Christians had little contact with mainstream Orthodox Christianity, whether Western or Eastern, until the end of the fifteenth century. Even the Syriac church that spawned the Thomas Christians gradually lost contact with its Indian flock. No other group of Christians of comparable size developed so independently.

II.

Anyone traveling to India will be warned about the likelihood of getting sick. I was, certainly, and thought nothing of it. I have had giardia in a war zone, been rushed to a French emergency room, and spent Christmas Day in a Vietnamese clinic. Travel is, for me, getting sick, being sick, or recovering from sickness. As long as I have a hotel room in which to burn away a sick day (or four) and a good book, I know I can and will endure. Indian sickness did not worry me.

I was throwing up by the time my Airbus A380 crossed into Indian airspace. When we began our descent into Chennai, one of the flight attendants had to pound on the bathroom door to get me back to my seat. The culprit of my sickness was one of two things: the (delicious) Mongolian barbecue I had during a stopover in Dubai or preemptive Indian diarrhea furies cruising at thirty-eight thousand feet. I stepped outside Chennai International Airport with a hundred-degree fever and splatters of stomach acid caked on my T-shirt. Confused, lost, and scanning the approximately two thousand Indian faces standing outside the airport, I could no longer remember the name of the hotel I was staying in. Eventually, the gentleman from my hotel found me leaning against a crowd-control barricade just off the terminal's entrance. I might or might not have been quietly weeping. He carried my bags to the car.

On the way to the hotel, the driver, who spoke only a little English, kept glancing back at me. When we arrived, he rushed inside to have a word about my condition with the staff. At the check-in desk, I was told that an appointment with an Indian doctor could easily be made. Nonsense, I said. An exceedingly kind Indian bellman helped carry me to my room. In the elevator, he kept going on about how terribly important it was that I drink tea. Much, much tea. Agreed, I said. Tea. In the room, I attacked with dull savagery five varieties of childproof packaging and gobbled down every type of medication I had on hand. Then I collapsed. When I woke up eight hours later, two pots of tea had been left outside my door.

I decided to become more acquainted with India the following day. "India," in this context, meant the people sitting next to me in the dining room of my hotel's first-floor restaurant while I tremblingly ate from a small plate of mangoes. After breakfast, I inquired with the front desk: Did any members of the hotel staff happen to be Christian? The woman manning the desk was not sure; she also seemed slightly troubled by my question. Historically speaking, India's Christians tended to keep to themselves and were often discouraged from marrying or even dining with those outside their community. To further my research, apparently I would have to venture outside.

India was too hot. That was my first impression. My second, equally forceful impression was that I could have spent a year in Chennai and had no better grasp of India than I did right now. It is that large, that instantly complicated. More than two hundred languages are spoken in India, and twenty languages are commonly spoken in Chennai alone.

I walked. The alleys smelled as if they'd been hosed down by India's hungriest asparagus enthusiast. Trash in the streets and choking the gutters. If there was any place trash reasonably *could* be, it was, and in gargantuan quantities. India's trash felt like some sort of philosophical précis on futility. But everywhere, too, I saw signs of attractive, normal Indian life: boys talking to girls, people going to work, men on their cell phones, movie theaters with charismatic posters written in Tamil, and mothers hugging their children in doorways. I had gone only around the block, but already the nostril-filling reality of India was intensely attractive.

When the first Western explorers landed in North and South America and called it "India," they were, perhaps, in their error, helpfully establishing for future generations a Western signpost for generic foreignness. This notional "India" is what a certain kind of traveler seeks above all else—a place where life is brighter, the spirituality is higher, and the animals are all named Babar. It was a delusion of having arrived somewhere, perceived something, more intense than oneself.

Later in the afternoon, I wandered outside once more and found a thirtyish Indian man standing in front of my hotel with his motorcycle. He was wearing blue jeans and a thin white linen shirt unbuttoned to display an adolescently hairless chest. His arms were folded, and an impressively unbroken unibrow gave his face a comical furiousness. When I raised my hand to him, though, he smiled and walked toward me. I told the man I wanted to see a little of Chennai but did not want to venture too far. He motioned toward his sidecar and, as I climbed in, told me his name: Dave. I laughed. He knew why I was laughing. "My real name is too hard to pronounce," he said.

At my insistence, Dave told me his real name, which had approximately eighteen syllables. Dave it was, then, and around the neighborhood we drove. Whenever we stopped, I asked Dave what kinds of people I was looking at: Tamil, Telugu, Hindu, Muslim, Christian? Sometimes Dave knew, but mostly he did not want to guess. I found myself studying the striking faces we passed for traces of India's painful histories of ethnic conflict and migration.

Despite being a basically impregnable geo-fortress—protected by shark-infested waters to the south and some of the highest mountains on earth in the north—India has attracted an uncommonly diverse number of peoples, some of whom derived from major empires (Persians, Macedonians, Greeks, Syrians, Arabs, Mongols, Turks, Huns, Chinese) and others from largely forgotten empires (Bactrians, Sogdians, Scythians, Kushans, Parthians). Two types of Indians have historically dominated cultural life on the subcontinent. These were the Aryans of the north, who are generally tall and lighter-skinned and genetically Caucasoid, and the Dravidians in the south, who are an older, more indigenous grouping of genetically Australoid peoples with shorter stature and darker skin. The Aryans have tended to lord over the Dravidians, literally and figuratively. Historically, the most subjugated members of the latter were referred to as *dasya,* or "slave" people, and today are called the Dalit.

Aryans ceded India much of its cultural heritage in the form of Sanskrit (literally "perfect sound"), an Indo-European language that became the Greek or Latin of the subcontinent: Hindi, Punjabi, Nepalese, and Bengali all grew out of Sanskrit, along with dozens of other languages. Chennai, however, was found in one of the strongholds of Dravidian culture, and its predominant language was Tamil (whose mystifying alphabet I spent several fruitless evenings trying and failing to memorize). Another Dravidian language was Malayalam, speakers of which tend to live along the Malabar Coast of western India. This area, today found in the state of Kerala, is where Thomas Christianity first developed, probably due to the trade centers there, which attracted Jewish—and possibly Jewish Christian—merchants. Thomas Christianity's first contact with India was via Dravidian culture. Its namesake apostle's final resting place in Chennai, on the other side of India, maintained that ancient cultural connection.

None of India's indigenous languages have a word for "religion." The "closest approximation," the historian Robert Eric Frykenberg notes, is *Sanskriti,* which does not describe spiritual practices but rather refers to "the whole of high, or classical, civilization and its literatures." *Sanskriti,* in this sense, has very little resonance in Dravidian southern India, whose "classical" period is linked to Tamil. According to Frykenberg, ethnic groups in India "never lost their elemental identities because, from the outset and for the most part, they did not allow members to intermarry across ethnic, cultural, and/or class lines." Thus, Indians understand their placement in society with an unusual degree of cosmological precision. This goes for India's Christians, Hindus, and Muslims alike. When wave after wave of people come into a place with strongly held fears of intermixing, various means of human accounting will naturally develop to allow these groups to keep track of one another. The most unfortunate reality to grow out of such social accounting is, without question, the Indian caste system.

India's caste system is old—so old that there does not seem to have been a time when some form of it was not practiced. However, it normalized and intensified during India's antiquity, when the powerful *Arya* of the north began to enslave the more numerous *Dasya* of the south. As Frykenberg notes, most human societies have at some point adopted slavery. "But of no other society on the earth," he goes on, "could one say that as many as one-fifth of the population were viewed as innately subhuman and, hence, relegated to a permanent, hereditary, and religiously sanctioned status of thralldom." Frykenberg harshly but fairly refers to Hinduism's systematized view of human subjugation as "perhaps the most sophisticated and reasoned doctrine ever devised that extolled the virtues of the intrinsic inequality of all mankind."

It is useful to compare Indian spiritual thinking, and how it affected India's Christians, with the quandary faced by the first Roman Christians, who were mostly slaves themselves. Yet within three hundred years, Roman Christians had worked their way into the highest echelons of their society. Indian Christians, meanwhile, remain less than 1 percent of the total Indian population (though in Chennai they make up almost 8 percent of the population). Indian Christianity, insofar as it proved upwardly mobile, did not often challenge or tempt the prevailing power structure. This gives Indian Christianity its noticeably different flavor and cultural imperative.

Historically, most Thomas Christians have come from high-caste backgrounds with long traditions of literacy. They were thus able to achieve social prominence within a scholarly culture. Yet every Christian in India, whether local or foreign, past or present, has had to wrangle with the caste system because it cuts directly across the central message of Christian fellowship.

Take, for instance, Communion, which ritualistically links Christians to one another. The Indian caste system, however, is rife with fears of "pollution," and few from a high-caste background would dream of drinking from the same cup as someone from a lower caste.

Because Dave, my tour guide, told me he was Hindu, I asked if we could visit a Hindu temple he liked. He told me I would get a better education about his beliefs by picking up and reading an issue of *The Hindu*, a widely read (and not overtly religious) left-leaning Indian newspaper headquartered in Chennai, which has been continuously publishing for more than a hundred years. I took that to mean Dave was not a religious man, but he said no, actually, he was. I already knew that Hinduism was a complicated set of codifications that attempted to explain every facet of existence—everything that grows, lives, and moves is covered by some facet of Hinduism, and even lakes and rivers are regarded as having divine properties by many Hindus—and that despite its disquieting core of social exclusion few other faiths so heroically championed scholasticism for scholasticism's sake. So I kept pushing; Dave finally relented to my wishes.

Outside a Hindu temple whose fronting and statuary looked (to my non-Hindu eyes) like an advertisement for an ambitiously surreal animated film, Dave calmly explained what Hinduism meant to him. Unfortunately, his relationship to his faith was not so easy for me to understand. Hinduism is the ultimate You Had to Be There faith—and if there is anything to Hinduism, you probably were.

"You know Christians," I said.

"Of course."

"What do you think about them?"

"I think of them as people, sir."

"I'm here to write about India's Christians. About Saint Thomas."

"I hope it will be interesting for you."

"Do you have any particular thoughts on Jesus?"

"We have many of the same stories, you know. Overcoming death? This is a Hindu concern. Life contains death, and we are pieces of life." Dave noticed me writing down what he was saying and smiled. "So, I think, Jesus makes very much sense to me, as an Indian, if I can be honest with you."

"Please do."

"Our goal as Indians is to escape the cycle of life and death. There is something beyond these cycles, something more . . . eternal?"

"Yes."

"So to me, as an Indian, Jesus is very Hindu."

"Jesus is Hindu?"

"I think so, yes."

"So by that you mean Jesus . . . successfully transmigrated his soul?"

Dave laughed. "Maybe this is what I mean, yes."

Suddenly a dozen firecrackers exploded near our feet. The tiny culprits who lobbed them at us ran off, giggling like gremlins.

"Dave," I said, "why are children throwing firecrackers at us?"

"Diwali," he said.

Diwali, the festival of lights. Today was the first day of this extremely loud holiday, which in high Hindu style celebrates so many things at once that to say what Diwali was about seemed beside the point. What Diwali felt like from an American point of view was the Fourth of July with an extra week plus 750 million additional fireworks. (The firecracker throwing was popularly thought to hold demons at bay.) Dave told me that the big-ticket citywide fireworks displays would start today at around 4:00 p.m. and would end after midnight. "What about the firecrackers?" I asked him.

"Those don't end," he said as we started back to my hotel. "Not during Diwali."

III.

The apostle known as Thomas appears in all of the New Testament's apostolic lists. Thomas's Greek name, *Didymus,* which means "twin," derives from the Aramaic word *Te'oma,* which also means "twin." Didymus was used as a name by Greeks in the first century but not, apparently, in Palestine and not, insofar as it is known, among Jews. There is a confirmed second-century Palestinian use of "Tomah," but that is a homophonic name with different etymological roots. What this probably means is that something is textually afoot with the name Thomas.

John, the only gospel writer to give Thomas anything to say or do, is curiously adamant about Thomas's name meaning "twin," mentioning it three times in his gospel: "Thomas, who was called the Twin," "Thomas (who was called the Twin)," "Thomas called the Twin." With this triple emphasis, John's author seems to be suggesting something to his original audience.

Some scholars believe Thomas/Twin might have its origins in a nickname, which was not uncommon among the Twelve; Simon, James, and John all are noted in various gospels as having earned their own. As it happens, the Syriac Christians who claimed Thomas seemed to think they knew their guiding apostle's "real" name: the apocryphal *Gospel of Thomas* refers to its hero as Didymus Judas Thomas, and in the apocryphal *Acts of Thomas* we meet "Ioudas ho kai Thomas," or "Judas, alias Thomas." But it is *only* the Syriac tradition that records this name for Thomas.

If Thomas really existed and his given Semitic name was Judas, why, then, was "twin" chosen for him? One possible answer is that he needed a nickname, as the Twelve already had at least two Judases among them: other than Judas Iscariot, Luke's gospel mentions a "Judas of James" where the other evangelists place Thaddaeus, and John's gospel contains reference to another potential Judas, called "Judas (not Iscariot)" (who in some ancient Syriac translations of John is referred to as "Judas Thomas"). Another answer holds that Thomas was indeed someone's twin brother, who a few early Christians believed was Jesus himself. As a postulation, this is less nutty than it sounds: Mark and Matthew record the names of Jesus's brothers, one of whom was named Judas. Obviously, the larger Christian church has done much to suppress this tradition, which confounds virtually everything Orthodox Christianity accepts about Mary, the virgin birth, and Jesus himself. Then again, as some have argued, Thomas's nickname could have derived from his resemblance to a person of no historical note. As one scholar puts it, "It is hard to imagine how the idea of a twin brother of Jesus could have been taken seriously in circles where the tradition of the virgin birth was current."

Yet the notion that Jesus had a twin, or at least someone within his inner circle who resembled him, turns up again and again in various pieces of heterodox (and sometimes even proto-orthodox) Christian writing.* A slightly different version of this "twin" figure surfaces in heterodox stories about the crucifixion, some of which imagine someone who looked like Jesus being executed in his stead. In the heterodox *Apocalypse of Peter,* Jesus tells Peter that a "substitute being" was crucified for him and that the "living Jesus," whom Peter also "saw on the tree," is "glad and laughing." A less ambiguous run at the same notion can be

---

* Some traditions record this look-alike disciple not as Thomas but as James son of Alphaeus, who (as we have seen) has his own complicated and potentially fraternal relationship to Jesus. According to Mark, Jesus was a *tekton,* like his presumed father Joseph. A *tekton* could denote anyone who worked with his hands, but Christian tradition evolved in such a way that *tekton* became synonymous with "carpenter." This tradition affected Thomas, whose symbol became the carpenter's square rule, though later Indian legends depict him as an architect of some kind. Thomas the carpenter might thus have grown out of the heterodox notion that he and Jesus were twins believed to have worked the trade of their earthly father. Two pseudonymous infancy narratives about Jesus are credited to Thomas and James, and these texts might have their origins in the hope that "Judas Thomas" and James, as Jesus's brothers, would be regarded as convincing eyewitnesses to his boyhood.

found in Sethian Christian literature, which imagines Simon of Cyrene (who in the synoptic gospels takes up Jesus's cross for him) being crucified in Jesus's place; this trick is assayed with the devious complicity of the Sethian Jesus, who laughs at Simon's misfortune. The "crucified other" motif has been carried over most spectacularly into modern times thanks to the Qur'an, in which we find this passage: "And they did not kill him [Jesus], nor did they crucify him; but [another] was made to resemble him to them. And indeed, those who differ over it are in doubt about it. They have no knowledge of it except the following of assumption. And they did not kill [Jesus], for certain."

Pretty clearly, the Christians whose beliefs informed Muhammad's misunderstandings of Christian theology were heterodox Christians, most likely from Syria. These later stories of Jesus's having a crucified twin or look-alike appear to be related in some way to the notion that among the Twelve was an apostle nicknamed Thomas/Twin, and Thomas, it must be remembered, has a storied place in Eastern Christianity generally and Syriac Christianity specifically. That Jesus avoided the cross with the help of an unnamed "twin" may be a theological elaboration on an earlier, heterodox notion that Jesus had a literal or possibly "spiritual" twin named Judas, alias Thomas.

In many ancient cultures, twins were looked upon as the likely result of magic, adultery, divine disfavor, or all of the above. First-century Palestine was, by all evidence, no different. As the scholar Glenn W. Most notes in his brilliant book *Doubting Thomas,* any man who earned the nickname Twin would almost certainly have been the younger, less favorably regarded brother. In many languages, "doubt" and "twin" have an etymological relationship, which can be seen in Greek (*distazein* and *dis*), Latin (*dubitare* and *duo*), German (*Zweifeln* and *Zwei*), and English ("doubt" and "double").

It is thus both fitting and a little strange that we refer to Doubting Thomas, as the apostle has come to be traditionally known. Thomas's "doubting" moniker derives from a story in the Gospel According to John in which Thomas, and Thomas alone, refuses to believe in the reality of Jesus's resurrection. The modifier leaves Thomas perpetually stranded in doubt, even though the purported point of the story is to demonstrate Thomas's conclusive *escape* from doubt. Thomas called the Twin. Twin called the Twin. Doubting Thomas. Doubting Double. Thomas, it would appear, is less an apostle than a semantic maze.

IV.

At several points in his gospel, John tries to establish Thomas's character and set down the narrative rails that account for why he would later doubt his master's resurrection. In John's eleventh chapter, Jesus announces to the disciples that he would like to return to Judaea. The disciples find this announcement worrying. Was Jesus not just threatened with stoning by Jews? Never mind that, Jesus tells them. "Our friend Lazarus has fallen asleep, but I am going there to awaken him." What follows are a few uncommonly dry New Testament sentences: "The disciples said to him, 'Lord, if he has fallen asleep, he will be all right.' Jesus, however, had been speaking about his death, but they thought that he was referring merely to sleep. Then Jesus told them plainly, 'Lazarus is dead.'" One can almost hear Jesus's disappointed sigh as he is reduced to explaining yet another metaphorical poeticism to his disciples.

Thomas is particularly block-headed. After Jesus suggests getting on with it and going to see their dead friend, Thomas says, "Let us also go, that we may die with him." No other disciple in John talks in such hair-shirt terms; no other disciple claims to be willing to pay the ultimate price for Jesus's sake. Thomas appears again during John's Last Supper sequence, when Jesus promises he must soon depart. Thomas tells Jesus, "Lord, we do not know where you are going. How can we know the way?" He has, yet again, misunderstood what Jesus is trying to tell him, and, yet again, this failure has to do with the nature of death and resurrection.

Jesus is doubted plenty of times in the gospels. In John, we find Jews who once believed in Jesus turning against him when he appears to claim parity with God—a telling passage that suggests John's awareness (and fear) of how a disciple can believe in Jesus sincerely yet also doubt his central claim. Matthew, too, contains a highly curious sentence near the end of his gospel, in which we learn that the "eleven disciples" go to Galilee to meet Jesus: "When they saw him, they worshipped him; but some doubted." This cryptic sentence, landing so close to the end of Matthew's gospel, has a strange and undeniable power. Matthew, like John, seems to recognize that belief and doubt are not always at war but kindred emotions within the same internal struggle. Note, too, that Matthew's doubters are not passersby or curious Pharisees but Jesus's chosen disciples. The typical scholarly argument holds that these passages exist because early Christian writers knew their stories were doubted and were forced to acknowledge that doubt as a rhetorical coping strategy.

Matthew's brief, glancing sentence about doubts felt by unnamed members of the Eleven becomes a brief but dramatically compelling scene in John.* We are presented with "the disciples"—who exactly or how many is not mentioned—in the immediate aftermath of Jesus's resurrection, holed up in a house in Jerusalem, the door of which is locked "for fear of the Jews." Earlier in the day, Mary Magdalene had visited the disciples and described her encounter with the risen Jesus outside his tomb. During that meeting, Jesus told Mary, "Do not hold on to me,

---

* Most scholars reject John as having any familiarity with Matthew, so Doubting Thomas was probably not the former's attempt to vivify the latter's mention of doubt among the Eleven. It is, however, highly likely that both stories grew out of the same core tradition—that some among Jesus's earliest followers doubted his resurrection.

because I have not yet ascended to my Father and your Father." Why the risen Jesus does not want to be held, and whether he *could* be held, John does not elucidate. His gospel nonetheless makes it clear that Jesus supernaturally enters the locked room in which his disciples hide. After greeting his disciples, Jesus blesses them with the Holy Spirit and promises that any sins they do not forgive will be "retained." With that, presumably, Jesus disappears.

John then reveals something interesting, which is that "Thomas (who was called the Twin), one of the twelve, was not with them when Jesus came." Where Thomas was, and what he was doing, are also not explained.* The disciples tell Thomas what has transpired ("We have seen the Lord"), but Thomas will hear none of it. "Unless I see the mark of the nails in his hands," he says, "and put my finger in the mark of the nails and my hand in his side, I will not believe." In Greek, these words, and the sentiment behind them, are even more vividly unpleasant. According to Glenn W. Most, the word Thomas uses to indicate his desire to "put" his hand in Jesus's side is actually much stronger in Greek; the verb means something akin to "throw" or "hurl." This is to say nothing of the pornographically ghastly vision of a man violating a friend's open wound with his fingers, which Most calls, with some understatement, "an unforgettable yet intolerable image."

The ideas at play here clearly have *something* to do with Jesus's earlier admonition to Mary Magdalene that she not hold him, but the most basic dialectic seems to be Thomas's desire to

---

* *The Book of the Resurrection,* which is attributed to Bartholomew, provides the reason for Thomas's absence from the locked room in John: Thomas was raising from the dead his own son, whom he promptly installs as a bishop in his local church. From there, Thomas travels back to his fellow disciples on a cloud. A more sophisticated Christian exegete such as John Chrysostom explained Thomas's absence by saying that God had arranged for him not to be there. The offering of his wounds was part of Jesus's plan to prove the reality of his resurrection, though one would think that Jesus's not being dead would stand as an equally persuasive piece of evidence.

be convinced that Jesus is not a ghost but something tangible—
someone who could be held if you wanted to hold him or touched
if you wanted to touch him.

Throughout Christian history, countless works of art and
exegesis have been based on Jesus's confronting Thomas and,
according to traditional understanding, allowing Thomas to
touch his wounds. Probably the most famous image devoted to
bringing the moment to life is Caravaggio's painting *The Incredu-
lity of Saint Thomas* or *Doubting Thomas,* which depicts Thomas
inserting his finger into the bloodless, almost labial wound in
Jesus's side, while Jesus firmly holds Thomas's probing hand
by the wrist. Like so many of Caravaggio's paintings, *Doubting
Thomas* is a deliberately erotic image, a case study in sacred/
profane balance-beam aesthetic gymnastics. One of the problems with the painting is that it helped popularize the notion
that Thomas did, in fact, touch Jesus's wounds. Among Christian intellectuals, the belief that Thomas touched Jesus's wounds
has been around since the second century, with Tertullian being
among the first to argue as much. Origen, who was later condemned as a heretic in part for his thoughts on the materiality
of Jesus's resurrected body, seems to have believed Jesus's ecto-
plasmic flesh could both resist Thomas's touch and pass through
doors. Augustine also believed Thomas touched Jesus, and the
vast majority of Christian exegetes since have followed suit.

Here, though, is how the Gospel According to John actually
describes Jesus's return the following week to convince Thomas
that he has been resurrected:

> A week later his disciples were again in the house, and
> Thomas was with them. Although the doors were shut,
> Jesus came and stood among them and said, "Peace
> be with you." Then he said to Thomas, "Put your fin-
> ger here and see my hands. Reach out your hand and
> put it in my side. Do not doubt but believe." Thomas
> answered him, "My Lord and my God!" Jesus said to

him, "Have you believed because you have seen me?
Blessed are those who have not seen and yet have
come to believe."

Obviously, imagining that Thomas touched Jesus's wounds
in the space between these sentences is an easy thing to do. The
mind almost wants or wills it to happen, given the savage terms
in which Thomas earlier framed his doubt.

Yet Most points out that "in supplying this kind of material
here, such readers are overlooking a small but decisive textual
fact," which is that Thomas's outburst is said specifically to have
"answered" Jesus's invitation. This may seem like a hairsplitting
argument, but the grammatical construction used in the scene
is, according to Most, quite clear. The New Testament, he notes,
contains over two hundred instances in which "quoted speech B
spoken by one person" comes after "quoted speech A spoken
by someone else." In every New Testament instance of this
grammatical construction, "speech B is a direct and immediate
response to speech A; speech B is caused directly by speech A,
not by any other event intervening between the two speeches."
John is giving us a scene in which Jesus offers Thomas the lux-
ury of touching his wounds, but Thomas is too stunned to do
so. Thomas, who has demanded a certain kind of proof, relents.

What is perhaps most remarkable about the entire scene is
how cunningly John appears to have escaped from the narrative
corner into which he has painted himself, even though the crux
of what Thomas wanted established—the nature of Jesus's resurrected body—remains an open question. Could the resurrected
Jesus be held or touched? Jesus's offer to Thomas ("Put your finger here") suggests that he could be. But in neglecting to depict
Thomas touching those wounds, John rather enigmatically failed
to resolve the issue.

The story of Thomas and the resurrected Jesus appears
nowhere else in the New Testament (though there is an echo
of wound touching in Luke), and Thomas has no other place

within the gospel tradition. Most believes that John, in perus-
ing lists of the Twelve, noted the etymological richness—the
doubleness—of Thomas's name, Twin, and settled upon him as
a perfect vessel to explore the nature of belief in Jesus's resurrection, which we know from asides in the gospels was being
attacked by doubters from the outset: John presents us with a
Jesus who is mistaken for a gardener outside his tomb; Luke
gives us a Jesus who does not resemble the man anyone remem-
bers; and Matthew describes a Jewish-devised cover story that
has the disciples stealing Jesus's body from its tomb while claiming their master rose from the dead. From this, we can deduce
that the gospels' various accounts of the resurrection were at
least partly defensive.

At the time of John's writing, there was precious little consensus about the meaning and mechanics of resurrection. The first
Christians were not at all certain of what the process entailed,
whether for Jesus or themselves. In John's gospel, Thomas wants
to touch Jesus's corporeal body; he wants to make sure the body
that died is the same body that has been resurrected. This is,
presumably, what a lot of Christians at the time wanted to know.

John seems to suggest that Christians have a literal, bodily
resurrection to look forward to but also that Jesus's resurrected
body is not quite a literal body. Jesus's resurrected body can eat
and (seemingly) be touched, but it is also a body that can appear
and disappear and pass through walls. Significantly, John's gospel contains another resurrection scene, which involves Lazarus.
Was there any difference between Lazarus's resurrected body
(which John's gospel assures us carried a "stench") and Jesus's
resurrected body? If so, whose resurrection did Christians have
to look forward to—a smelly resurrection like that of Lazarus or
a presumably pristine resurrection like that of Jesus?

Paul's Christian friends in Corinth had their own questions
about the resurrection. Prior to meeting Paul, many if not most
of the Corinthian Christians had been pagans. When it came to
questions of immortality, pagan ideas were less concerned with

the body than with the soul. The *bodily* resurrection of the dead was an entirely foreign concept to pagan thought, as it derived from relatively new ideas within Pharisaic Judaism. Despite the strenuous attempts of Paul, a former Pharisee, to communicate his ideas about bodily resurrection, the Corinthians remained bewildered.

In his first letter to the Corinthians, Paul quotes one of his Corinthian doubters: "How are the dead raised? With what kind of body do they come?" That Paul deems the person who asked this question a "fool" surely says something about his frustration. In Paul's mind, the resurrection of the dead is the soil of Christian belief: "Now if Christ is proclaimed as raised from the dead, how can some of you say there is no resurrection of the dead? If there is no resurrection of the dead, then Christ has not been raised, and if Christ has not been raised, then our proclamation has been in vain and your faith has been in vain." The careful reader of Paul will note that whenever he hits the thrusters on circular restatement, he knows he is in a philosophical black hole and is desperately trying to escape it.

Most of Paul's thoughts on the resurrection of the dead can be found in 1 Corinthians, and scholars and Christian exegetes alike have long been puzzled by what exactly he was trying to say. The main thrust of his argument appears to be that the body will be raised but in different form: "Not all flesh is alike, but there is one flesh for human beings, another for animals, another for birds, and another for fish. There are both heavenly bodies and earthly bodies, but the glory of the heavenly is one thing, and that of the earthly is another." Both the zoology and the astronomy here are flawed, to say the least,* but we can at least

---

* The second-century anti-Christian writer Celsus was apparently aware of Paul's teaching on this issue, to which he issued a stern, professorial rebuttal: "All animals have a single common nature; this nature passes through changes and subsists in many different forms, returning in the end to what it originally was; yet no product of matter is immortal."

appreciate Paul's metaphorical zeal. "What is sown is perishable," Paul goes on, "what is raised is imperishable. . . . It is sown in weakness, it is raised in power. . . . If there is a physical body, there is also a spiritual body." Later in the letter, Paul argues that Adam, the first man, and Jesus are forever linked through sin and resurrection: "For since death came through a human being, the resurrection of the dead has also come through a human being, for as all die in Adam, so all will be made alive in Christ."

Paul could not deny for his faith's sake that what is resurrected is a body of some kind, but he was also too smart to maintain that what is resurrected is *merely* a body. He thus created a kind of third body, earthly and familiar yet also elevated and spiritually endowed. To make any argument that eschewed the importance of an earthly body seriously harmed early Christians' enthusiasm for resurrection, the area in which they needed (and today's Christians continue to need) the most reassurance.

The resurrection of the dead is where Christianity offers the greatest hope and the least conspicuous guidance. As Paul's letter to the Corinthians and the Gospel According to John establish, the resurrection probably cannot be convincingly expressed, dramatized, or conceptualized in any language human beings are capable of. The thing that Thomas doubted is the thing we continue to doubt; the proof that Thomas wanted is the proof we continue to want. According to John's gospel, Thomas never got his proof on the terms he originally desired. Doubting Thomas doubted for good reason.

V.

I had booked my Chennai hotel room over the phone, making sure to ask the reservation manager whether his hotel was within walking distance of Saint Thomas Basilica, the supposed resting place of Thomas. The reservation manager was happy to tell me that Saint Thomas Basilica was most certainly within walking distance, as was St. Thomas Mount, where Thomas was supposedly martyred. I booked a room. Then I looked at several maps of Chennai.

The next day I called the hotel and told the manager I was having a hard time reckoning how what he told me could possibly be true. He said, "No, sir. Both are in walking distance, sir." As it turned out, he was correct, at least in the sense that New York and Philadelphia are also within walking distance. The basilica, found in a neighborhood called Mylapore, was a four-mile stroll from my hotel's front door. St. Thomas Mount, meanwhile, was almost eight miles away from the hotel in the opposite direction. Months later, once I had settled into the hotel, I asked if I could have a friendly word with the reservation manager who had so misled me. He no longer worked for the hotel, I was told.

I tried to get to know the exhaust-choked commercial district of Chennai in which my sickness had sequestered me. Until 1996—when many Indian cities were renamed in accord with resurgent feelings of nationalism—Chennai was called Madras; many today still refer to the city as Madras. (Chennaipatnam and Madraspatnam were the names of small adjacent villages out of which the city later grew. Chennai was apparently thought to be the more historically authentic of the two names.) The capital of the Tamil Nadu state and the fourth-largest city in India, Chennai is known as "the gateway to the south," and, indeed, every non-Indian tourist I met was headed south (or north, east, or west) as fast as he or she could go. Why? "Because," I was told, "Chennai is India's most boring city." A backpacker I ran into told me he was getting out of Chennai, too, because it was not the "real India."

On my second day in Chennai, I dammed my GI tract with Imodium and set out to find some Indian food, which I imagined would be cheerfully vended on every corner. I walked for twenty minutes and passed several bakeries and two Domino's Pizzas before coming upon an Indian restaurant that promised "high-class all only vegetarian" food. The offerings looked fantastic; the long line of waiting patrons was doubly heartening. After thirty minutes in line, I arrived at the counter to discover there was no menu. Everyone here was ordering his or her favorites and eating with his or her hands out of wicker baskets. I wound up asking the man behind the counter to make me the house special. A moment later, I was eating something he called "cottage cheese chile" out of my own wicker basket. Delicious. Three hours later, I was back in my hotel room, my internal Imodium dam having suffered a severe structural breakdown. That night, for dinner, I enjoyed a plain slice of pizza courtesy of Domino's, whose customers were the only overweight Indians I saw in Chennai.

What Chennai lacked in Indian restaurants it made up for in twenty-four-hour emergency care hospitals. On my way back from Domino's, I walked past several such establishments, including one called the Fracture and Chest Injury Clinic. What I needed was the Ceaseless Diarrhea Clinic. I began to wonder, not unseriously, if I would ever get well. Then, on my third morning in Chennai, I ventured into the city for the first time with no stomach medicine coursing through my system.

It was a good day: only slightly hellishly hot, the sky so densely blue it seemed as though it were a smooth, cool cove ceiling I could reach up and place my hand against. I had planned to go for a short walk, but suddenly thought, *Why* not *walk eight miles to St. Thomas Mount?* In the sixteenth century, Portuguese missionaries had built a small, pretty church (I had, by now, looked at its picture on the Internet many times) atop the mount, at the sight of which arriving Portuguese ships would joyfully fire their cannons. Today the church housed a museum with an audacious collection of supposed relics. Among its treasures was the cross Thomas collapsed on when he died, which was "discovered" by a Portuguese priest during an early renovation of the church and which wept copious tears of blood and water on the eighteenth day of December every year from 1558 to 1704. ("It is strange that since the year 1704," one local Christian writes, "these wonderful occurrences have stopped short."

Strange indeed!) Hanging above the church's altar, meanwhile, was one of the seven paintings of Mary tradition attributed to the multitalented evangelist Luke; Indian Christians believe that Thomas somehow hauled this Mary portrait with him to India.

One odd thing about Indian Christianity is its unsmiling absolutism about legendary material. Indian Christians are fundamentalists about legends. The cross did not become a common devotional object until the fourth century, so the idea that one of the Twelve was carrying one when he died is historically risible. Every Indian Christian I spoke with about this matter maintained, no, that cannot be accurate, that was the cross Thomas held as he died, that is our tradition, our traditions are accurate.* It is also well-known that Mary was of relatively little interest to the first Christians, and there is absolutely no record of cultic devotion to her until the mid-second century. Any notion of Luke's painting Mary's portrait is obviously ahistorical—a third- or fourth-stage development in the legends that grew around her. Share this with a serious-minded, intellectually sophisticated Indian Christian, however, and prepare yourself for a lecture arguing the contrary.

In 1955, Rajendra Prasad, the first president of India and a Hindu, said something very revealing at a Thomas celebration in New Delhi: "Saint Thomas came to India when many of the countries of Europe had not yet become Christian, and so these Indians who trace their Christianity to him have a longer and higher ancestry than that of Christians of many European countries. And it is really a matter of pride to us that it so happened." Christianity came to India early; of that there is no doubt. It is even possible that someone named Thomas was responsible for bringing Christianity to India. The idea that this man was born in Roman Palestine in the first century, and served as

---

* There are some extremely old stone crosses in Kerala, where Thomas is supposed to have begun his missionary activity. A few are older than many extant Hindu sculptures in the same region. However, they do not date back to the first century.

one of Jesus's original followers, is not likely. But Indian Christians* want something more than the bragging rights of having encountered the Christian faith six hundred years before Russia, nine hundred years before Sweden, or a thousand years before Lithuania.

Most Christian communities have imagined fanciful pasts for themselves; you might say this is a very Christian thing to do. However, not even the pope claims with absolute certainty that Peter's remains lie beneath the Vatican. Yet one recently published book—by an Indian Ph.D., no less—contains this sentence: "The date A.D. 52 is now accepted by most scholars as the one that marks the arrival of St. Thomas at the then well known port of Cranganore, in Malabar." No non-Indian scholar accepts any such thing. The date, as with all dates involving the Twelve, is historically unverifiable.

It was now 8:30 a.m. If I made it to St. Thomas Mount in three or four hours, I could take an auto rickshaw back to the hotel by mid-afternoon. I had with me a decent map. This was no problem. Walking to St. Thomas Mount? Yes. Good to see the real India.

Problem 1: Chennai is not a walking town. A lot of sidewalks along major roads (the roads, in other words, I had mapped for) terminated without warning, meaning that, quite suddenly, I was walking down a laneless road, horns beeping everywhere, cars just missing me, rickshaw drivers covering their eyes from the flying dust and tire-launched gravel. After my fifth near visit to the local Fracture and Chest Injury Clinic, I attempted to take a different path to St. Thomas Mount, becoming gradually aware of:

Problem 2: A large number of Chennai's streets are

---

* And not just Indian Christians. The scholar Robert Eric Frykenberg, after summarizing some of the legends behind Thomas's missionary activity, writes that it is "entirely plausible to conclude that such events might have involved the Apostle Thomas himself."

unmarked, and many that are marked have no English translation. Not that this mattered anyway, because:

Problem 3: Much of Chennai looked identical to me. I should have been ready for this. When my driver Dave was showing me around Chennai two days before, he would tell me we were in a wealthy neighborhood, or a university neighborhood, or a bad neighborhood, all of which looked exactly the same. You saw this in a certain kind of Asian city. It was often unclear whether a home was a roofless barnyard or a queenly palace until you ventured past the compound walls. In all but the most ostentatious cases, personal wealth in many Asian countries was not easily gauged from a sidewalk. You had to go inside. This was interesting to think about, but not right now, because right now my stomach problems were returning, which horribly revealed:

Problem 4: Chennai has no public restrooms—not unless quiet alleyways counted as public restrooms. (Apparently, to many, they did.) Great molten marbles of gastrointestinal agony rolled through me as I staggered from bread shop to furniture store, asking if anyone had a restroom. No one did. I finally found a public restroom, in, of course, Domino's Pizza, from which I emerged sadly resigned to taking an auto rickshaw for the remainder of my long trip to the mount, which brought me up against:

Problem 5: Rickshaw drivers in Chennai did not seem to know where anything in Chennai was located. "St. Thomas," I said to the driver, a drowsy, older man whose face had turned into dark crocodilian armor under the Indian sun. He stared at me diffidently. With his big white bushy mustache, he looked like the negative image of some tiger-stalking British hunter in his sunset years. "St. Thomas Mount. Do you know?"

"Yes, yes," he said. "I know."

We drove for a while. I could see what I assumed was St. Thomas Mount in the distance. We were moving in an opposite direction from it. "Excuse me?" I said, and pointed. "Isn't that the mount over there?"

"Church coming," he said.

The mount grew more distant. When we stopped at something called Our Lady Chapel, the driver said that would be three hundred rupees, please. "Sir," I said, "this is not a mount. This is a chapel."

The man climbed out of his auto rickshaw and went and discussed the issue with a fellow rickshaw driver. Broken glass and small sharp rocks covered the street, over which my driver trod without noticeable reaction. When he returned, he nodded at me reassuringly and started up his rickshaw. Ten minutes later, we stopped at the New Life Church, a plain white wooden building. Outside the New Life Church, a dozen young Indians were handing out pamphlets, one of which said, "'How can you believe when you accept glory from one another and do not seek the glory that comes from the one who alone is God?'—John 5:44." The quotation seemed to be a Christian torpedo aimed directly at the dreadnought of Hinduism. So the New Life Church's partisans were hard-core Protestant Indians hectoring Hindus, Muslims, and fellow Christians alike to heed the words of the most inflexible, cartoonish brand of Christianity foreign missionaries had to offer. By all evidence, these missionaries were having a good deal of success in India: Evangelical Christianity is one of the country's fastest-growing sects, and today India has at least ten times as many Christian missionaries preaching within its borders as it has had at any other time in recorded history.

The New Life Church had one thing going for it. This was its outstandingly clean bathroom, which I took great pleasure in defiling. Afterward, I walked outside, booked another auto rickshaw driver, and told him where I wanted to go. Minutes later, my face was plunged into my hands as I noticed that, once again, we were traveling *away* from St. Thomas Mount. The driver, thankfully, turned around.

The most prominent description of Thomas's supposed martyrdom occurs in the apocryphal *Acts of Thomas* but does not specify on which of Chennai's two mounts Thomas met his end. Tradition has evolved to place his death on the larger of the two mounts, which at three hundred feet above sea level was not terribly large. In Tamil, St. Thomas Mount is called Parangi Malai. Its name derives from *Pfarangi,* a term used in India to describe the Portuguese. *Pfarangi,* or "Frank," was apparently first used by Middle Eastern Muslims to describe Christian crusaders, and its employment by Indians suggests how deeply Muslim thought patterns and designations penetrated even distant lands to which Islam spread. The mount was called Parangi Malai due to the number of Portuguese who had once settled at its base; the Portuguese themselves called it Monte Grande. Once upon a time, the mount was a densely forested area filled with tigers and cobras, but today its grounds had been groomed with public-park efficiency. Along the mount's main road, one of India's best military academies was located.

At the base of the mount, in what I gathered was a poor neighborhood, I asked the driver to stop. I thought it would be nice, or nicer, to walk up to the church rather than ride. The driver seemed to think this was an unusual request. Only when I insisted on paying him did he shrug and drive away. I had taken perhaps a hundred steps when another rifle shot sounded in my stomach, one so intense I staggered to a nearby fruit stand and steadied myself against its rusty blue frame. I stood there, breathing, watching some black piglets roll around near a pile of fragrantly burning garbage. Whether the piglets rolled from joy or madness I could not decide. Also watching the piglets were four young Indian men, who noticed me watching them. They walked over.

I knew I could only imagine—and probably not very accurately—the irritation felt by a poor young Indian living at the base of St. Thomas Mount, who day after day watched rickshaws and taxis carry Westerners and wealthy Thomas Christians through their neighborhood and beneath the mount's grand arched entrance. I stood there, hunched over in pain, leaning against the fruit stand, doing my best not to look at or challenge the four young Indians, whose wide, mean grins said everything there was to say about their feelings for who I was and what, to them, I represented. My eyes found the face of the ancient shopkeeper whose rusty booth I was leaning against. My shy, pleading smile at her was not returned. One of the four young men said something in Tamil, and the others began laughing in the weird, synchronous way young men laugh when unified in malign intent. I looked over at them.

They were barefoot. The knees of their pants had been worn thin against the orb of their patellae. Their collared shirts were dirty, opened, buttonless. Their teeth were cavitied. Two of the boys had managed to grow tiny maître d' mustaches. They were still speaking in Tamil. I waited for them to go away; I would be a good sport. Poor, powerless kids laughing: surely that was their prerogative. The figure I cut was not exactly dashing, after all. I was sweaty and pale; I had not shaved in a week. Too much travel, too much food, too many hotels, not enough exercise. I always figured that being challenged by young men when I traveled was the insider's grand but harmless nihilistic gesture against the outsider. With young men, we are essentially talking about cavemen living according to cavemen rules and cavemen assumptions. But I was no longer in my twenties; I was a long way from my twenties. Cavemen logic had long since ceased to make any emotional sense to me.

I posed no challenge to the young Indians. Graying, overweight, physically unimpressive. I was probably the same age as their fathers. But okay. They could watch me suffer. They could watch me fight back my opening bowels. After the pain passed and I had straightened up, the young men rearranged themselves so that I had no way to walk toward the mount's arched entrance without brushing past one of them. And this, it turned out, was too much to ask of me.

I said, "Could one of you idiots fucking move, please?"

The ancient shopkeeper said something to the young men in Tamil, dispersing them. I walked away from her food stall, toward the mount's arched entrance. The young men, meanwhile, walked across the street but stayed close to one another. I became fairly sure they were going to regroup and reengage with me as I made my way up the hill, away from the eyes of the shopkeeper. This was exactly what they did. I heard them fall in behind me, still muttering, still laughing. The mount's arched entrance was thirty yards ahead.

Tonight I would sleep on sheets as white as tundra; they would descend into dreams with the stench of burning garbage in their nostrils. I tried to remember that. Not as comfort, but as a way to remind myself why my obvious unhappiness could give anyone else pleasure.

The arch was now twenty yards away. Above it arced the words of the Twenty-Third Psalm: THE LORD IS MY SHEPHERD. Then I stopped, turned around, and planted myself there in the middle of the street. The young men seemed surprised that I decided to confront them. I scanned their faces, trying to find the leader. Nothing. No one. Here was a quadrumvirate of leaderless equals.

"Look," I said. "What do you want?" I threw my arms out. "What do you want? I'm a guest here. A visitor. I'm visiting this mount, which is important to many Indians. What do you want?"

None answered. Less than a quarter of Indians speak English, I recalled reading. So, without really thinking about it, thinking only of my frustration, I kicked some dirt at the young Indians. A few older Indians were watching us now, though not with much concern or interest. One of the young men kicked dirt back at me. I took a step closer, which caused two of them to burst out laughing, and the others quickly joined in. I looked defeatedly around the neighborhood. Inside the nearby, dark little houses I could see six, seven people stirring. Chickens high stepped around, dragging manure and animalcules everywhere they went. Cows standing around, huge and stupid, shit pouring out of them. The Indians in this and many neighborhoods used that shit as a reliable fire source.

I turned around, the twisty road ahead of me lined with palm trees and bushes as spiky and perilous as medieval armaments. I passed beneath the mount's gateway arch—the young men did not follow—and walked until I found a small, fenced-in area, called "Jesus in Gethsemane," its resident statue a brightly painted, magnificently bearded, unusually tacky Jesus who stood at least fifteen feet tall. I kept walking up the road. As I climbed, a vista of Chennai pooled out before me, the mostly low buildings seeming to huddle protectively under a gauzy layer of smog. For the first time, I saw how huge Chennai was, how like a vast smoke sea. A taxi came at me, down the road, on its windshield a sticker that read, PRAISE THE LORD. At the top of the mount, finally, was a big parking lot scattered with bright red dirt and lined with tropical trees, rickshaw drivers everywhere, and over yonder a stone stairway that led up to the church itself.

Once again, I was sick, but up the stairs I went, up to the white church, do I really need to describe it, a white church on a hill, the Christian tracts sold everywhere, little pamphlety broadsides filled with blurry photographs and an array of fascinating misspellings, tell me where on earth is the bathroom, sweat pouring down my back, put away your notebook, it is no longer needed, do not care about Thomas, he was not martyred here, please India give me a break, please India praise the Lord, throw the latch on the door and squat and *actually* is it *really* are you *really* are those tears? Oh you *are* sick are you not dear boy weeping in a church bathroom where your namesake was run through with a spear.

VI.

By the end of the first century, what scholars call the Thomas movement was operating in Syria; by the third century, it was active in India. Today, many of the world's surviving non-European Christian communities trace themselves back, wholly or partially, to Thomas. The great thirteenth-century

Christian philosopher Gregory Bar Hebraeus, a bishop in the Syriac Orthodox Church, went so far as to call Thomas "the first pope of the East." That Thomas traveled to eastern lands, and saw great missionary success within them, is one of the earliest and most widely attested pieces of apostolic lore.

The Thomas movement was, at least in part, a missionary effort on behalf of the Church of the East, which survives to this day in the form of the Assyrian Church of the East, whose patriarch, oddly, lives in exile in Chicago, Illinois. This theologically and culturally distinct church claims as its founders Peter (due to his having supposedly founded the church in Antioch and a mention in 1 Peter of having been written from "Babylon"), Thomas, Bartholomew, Thaddaeus, and Mari (whom tradition cites as having been one of Luke's Seventy Disciples). Its theology, however, earned it a different name in antiquity: the Nestorian Church.

Nestorius, the fifth-century bishop of Constantinople, did not formulate the theological position to which he inadvertently gave his name, but his prominence, not to mention his argumentative and unbending nature, has made him one of history's great scapegraces in the eyes of Christian orthodoxy. The difficult issue was the nature of Jesus's humanity. Nestorius argued that Mary, whom he regarded as fallibly, sinfully human, was incapable of bringing to term a fully divine Jesus. Nestorius argued that Jesus was, in effect, human on his mother's side and that his human and divine selves were separate entities within him. Jesus's humanity (or lack thereof) had been troubling Christian intellectuals for centuries; the formulation of the Nicene Creed in 325 did little to define terms. Nestorius's argument was opposed by proponents of the rapidly growing cult of Mary, and Cyril, the bishop of Alexandria, led a campaign against what was becoming known as Nestorianism, even though Nestorius was far from its only proponent.

The emperor Theodosius attempted to settle the matter at the Council of Ephesus in 431. When Nestorius arrived, unfortunately, he was not allowed to speak. Nothing was settled beyond the mealy compromise that Jesus Christ was both fully divine and a perfect human; all sides of the debate left the council displeased. Nestorius was driven out of his bishopric and exiled to Egypt.

How Jesus's human and divine natures coexisted was again addressed at the Council of Chalcedon in 451. (Nestorius was invited to participate but died days before he received his invitation.) The council's ruling—one of the most important rulings in the history of Christian orthodoxy—held that Jesus was "perfect in divinity and perfect in humanity, the same truly God and truly man, of a rational soul and a body; consubstantial with the Father as regards his divinity, and same consubstantial with us as regards his humanity." This compromise-driven definition remains the mainline position among Eastern Orthodox, Roman Catholic, and Protestant Christians, but it drove away many ancient believers in Jesus. Among them were those who believed Jesus's nature was that of one fully divine being (Monophysites), those who believed Jesus's humanity and divinity were of one insuperable nature (Miaphysites), and those who believed within Jesus were separately human and divine selves traceable to his uniquely complicated parentage (Dyophysites). After Chalcedon, these Christians (Armenians, Copts, Nestorians) broke free from the imperial church. In many cases, they also broke free from one another: even today many non-Chalcedonian churches refuse formal contact. To spread its good news, "Nestorianism" traveled elsewhere, far beyond the borders of the Roman world and its theological enforcers. By the seventh or eighth century, any form of Eastern Christianity that ran afoul of Christian orthodoxy was being called Nestorian.

The most powerful and populous non-Chalcedonian church was, for centuries, the Church of the East. Syriac Christianity had a major influence on the Church of the East, and Syriac Christians, of course, claimed Thomas the apostle as their founder and legitimizer. In the fourth chapter of Matthew, we read of how Jesus's "fame spread throughout all Syria," which reminds us how easily Christianity could have remained a predominantly Middle Eastern or Asian faith, with its capital planted not in Rome but in Babylon or Edessa. Syriac Christian missionaries were active in Central Asia, China, the islands of the Persian Gulf, the foothills of the Himalayas, and Sri Lanka. The Church of the East even managed to win over a family of Mongols to the Christian faith, among them a princess who married one of Jenghiz Khan's sons.* Initially, at least, these Christians met with little hostility; the Parthians in particular seemed unusually open to Christian thought. But eastward-moving Christians had little institutional protection or support and were largely cut off from the rest of Christianity. Theirs was also often a deeply monastic and combative form of Christianity, waging what one scholar describes as "Christian life-warfare against the world." But the Church of the East, which at one point was well positioned to lead a large part of the Christian world, was inexorably affected, and hindered, by the rise of Islam.

When, in the second century, Christianity first entered Edessa, the capital of the tiny independent kingdom of Osrhoene (today found in Turkey, about four hundred miles northeast of Palestine), it was an independent city-state relatively uncolored by the philosophical influence of Hellenism or the civic influence of Rome. Furthermore, Syriac, the language spoken throughout Edessa and Osrhoene, was closely related to Aramaic, the language used by Jesus and his original followers, which allowed Syriac-speaking Christians to feel a certain amount of (arguably justified) linguistic chauvinism.† The original founders of

---

* These modest success stories eventually gave rise to the medieval legend of Prester John, who was said to rule a fantastical Christian kingdom in the middle of the Orient replete with a fountain of youth, a mirror that allowed the viewer to gaze upon any region in the world, and the palace of the patriarch of all Thomas Christians.

† Greek overtook Aramaic as Christianity's lingua franca shockingly quickly. Many later Greek- and Latin-speaking Christians thought poorly of Jesus's linguistic descendants. When Jerome tried living in Chalcis among Syriac-speaking monks, he

Osrhoene were Nabataean Arabs. They had no natural place in the Roman Empire to the west or the Parthian Empire to the east, both of which routinely squeezed the region and its capital city. In this challenging religious and geopolitical climate, Edessa somehow managed to become one of the greatest centers of Christian learning of its age.

Eusebius, in his fourth-century history of the church, said virtually nothing about Syriac Christianity. He did, however, tell a story about Edessa that involves Thomas. In Eusebius's account, a "brilliantly successful monarch" named King Abgar V Ukkama was "dying from a terrible physical disorder" in Edessa. But Abgar heard "continual mention" of a Galilean healer named Jesus, to whom he dispatched a royal messenger. Abgar, who wanted Jesus to come to Edessa and miraculously heal him, concluded his letter in this way: "I may add that I understand Jews are treating you with contempt and desire to injure you: my city is very small, but highly esteemed, adequate for both of us." The first line of Jesus's response letter to Abgar: "Happy are you who believed in me without having seen me!" (This is, of course, a gloss on what Jesus says to Thomas in John's locked room: "Blessed are those who have not yet seen and yet have come to believe.") Jesus, according to Eusebius, "did not immediately accede to [Abgar's] request," explaining, "I must complete all that I was sent to do here." However, Jesus assured Abgar that once he was "taken up to the One," he would send a chosen disciple to heal him. "In a very short time," Eusebius wrote, "the promise was fulfilled. After His resurrection and ascent into heaven, Thomas, one of the Twelve apostles, was moved by inspiration to send Thaddaeus, himself in the list of Christ's seventy disci-

---

referred to their language as "barbarous gibberish," even though Syriac was widely spoken among Christians outside the Roman Empire. Indeed, Syriac served as the literary and liturgical language of most "Eastern" Christians, whether Syrian, Babylonian, Persian, or, later, Chinese and Indian. It remains the liturgical language of several Christian sects today, including Lebanon's Maronite Church.

ples, to Edessa as preacher and evangelist of the teachings about Christ."

Eusebius assured his readers that "written evidence of these things is available, taken from the Record Office at Edessa," and further claimed that he had "extracted" various other documents from the Edessan archives, including a Syriac document describing Thaddaeus's visit, which begins, "After Jesus was taken up, Judas, also known as Thomas, sent to him as an apostle Thaddaeus, one of the Seventy." Here we find ourselves in a predictable apostolic bramble; yet again the tricksy name Judas complicates the proceedings. Thomas is never referred to as Judas in the New Testament, and Thaddaeus—whose place among the Twelve Eusebius makes quite unclear (it is possible he means another Thaddaeus)—is replaced with "Judas of James" in Luke's and Acts' apostolic lists. So who is actually who? A few later retellings of this tradition are highly confused as to whether someone named Thaddaeus, Judas, Thomas, or Judas Thomas delivered the letter to Abgar.

Although Abgar was a historical figure, the story of his letter swap with Jesus is legendary. Even many ancient Christians disputed the story, among them Augustine and Jerome, who were adamant in their belief that Jesus wrote nothing down. While Eusebius might have been fibbing about personally "extracting" the documents from the Edessan archives, a more reasonable explanation is that such documents did exist, and Eusebius did in fact find them, but they were fabrications written by Syriac Christians wishing to give themselves and their church ecclesiastical authority.

Edessa, which thought of itself as the Rome of its region, was home to a busily scribbling group of Christian storytellers and fabulists whose stories proved remarkably successful in passing into the wider Christian tradition, even though the Syriac-speaking Christians responsible for these stories were regarded as Nestorian heretics by many other Christians. The city was also home to an evangelical missionary movement to the east, especially into Parthia (northeastern Iran), which is where Eusebius, and many other ancient Christians, placed Thomas the apostle's primary activities.

Much of this story is told in *The Acts of Thomas,* which one scholar calls "the oldest surviving account left by any congregation beyond the frontiers of the Roman Empire in the East." Most likely, *The Acts of Thomas* was originally written in the second or third century in Edessa. Its ancient popularity is obvious: versions of the text turn up in Arabic, Coptic, Greek, and several other languages. Although Western Christians looked askance at many aspects of Thomas's *Acts,* its official denunciation by the church did not occur until the sixteenth century.

You know you are in for a strange reading experience—even by apocryphal standards—when in the opening moments of *The Acts of Thomas* Jesus sells Thomas into slavery. Jesus is forced to do this because Thomas tells him flatly, "I am not going to the Indians." Unfortunately for Thomas, a merchant by the name of Abban happens by. Abban has been dispatched by a certain king Gondaphorus to find a suitable carpenter or builder for a new palace. Jesus approaches Abban, slyly introduces himself as "son of the carpenter Joseph," and tells him that Thomas is his slave and a good builder to boot. Jesus will, he says, sell Thomas to Abban if Abban wishes. Abban agrees to the deal, approaches Thomas, and asks if Jesus is indeed his master. Thomas says, "Yes, he is my Lord," thus stepping into the semantic trap Jesus has laid for him.

Eventually, Thomas meets Gondaphorus and agrees to build for him a large, splendid palace. Thomas tells Gondaphorus what he needs ("wood, ploughs, yokes, balances, and pulls, and ships and oars and masts") and Gondaphorus, impressed, immediately hands him the money to begin work. But Thomas spends all of Gondaphorus's money on the poor and needy in the surrounding villages. When Gondaphorus gets wind of this, he begins to ponder the manner in which he will kill Thomas. Before Gondaphorus can act, his brother, Gad, falls into a deep sickness and has a vision of Gondaphorus's palace, which has indeed been built by Thomas, but in Heaven rather than on earth. When Gad returns from his dream, he tells his brother what he saw. Soon enough, the brothers' souls are put "at ease" by Thomas, and both are baptized.

It is, of course, possible that Thomas, or someone like him, reached India in the first century. Certainly, we know Rome traded with India during that time. It is also true that Judaism had been a small part of life on the subcontinent as early as the fifth century BCE, shortly after the end of the Jews' Babylonian captivity. India's ancient trading cities and villages on the Malabar Coast, many of which are today associated with Thomas's missionary activity, were once known for their Arab and Jewish merchant communities. One of the first churches supposedly founded by Thomas, in a river port village known as Niranam, claims to serve the oldest Christian community in the world, having been continuously operating, according to local tradition, since 54 CE. What seems distinctly less possible is that *The Acts of Thomas* has anything to tell us about what happened to Thomas the apostle in India. Several scholars argue that when ancient Christians wrote of Thomas traveling to "India," it could have meant, literally, anywhere. Certain historical findings, however, have led a small group of scholars, most of them Indian, to argue even more vociferously that the stories in *The Acts of Thomas* are true in their broad outlines.

Take, for instance, King Gondaphorus. In the mid-nineteenth century, several coins bearing his Greek name (Gondophares) were found around Kabul. (They are today displayed in a museum in Lahore, Pakistan.) Gondaphorus, or Gundaphar, far from being a figment of some Edessan storyteller's imagination, appears to have ruled a kingdom in the Parthian Empire near modern-day Peshawar from 19 to 55 CE, and his name may have some relation to the Taliban stronghold city Kandahar

in Afghanistan.* The Parthian king's proclivity for building is
recorded on one of the coins bearing his name, greatly excit-
ing those who wish to believe the historical Thomas had deal-
ings with him. However, most kings tend to be builders, because
building is what ensures a king's legacy. It would probably be
harder to search through history for an ancient king *not* inclined
to build things. Surely, word of the real Gundaphar could have
easily passed into the hearing and consequently the imagination
of the anonymous Syrian Christian or Christians who wrote *The
Acts of Thomas*. For these writers, finding out the name of the
king who lived in roughly the right place at roughly the right
time might well have been as easy as dropping by the Edessan
"Record Office" mentioned by Eusebius.

Whether fantasy, fact, or some mixture thereof, *The Acts of
Thomas* is not an Indian document; Indian Christians did not
write it. In fact, no Tamil or Dravidian source has anything at all
to say about Christians or Christianity until the fourth century.
But the stories told in the *Acts* are clearly related in some way to
the earliest sagas and songs Indian Christian families have been
sharing with one another for at least seventeen hundred years.

Within India, there are two competing stories about Thomas's arrival. A "northern" or "western" tradition (which appears
to have its origins in stories told by Christian missionaries from

---

* He might also be related in some way to Caspar (also known as Gaspar, Gathaspa,
Jaspar, and Jaspas), one of the "three wise men from the east," who, in the Gospel
According to Matthew, uses a star to seek out the birth of Jesus. (The names of the
Magi are not provided by Matthew, however, and apparently derive from a Greek
manuscript probably composed in Alexandria around 500 CE.) A question not often
asked: What on earth are these thuriferous and presumably Zoroastrian wise men
from Persia even *doing* in the New Testament? The scholar Martin Hengel refers
to the Magi's prominence in Matthew as a vestigial mark of Hellenistic respect for
"the mysterious, age-old wisdom of barbarian peoples . . . from whom answers were
sought to questions of life which remained inaccessible to rational thought." In later
Christian stories, Thomas became a kind of guided missile toward these archetypal
wisdom lovers. John Chrysostom approvingly noted the legend that has Thomas
coming across the Magi in Persia and baptizing them.

Persia and Syria) claims that Thomas arrived in India overland,
via Persia or Central Asia. A "southern" or "eastern" tradition
(bolstered by internal Indian sources almost entirely derived
from local languages) maintains that Thomas arrived from the
sea and landed on India's western Malabar Coast. Beyond that,
the two traditions have a few commonalities, including tales
of Thomas's building a palace for a local ruler and the manner
of his death. While the earliest manifestation of the northern
tradition remains unknown, *The Acts of Thomas* is its literary
apotheosis.

The southern tradition, conversely, is exemplified in the
songs and oral traditions of Indian Christianity. The *Thomma
Parvam*, or "Song of Thomas," is the oldest internal account of
Thomas's arrival and is still sung at some Thomas Christian wedding ceremonies. It establishes the key elements of the southern
tradition: Thomas landed on an island off the coast of Malabar,
sailed around India, and stopped at Mylapore (or modern-day
Chennai); went to China; came back to Malabar, settled in Thiru-
vanchikulam (near the ancient city of Muziris), and oversaw the
seven Christian communities with which he became associated;
attracted high-caste Indians with his uprightness; left again for
Mylapore; and was martyred by angry Brahmans. The various
local traditions that place Thomas in India were not fully collated until the twentieth century, and the first major book on
the subject appeared in 1905. Most of the writers to cast their
eyes on these traditions since have been bishops, vicars, rever-
ends, priests, or scholars belonging to or associated with various Thomas sects. These Christians have sought to preserve the
Thomas stories' historical integrity, pointing out the numerous
similarities within competing strands of the Thomas tradition.
These similarities exist, but *The Acts of Thomas* has much more
in common with other apocryphal *Acts*. It opens with an apostle lamenting his chosen site of missionary activity, includes a
detailed naval journey, describes the apostle being held and tortured by a foreign king whose wife proves susceptible to apos-

tolic teaching, and so on. Very clearly there developed in early Christian storytelling a useful narrative template into and out of which various apostles could be swapped.

Undoubtedly, the most famous piece of heterodox Christian literature associated with Thomas is *The Gospel of Thomas,* which was discovered in a Coptic translation in 1945 at the Egyptian village of Nag Hammadi. Once the Coptic text was published, scholars recognized that it was similar to fragments of an earlier Greek text found in an ancient dump near the Egyptian city of Oxyrhynchus in the 1890s.

Most scholars believe *The Gospel of Thomas*'s original language was Greek, and its estimated dates of composition range from the 50s to the 150s. Although the text's author puts himself forward as Judas Thomas (actually, "Judas Thomas the Twin"), as does the author of *The Acts of Thomas,* and though this author claims to have received secret knowledge from Jesus, as does the author of *The Acts of Thomas,* the works are not believed to have any literary connection, though they may have a distant theological connection. As it happens, *The Gospel of Thomas* is not a gospel at all; it is, rather, a narrativeless series of sayings, some of them quite odd. (An especially strange saying likens God's Kingdom to an assassin!) Many revered teachers in the ancient world saw their words enshrined in "sayings" documents of this type. And while a circle of eager students could be moved to delighted perplexity by the sayings contained in *The Gospel of Thomas,* it is hard to imagine a social or religious movement being inspired by it.

Roughly half of *The Gospel of Thomas* will seem familiar to the close reader of the canonical gospels. For instance, *The Gospel of Thomas* has Jesus boldly flouting circumcision, just as he occasionally flouts the Law in the canonical gospels: "If [circumcision] were useful, children's fathers would produce them already circumcised from their mothers." One brash saying corresponds to John's depiction of Jesus as the root of all earthly creation: "I am the light that is over all things. I am all: From me all has come forth, and to me all has reached. Split a piece of wood; I am there. Lift up the stone, and you will find me there." Among the most interesting correspondences is *The Gospel of Thomas*'s version of what is appropriately rendered unto Caesar. "Give Caesar the things that are Caesar's," *The Gospel of Thomas*'s Jesus says, "give God the things that are God's, and give me what is mine." The final clause, which is unique to *The Gospel of Thomas*, thoroughly scrambles the assumed point of Jesus's foxy answer to the Pharisees in the canonical gospels and hits any reader familiar with the canonical gospels like a smack across the face. Who *is* this Jesus, anyway?

One thing *The Gospel of Thomas*'s text utterly lacks compared with the canonical gospels is what the scholar Marvin Meyer calls "spiritualization," which is to say a dramatic or scenic context that enriches or challenges one's understanding of what Jesus is actually saying. A telling example occurs in Saying 9:

> Jesus said, "Look, the sower went out, took a handful [of seeds], and scattered [them]. Some fell on the road, and the birds came and pecked them up. Others fell on rock, and they did not take root in the soil and did not produce heads of grain. Others fell on thorns, and they choked the seeds and the worms devoured them. And others fell on good soil, and it brought forth a good crop. It yielded sixty per measure and one hundred twenty per measure.

We find parallel passages in the thirteenth chapter of Matthew and the eighth chapter of Luke, but the story of the sower is allegorized into having something to do with the Kingdom or the Word of God. In Meyer's view, the story of the sower in *The Gospel of Thomas* is "more original" than the canonical gospels' allegorized version. The way the story has shifted overtly toward parable, Meyer goes on, suggests that the early church used details "about farming in rural Palestine" to explain to later Christians how faith might endure in hostile times.

The briefest, most enigmatic saying attributed to Jesus in *The Gospel of Thomas* is this: "Be passersby." While such sentiment probably has a relationship to Jesus's recommendation in the canonical gospels that his disciples travel widely and partake of strangers' generosity, "Be passersby" has an apothegmatic elusiveness. Apparently, it has something to do with keeping away from the corrupting world, remaining alone. (Not for nothing does the word "monk" derive from the Greek *monachos,* or "solitary.") These two words never found their way into canonical Christian scripture, but they obviously struck others in the ancient world as worthy of immortalization: a nearly identical saying attributed to Jesus, and inscribed in Arabic, can be found in a tenth-century mosque in India.

VII.

The morning after my cataclysmic visit to St. Thomas Mount, I read a book while drinking a six-dollar bottle of water on one of my hotel's open-air inner courtyard patios. I felt quite a bit better that morning, my body a plague-cleansed city. My only real malady was a dehydration headache glowing inside my skull and possibly a slight fever. All the same, today was the day I had to visit Saint Thomas Basilica.

On the cab ride over, a liquid seesaw rocked back and forth in my stomach. I gazed out the window, squinting the world into liquidy vagueness, trying not to focus on the dark shops packed with what looked to be detergent boxes; the colorful, ghostly drift of women in saris; the overturned bicycle pinned under a diagonally parked car, the gathered crowd, two hotly arguing men. Sweat poured out of me, and not the honest, gritty-textured sweat of exertion, but sweat that felt sour and contaminating.

The cabdriver had no trouble finding Saint Thomas Basilica,

or Santhome Basilica, as it was locally known. Weak and ravenous for caloric strength, I climbed out of the cab and looked around. This was one of the cleaner, more verdant neighborhoods I had seen in Chennai. I had come to associate such neighborhoods with two things: clean toilets and Domino's Pizza. I walked off in search of the latter, past the basilica, its sign of annunciation an overturned Kubrickian black marble obelisk emblazoned with INTERNATIONAL SHRINE OF ST. THOMAS BASILICA. I did not find Domino's Pizza. I did, however, stumble across something called the Image College of Arts, Animation, and Technology, which offered courses in game development, game design, and game journalism. I found the stately colonial-era building that provided residence to the diocese's archbishop. I found a home for retired Indian clergy, one of whom I saw smilingly leaning out of a second-story window to water his flowers. I found a number of parochial schools, around the playgrounds of which trundled happily screaming Indian children in Catholic plaid. I watched two boys kick a soccer ball back and forth until the nuns called them in.

Even though several of the Catholic priests I had known in my life were Indian Christians from Goa, I knew I would never get used to steeples towering above equatorial palm trees or school-uniform plaid worn in tropical heat. However anachronous it could sometimes seem, Christianity came into India quietly and, for the most part, accommodatingly. The same cannot be said for Islam, which arrived in India in three waves. The earliest Arab Muslims did not come bearing swords. As educated merchants, India's first Muslim visitors were deeply curious about the wider world and won many converts along the coasts of India. Shia Muslims from Persia were less accommodating but more successful and influenced Indian religious and bureaucratic life in ways that are still felt today. In the thirteenth century, however, Allah's final messengers to India arrived from the resource-deprived steppes of Central Asia. Brutal and efficient, these Turkic Muslims were not merchants or scholars or chroniclers or mystics but inveterate warriors who regarded the people of Hindustan as infidels. The Turks established the first Islamic empire in India, partly due to their success at converting low-caste Indians, who were understandably enlivened by Islam's seemingly promising, spiritually mandated demolition of the caste system. While several of the first Muslim rulers of India's Mughal Empire displayed a wise public deference to Hinduism (one stopped eating beef as a mark of respect, for instance), their rule eventually came to be characterized by internal instability, geopolitical ambition, and fundamentalist harshness. By the end of the sixteenth century, many Christians and Hindus were actively collaborating with India's eager European colonizers.

Unfortunately for India's Christians, the European Christians who rediscovered them were Portuguese sailors—both fanatically Catholic and deeply suspicious of anyone and anything that seemed Moorish, Muslim, or otherwise "heretical." Less than two hundred years prior to their arrival in India, the Portuguese had lived under the humiliating yoke of Islam. From this they emerged with an angry, aggressive, post-traumatic-stress Christianity and "crusading ethos and religious intolerance as extreme as anywhere in western Europe," in the words of one historian. Indians, meanwhile, had no frame of reference for what the Portuguese actually represented. India's earlier Christian incursions had been small and mostly peaceful, and while many Christian visitors sneered at Indian Christianity's "Nestorian" ways, they were never numerous enough to do anything about it.

Yet the first contact made between Portuguese and Indians, in 1498, was also peaceful. Initially, the Portuguese worked with local Thomas Christians, who were frequently oppressed by non-Christians. Conveniently, the local spice trade, which the Portuguese sought to control, was mainly a Thomas Christian operation, and so both sides agreed to a treaty of formal cooperation in 1503. By 1510, the Portuguese had built a fortress in Goa (which eventually became the largest Christian cathedral in Asia), and some Thomas Christians were drawn into Catholicism. The alliance cracked after five decades due to the fanatical nature of Portuguese Catholicism and the ingrained resistance of Indian Christianity.

By 1550, the Portuguese had massacred thousands of Muslims, outlawed the practice of Hinduism in the lands they controlled, and turned most Thomas Christians against them. Yet the Portuguese had also persuaded the Roman Catholic Church to allow the archbishop of Goa "rights of patronage" over India. The missionary activity the Goan church sponsored was some of the most confrontational and destructive in Christian history. Rome eventually came to regret the carte blanche it had granted its Portuguese messengers, but not until the 1830s did it reassert its authority over Indian Catholicism.

India's Christians had never been given a reason to think much about the doctrinal disputes that had separated so many European Christians from one another. Having no history of evangelism themselves, many Thomas Christians regarded European conversion drives as behavior more fitting of a Muslim than a self-professed Christian. By the end of the sixteenth century, frustrated Portuguese-sponsored missionaries in India began to subvert and sometimes even destroy the legacies and traditions of Thomas Christians. Around 1560, the Portuguese brought an Inquisition in miniature to the subcontinent. Ancient and revered works of Syriac scripture were scrubbed of "Nestorian" thinking; many other texts were destroyed; all contact with Syria's Christian patriarchs was forbidden; several libraries were burned. Indian Christianity hardened against all these incursions, and by the seventeenth century the Christians of Portuguese-controlled land lived in a state of open acrimony.

The Portuguese were not the only European Christians in India. In 1639, not too far from Saint Thomas Basilica, a confederacy of largely English merchants landed their ships on a five-mile-long beach and set out to build a "factory," or trading post. Along the coast were four separate villages, whose Christians the English quickly turned to for help and alliances. Like the Portuguese, with whom they competed, the English traders built a fort, which they named after their patron saint, George. With a foothold trading post already in Surat, on the west coast of India, the Governor and Company of Merchants of London Trading into the East Indies—soon mercifully shortened to the East India Company—was on its way to becoming the first truly multinational corporate entity in human history.

To an extent far surpassing that of the Portuguese, the East India Company leveraged the knowledge and skills of local people. It also routinely exploited and sometimes tormented local people, but Frykenberg argues that the nature of this power balance was more complicated than most colonial relationships. Many towns in the area saw their populations increase fivefold in a decade. While the city-state of Madras/Chennai was overseen by the administrator of Fort St. George and backed by English (and, later, British) sea power, "Indian money, Indian manpower, and Indian methods of collaboration" were all equally crucial to its success. Madras's central defining component, Frykenberg writes, was that it "permitted and encouraged unrestricted entry and enterprise. . . . Any and all who came to seek shelter within its walls found refuge and opportunity."

Fort St. George was built only a decade after an earlier Portuguese-designed Santhome Basilica had gone up. The basilica's spire, which could be seen from the fort walls, must have been a reassuring sight to the English merchants. As Madras/Chennai grew, however, the number of temples and mosques increased apace; by the nineteenth century, the city was a bastion of Hindu nationalism and a favorite city of Indian Muslims. It was also home to large Armenian and Jewish communities, a growingly Evangelical Anglican movement, and an increasingly resentful community of Thomas Christians.

Anglican missionaries attempted to adjust Thomas Christians' doctrinal peculiarities. When that did not work, they, too, resorted to altering and vandalizing their sacred scriptures. However, a few small groups of Thomas Christians wound up converting to Anglicanism, and some even went so far as to break the cultural taboo of ministering to low-caste Indians. One legacy of this was sharply worsened relations between Hindus and Indian Christians, with the former regarding the latter as social heretics for reaching out to people categorized, literally, as "crushed." By the mid-nineteenth century, Madras/Chennai had "a special reputation for the vehemence of its Hindu-Christian conflicts," Frykenberg writes. The Brahman elite frequently attacked Thomas Christians, some even going so far as to hold mocking travesties of the Christian Mass. A consolidated movement of Brahmans and their allies worked to blackball any and all Indian Christians from positions of local power, and because the Brahmans were powerful, and crucial to British business, it became de facto British policy to appease them at every turn, even if it meant shunning Thomas Christians, which struck many Britons within and without India as an appalling turn of events.

Not everything in the story of Indian Christianity's painful reintroduction to the modern world concerns fragmentation and abeyance. Despite the damage caused in India by agents of Catholicism, the church, in 1894, finally sanctified the use of the Syriac rite for many Indian Catholics and later granted Thomas Christians representation by their own bishops. Today, India's various Thomas Christian churches, Eastern Catholic Church, and Roman Catholic Church coexist in a state of relative comity. For more than a century, the Catholic Church has overseen the operation and maintenance of Saint Thomas Basilica, which it elevated to the status of minor basilica in the mid-1950s.

VIII.

The first thing visitors encountered when turning off San Thome High Road and onto the basilica's grounds was an attractive little jungle glen landscaped directly into the compound's surrounding wall. Behind the glen, an artificial waterfall quietly spilled. Standing tall amid the vines and fronds was a creamy white statue of the Virgin Mary, who Indian Christians claim appeared to Thomas at several locations around their nation and who might also be Thomas's sole rival as India's most beloved Christian figure who is not Jesus.*

A pair of silent, down-staring beggars were camped nearby the landscaped glen, one of whom wore a T-shirt that read, AT LEAST LIFE SUCKS FOR FREE, which made my giving him a hundred rupees less a matter of choice than reaction. Once I stepped past the beggars, I was in a sunny, orderly place that felt more like Florida than India. I glanced back at San Thome High Road, twenty feet behind me, and saw small but tragic manifestations of workaday Indian catastrophe: a filthy child walking alone down the street, a half-naked man passed out under a tree, a loudly backfiring auto rickshaw. The comparative calm of this basilica's courtyard suddenly felt like that of a naughty student on his best behavior.

Indians and Westerners strolled about on the courtyard's albedo white flagstones, the Indians looking perfectly cool in their loose linen clothing and saris while the Westerners were mostly dripping, wet-faced, armpit splotched, camera strapped, fanny packed, and dabbing, dabbing, dabbing at their foreheads. The wall-enclosed courtyard was smaller than I had been expecting, while the basilica itself was larger.

The Gothic cathedral before me had been built in 1893, on land previously occupied by a Portuguese church that dated from the seventeenth century. The Portuguese church was merely one in a long line of Thomas-devoted churches, many of which came to grief. As a local guidebook put it, "Down the

---

* In various legends, Thomas assumes care of Mary's holy girdle as she is being taken up into Heaven from the Mount of Olives. In one version of the legend, Peter expresses some surprise that Thomas has been so honored with Mary's garment, for Thomas was "always unbelieving" in life. Today Mary's girdle is supposedly housed in Prato, Italy.

centuries this holy shrine had suffered damages beyond reckoning." In the late eighteenth century, for instance, the Portuguese church was occupied by Muslims for eleven years, and during that time all Christians were forbidden to enter. Prior to that, Thomas's shrine had been attacked and burned during various spasms of religious violence. Despite a turbulent twentieth century in India, Santhome Basilica reached the present day largely unscathed. The stark, Gothic design—particularly that of the basilica's main spire—made it seem dislocated here in the tropics, to say the least, as though a sharp piece of Middle Europe had dropped from the heavens and embedded itself immovably in Indian soil. Most striking was the basilica's grayish, deracinated whiteness—the whiteness of having been attacked and scoured for nutrients—though a bit of color was provided by its orange roof. Santhome Basilica was the single cleanest thing I had seen in India this side of Domino's Pizza bathroom porcelain. It must have been washed hourly, I thought. As though on schedule, two workmen appeared and began cleaning the basilica facade with long-handled mops.

For more than a thousand years, non-Indian Christians have been coming to the shrine of Thomas and the various churches built around and atop it. (The first church in Mylapore is, of course, locally credited to the carpenter's rule of Thomas himself.) There is record of two British monks having visited Thomas's shrine in the ninth century. Five hundred years later, a Franciscan missionary visited the shrine and wound up staying in Mylapore for thirteen months. Around the same time, Thomas's shrine welcomed one of its most celebrated Western visitors, Marco Polo.

While Polo never specified the name of the town in which Thomas's remains were kept—he referred to it as "a small city not frequented by many merchants" within the "province of Ma'abar," which is apparently what Indian Muslims once called the modern-day state of Tamil Nadu—he obviously meant Chennai. Polo described how some Indian holy men, as "descendants of those who slew Saint Thomas the Apostle," were supernaturally repelled from entering Thomas's tomb. He also noted that "Christians and Saracens" alike venerated the apostle and that the local nut trade was in the hands of Christians. In the fourteenth century, an ill-tempered friar complained about "the vile and pestilent heretics"—that is, Thomas Christians—who oversaw the shrine's operations. Shortly before the Portuguese first arrived in India in 1498, a Venetian with a more forgiving turn of mind visited the shrine and noted that the "body of St. Thomas lies honorably buried in a large and beautiful church," where he was worshipped by "a thousand Nestorians who identified themselves with the Apostle."

The possibly fictitious fourteenth-century traveler John Mandeville also claimed to have visited Thomas's "beautiful tomb" in a city he called "Mailapur." Thomas's body, Mandeville noted wondrously, remained uncorrupted, and he described how Thomas's arm—believed, of course, to have touched Jesus—was displayed outside the reliquary: "Men of that country judge who is right by [Thomas's] hand. For if there be a quarrel between two parties and each affirms right is on his side, they cause the case of each party to be written in a scroll and put these scrolls in the hand of Saint Thomas; quickly the hand casts away the scroll that contains the false case."

The suite of buildings along the edge of the basilica courtyard contained a souvenir store, a liturgical center, and a management office. Outside every doorway, I noticed, was a small pile of Indian shoes, though some Indians, I also noticed, went inside these buildings without taking off their shoes. Whether this was a Christian thing or a caste thing or a Hindu thing or simply an individual thing, I was not sure, but to remain on the safe side, I removed my shoes before entering the shrine office. A jowly, dark-eyed Indian woman sat behind an uncluttered desk, writing in a ledger. She looked up at me as I came in. I asked her if the basilica had a resident historian or public affairs person with whom I could discuss its history and relics. No, she said, though there was a priest here who was normally happy to discuss such matters with visitors. Wonderful, I said. Was he available? He was not. That was a shame. When would he be back? Next week. She frowned. I frowned. Her office was small and airless, infused with a warm, rotting-fruit smell. I asked her, "What do you think of the Thomas relics your shrine contains?"

She put down her pencil. "Sir, I think they are what give us our church and our faith."

"Can I ask you a question?"

"Please, sir."

"To you, is there any doubt whether the apostle Thomas came to India?"

"There are many scholars saying this, sir."

"That Thomas came to India?"

"Many scholars, sir."

"Yes," I said.

"Many scholars, sir."

"I see. Thank you."

"Thank you, sir."

Once again I removed my shoes outside the basilica's souvenir store, as had all its Indian customers, but a friendly Indian nun approached me and said there was no need for me to remove my shoes. I put them back on. Another Westerner came in, however, and, in full sight of the nun, removed his shoes. Alarmingly, she said nothing to him. This sharpened my anxiety that shoe removal was yet another aspect of Indian life governed by an invisible rule set, which I had blunderingly violated not once but twice. I began to peruse the shop's bookshelves.

The books, many of them crypto-Christian, had titles like *31 Tips for Youth: How to Develop a Pleasing Personality, Making the Most of Your Business, Coping with Criticism (Made Easy!),* and *Strategies for Effective Leadership—at Home and the Office!* Here, perhaps, was a sign that Indian Christianity was at long last tolerant of, and vulnerable to, conversion-minded outreach. This mingling of profits and spirituality was not much different from graspier versions of American Protestantism, wherein faith in Jesus and economic success were regarded as similar types of accredited investing. The uncritically acquisitive model of Christianity on display here in the souvenir store was evident elsewhere in India. A church in Kokkamangalam, which was supposedly founded by Thomas, contains a relic that, according to one account, is prayed to on Friday evenings by Indians who "aspire to employment, especially abroad." My eyes wandered along the souvenir store's bookshelves, stopping at a title that suggested another correspondence between self-help-inflected Indian Christianity and American Fox News Christianity: *The Indian Media: How Credible?*

I asked the nun in the bookstore if I could have a seat for a moment. Just a moment. "I'm not feeling well," I told her. She nodded and rose and got me a cup of water. She had round, kind eyes and a small, humorless mouth.

I was uncertain as to whether this water was potable. She noticed my hesitation. "Drink the water, sir. You look warm."

After I drank, she nodded and said, "You may go to the church and pray now, sir."

I walked across the courtyard to the basilica, removed my shoes, and made my way to an empty pew. The floor was surprisingly cool against my feet, but an empty pew was not so easy to find, given the number of worshipping Indians present, despite its being a weekday. The interior of the basilica was just as handsome as its exterior. The ceiling and walls were white; the floor, pews, wooden chandeliers, and joinery were cocoa brown; the stained-glass windows had a candy maker's splash of red and blue and orange. Above all fourteen stations of the cross, a giant fan turned quietly, which proved magically effective in cooling the church down. Before many of the stations of the cross were freestanding easels that held large, garish portraits of the Twelve. The portraits had pretty obviously been hijacked from the Internet, blown up, printed onto poster board, painted over, and attached to the easels. Quite a few of the Twelve resembled mid-1980s American television hunks. James the Lesser looked quite a bit like Thomas Magnum, and John had a mullet gloriously similar to Greg Evigan's from *My Two Dads*. Now that I was looking at these portraits closely, it seemed increasingly likely that they *were* repurposed photographs of Thomas Magnum and whatever the name of Greg Evigan's character in *My Two Dads* had been.

Jesus was on his cross in the back of the basilica, behind the altar, distant, wan, and violated, as he always was. Had any other religion settled upon such a pessimistic, but demonstrably true, organizing symbol as to how the mechanisms of earthly power really worked? Nearby, beneath the sixth station of the cross—wherein Veronica wipes the face of Jesus, which has no scriptural basis—was a portrait of Thomas, which seemed to be one of the few apostolic portraits here that had not been based on a cast member of *Riptide* or *Simon & Simon*. The resulting image, muddy and only partially competent, was of a balding man holding a spear.

My knees sank into the pew's plush, comfy kneeler—a sensation I had not felt in two decades. The last two times I attended Mass with my father, during my senior year of high school, I refused either to kneel or to pray. I no longer believed, I told my father, so why should I go through the motions of celestial obedience? Many members of my family initially regarded my loss of faith as part of my "journey." They were sure my journey would eventually bring me back around. Sitting there, I remembered two things about going to Mass with my father: he never took Communion because of his and my mother's divorce, and he always tapped his heart three times, with solemn insistence, after the recitation of the Apostles' Creed. I asked him about his ritual once. His eyes filled with such alarm that I instantly knew his heart tapping had something to do with a loss or devastation: his parents' early deaths, his divorce, his wounding in Vietnam. There was no reason for me to invade that space. Maybe that was the best simple explanation for religion: it filled our spaces.

I stared at bald, spear-carrying Thomas, whom I had come to see, whom I had become unwell to see. I tapped my own heart three times, just as I had once watched my father do. Thomas, I am sick. Thomas, I ask you here today, how credible is the Indian media? Thomas, where is the nearest Domino's Pizza?

To my utter surprise, part of me wanted to pray right now, but prayer without a direct object was merely thought. I lifted myself off the kneeler and sat back against the hard, handsomely carved pew and closed my eyes. When I opened them again, my notebook and pen were on the floor. I had been asleep, it turned out, for thirty minutes. Falling asleep in church had an esteemed tradition that went all the way back to the Acts of the Apostles, when, in Troas, a young man named Eutychus nods off while Paul speaks, falls out of a window, and dies, thereby becoming what one scholar calls the "first recorded Christian to fall asleep during a long-winded sermon."

The only remaining building left to visit was Thomas's shrine, which was located under the basilica's altar. Even so, to get there, you had to move through a separate building, part of which was a museum and part of which offered blessings, Communion, and counseling from an on-site priest. Before entering the shrine, I drank six glasses of gaggingly sweet iced tea from the basilica concessions stand, which despite the heat was doing a mean business selling cup after paper cup of hot coffee and tea to thirsty Indians.

I removed my shoes at the museum door. The museum was small, as was its selection of artifacts: a painting of Chennai in the seventeenth century, another painting of Chennai's old Saint Thomas Church, yet another painting of the modern Santhome Basilica. Various bronze friezes commemorated India's Christian history. A few unusually dubious relics were on display, including the tip of the alleged spear that killed Thomas.

I headed down into the shrine, where I was greeted by this plaque: ONLY THREE CHURCHES IN THE WHOLE WORLD ARE BUILT OVER THE TOMB OF AN APOSTLE OF JESUS CHRIST. It smelled as though many barrels of incense had been burned down here over the years: two shallow sniffs turned into a headache annunciation. In the middle of the first room I passed through was a water-filled brass bowl the size of a semitruck tire; floating on the water's surface were two dozen red and white carnations. Two side doors—an entrance and an exit—angled off toward the shrine itself.

Beside the shrine's entrance was a diorama habitat, the kind you find in old-school natural history museums, with plaster people, fake greenery, molded wax water, and matte vistas on the too-close back wall. The action portrayed within was that of a huge-nosed, swarthy man preparing to spear Thomas in the back. This aggressor, a pop-eyed murdering beast, wore a turban and had a scorpion tattoo on his forearm. The saintly, kneeling figure before him did not resemble a first-century Palestinian Jew so much as a nineteenth-century Englishman.

The cheap reverence of the appalling diorama nicely prepared me for the shrine itself, which was even worse. Low ceilings. Poundingly artless light. Dirty Formica floor. Cheap wood-paneled walls. Dusty corner-mounted stereo speakers, the covers of which were frayed and shroudy with cobwebs. An empty keyboard stand pushed off to the side of the space. It looked like some VFW hall devoted to servicing the veterans of a disgraced war. According to one of the books I picked up in the bookstore, Thomas's shrine had been built in 1906 and was once faced "with beautiful marble, so that pilgrims could have easy access to the bottom of the crypt and that mass could be conveniently held right over the grave." The beautiful marble was no more, but the pilgrims remained present in force.

Thomas was kept in a glass case near the back, over which a white tablecloth had been draped, Thomas's famous words "My Lord and my God" written across the hem. This was the busiest, fullest apostolic shrine I had yet seen. Two Indian women were kneeling in front of Thomas's case, praying quietly, and from time to time kissing the glass. About two dozen other Indians were in the room, most of whom were sitting motionless in their pews. I walked back into the anteroom and asked the woman sitting at the information desk (a fold-out card table) if I was seeing a normal amount of visitors today. She waggled her head and said she believed so, yes.

What exactly Thomas's Indian shrine contained was a matter of historical confusion. At least since the fourteenth century, Indian Christians have affected to believe Thomas's remains were here in Chennai. But the traditions associated with his remains are equivocal even by apostolic standards. Clement of Alexandria, one of the first Christians to weigh in on Thomas's death, believed Thomas perished from natural causes in an unspecified place, information he credited to a heterodox Christian named Heracleon; other early reports place his death in Edessa rather than India. Later, a different death tradition developed, and from that grew another tradition, which was that in the third century Thomas's remains and relics were carried by Syrian Christians from India to Edessa on July 3, which has since become Thomas's feast day.* His relics were apparently kept in a grand Edessan martyrium until 1258 (a fourth-century visitor described it as "very great, very beautiful and of new construction, well worthy to be the house of God"), after which they were sent to Ortona, Italy, by way of the Greek island Chios, due to fears of Muslim ruination. In Ortona's Concattedrale di San Tommaso Apostolo,† Thomas's relics are still displayed and venerated. One of Thomas's arms was supposedly brought from Ortona to Kerala, on the west coast of India, in 1953, where it is

---

* Until the Middle Ages, Thomas's feast day was typically celebrated, by Christians as early as Jerome, on December 21. As Glenn W. Most points out, July 3 is literally "as far from Jesus' birthday as the calendar permits." Most believes this feast day shift indicates a possible calendrical squelching of the ancient belief that Thomas and Jesus were twins, as December 21 and December 25 might have been too temporally close for Orthodox comfort.

† Which was largely destroyed by German troops during World War II—on December 21, Thomas's former feast day!

still displayed in a church. Meanwhile, a Roman church, Santa Croce in Gerusalemme, claims Thomas's finger, which is kept in a silver repository affixed with a wax seal that attests to the finger's authenticity: the doubter himself now protected from doubt. What possible piece of Thomas did that leave for Chennai? His toe? Eyelid? According to local tradition, Thomas's reliquary in Chennai had been opened on four occasions: at some ancient time no one agrees on; in the thirteenth century; in the sixteenth century, by the Portuguese, when they were building their church; and in the early eighteenth century, by the bishop of Mylapore, who sprinkled local Christians with a handful of dust gathered up from the tomb itself. Perhaps that was all that was left of Thomas in India. Dust.

When I walked back into the shrine, half of Thomas's visitors were asleep in their pews. I wanted very much to join them but instead walked up to the reliquary. Behind the glass was a supine statue of Thomas covered by a red cloth robe. Parallel to Thomas, set just against his arm, was a spear. While I scribbled impressions in my notebook, two Americans, a man and his daughter, came in and stood next to me. The man was in his fifties, overweight and overdressed, wearing expensively tasseled brown loafers. His daughter was a small, pale girl with the straight black hair of a young squaw in some patriotic Thanksgiving painting. I gathered they had not been in Chennai for long because they still seemed relatively happy.

"Terrible," I said, while scribbling a spirited jeremiad in my notebook, "isn't it?"

The man sighed. "It's not great, no."

"This is the worst apostolic tomb I've ever seen."

The man looked over at me. "Seen a lot of apostolic tombs, have you?"

"Dude, you have no idea."

His daughter peered into the wall-mounted glass case next to the reliquary and made a bright sound of discovery. "One of Thomas's bones," she said. I had a look for myself. The fragment was no bigger than a piece of perforation plucked from the edge of a postage stamp.

IX.

A young man who worked at the hotel put me in touch with a family friend of his, an Indian writer, he said, who knew a bit about Chennai and its Thomas cult—and what the Indian church had to gain from preaching its inviolate Thomas traditions. When I called the man, I asked him if he believed Thomas had made it to India. The man laughed and said, "No, of course not."

We agreed we would meet at Saint Thomas Basilica the day before I left Chennai, walk around, do an interview, and have lunch. The morning of our interview, I was feeling well enough to walk to the basilica. I made it perhaps a fourth of the way to Mylapore when there descended upon Chennai a storm of black-skied savagery. The streets filled up with rain almost instantly, saturating the air with the smell of waste. The clouds seemed to squeeze the light itself out of the morning, and the trees shook as though some mighty hand were distressing them at their base. Everyone ran for cover. In my case, this meant the lobby of a hair-removal clinic, where I was joined by at least twenty Indians. The nurse of the clinic was at first annoyed. Then she got a look outside and sighed. The storm went on for ninety minutes and left much of the city flooded and without power. I already knew, standing shoulder to shoulder to shoulder with my fellow refuge seekers in the lobby of a hair-removal clinic, that I would not be seeing or interviewing the Indian skeptic today, or ever. My time in India would end in disaster, just as it had begun.

Beside me, a young Indian man was scanning that day's *Chennai Chronicle,* the water from his hair plinking loudly on the newspaper. I read the gossip page over his shoulder about some reality television star's recent impregnation by an English soccer player. It was comforting, somehow, to know Indian gossip pages were as abominable as everyone else's. He turned to the local news. Last night, an Indian filmmaker's daughter had fallen to her death only a few blocks from my hotel. The article made clear that falling off roofs was a problem for partying Indians. It had happened before and would happen again. The young man turned to world news. President Obama, who recently visited the country, had told the Indian Parliament that India was not emerging; India had *emerged*.

The world outside the window of the hair-removal clinic looked neither emerged nor emerging. It and its rivers of floating garbage looked devastated, Noachian, especially when a small car floated by the window, down the street, turning slightly clockwise, its two male passengers smiling hopelessly. *My Lord,* I thought. *My God.*

CHRISTOS:
ON JESUS CHRIST

ANOINTED ONE • "RECONCILING THE WORLD TO HIMSELF" • ANOTHER JESUS • ADOPTIONISM • LETTER TO THE HEBREWS • LAST WORDS • "ONCE HE WAS NOT" • THE CREED • *ON THE INCARNATION* • JULIAN THE APOSTATE • "THE SUN IS NOT PRIOR TO ITS LIGHT" • THE BEST MINDS

I.

The moral teachings of a man named Jesus are not, and never have been, the defining component of Christianity. Some of what Jesus had to say was striking, certainly, but other ancient ethicists said similar things. Jesus compelled his followers to turn the other cheek, but, as Socrates told Crito, "We should never take revenge and never hurt anyone even if we have been hurt." Putting aside any question of their originality, Jesus's moral teachings were often highly impractical. As the scholar Paula Fredriksen notes, "No normal human society could long run according to the principles enunciated in the Sermon on the Mount." This is probably why, to be considered a Christian by most Christians, you must accept that Jesus was the Messiah; that he rose from the dead; that he was, at the same time, both man and God; and that his death had immense cosmic significance.

All of these postulations are somehow contained in the roomy word "Christ," a transliteration of the Greek word *christos,* which is itself a literal translation of the Hebrew word *meshiah*. In its original Jewish context, *meshiah* meant "anointed one." Neither a mystical nor a cosmic appellation, *meshiah* is applied liberally to kings throughout Jewish scripture—even to the pagan Cyrus in Isaiah 45:1—and hinged on what one scholar describes as "the continuing approval of the people." For the everyday Greek speaker of the first half of the first century CE, *christos* was the word used for "ointment." How these Jewish and Greek concepts fused and came to stand for the inexplicable presence of an intervening God among his earthly creations was, unsurprisingly, a complicated process.

For even the most proto-orthodox-minded early Christians, the philosophical conundrums posed by Jesus Christ were profound. How could the divine descend into the human while remaining unaffectedly divine? Exactly what part of Jesus was divine? How could the Son of God also be God? What use was Jewish scripture in describing or anticipating Jesus Christ? Why was Jesus Christ necessary, and what did his death actually accomplish? How can God's love for us (or his son) be expressed through torture? In the first and second centuries, not everyone who posed these questions came to similar conclusions. Some who considered themselves sincere, right-thinking Christians believed that Jesus Christ was not and had nothing to do with the god of the Jews; that he was solely human; that he was solely God; that the "god" inside him was merely a spirit sent to the earth by God; that he was never really crucified; that he was crucified but did not suffer.

That Jesus's original followers never called him "Jesus Christ" while he was alive is a near certainty, or as close to a certainty as conjecture about the first century allows us. When exactly Jesus became "Jesus Christ" in the minds of his followers is not known, but it happened very early in the Christian tradition, as Paul's letters confirm. The synoptic gospels almost always precede *Christos* with the definite article: "the Christ."

For John and Paul, it is less of a title and more akin to a proper name.

Difficult philosophical questions arose once Jesus became Jesus the Christ, much less Jesus Christ. The first, which the gospel writers endeavored mightily to answer, was how worshipping Jesus Christ maintained continuity with the god of the Jews. The second, which carried Christian thinkers deep into the third century, was whether God and Jesus Christ were one God. The third, which occupied Christian thinkers until the fifth century, was exactly *how* God and Jesus Christ were one God. It says much about Christian tenacity that these questions were eventually answered to the satisfaction of most Christians—and much about the opacity of scripture that the answers were so long in coming.

II.

The earliest chronological mention of Jesus's death occurs in 1 Thessalonians, which was written by Paul around 50 CE, probably in Corinth. In this epistle, Paul assures his audience that they have "suffered the same things from your own compatriots as they did from the Jews, who killed both the Lord Jesus and the prophets, and drove us out." That the Jews, rather than the Romans, are identified by Paul as having been chiefly responsible for the death of Jesus means that corporate Jewish guilt was resonantly part of the Jesus tradition from the beginning. Yet Paul also writes how those in Thessalonica who "grieve" after "those who have died" must take heart, for "since we believe that Jesus died and rose again ... God will bring with him those who have died." This is a frankly astounding thing to declare about someone who had died less than twenty years before. Martin Hengel has written that within the first twenty years after the death of Jesus more happened in Christology "than in the whole of the next seven centuries." This is debatable, but Paul's letter to the Thessalonians is obviously reflective of this early Christological earthquake.

If Paul's own testimony is accurate, he understood Jesus, a little over a decade after Jesus's death, as the single-named entity "Christ," "the Son of God," and as one who had "died and rose again." According to 1 Thessalonians, Paul had already been all over Greece and Macedonia preaching this Jesus, and he included in his preaching an ominous promise that "the day of the Lord will come like a thief in the night," which Paul believed would happen relatively soon. Where Paul picked up these ideas remains an open question—perhaps *the* open question. As one scholar writes, "The origin of the cult of Christ . . . is the secret of the earliest Palestinian community." In 1 Corinthians, Paul claims to preach the same message as the apostles ("we proclaim and so you have come to believe") while using the occasion to take a shot at the apostles ("I worked harder than any of them"). What seems evident is Paul's ideas about Jesus were probably not the creation of Paul alone.

One of the most startling Pauline insights into the precise role of Jesus Christ occurs in 2 Corinthians, when he writes, "All this is from God, who reconciled us to himself through Christ, and has given us the ministry of reconciliation; that is, in Christ God was reconciling the world to himself." What exactly this means has challenged theologians for two thousand years. Other aspects of Paul's letters are even more mysterious. In Romans, he cites an early hymn that Jesus was "declared to be Son of God with power according to the spirit of holiness by resurrection from the dead." Needless to say, the suggestion that Jesus was not yet fully divine until his resurrection is far from the beliefs of what later became Christian orthodoxy. In Philippians, Paul quotes another early Christian hymn in which we learn that Jesus, "though he was in the form of God, did not regard equality with God as something to be exploited." In 1 Timothy, Paul (or a follower of Paul) cites yet another early

Christian hymn, which proclaims, "There is one God; there is also one mediator between God and humankind, Christ Jesus, himself human, who gave himself as a ransom for all." Jesus might have been only in the *form* of God? Jesus mediates between God and humankind? Had Paul given voice to these views in the fourth rather than the first century, he would have been condemned as a heretic.

Early critics of Christianity had a field day with the faith's initial inability to clearly describe the ultimate purpose of God's earthly visitation. As the anti-Christian philosopher Celsus wrote, "Now what I should like to know is this: What is God's purpose in undertaking such a descent from the heights? Does he want to know what is going on among men? . . . [W]hy does he not simply correct men by his divine power?" A Christian might consider it altogether reasonable that Jesus Christ's mission and purpose took human beings so long to understand, because his nature and intent were so unprecedented. Yet the professional atheist looking to undermine the purported uniqueness of Jesus can point to a wide variety of echoes. One of the most famous is Apollonius of Tyana, a wonder-working, countryside-wandering ascetic philosopher from Asia Minor who was born sometime between 10 and 20 CE. Apollonius had disciples, taught widely but left no writings himself, and was said to have confronted a Roman authority figure (though, unlike Jesus, he lived to tell the tale). Despite the similarities found in stories told about Apollonius and Jesus,* particularly when it comes to miracle working, it is not at all clear in which direction primal influence flows. The first life of Apollonius was not written until the fourth cen-

---

* These similarities gave Edward Gibbon, in his *History of the Decline and Fall of the Roman Empire,* the occasion for a footnote daring in its asperity: "Apollonius of Tyana was born about the same time as Jesus Christ. His life (that of the former) is related in so fabulous a manner by his disciples that we are at a loss to discover whether he was a sage, an imposter, or a fanatic."

tury, and though it clearly collated folktales concerning Apollonius, it might also have been informed by Christian stories of Jesus.

One odd story involving Jesus has him turning up in Jerusalem. While walking the city streets, Jesus began calling out, "A voice from the east, a voice from the west, a voice from the four winds, a voice against Jerusalem and the Sanctuary, a voice against bridegrooms and brides, and a voice against this whole people!" According to the story, the "more prominent" people of Jerusalem—the priests and aristocracy, in other words—were upset by Jesus's words, seeing in them "some supernatural force." Jesus was dragged before the Roman procurator and whipped "till his flesh hung in ribbons." During his torture, Jesus made no statement for himself and was specifically noted not to have cried out in pain. When the procurator questioned Jesus, furthermore, he refused to answer beyond wishing further woe unto Jerusalem. The procurator dismissed Jesus, regarding him as a simple lunatic. Jesus wandered the streets of Jerusalem for seven more years. "Those who daily cursed him he never cursed; those who gave him food he never thanked: his only response to anyone was that dismal foreboding." According to Josephus, in whose *Jewish War* this story can be found, the strange, tormented man known as Jesus the son of Ananus was finally killed around 70 CE, during the Roman siege of Jerusalem, by a stone projectile launched by a war engine.

Jesus the son of Ananus and the Christian Jesus of the Passion narratives have a few things in common. Both are public troublemakers who wish woe on the Temple. Both are dragged by Jewish priests before a Roman authority figure and flogged. Both remain silent about the charges brought against them. These two Jesuses diverge in other ways—their final fates, obviously, are drastically different—but it bears repeating that the gospels, as a literary form, almost certainly came to be as a reaction to the Jewish War, the Roman destruction of Jerusalem's

Temple, and Jesus's failure to return as (apparently) promised. After 70 CE, figures like Jesus the son of Ananus were likely familiar to Christians and Jews alike. More than that, the types of people who edited the gospels were probably aware of the work of Josephus—as well as the work of, say, Plutarch, in which we can find a crucified rebel being stabbed with a spear to confirm his death, just as John describes Jesus being pierced with a Roman lance to confirm his death. The synoptic gospels describe an eclipse occurring on the day of Jesus's crucifixion. According to Josephus, an eclipse also occurred when Herod the Great burned the young rebel Matthias alive in punishment. Matthew tells us that after the crucifixion of Jesus, the tombs around Jerusalem "were opened," apparently by an earthquake, "and many bodies of the saints who had fallen asleep were raised." The historian Lucius Cassius Dio reported that the death of Claudius was heralded by the temple of Jupiter opening up and a shower of blood, and Virgil's *Georgics* describes how the death of Julius Caesar caused the Alps themselves to rumble.

"The Son of God," Jesus's most significant and difficult-to-comprehend title, would have been conceptually familiar to many living in the Roman Empire; the halls of paganism were crowded with God-sired demi-deities.* As a title for a human being, however, "the Son of God" does not occur in pre-Christian sources, with the exception of two highly obscure passages in the Dead Sea Scrolls, one of which reads, "The Son of God he shall be said to be, and the Son of the Most High they shall call him." (The identity of the "he" here appears to be an unnamed and presumably Jewish king.) As belief in Jesus Christ developed, Christian thinking seems to have incorporated a number

---

* Jesus's resemblance to mythological figures such as Osiris, Hercules, and Mithra, which is sometimes argued as evidence that he, too, is a purely mythological figure, is both vastly overstated and not nearly as interesting as the Christ-as-myth theory's proponents appear to believe.

of phrases and divine honorifics already in circulation among pagan Romans. An Ephesian inscription, for instance, refers to Julius Caesar as "god made manifest"; another emperor's birthday was referred to as "good news." In the Gospel According to John, Thomas says to Jesus, "My Lord and my God!" which resembles an imperial formulation used to describe Domitian: "Dominus et deus noster," or "Our Lord and God." However, as Martin Hengel writes, Christians might have regarded this language as "a negative stimulus" rather than some kind of titular model to pursue.

Christianity seems to have begun relatively modestly, as a sectarian Jewish personality cult founded upon Jesus. A larger, more spiritually inclusive version of that personality cult, founded upon Jesus Christ, emerged from within a framework of missionary outreach led by Paul. (Most Christians, of course, would argue that the latter cult began to form on the day of Jesus's resurrection, if not sooner.) Safe assumptions to make about the historical Jesus include his baptism by John, his large popular following, his reputation for miracle performance, his wont to speak parabolically, his preaching of a coming kingdom, his belief that he was somehow an envoy or prophet of God, and his familiarity with at least some Jewish scripture. It also seems reasonable to assume that at some point in his career, Jesus attracted the notice of the Temple and Roman authorities and was condemned to death, which greatly astonished and disappointed his followers, who nevertheless continued to preach, at least for a time, something similar to what he had preached. Our inability to determine much more than that about the historical Jesus moved the twentieth-century German scholar Rudolf Bultmann to famously declare the impossibility of ever encountering the historical Jesus. Those who go looking for Jesus mostly just find some version of themselves. The Jesus story, as a story, can be understood in a few ways. One way is to accept that it all happened, but this necessitates an additional acceptance that the known laws of the universe were put on hold during a brief period in first-century Palestine and the only people who noticed were Christians.

III.

A difficulty in figuring out how the earliest Christians understood Jesus is the paucity of surviving texts. The gospels, Acts, and epistles survive only because they tell us what Christians of later centuries agreed to be true. Of all the Christian texts mentioned within surviving second-century sources, only 15 percent of them are partially or completely extant. What these lost works might have contained is as irrecoverable as the life and times of the historical Jesus. In this light, what is most remarkable about the Christian texts that do survive is the variety of ideas they contain about Jesus's divinity, ideations of which we can see float in and out of focus within all four gospels. A few of these Christological notions blossomed into types of "heresy"—a word that originally meant only "choice"—which Irenaeus and others would later energetically condemn.

As the scholar Bart D. Ehrman demonstrates in his fascinating textual study *The Orthodox Corruption of Scripture,* the first genuine battle over the meaning of Jesus Christ did not take place in the gospel writers' minds; instead, it took place on the battlefield of the text, as scribes and copyists made tactical changes to highly contested passages. That early Christians were aware of the problem of textual corruption is evident in the New Testament itself: Revelation promises that God will visit upon anyone who meddles with the text "the plagues described in this book." Ehrman, however, argues that many of the corruptions made to early New Testament texts were inserted not by scribes attempting to change the meaning of a text but by scribes wishing to make clearer what they believed the texts said. In texts that date from the second and third centuries—the period in which the Christology of Jesus was least settled—many scribal changes swarmed around passages with Christological implications.

Some of the most prominent competing Christologies within the early days of Christianity were what we now call Adoptionism (which envisioned an entirely human Jesus in whom Christ temporarily dwelled), Docetism (which envisioned an entirely divine Christ whose humanity as Jesus was a calculated illusion, from the Greek verb *dokein,* "to seem"), and Modalism (which envisioned a Jesus who was not the Son of God but fully, patriarchally God), though none describe merely one type of Christian or Christianish thinking.

The Adoptionist view of Jesus's divinity is probably the most fascinating. The Gospel According to Mark carries the strongest whiff of Adoptionism—its original draft might have been explicitly Adoptionist; according to Irenaeus, those "who separate Jesus from the Christ" used Mark's gospel solely— which helps explain why it was the least frequently copied gospel by ancient scribes. For many Adoptionist Christians, Jesus became Jesus Christ at the moment he was baptized by John. Mark's gospel suggestively opens with this scene, telling us that as Jesus emerges from the water of the Jordan, "he saw the heavens torn apart and the Spirit descending like a dove on him. And a voice came from heaven, 'You are my Son, the Beloved, with you I am well pleased.'" Mark contains none of Matthew's or Luke's legendary nativity material,* much less John's postulation

---

* Matthew's and Luke's accounts of Jesus's birth and descent from David pose a number of problems. Not only are their genealogies in disagreement, but Jesus's Davidic descent is traced through Joseph, his supposed stepfather, though it may be that both Matthew and Luke were interested primarily in the potent symbolism of Davidic descent rather than literal bloodlines. (That Paul was familiar with the tradition of Jesus's descent through David suggests it was a hugely important part of the earliest ideations of him. Most likely, it gave Jesus's salvific purpose on earth historical context.) In Luke, though, we are told that Jesus "was the son (as was thought) of Joseph son of Heli." That "as was thought" is almost certainly the insertion of an

that Jesus existed at the dawn of creation. From an Adoptionist Christian perspective, Mark's gospel, purposefully or not, was highly complementary to their beliefs.

Matthew's and Luke's portrayals of the baptism of Jesus contain their own peculiarities. Matthew's Spirit, for instance, is said to have "alighted" on Jesus, which possibly deemphasizes Mark's implication that Jesus's contact with the Spirit had any absorptive quality. Some of the earliest copies of Luke, on the other hand, contain the most overtly Adoptionist language in the entire New Testament. In these early variants of Luke, the voice that calls down from Heaven tells Jesus, "You are my Son, today I have begotten you." With this language, Luke is citing Psalm 2:7, though the Greek Septuagint version rather than the original Hebrew. In doing so, however, he opened up his gospel to a boldly Adoptionist interpretation.* Rest assured, Christian scribes quickly took care of the problem, and the language eventually disappeared in later Luke manuscripts. The presence of Adoptionist ideas in the earliest copies of both Mark and Luke indicates that Adoptionism was not necessarily a Christological heresy so much as a Christological first draft.

Given what we know about early Christianity, this makes a certain amount of sense. For the Gentiles to whom Paul appealed, the Son of God was a powerful, startling thing to imagine floating unseen among them. For Jewish Christians living in Palestine under the increasingly heavy yoke of Roman power from the 40s on, the Son of God had seditionist, attention-getting insinuations many of them would likely have wanted to avoid.

---

alarmed early copyist who worried that any ambiguity on the matter of Jesus's patrimony would be exploitable by Adoptionist Christians.

* Luke uses the phrase again, in Acts 13:33, but frames it as pertaining to Jesus's resurrection (much as Paul did before him) rather than to his baptism. The idea that Jesus was elevated to a new stratum of divinity at the moment of his resurrection was never as controversial within the early church, even though it is far from the eventual position reached by Christian orthodoxy.

By all evidence, the Jewish Christian Jesus fit into established cultural traditions. The titles "Son of Man,"* "Lord,"† and "Rabbi"‡ were all products of Jewish traditions, two of which titles were not explicitly divine. "Lord" had traditional insinuations of divinity, but only when used in an absolute way, which is not necessarily how it was always applied to Jesus. (Only Matthew uses the phrase "the Lord" [ho kurios] with regard to Jesus and does so

---

* In the gospels, Jesus refers to himself as the "Son of God" only in John. In Mark and Matthew, the phrase Jesus uses to refer to himself is "the Son of Man." (Luke, later than both, avoids the term, probably due to its strong apocalyptic insinuation.) A version of the phrase appears in the book of Daniel, one of the youngest works of Hebrew scripture and a crucially important text for early Christianity. (It was so important to early Christianity that the rabbis at the forefront of second-century Judaism effectively downgraded Daniel from its position among the "prophetic" books to a less exalted category: "writings.") Within Daniel, we find an early mention of the "Kingdom of God," along with a vision of "one like a son of man coming with the clouds of Heaven." Daniel's "son of man" is bracketed by much odder visions of a horn with human eyes and a lion with eagle's wings, and it is possible that much of Daniel's vision, including the "son of man" language, was borrowed from Canaanite mythology. No one knows if anyone in Jesus's time would have even recognized "Son of Man" as a special title with special meaning. Nothing in Daniel underlines the phrase as prophetic of a cosmic redeemer. The noncanonical 1 Enoch, however, in which the term also appears, anticipates something closer to a redeeming Messiah, with mentions of his sitting on a "throne of glory" and being referred to by God literally as "little Yahweh." The difficulty posed by early Christian use of "Son of Man" is exemplified by a simple fact: but for one mention in Acts and two in Revelation, the title does not appear outside the gospels.

† Paul closes his first letter to the Corinthians with an Aramaic saying: "Marana atha!" (Our Lord, come!). With the exception of his two uses of Abba (father) in his letters to the Galatians and Romans, this is the only time Paul cites Aramaic language in his surviving letters. Quite clearly he is quoting a then-familiar Christian saying, possibly one derived from the Jerusalem or Palestinian church. The phrase was also used during reenactments of the Lord's Supper (as The Didache, at least, has it). What this suggests is that "Lord," when used for Jesus, had a clear eschatological inference—that Jesus, when he returned, would somehow govern on God's behalf how the present reality gave way to the next.

‡ Usually rendered in the gospels as didaskalos, Greek for "teacher." It does not refer to "rabbi" in any modern sense of the word. The foundations of rabbinic Judaism did not begin to cohere until a century after Jesus's death.

only once. In first-century Koine Greek, *kurios* could also mean "sir.") A Davidic Messiah who had come to wield the authority of God was not necessarily the Son of God. Even if he were so conceptualized, "Son of God" probably meant something very different in first-century Palestine than it did in the doxological pressure cooker of fifth-century Byzantium.

IV.

One of the most riveting scenes in the Passion tradition, which is found in some form in all four gospels, has Jesus praying in Gethsemane right before his arrest—the sole instance in which the gospel writers endeavor to portray the inner life of their subject.

That the historical Jesus prayed there can be little doubt. However, the very notion of orthodox Christianity's Jesus praying challenges the most diligent and searching Christian explanation. The author of the Gospel According to John, whose Jesus is least ambiguously divine, understood the difficulty here; he never depicts Jesus praying, not even while dying on the cross. If Jesus was one of three omniscient beings within God incarnate, to whom exactly would he pray? *To what possible purpose* could *he pray?* Here is Origen's valiant attempt to justify the inexplicable prayers of Jesus: "Now if Jesus prays and does so not in vain, since He gets what He asks for in prayer when He might not have done so apart from prayer, which of us would neglect to pray?"

The synoptic gospel writers were as puzzled as anyone when it came to Jesus's prayers. In Mark, Jesus's grief at what he faces at Gethsemane is most pronounced: "And going a little farther, he threw himself on the ground and prayed that, if it were possible, the hour might pass from him. He said, 'Abba, Father, for you all things are possible; remove this cup from me.'" Mark's Jesus even claims to be "deeply grieved." Matthew's version of the scene is virtually identical. John includes the trip to Geth-

semane (which goes unnamed) but does not bother with depicting Jesus at prayer. He does include language about a cup but
frames it as something Jesus says to Peter, who has just finished
hacking the ear off one of Jesus's aggressors: "Put your sword
back in its sheath. Am I not to drink the cup that the Father has
given me?" Mark's rendering of the scene, with its frank depiction of Jesus as doubtful and scared, becomes, in John's hands, a
rhetorical question with an obvious answer. Clearly something
has happened to the Christian understanding of Jesus between
these two gospels.

Luke's version of the scene may have something to tell us
about the intervening stages between Mark's and John's Jesus.
Of all the gospels, Luke's Jesus prays the most frequently, and
this typically occurs at some crucial point in Luke's story. Yet
throughout his gospel, Luke, like John, portrays a Jesus in firm
control of his fate. During his prayer in Gethsemane, Luke's Jesus
does not appear to suffer much doubt at all: "Then he withdrew
from them about a stone's throw, knelt down [recall that Mark's
Jesus throws himself to the ground], and prayed. 'Father, if you
are willing, remove this cup from me; yet, not my will but yours
be done.'" In the next passage, however, Jesus succumbs to Mar-
kan anguish: "Then an angel from heaven appeared to him and
gave him strength. In his anguish he prayed more earnestly, and
his sweat became great drops of blood falling on the ground."
This is one of the more troubled passages in the New Testament,
with scholars evenly divided as to whether it is original to Luke
or a later scribal addition. In any number of ways, it is a strange
passage, particularly in its assumption that an angel could give
Jesus, who is supposed to be God, strength.

Ehrman believes the passage is a later addition for several reasons. It undermines the controlled, fate-accepting Jesus
that Luke largely endeavors to portray elsewhere; it contains
language found nowhere else in Luke or Acts; it expresses an
idea—Jesus being humanly capable of sweating (even if what
he sweated was blood)—that later proved helpful in combating

Docetist Christians who argued against Jesus's having a literal body. Perspired blood finally has no place in any of the other texts that present us with a tempted Jesus.

In the Letter to the Hebrews, we see an altogether different angle on the tradition that Jesus was, in some manner, tested. One of the key points the letter's unknown author* makes is that Jesus Christ is the perfect high priest, for in him "we do not have a high priest who is unable to sympathize with our weaknesses, but we have one who in every respect has been tested as we are, yet without sin." The mention of Jesus's having been "tested" has almost nothing linguistically in common with the gospels' depiction of the prayer at Gethsemane, but it appears to confirm the apparently widely familiar tradition of a Jesus who momentarily questioned his fate.

Thankfully, Hebrews goes much further in its approach of Jesus. In this sense, it may be the most sophisticated, interesting, and coherent work in the New Testament on the issue of Jesus Christ. Among New Testament works, only the Gospel According to John rivals its thermospherically high Christology. Nowhere else does a New Testament author argue so passionately that the figure of Jesus Christ has effectively displaced Hebrew scripture. The homely wandering Jesus of the synoptic gospels is nowhere apparent in Hebrews; neither is Paul's soaring, spiritual, some-

---

* Clement believed Paul was the author of the Letter to the Hebrews and suggested that Paul left the letter unsigned out of recognition of having been divinely commissioned as the apostle to the Gentiles. Jerome followed Clement in this belief, and for more than a thousand years the Vulgate Bible that Jerome was central to translating and compiling listed the work as "The Epistle of Paul to the Hebrews." This view did not prevail among all, as Hebrews has almost nothing linguistically or conceptually in common with the authentic Pauline writings. The author was a highly educated Jewish Christian, knowledgeable about Jewish scripture, and conversant with Hellenistic philosophy. Some (including, apparently, Tertullian) identified the author of Hebrews as Paul's friend Barnabas, but several modern scholars have pointed to Apollos, "an eloquent man, well-versed in the scriptures," whom Paul, along with Aquila and Priscilla, meets in Ephesus in Acts of the Apostles; Paul refers to Apollos several times in 1 Corinthians, sometimes tensely.

what fragmentary Jesus. The Jesus of Hebrews is the "appointed heir of all things," the vessel through which God has chosen to speak to the ancestors of Abraham and Moses. He is a new high priest, "according to the order of Melchizedek, rather than one according to the order of Aaron." The Levitical priests of Aaron's order inherited their priesthood "through a legal requirement," the author of Hebrews argues, but Jesus, like Melchizedek, "holds his priesthood permanently, because he continues forever."

For those of you at home, Melchizedek is a king in Genesis who presents Abraham with bread and wine and later turns up in Psalms as a priestly ruler whose prominence David appeals to after having conquered Jerusalem. The name appears to derive from that of a Phoenician deity and translates literally as "my king is Zedek." Although the third-century Roman theologian Hippolytus recorded the existence of a Christian sect called the Melchizedekians (who apparently believed Jesus Christ was "the only image" of Melchizedek), it was not until the twentieth century, with the discoveries of the Dead Sea Scrolls and Nag Hammadi literature, that Melchizedek's prominence in Hebrews was better contextualized. He was on a lot of people's minds around the first century, Jew and Christian alike. The Essenes possessed scrolls in which he was likened to the archangel Michael, a pre-Christian "mediator" between God and man, much as Paul argued Jesus was. *Melchizedek,* an obscure third-century Christian tract found at Nag Hammadi, portrays him as a "warrior" priest fated to return during the end of days. The author of Hebrews might have been appealing to Melchizedek, much as the psalmist's David attempted to use Melchizedek, as a mystically unifying figure. (In modern times, Melchizedek has proved a figure of great interest within Mormon theology.)

One of the most intellectually adventurous passages of Hebrews argues that Jesus was not only the perfect priest; he was also the perfect sacrifice. Before Jesus, priests entered the Temple to spill the blood of animals, thereby cleansing the slate of sinfulness between God and his chosen people. But this process never worked in the way God's people wished it to. A sacrifice that had to be rendered again and again was imperfect—"a shadow of the true form" of what the ritual was intended to enact, "a reminder of sin year after year. For it is impossible for the blood of bulls and goats to take away sin." In Jesus, however, humankind encountered the perfect sacrifice: "just as it is appointed for mortals to die once, and after that the judgment, so Christ, having been offered once to bear the sins of many, not to deal with sin, but to save those who are eagerly waiting for him."

Part of what makes Hebrews such a remarkable document is its assumed date of composition. Given the text's focus on priestly legitimacy, and the fact that the traditional Jewish priesthood was exterminated following the destruction of the Temple in 70 CE, the original basis for Hebrews might well have been written prior to 70. This somewhat belies the common belief that the later the composition date of a given New Testament text, the higher its Christology will probably be. (Paul's letters are an admitted and crucial exception to this.) Hebrews could predate Mark and Matthew by as much as a decade, yet its view of Jesus's divinity surpasses both.

By the time the gospels were written, Jesus's resurrection (at least in some form) was an established fact of Christian belief, but the explanation for what his death accomplished proved more elusive. In the second and third centuries, Christian thinkers, many of whom had read and appreciated the Letter to the Hebrews and certain letters of Paul, developed further what is now called atonement theory, which has to do with the belief that Jesus's shed blood redeemed earthly sinners by negating the original sin of Adam. Among the gospel writers, Luke seems to have explicitly rejected atonement theory as an explanation for Jesus's death, for he chose to suppress Mark's endorsements of primitive atonement theory whenever he came across them. The one exception is when Luke's Jesus addresses the Twelve during the Last Supper: "This cup that is poured out for you is the new covenant in my blood." The problem, yet again, is that this is most likely an interpolation inserted by a later scribe, for it is not found in many early copies of Luke and nowhere else does Luke show any leanings toward primitive atonement theory. Jesus's *innocence* of the charges against him seems to be the always-decorum-minded Luke's primary concern, not whether his spilled blood washed away terrestrial sin.

The clearest demonstration of the uncertainty with which the gospel writers regarded Jesus's death can be found in how they chose to portray his last words on the cross, which vary greatly. As many have pointed out, it should not have been terribly difficult to reach consensus on the last words uttered by a dying, beloved man, so Jesus's "last words" were obviously viewed by the gospel writers as having theological rather than historical value. Indeed, almost everything the synoptic gospel writers depict Jesus as having said on the cross has roots in various psalms. After he is crucified, Mark and Matthew have Jesus speaking once ("My God, my God, why have you forsaken me?"). Luke has him speaking three times, once to God ("Father, forgive them; for they do not know what they are doing"), once to the so-called good thief crucified beside him ("Truly I tell you, today you will be with me in Paradise"), and once again to God ("Father, into your hands I commend my spirit"). John, too, has him speaking three times, once to his mother and the Beloved Disciple ("Woman, here is your son," and "Here is your mother"), and twice, with elegant bleakness, to, seemingly, himself ("I thirst," and "It is finished").

Mark and Matthew were both attempting a gloss on Psalm 22 of the Septuagint. Many heterodox Christians regarded the passage as an indication that the spirit that inhabited Jesus had left him to die on the cross. Proto-orthodox Christians, on the other hand, understood the words as spoken by a deity who felt forsaken by the burden of taking humanity's sin onto himself, of reconciling the world to himself. John and Luke, too, mention that at the moment of Jesus's death a "spirit" was given up, which provided Adoptionists with more theological ammunition. Whereas Luke's last words seem fixated on making the dying Jesus out to be a respectable, innocently persecuted man, John's last words subtly and beautifully portray both the despair of Jesus's death and its glorious, painful accomplishment. Either way, the lack of a coherent intra-scriptural explanation for the meaning of Jesus's death, much less the makeup of his being, would bedevil Christian theology for centuries.

V.

The Lamb of God, the Son of Man, the Word, the Way: as early as can be figured, Christians have thought about Jesus metaphorically. In the early third century, Origen argued that allegory and metaphor were profoundly important Christian tools in interpreting the meaning of scripture. In his *Homilies on Genesis,* Origen dismissed literalist interpretations of the stories in Genesis as "silly" and described the "stupidity" of literalist Christians as "heavier than the sand of the sea." To him, the story of Noah's ark was an allegory for how to survive within a church surrounded by a hostile world.

Prior to Origen, Christian theology was in a tenebrous place. The prominent second-century Christian writers whose work has survived were primarily polemicists. Origen was particularly instrumental in deepening early Christianity's understanding of Jesus, to whom he referred as "the image of [God's] being," employing a term—*hypostasis*—with great importance to Hellenistic philosophy but that also helpfully appears in the Letter to the Hebrews. (*Hypostasis* literally means something like "underpinning" but can mean "beingness" as well.) Origen additionally crafted one of the most brilliant metaphors in the history of Christian apologetics to explain how God and man could coexist in one being: Metal and fire coexist within the tip of a red-hot iron, do they not? Origen loved and worshipped Jesus but was also unsure whether Jesus and the Holy Spirit were as powerful as God. He wrote openly of the Holy Spirit's being sub-ordinate to Jesus. In Origen's view, Jesus Christ was born before all earthly creatures but was not co-eternal with the Father.

Today, historians of religion refer to such a belief system as subordinationism, which envisions a Trinity of divine but hier-archical beings, with God the Father typically sitting on top and a subordinate and less powerful Son (and Holy Spirit) below him. The vast majority of early Christians, including Origen and most of the authors of the New Testament, were either subordi-nationists or had strong subordinationist leanings. When Origen died of injuries sustained during torture in the persecution led by the emperor Decius in the mid-third century, many Christian thinkers still regarded him as their North Star. But his subordi-nationist views on the relationship between Jesus Christ, God, and the Holy Spirit were deemed controversial later in the third century, and Origen's many admirers were forced to back away from (and, in some cases, denounce) one of the most learned, optimistic, and brilliant theologians to ever call himself a Chris-tian. Consequently, most of Origen's work was destroyed. Of his 574 homilies, only 21 survive in their original Greek.

The Christianity of the first, second, and early third centu-ries was not about maintaining theological union among many. It was about accepting the reality of theological federalism. Dif-ferent Christians in different places used different texts and believed different things. Christianity at this time was largely concerned with principles rather than details. The works that became the New Testament were not selected for the clarity—much less the consistency—with which they explained who and what Jesus was. But a Christianity whose theological details remained in debateful flux had little chance of intellectual or institutional survival.

As the scholar Edward R. Hardy writes, "The history of the-ology can be written in large part by the explanation of a series of technical terms." Christianity holds up a Galilean prophet and transforms him into the Son of God while promising salvation eternal. Its scriptures, unfortunately, speak of such weighty matters confusingly. In the second, third, and fourth centuries, terms sprang up, some hijacked, some coined, some still trailing the contextual tatters of other disciplines behind them: *hypostasis, trinitas, substantia, ousia, homoousios, prosopon, persona, homoiousios*. This is the language of theological Christianity, yet few of these words appear in scripture.

Of the many concepts Christian theologians projected into scripture, none was more significant than the Trinity, which has no scriptural basis beyond that which has been detected by desperate exegetical bird dogs. The first Christian to formally propose a formula for the Trinity, and coin the term *trinitas,* was Tertullian. This occurred roughly 170 years after the death of Jesus. A dour if rigorous thinker, Tertullian displayed little of his contemporary Origen's curiosity, having come of age in Carthage, in North Africa, the indigenous religions of which were often violently resistant to Christianity. ("With our faith," Tertullian wrote, "we desire no further belief. For this is our primary faith, that there is nothing which we ought to believe besides.") Prior to Tertullian, other Christians had used Trinitarian language but not with much philosophical consistency. In Tertullian's formulation, the Trinity comprised "three persons [*personae*], one substance [*substantia*]." To indicate a Father, Son, and Holy Spirit that shared an underlying being while maintaining distinct individual personas, Tertullian used *consubstantialis,* or "of the same substance." This idea was within range of Origen's idea of Jesus's being the *hypostasis* of God, but it was not quite the same thing. Nor was *substantia* quite the same thing as the Greek equivalent of "substance," *ousia,* which was a more conceptual, abstract word. *Ousia,* which derives from the Greek "to be," transmits a sense of identity; *substantia,* significantly, does not.

A number of Greek Christians had already begun to employ *ousia* to describe their ideation of the Trinity, but the word was first used in heterodox Christian circles and initially feared for that reason. Also, neither *ousia* nor *substantia* appears within

the New Testament. The paradox of primitive Trinitarian thinking was already pronounced—three beings defined by their
omniscient, infinite nature sharing the same "substance" or
"essence" defied logic in any language—but scripture's refusal
to provide a vocabulary to talk about what it seemed to be positing presented Christian thinkers with a more or less insuperable
problem. Thus, as Christianity journeyed into its fourth century,
numerous ideas about Jesus remained within the pale of serious
Christian discussion. Subordinationism, meanwhile, continued
to field a strong body of support. Without coming to agreement
on how Jesus fit into this jigsaw of divinity, Christianity was in
danger of becoming another mystery cult vestigially attached to
Judaism.

Some Christians regarded the persecutions of Decius, Valerian, Diocletian, and Galerius, which occupied discrete chunks
of the mid-third to early fourth centuries, as proof that internal
theological divisions had caused the faith to lose the support of
God. But these persecutions, as bad as they were in some areas,
were unevenly enforced and most gravely affected Christians
in the East, leading to lasting divisions between young and old,
between eastern and western believers, and between those who
had renounced their faith under torture and those who gladly
accepted the lash. Despite Christianity's theological disarray, the
persecutions established the degree to which faith had developed
a sturdy framework of hierarchical administration. The future
emperor Constantine, whose father, Constantius, had skillfully
navigated a complicated system of imperial governance instituted by Diocletian, took intrigued note of Christianity's organizational sophistication. Also significant was that Constantine's
father had come to regard Christians positively and did little to
enforce the Diocletianic persecution in his areas of administration, which might have further influenced his son's eventual
openness to the faith.

That Constantine dreamed he saw Christian portents in the
sky on the eve of the Battle of the Milvian Bridge in 312, foretell-

ing his victory, as Eusebius later reported, is unknowable. The Christian version of the story does not emerge until a decade after the fact, and coins minted under Constantine's rule held pagan images until 320. But there is no question Constantine believed the battle's favorable outcome was due to the auspices of the Christian god. Constantine's attraction to Jesus Christ seems to have been real, but he probably viewed him as a potential deliverer of order rather than as a guarantor of personal salvation. (The man himself had an unsurprisingly sordid personal life.) Imagine Constantine's surprise, then, to discover that the seemingly rising faith on which he had staked his rule was rife with internal divisions, all of which became more severe under the spotlight of imperial power.

In 318, five years after Constantine's Edict of Milan, which granted Christians the right to practice their faith unmolested, a respected presbyter in Alexandria named Arius began teaching his subordinationist formulation about Jesus: "Once he was not." Arius believed Jesus Christ was not co-eternal with but rather a creation of God the Father, whose will he enacted on the earth. In this belief, Arius had the backing of numerous passages of the gospels, certain lines within Paul's letters, and the work of greatly esteemed theologians such as Origen. What would later be called Arianism had much going for it, not the least of which was its philosophical coherence. Arianism's one glaring problem was that a Jesus subordinate to God was and always would be sideways polytheism.

Constantine was forced to focus on Christianity's internal divisions, especially with regard to Arianism, after he became sole emperor in 324, by which time a unified church had become central to his success as emperor. In 325, Constantine arranged transport for hundreds of bishops and presbyters from around his empire, Arius included, and ferried them all to an imperial residence in Nicaea in modern-day Turkey. In so acting, Constantine placed the theology of the church and the goals of the empire on contiguous tracks for the first time.

At the General Council of Nicaea, Arianism was the main point of discussion, according to the few (and no doubt somewhat distorted) accounts we have of what went on there. Christians had never before gathered together to find theological common ground, and the Arian faction, which was internally divided, found itself outnumbered. (Arius was of too junior a position to formally participate.) Even so, no one could agree on terms. The historian Eusebius, who was sympathetic to Arius, petitioned the council to adopt as a general statement of faith a creed (or confession of faith) that he claimed was used in his native Caesarea:

> We believe in one God, Father, Almighty, the maker of
>   all things visible and invisible.
> And in one Lord Jesus Christ, the Word of God, God
>   of God, Light of Light, Life of Life, unique Son,
>   first-born of all creation . . .
> We also believe in one Holy Spirit. . . .
> [A]nd so I am convinced, and so I have held, and will
>   stand for this faith till death, anathematizing every
>   godless heresy.

At Constantine's urging, a newish, non-scriptural, and somewhat disputed word, *homoousios* ("of one essence," similar to— but not the same as—the Latin equivalent, *consubstantialis,* "of one substance"), was introduced into Eusebius's creed. But enemies of Arius wanted to further isolate the man and his supporters, so the creed had an additional phrase about Jesus Christ inserted into it, "begotten, not made," and ended with a condemnation of those who "say 'there was a time when he did not exist.'"

Quite a few of the Christians who chose to publicly accept the new creed were privately unhappy with *homoousios,* which had hitherto been used in mostly heterodox Christian circles.

While the original Nicene Creed* solidified the Christian definition of how Jesus and God were the same, it was less successful
in accounting for how they were distinct. On top of that, the
creed contained no explicit mention of the Trinity. This did nothing to clarify the hitherto ambiguous stature of the Holy Spirit,
which the creed mentioned in one sentence. Finally, the Nicene
Creed did nothing to challenge Arius's core point. If anything,
it intensified Arius's core point. How could something begotten
not also be made? How could something eternal be begotten?

A cowed Arius withdrew from church life after his friend
Eusebius arranged for him an official pardon, but the debate
over Arianism, and "of one essence/substance," darkened Christianity for decades more. One of the angriest and most vocal
opponents of Arianism in all its forms was an ambitious young
intellectual named Athanasius, who attended Nicaea under the
auspices of his boss, Alexander, the bishop of Alexandria. (Athanasius, who is believed to have coined the term "Arianism," which
he applied liberally to those he disagreed with, later persuaded
Constantine to formally excommunicate all self-professed Arians, though that ban was lifted after only two years, again thanks
to Eusebius.) What helped Athanasius's hand after Nicaea was
that despite his youth he had already written quite a bit about
Christian theology.

Athanasius, too, lived and taught in Alexandria, though
unlike many products of that city's Christian tradition he
resisted any intrusions of Neoplatonic thought into his faith.
He was born a few years before 300, just as the Diocletianic
persecution began, and had probably seen members of his
church tormented, humiliated, and killed. The persecution filled
the deserts outside Alexandria with monks, one of whom, the
famed ascetic Anthony, Athanasius knew and followed in some

---

* The creed we typically refer to as the Nicene Creed was actually formulated in
Constantinople several decades later.

capacity, which may explain how quickly he was able to achieve prominence within the Alexandrian church. By the time Athanasius was in his early twenties he had already written a diatribe against paganism, his hatred of which was pronounced even by early-Christian standards. His next book was *On the Incarnation,* one of the first proto-orthodox works intended to elucidate Jesus's position within the Godhead.*

Athanasius was intent on establishing the eternal nature of the Word, its role in the creation of the world, and its logical continuance in the person of Jesus Christ: "There is thus no inconsistency between creation and salvation; for the One Father has employed the same Agent for both works." God made us "reasonable" and even lovable creatures, Athanasius goes on, and so, when God discovered us perishing on the earth, his only loving option was to save us, "to bring again the corruptible to incorruption and to maintain for the Father his consistency of character with all. For He alone, being Word of the Father and above all, was in consequence both able to recreate all, and worthy to suffer on behalf of all and to be an ambassador for all with the Father." This is an interesting piece of theodicy, certainly, but certain questions remain: Why is an all-powerful God not powerful enough to make right what is wrong without the extraordinary intercession of the Son? Athanasius came up with one possible answer: "The death of all was consummated in the Lord's body; yet, because the Word was in it, death and corruption were in the same act utterly abolished. Death there had to be, and

---

* Athanasius's influence on Christianity goes beyond theology. A festal letter he wrote in the late 360s—one of Christianity's most difficult decades—is one of the first attempts to define the canon of the New Testament. Apparently, the letter was successful, for the books Athanasius listed are, by and large, the accepted New Testament canon. Amazingly, Athanasius's letter is one of the only glimpses we have into the formation of the New Testament. As one scholar writes, "Nothing is more amazing in the annals of the Christian Church than the absence of detailed accounts of so significant a process."

death for all, so that the due of all might be paid." For a quickly expanding church, this might have seemed an empirically sound position: death for all, and so life for all. Nevertheless, if Jesus Christ redeemed all, why were so many excluded from the grace of his sacrifice by the sheer accidents of parentage and geography? The magical thing Athanasius argued that Jesus Christ had accomplished was not successful even on its own magical terms.

Finally, Athanasius tackled the contentious question of how human Jesus Christ's mind was: "The Word was not hedged in by His body, nor did his presence in the body prevent His being present elsewhere as well. When He moved His body He did not cease also to direct the universe by His Mind and might." A Jesus Christ who wandered the Galilean countryside while simultaneously maintaining the stars' passage across the sky presents us with a galactic funambulist far beyond anything imagined by Paul or the author of Hebrews.

Athanasius's disagreeable and ruthless nature endeared him to few. When Constantine welcomed Arius back into the Alexandrian church, Athanasius refused to recognize Constantine's authority; in response, Constantine exiled Athanasius to Trier for a few years to think on his obstinacy. In the late 330s, Athanasius returned to Alexandria and rededicated his public life to addressing Arianism's mephitic refusal to die. From Athanasius's perspective, the problems were dire, because the philosophical weakness of the Nicene Creed had led to a revival of Arian thought. Constantius II, who became sole emperor in 351, believed, as did all of Constantine's sons, that Jesus Christ's divinity was not equal to that of the Father. This led to several Constantius-sponsored creeds, including one that specifically denounced *homoousios* and posited a Jesus Christ who had been "begotten before all ages" but was not co-eternal with the Father. These creeds were almost uniformly rejected in the western empire, where Nicene thinking was stronger, in part because the Latin terminology used to describe the Godhead was generally less abstract. In the East, however, the Arian position was strong enough to persuade Constantius to send Athanasius into yet another exile.

During the 350s, a group of Christians called the Homoiousians (from their position that the Father and the Son were like [*homoios*] but not identical to each other) emerged to present Christianity with yet another way of thinking about Jesus Christ's position within the Godhead. Unfortunately, the Father and the Son being "like" but not "identical" to each other was even vaguer than the Nicene Creed! By the end of the decade, Constantius pushed to resolve the issue. The result was utter confusion, with several creeds and councils succeeding primarily in sharpening the divide between eastern and western bishops. One of these synods, the Council of Rimini, resulted in an official creed of the church that endorsed a variety of Arian positions. It proved so influential that many Goth tribes in northern Europe would maintain their Arian faith until the seventh century. Constantius died of fever in 361, while on his way to meet his usurping cousin in battle, whereupon Christian theology went adrift for two decades. Had Constantius not perished, we might today be living in an Arian Christian world.

Constantius's usurping cousin, Julian, was the last member of the Constantinian dynasty. Raised a Christian, he rejected the faith while still a young man, having come to regard the debates over the substance or essence of the Godhead as a calamitous waste of mental energy. When Julian attempted to re-paganize the empire, he became the last imperial champion of classical Roman culture.* During his two-year rule (he was killed in 363 during a military campaign in modern-day Iraq), Christian divisions deepened, much to Julian's delight, if not exactly to his shock. The eastern emperor Valens, who ruled from 364 to

---

* Julian's most diabolical plan? To rebuild the Jewish Temple in Jerusalem, in defiance of Christian claims to have made its mother faith obsolete. In Julian's mind, Jewish beliefs were marginally more acceptable by virtue of being ancient.

378, was convinced by Homoiousian logic and drove into exile several bishops who disagreed with him. Athanasius, who was now an old man, attempted to rally Christians by holding up the Nicene Creed as a starting point of philosophical agreement, having forgotten that the Nicene Creed was an ad hoc solution few Christians at the time admired. Eventually, Athanasius was moved to revive the now widely discredited word *homoousios* to describe the Godhead. By this time, Athanasius's stature was such that Valens, who greatly disliked the old Nicene, allowed him to die in 373 while still holding his episcopal office. But Christian theology, literally and figuratively, was still very much up in the air.

Athanasius had trouble convincing those who disagreed with him because his keenest interest was in destroying his opponents, not winning them over. In this sense, a group of Christian thinkers known as the Cappadocian Fathers—Basil of Caesarea, Gregory of Nyssa, and Gregory of Nazianzus—became Athanasius's most important theological inheritors. Hailing from an insignificant province of Roman Asia but born to a wealthy family, Gregory of Nazianzus quickly developed a reputation as having one of the strongest theological minds of his time. After the catastrophic battlefield death of the Arian eastern emperor Valens in 378, Gregory made his way to Constantinople just as a bishop named Eunomius began to preach an extreme form of subordinationism that denied that Jesus Christ and the Father had *any* substance or essence in common. Gregory responded to Eunomius, as well as to milder Arians, with a series of lectures today known as *The Five Theological Orations.*

Gregory helped change the tenor of the debate in Constantinople by refusing to discuss the Trinity via elaborate analogies to the physical world, which Latin-speaking Christians generally found to be persuasive but which left many Greek-speaking Christians cold. He readily admitted that the Trinity appeared to defeat logical explanation and thus appealed to the deeper, more mystical logic of the universe and often used pagan thinking to support his points. He explained the co-eternal nature of the Trinity by pointing out that "there never was a time when [God] was not. And the same is true of the Son and the Holy Ghost. Ask me again, and again I will answer you, When was the Son begotten? When the Father was not begotten." Anything that is a part of God, Gregory argued, must necessarily be viewed as co-eternal with him: "The sun is not prior to its light. . . . [T]he sources of time are not subject to time." This was not know-nothing mysticism or angry invective but actual Christian philosophy. Gregory of Nazianzus helped make the logic behind the Nicene Creed—and full Trinitarian thinking—intellectually acceptable to Greek-speaking Christians.

VI.

In many ways, the best thing to happen to Christianity was imperial backing; the faith might not have risen so meteorically to prominence without it. The worst thing to happen to Christianity was also imperial backing, for rarely has any clergy deeply entangled with power politics made wise decisions. This is why the various councils that had convened in the fourth century saw so little lasting consensus. As the historian Diarmaid MacCulloch writes, once Christians had "absorbed one set of explanations about what the divine was, anything from outside which disrupted those explanations threatened their access to divine power." Yet Christianity was no longer about access to divine power through table fellowship and baptism and carefully reasoned epistles; it was about access to divine power through bizarrely complex doctrinal adjustments and naked appeals to earthly authority—and every bishop knew it. This explains the great derangement that affected Christian thinking throughout the fourth century and that came to a head in Constantinople in the 370s. The Cappadocian father Gregory of Nyssa, who was visiting at the time, famously noted, "If in this city you ask anyone for change, he will discuss with you whether the son is begotten or unbegotten. If you ask about the quality of bread, you will receive the answer that 'the Father is greater, the Son is less.' If you suggest that a bath is desirable, you will be told that, 'there was nothing before the Son was created.'" What few realized was that this atmosphere of open Christian debate was about to vanish off the face of the earth.

No one could agree on what early Christian writings said about Jesus Christ because, on this issue and others, Christian writings were either unclear or contradicted themselves. Many Christians used the same books—in some cases, the same *scenes*—to come to radically different theological conclusions. A Roman emperor was incapable of making that problem go away. When the western ruler Theodosius I assumed power in 379, the empire was in conceivable danger of military collapse. On the issue of Christian discord, however, Theodosius had a novel idea: rather than find authority for his views within Christian scripture, he would wield his authority over Christian scripture. A fervent believer in the Nicene Creed, which in his native Spain went largely unquestioned, Theodosius entered Constantinople, long an Arian power base, with the purpose of uniting all Christianity under the Latin-speaking world's understanding of God. One of his first decrees was that the Father and the Son had to be referred to jointly; any belief that fell short of proper Nicene thinking was condemned as "insane." Theodosius sacked the local Arian bishop and replaced him with Gregory of Nazianzus. He stationed soldiers outside churches so newly appointed Nicene priests could preach without being torn apart by Arian parishioners. Finally, he called for yet another synod, the First Council of Constantinople, which convened in 381 and whose attendees Theodosius himself selected.

While many matters were discussed during the council, its importance to church history derives from its renewal of the Nicene Creed, which now came backed by the full force of a hard-nosed emperor and a battery of theological quislings. (Gregory of Nazianzus was a noble exception to this. Disgusted by the council's strong-arm political tactics, he left and resigned his bishopric.) Once again, Jesus Christ was said to be "consubstantial with the Father," and, once again, there was no explicit mention of the Trinity. In exchange for support of his neo-Nicene Creed, Theodosius did not blink at offering wavering bishops various emoluments. (He had already made it illegal for any non-Nicene Christian to be appointed bishop.)

The historian Charles Freeman argues there were "ideological reasons" for why Theodosius and the Nicene faction were so eager to argue on behalf of a Son who was co-eternal to, and as powerful as, the Father. The Jesus of the gospels was in no position to justify the hierarchy of the imperial church. He had been executed by the Roman authorities and preached a coming kingdom in which the poor had an honored part. An indisputably divine and kingly Jesus served as a different sort of lodestar. Freeman calls this latter Jesus "a bizarre distortion of the historical reality but one that reflects the imperial ideology within which the church now operated." The Nicene Creed and the relationship between Jesus Christ and God it put forth thus became a "mystery of the faith," but only because the Nicene Creed was, and remains, such a theologically frustrating explanation for who and what Jesus Christ was. Unlike the original Nicene Creed, which was never intended for liturgical use, the neo-Nicene Creed began to be used during baptisms and later crept into the liturgy itself. The strange words it contained imprinted on the minds of Christians, who learned to recite them without fully thinking about what they said. (As an erstwhile altar boy, I can personally attest to this phenomenon.)

Even with Theodosius's backing, many Greek-speaking Christians remained unsatisfied with the results of the first Council of Constantinople. The following year, a second, smaller council was convened in the city, which approved the Greek use of *hypostasis* to describe the three substances of the Trinity (long a point of contention between East and West) and officially codified the Holy Spirit's inclusion within that Trinity. These became, and remain, the tent-pole postulations of orthodox Christianity, which now came into formal existence. Arianism, in all its guises, real or perceived, was outlawed. By the late fourth century, the agents of Theodosius wielded largely unchallenged power. In the next century and beyond, that power would be used to dismantle the classical world: the Olympic games were shut down, non-Christians were forbidden to hold office or serve in the military, and many important pagan temples were destroyed.

The hard, strange work of Christology was not yet complete, of course. Augustine's thoughts on the Trinity yielded the beautiful insight that the Holy Spirit was, among other things, the conduit through which the Father and the Son expressed their love for each other. Nestorianism, and the questions it raised about the nature of Jesus's humanity, were addressed at the Council of Ephesus in 431 and divisively settled at the Council of Chalcedon in 451. The answer was yet another adjusted restatement of the Nicene formula: his divinity was consubstantial with the Father, and his humanity was consubstantial with ours— two natures (or substances) united in one divine man, whose essential being remained unchanged throughout his spiritually eventful life. Finally, at the Third Council of Constantinople in 681, Christian theologians put to rest questions about the nature of Jesus Christ's will. He had not one will but two, and his two wills—one divine, one human—did not and could not conflict but were perfectly (if paradoxically) complementary. It was the last important theological ruling issued by an imperial council. The best of Christianity's many, varied minds finally knew who and what Jesus Christ was, right down to the God-sparked molecules of his *hypostasis,* and it had taken them only 650 years to work it all out.

SIMON THE CANANAEAN
& THADDAEUS

Saint Sernin's Basilica: Toulouse, France

PINK CITY • SATURNINUS • IDENTITY PROBLEMS • ZAROËS & ARFAXAT • SUNDAY MARKET • THE ZEALOTS • BANDITS • BROTHERS OF THE LORD • THE GREATEST RIDDLE • *I ENOCH* • APOSTLES NOT OF THE TWELVE

I.

Ihad been there only a few hours, but I could tell already there was a lot to admire about Toulouse, also known as the Pink City, the Cape Canaveral of the European space program, and, long ago, the finest city in all of medieval Gaul. Then I began talking to Gérard, a native son determined to tell me all the things about Toulouse I was supposed to hate. Gérard first noticed me writing in my notebook while I stood across the street from Saint Sernin's, Toulouse's central basilica, which held the relics of the apostles Simon the Cananaean and Thaddaeus. It was eleven o'clock on a misty Saturday night in late May: above us, all around us, summer air was humidly annexing the spring.

Gérard began by detailing his problems with the Muslims, moved on to the blacks, proceeded on to the Asians, shifted over to the Africans, drifted back to the Muslims, and ended, forcefully, with the Muslims. The nutshell version of his argument was that none of these people were French. Hundreds of years ago, he told me, not terribly far from where we stood, at Pamiers, the Muslim horde was once pushed back by spear and sword. Once, he said, they came as warriors, carrying banners and weapons. Now Muslims came pregnant, carrying visas.

Gérard apparently believed I was a student and with flashing troublemaker eyes kept indicating my notebook and telling me to "include" this or that bit in my "research." When he started in on the Muslims again, I stopped pretending to take notes. Five five in his amply heeled shoes, Gérard wore a thin blue sport coat and tie whose fat paisley knot was loose and miscentered. Suddenly I could see the small, shabby apartment to which he had no wish to stumble home: the stale sandy crumbs in the bread dish on the plain wooden table, the stained coffee cup he rarely washed, the photograph of the wife long dead, the phone that no longer rang. His hands were palsied with something like Parkinson's or alcoholism or both.

It had not rained enough to leave any puddles, but the streets and sidewalks gleamed like black rubber. Not many people were out walking tonight. In a café across the street, a few youngish French drank and chatted. On the corner nearest to us, a street musician played his accordion, though its sad, strangled sound suggested something traumatic had happened to its bellows. A young Frenchman hurried into view on the opposite street, carrying a bottle of wine and delicately cradling a light brown torpedo of fresh bread. An archetypal French sight, but for his dreadlocks and iPod earbuds. Gérard watched him without expression.

I told Gérard I had to be going. He nodded in a way that seemed to recognize that he had taken one or two (or twelve) unnecessarily alienating rhetorical steps. We headed off in separate directions, him to his lonely apartment, me to my lonely hotel room. Once Gérard disappeared around the corner, though, I doubled back and walked around Saint Sernin's Basilica a second time. This took several minutes. A large Romanesque cross-shaped church—the largest such church in Europe, and a UNESCO World Heritage Site—Saint Sernin's was snugly enclosed within an ovular huddle of distinctively pink Toulouse buildings, which meant it was virtually impossible to see the basilica from a distance. On approach, you caught glimpses of it, looming between the cracks of narrow streets, almost as though you were stalking an elephant through thick jungle, but to really see Saint Sernin's, you had to get close. Only its six-story octagonal slit-windowed stone belfry could be seen from a distance.

Saint Sernin's was built on the supposed remains of a shrine devoted to Saint Saturninus, who is known in French as Sernin. According to legend, Sernin was the first bishop of Toulouse, leading its small community of Christians in the first half of the third century. In 249, however, the Roman emperor Decius issued a decree that affected nearly every living Christian in the empire. Rome's fortunes had declined, Decius believed, because not enough Roman citizens were making the necessary sacrifices to the gods. Thus, he demanded that every Roman citizen (males were allowed to sacrifice on behalf of their households) make a sacrifice. Once this sacrifice was enacted before an imperially recognized witness, Romans were given a certificate. Those who refused to sacrifice and were not granted their certificate were vulnerable to punishment and, sometimes, execution. Decius's order was at least partially directed at the empire's Christians, most of whom obeyed and sacrificed. One feels for these ancient Christians: on this particular issue, their scripture offered little guidance, containing, as it did, as many recommendations to kowtow to earthly authority as it did to reject pagan idols.

The damage done to Christianity by Decius's decree was considerable, and the persecution helped generate a copious amount of martyr literature in which Christians depicted themselves as the always-resistant victims of continuous pagan harassment. This literature was fanciful in two ways: most Christians did not resist, and most persecutions were minor (though Decius's eventual successor, Valerian, was rougher on Christians). There is no question that some Christians resisted Decius's decree; most, however, were community leaders, such as Sernin, whose supposed end came when he refused to sacrifice and was arrested in front of Toulouse's pagan temple and tied to a sacrificial bull. The bull was then goaded until it went berserk; it charged through town with an increasingly mutilated Sernin in tow. (As *The Golden Legend* has it, "Thus Saturninus, with his skull shattered and his brains spilled out, happily consummated his martyrdom.") Sernin's broken body was secreted away by his followers and buried. At some point in the following century, a local bishop "found" Sernin's relics and body and ordered the construction of a small wooden shrine over them, though no archaeological remains of this structure have ever been found.

There seem to have been a few early Christian bishops named Saturninus (an African name), all of whom were gruesomely martyred. This, along with the fact that Sernin was said to have been a member of the Seventy Disciples, which is temporally impossible given the century of his death, indicates a high likelihood that Sernin of Toulouse is a purely legendary figure. Either way, by the fourth century Sernin was the center of an active cult. With Christianity triumphant throughout the empire, a basilica was built in his honor over or around his Toulouse shrine, though its layout and size are, once again, unknown. In the eleventh century, Toulouse's Christian community laid the cornerstones of a new and grander Saint Sernin's Basilica, work on which continued for several hundred years. Despite the town's efforts, ancient and modern, on behalf of Saint Sernin's, certain structural elements were never completed, such as the two intended towers on the basilica's western front. Many of its ornamental exterior carvings have today eroded beyond any hope of restoration.

By medieval times, Saint Sernin's had become an important stop on the Camino de Santiago, Europe's greatest Christian pilgrimage walking route, which terminates at the tomb of James son of Zebedee in Santiago, Spain. Scholars have debated where the European Christian impulse toward peregrinative piety—which has no basis in scripture—derives from, but it may have something to do with Cluny, a village in France's Burgundy region, which was founded in the early tenth century. Today, Cluny is a mere village, but its vibrant determination to promote itself and its millennial vision changed European Christianity for good and ill. Although Cluny's monks built many spectacular buildings within Cluny itself, including one of the largest churches in Europe—many of the town's devotional structures were destroyed by mobs during the French Revolution—they reserved their greatest propagandistic efforts on behalf of James son of Zebedee's then-hard-to-reach shrine in distant Santiago, Spain.

It is unknown whether the monks and abbots of Cluny were the first to propose walking hundreds of miles to Santiago or simply seized on the fact that Christians were already doing so. What is known is that from the eleventh century on the Christians of Cluny built and promoted numerous way-station churches, sanctuaries, and monasteries along the pilgrimage path, including Saint Sernin's, which was concocted as a tourist church and today remains primarily a tourist church.

Saint Sernin's Basilica was not a magnificent or overpowering building. It had a lovely, comforting homeliness to it, almost as though it were a brick cassoulet. Perhaps the most striking exterior aspect of Saint Sernin's was the pair of gargantuan wood double doors that opened onto its transept crossings. Adjacent to the door were cornices and modillions festooned with carvings of biblical scenes, along with some figures whose meaning was not easily surmised. Two of the better preserved modillion carvings, above what is called the Miègeville Door, show a mysterious man's and woman's faces. Other bits of ornamental art were stranger yet: human figures imprisoned within scrolls, an angel-flanked Peter holding out cruciform wafers, two women riding

lions.* Nearby were relics of Toulouse's paleo-Christian community, including an ancient funereal niche filled with large marble
coffins that probably dated from the eleventh or twelfth century.
These were in grievous condition, appearing to have been periodically hosed down with sulfuric acid.

I had stood before and within the churches of many cultures: Indian, Roman, Palestinian, Byzantine, Vietnamese,
American, Greek, German, Russian, and Tanzanian, to name but
a few. I knew this: no other culture's churches were as strangely
distancing—even alienating—as those of medieval Europe. I
thought of Kingsley Amis's famous line: "Had people ever been
as nasty, as self-indulgent, as dull, as miserable, as cocksure, as
bad at art, as dismally ludicrous, or as wrong as they'd been in
the Middle Ages?" Never before had such intellectually hermetic,
helplessly superstitious people endeavored to build more utterly
astonishing things across such a wide sweep of lands and cultures. The Christians of medieval Europe had no computers or
machines. They had only their brute strength and cruel mastery
over various beasts of burden. From this: Notre Dame, Chartres,
Saint Sernin's, Santiago de Compostela. How was this possible?
How on earth did they complete these structures that would
challenge the finest architects and engineers of the twenty-first
century?

But they were not building churches or basilicas so much as
universes in miniature. Every portal sculpture, every modillion,
every stone face above every capital—this was their philosophy,
their theodicy, their genome of brick and mortar. It was faith
literalized and semiotized, for all eternity. Put aside thoughts

---

* Christian art in medieval Europe got weird in some places, especially in the
churches found along the Camino de Santiago. The intrusion of once-forbidden
pagan and shamanistic creatures became so common that a medieval monk complained, "What are these ridiculous monsters doing in the cloisters? What are these
filthy apes, ferocious lions, monstrous centaurs doing here?"

of the colossal waste of such buildings being constructed in a time of poverty and social deprivation: architectural historians will tell you that the vast majority of medieval churches were subsidized by their communities with pride-fattened hearts. Medieval churches occupy the highest points within their cities for a reason. The medieval architects and craftsmen on the church-building circuit were the Hollywood film crews of their time, traveling widely (and almost always by foot), exchanging techniques, and feasting on the celebratory banquets of their wealthy benefactors. The peasants who lived in the shadows of these costly, otherworldly churches must have accepted all this as reasonable, just as we somehow accept that earning tens of millions of dollars for pretending to be Iron Man is reasonable.

When I rounded the final corner of Saint Sernin's, I found two teenagers sitting in the jamb of the western door amid a small palisade of empty Kronenbourg beer bottles. Both watched me mutely, and I realized quickly they were sitting there to make out. "Bonsoir," I said, and asked if they spoke English. "A little," the young man said. "She speaks more than me." His spotty beard made his face seem as though it were wearing an old moth-eaten sweater. She just looked at me: short black hair, small face, the dejected eyes and mouth of a goth girl with no makeup. I asked them if they knew anything about the church. The young man looked to the young woman. "It's a very old church," she said. "A lot of tourists come here." Did she know about any of the relics inside? She did not. Neither did he. "Have you," I asked her, "ever heard of Simon the Cananaean or Thaddaeus, the apostles?" These names were utterly unknown to her. Her boyfriend asked what the hell we were talking about. When she translated for him, he laughed at the outrageous notion of his caring about such things.

I wished them a good night and walked around Saint Sernin's a third time. The next time I passed the doorjamb, they were gone.

II.

Simon the Cananaean and Thaddaeus are probably the most obscure members of the Twelve. They are also the only members of the Twelve traditionally imagined to have met their martyrdoms together. Simon is primarily notable for being regarded as something he was not, and Thaddaeus is primarily notable for being regarded as someone he was not. Even their placement in the New Testament's apostolic lists establishes the lack of interest they generated among the evangelists. In Mark and Matthew, "Simon the Cananaean" holds down the Twelve's eleventh position, followed only by Judas; Luke, however, promotes the apostle he calls "Simon, who was called the Zealot" to the tenth position. In Mark and Matthew, meanwhile, Thaddaeus occupies the tenth position; in Luke, an apostle literally referred to as "Judas of James" is listed eleventh, before Judas. What these traded places and swapped names actually amounts to cannot be known, especially when neither Simon nor Thaddaeus is mentioned within the New Testament beyond the lists of the Twelve,* though John's gospel mentions one "Judas (not Iscariot)," who some commentators have argued must be the same person as Luke's "Judas of James."

Another mystery is why the gospels disagree on the names of these two apostles. Possibly Luke was aware of traditions that provided Simon with a different epithet and Thaddaeus a different name. Most scholars agree that the apostle Mark and Matthew deem "Simon the Cananaean"—Simon *"ho Kananaois,"* which is to say, Simon from Cana or Simon the Canaanite—is the result of a transliteration error. "Cananaean" is not a place-of-origin epithet but a derivation of *qan'ana*, the Aramaic word for "zealous." Luke, who otherwise shows little interest in Aramaic

---

* Thanks to Epiphanius, we know that *The Gospel of the Ebionites* (also known as *The Gospel of the Twelve Apostles*) included Simon and Thaddaeus as being among the first apostles to be called into the Twelve by Jesus.

words, apparently recognized Mark's and Matthew's mistake and provided a presumably more accurate Greek rendering of the epithet: Simon *zelotes,* or "Simon, who was called the Zealot."

Thaddaeus (in Greek, *Thaddaios*) is a diminutive of a few Greek names, including *Theodosios* and *Theodoros;* the Semitic version of Thaddaeus was rendered as *Taddai* or, possibly, *Addai.* It was not a common name in first-century Palestine; there are only a handful of other confirmed instances of its use. Christian tradition has generally evolved to regard Thaddaeus as the nickname of Luke's "Judas of James" and John's "Judas (not Iscariot)." No one, after all, would have wanted to go by the name of the apostle who betrayed Jesus. This consequently gave rise to a tradition of referring to the apostle Jude Thaddaeus, who, as Saint Jude, is perhaps best known to modern Christians as the patron saint of lost causes. However, there is nothing in the New Testament to indicate the existence of Jude Thaddaeus.

A few early Matthew manuscripts give Thaddaeus's name as "Lebbaeus" (Greek: *Lebaios*) or "Lebbaeus surnamed Thaddaeus," which complicates things further. In the Vulgate Bible, Jerome referred to Thaddaeus as "Trinomius," or "the man with three names," but he is actually Quadrinomius: Judas of James, Thaddaeus, Jude Thaddaeus, and, simply, Jude. The confusion surrounding Thaddaeus's name makes him a significant apostle historically, if only because it suggests that by the time the gospels were written, the individual identities of the Twelve were no longer regarded as important to Christians. If they were, the gospels' earliest copyists would surely have done more to harmonize the apostolic lists' discrepancies. That they generally did not establishes the low-priority nature of the issue.

Another minor mystery pertains to whether Luke meant "Judas of James" to mean "Judas the son of James" or "Judas the brother of James." In standard first-century Greek usage, "of" formulations usually indicated a father-son relationship. That appears not to be the case here, or so tradition has assumed. But which James is Jude "of"? James the brother of Jesus, James the brother of John, James son of Alphaeus, or some other, historically insignificant James? Arguments on behalf of all these candidates have been waged. Because James the brother of Jesus had a brother named Judas, and because Judas eventually became a prominent figure in Jewish Christianity (the canonical Letter of Jude's author self-identifies as "Judas the brother of James"), one traditional understanding is that "Judas of James" was the brother of James son of Alphaeus (which is actually James the brother of Jesus but, in the Catholic mind, becomes James the cousin of Jesus). In the early second century, the Christian writer Papias wrote of his understanding that Simon and Jude were brothers to James "the bishop," meaning, probably, James the brother of Jesus. Origen, in the third century, identified Jude as the brother of Jesus and James but not Simon. The mid-fourth-century Christian Ephraem the Syrian wrote a commentary on Acts that connected "Simon the Zealot" and "Judas of James" with Jesus's brothers Simon and Jude, but few later commentators have chosen to explore this path, due to the gospels' insinuation that Jesus's brothers were not members of the Twelve. Others have proposed that Judas of James is the son of James son of Zebedee and thus nephew to the apostle John.

Many ancient legends conflate Simon the apostle with Simon the brother of Jesus and Simeon the second bishop of Jerusalem, as in this introductory processional to a Coptic legend: "The preaching of the blessed Saint Simon, the son of Cleopas, who was surnamed Judas, which is interpreted Nathaniel, who became bishop of Jerusalem after James, the brother of our Lord." (Actually, Simon has been confused with *three* different men here: Simon the brother of Jesus, Judas of James, and Nathanael the disciple.) Attempts to zero in (even generally) on Jude/Thaddaeus's identity are equally hopeless. Someone called "Judas the Zealot" appears in a few early New Testament manuscripts and Christian legends, and in the fourth century Eusebius wrote of the Syriac Christian legend in which "Thomas, one of the twelve apostles, was moved by inspiration to send Thaddaeus, himself in the list of Christ's seventy disciples, to Edessa as preacher and evangelist of the teaching about Christ." While in Edessa, the legend holds, Thaddaeus met King Abgar and later muled letters back and forth between Jesus and the king; in the meantime, Thaddaeus "amazed all [Edessa's] inhabitants [with] his wonderful miracles." Despite Eusebius's testimony that this particular Thaddaeus was a member of the Seventy Disciples, the actual Syriac legend, which Eusebius also quoted, refers to Thaddaeus both as "an apostle" and as "one of the Seventy." Even more confusing is the Syriac legend's attestation that "Judas, also known as Thomas," sent Thaddaeus on his way. This leaves us with an apostle saddled with the alternate name of Judas being dispatched by a different apostle saddled with the alternate name of Judas. The traditions of Syriac Christianity regard the "apostle" Addai as the faith's co-founder with Judas Thomas, the supposed twin brother of Jesus. Addai, in all likelihood, is Thaddaeus from the gospels transplanted. Manichaeism, the great enemy faith of early Christianity, which incorporated many crypto-Christian elements and directly competed with Syriac Christianity in some areas, contains a tradition that its founder, Mani, had two great disciples named Addai and Thomas. These legends are probably connected in some way.

Very little mention is made of Simon the Cananaean/Zealot during the first three hundred years of the church. Basil of Caesarea, who died in the late fourth century, mentioned that Simon expired of natural causes in Edessa, of all places—one of many instances in which a legend associated with Jude/Thaddaeus intermixed with a legend associated with Simon. A later, more whimsical legend places a youthful Simon among the "shepherds living in the fields, keeping watch over their flock," to whom, in the Gospel According to Luke, an angel announces the coming of Jesus. In the fifth or sixth century, various Coptic legends developed that had Simon traveling to Britain.

Thaddaeus, along with Bartholomew, is one of the "first illuminators" to which the Armenian Church traces its origins.

Indeed, Thaddaeus has been called the "first patriarch of the Armenian Church." Other legends land him in Mesopotamia and Syria. A Coptic legend called *The Preaching of Judas Thaddaeus in Syria* describes Peter and Thaddaeus's highly tedious adventures, one of which involves a "harlot" being stripped of her clothes before the apostles and magically levitated and twirled around as a plaything by Peter. At the end of the text, we are told that Thaddaeus died nonviolently in Syria after he and Peter "built them a church, and . . . wrote for them a Gospel and a Book of commandments."

A legend in which Simon and Jude/Thaddaeus preach and travel together can be found in a compendium work once called *The Apostolic History* but now known as *Pseudo-Abdias,* so named for its pseudonymous author, Abdias, a supposed bishop of the Babylonian church and member of Luke's Seventy Disciples. The relevant section of *Pseudo-Abdias,* called *The Acts of Simon and Jude,* is actually a section of a section called *The Acts of James the Less,* though scholars assume that Simon and Jude's adventures were once part of a separate longer text. In the story, Simon and Jude battle the Persian sorcerers Zaroës and Arfaxat, who were driven out of Ethiopia by Simon and Jude's fellow apostle Matthew. They also somehow become entwined in an Indo-Persian land war. During the pair's travels, however, the wizards Zaroës and Arfaxat continue to bedevil them and eventually gather together enough priests to attempt to force the apostles to sacrifice to their gods. The apostles consider their options: destroy every heathen in sight or accept the palm of glorious martyrdom. According to this legend, "They chose the palm. . . . The priests and people attacked the apostles and slew them."

In Eastern Christianity, traditions about Simon and Jude/Thaddaeus's martyrdoms are not prevalent, but the Western tradition typically assumes they met their end together in what would today be Iran. When it comes to how exactly Simon and Jude/Thaddaeus died, Christian storytellers did not skimp on the gorier details. The implement purportedly used to cut the Simon of legend from skull to groin was the two-man ripsaw, which accounts for the numerous statues and paintings of Simon carrying such a saw. Earlier legends of Jude/Thaddaeus's death mention a club or cudgel, but later legends imagine him as having been killed by the helmet-splitting medieval European weapon known as a halberd, which, like Simon's saw, has proved to be its victim's ghoulishly enduring symbol.

III.

The following morning, Sunday, I arrived at Saint Sernin's at around 6:30, just in time to watch a fleet of white vans pull up and park around the basilica and several dozen French Arab men climb out and throw up their Sunday-market tent stalls. Many of these Arabs were recent immigrants to France, or at least I imagined they were due to their many layers of clothing and how often they blew into their hands. It was fifty degrees, yet many of them seemed to think they were hiking across southern Greenland. Shortly after the Arabs came the Chinese merchants, and then the African merchants: by 7:30 a.m., the stalls were open for business. I could suddenly, sort of, understand why a man of Gérard's generation was so alarmed. The sight of Toulouse's grandest basilica surrounded by Arabs and Asians and Africans—even if they carried French passports— would have been enough to make a crusader soil his armor.

Toulouse's Sunday market offered wares both predictable and not. Predictable: stall after stall of soccer jerseys with FLY EMIRATES and VODAFONE stenciled across the breast. Less predictable: dangling carousels of saucy ladies' underwear, which several head-scarfed Arab women were buying in gross. One of the Chinese stalls sold only batteries and complicated hair dryers whose accompanying voltage adapter sets were larger than the hair dryers themselves. Several African stalls sold tribal masks and carved wooden statues, because when one is strolling the edge of a Christian basilica on a Sunday morning in southern

France, a child-sized Namibian fertility idol is the very definition of an impulse buy. Most of the market's customers were Arabs. Quite a few of the police officers patrolling the market in their light blue short-sleeved shirts were also Arabs. The only French vendors I saw were the older hippie Frenchwoman with flyaway hair selling her handmade jewelry, the young Frenchwoman selling bicycles that appeared to predate the invention of the automobile, and an older Frenchman, whose face bore the haggard gravity of an actor condemned to performing Beckett for eternity, hawking dirty cardboard boxes of books, which contained such classics of French literature as Malraux, Flaubert, Valéry, Crichton, Ludlum, and Auel.

A while later I stood outside the western entrance of Saint Sernin's, where an elderly white French couple was waiting for the doors to open for Sunday's service. (The Kronenbourg beer bottles from the previous evening were still there.) The couple and I chatted a little—they spoke English—and they seemed intrigued to learn of an American who had come all this way to see the resting place of Simon and Jude (as Saint Sernin's referred to him). The couple knew the relics were here, they said, but they had never visited the actual reliquary. How long, I asked, had they lived in Toulouse? "Thirty-five years," the woman said. And how long had they been attending Mass at Saint Sernin's? "Thirty-five years." My hopes for finding an interesting apostolic site here correspondingly dimmed.

The gears and tumblers within the smaller door to the right of the basilica's main doors began to click and turn. The smaller door opened, and a young French Vietnamese man with blond streaks in his hair, a diamond earring, and a boxy hit-man suit welcomed us in. He was holding what looked to be several bastilles' worth of forearm-sized keys. I spontaneously requested an interview with this intriguing young man, which he agreed to do with a bright, surprised smile. We sat down in his basilica's last pew.

His Vietnamese name was Tuan, but he had long adopted

the French name Henri. His grandparents were from Haiphong, in North Vietnam, and in 1955 they fled to South Vietnam with a quarter million other Vietnamese Catholics during the mass exodus known as Operation Passage to Freedom, which was conducted by the French military and overseen by the United States. After two years in Saigon, his grandparents fled again, to Paris, and from Paris to Toulouse. Henri was born in Toulouse, spoke better English than Vietnamese, and had no wish ever to travel to Vietnam. It quickly became clear that Henri was as uninterested in hearing about my experiences living in Vietnam as he was in what I ate for breakfast that morning.

Henri's tasks as a layperson included welcoming parishioners for the morning Mass. Whenever a member of Toulouse's large immigrant population peeked into Saint Sernin's, Henri said, he did his best to make him or her feel at home. It was only reasonable, he said, and Christlike, to extend to other immigrant families the same welcome his family had been afforded, even if these immigrant families were not interested in full conversion. Hearing such sentiment spoken aloud by an agent of French Catholicism, which had become the roach motel of France's unusually scary right wing, was heartening.

I asked Henri whether members of Toulouse's Arab community ever visited Saint Sernin's. "Sometimes," he said. "Not very often. In our congregation, we have many Africans, many Asians. But we have few Arabs."

"What about native French people? Are they a large part of your congregation?"

"Older French people, of course. The younger people do not always come here. I don't know why." He smiled. "I wish I did."

"Last night," I said, "I found two young French people drinking beer on your basilica's front steps."

Henri sighed. "Yes," he said. "Sometimes they do this. I don't know why. Again, I wish I did."

"What can you tell me about the relics of Saint Simon and Saint Jude?"

Henri turned and looked down the basilica's long, narrow nave toward the altar, beneath which were many crypts, including the reliquary of Simon and Jude. "Their relics have been part of our basilica for many centuries. We honor them as well as our other beloved relics."

"Do you have any thoughts or beliefs about Simon and Jude?"

Henri thought for a moment. "They were the"—he searched for a word—"companions of Christ. *Les douze apôtres.*"

"They're not very well-known."

"No, this is true," he said, "but we know the legends, yes? How they died in glory for Christ."

"Do you think it's possible they died together, side by side, like some of the legends say?"

Henri held my gaze. "I think anything is possible."

Our interview done, Henri went back to working the door, and I began my Saint Sernin's walk-through, bidding the world of functional architecture—rooms, hallways, doorknobs, translucent glass—farewell. As a pilgrimage church, Saint Sernin's was designed to accommodate thousands of Christians at once. Its layout thus adhered to what is called a pilgrimage church plan, as opposed to the more conventional layout of a basilica that did not periodically find itself awash with seven thousand sweaty Christians who had been walking for weeks. What determined the pilgrimage church's layout was relics. As the historian Bamber Gascoigne notes, "Nowadays a place becomes a tourist resort if it has a good beach, or famous buildings and works of art. In the Middle Ages, when every tourist was a pilgrim, what mattered was relics."* Radiating chapels were needed to properly display a basilica's showcase relics, and these chapels needed to be accessible even while Mass was being conducted. This

---

* Some of European Christianity's more demented relics: a bone from a child massacred by Herod; Jesus's foreskin, swaddling clothes, milk teeth, and tears; a piece of Mary's placenta; clay left over from God's creation of Adam; and bread left over from the Last Supper.

accounted for Saint Sernin's ambulatory, which traveled along the side aisles adjacent to the nave and past many chapels once crammed with relics.

The most interesting thing inside Saint Sernin's was its high, multiply barrel-vaulted ceiling, which must have mesmerized every pilgrim to have ever stepped inside. Everything about the interior of this basilica, from the nave's seemingly endless rows of thick white pillars to the chapels' forty-foot-high arches, resulted in a fascinating spatial dementia, so that virtually everywhere you stood in Saint Sernin's you felt as though you were at the end of a forbiddingly long hallway. When you looked up at the barrel-vaulted, many-ribbed ceiling, meanwhile, you were overcome by the sensation of having been swallowed by some great alabaster whale. Contemplating this basilica's enigmatic and cave-like immensity, I was reminded that the word "basilica" comes from the vocabulary not of religion but of royalty. I touched one of the massive chalk-white columns along the nave: ice cold, graphite smooth. How inhuman the home of a king can seem.

The interior of Saint Sernin's was restored in the 1970s to get the stonework's famed, long-faded red-white tint back to what it was imagined to have been a thousand years before. The result was not quite reddish or whitish but both—the color of blood with milk poured into it. In the middle of my journey up the nave, I turned and looked back at the organ loft, which housed a tremendous agglomeration of black wood and silver pipes, looking like some fiendishly ornate weather-controlling machine.

At the baroque high altar—an infestation of golden eagles and cherubs—the ambulatory became a rotunda that wended around and led into the chancel, along with its apostolic crypts. But now more people were entering. When I first walked into Saint Sernin's, there were only four parishioners inside, all of whom were white French in their sixties (at least). As I waited, younger parishioners arrived. As Henri had indicated, all were immigrants. One young man told me he was from Cameroon, another was from Ivory Coast, yet another was from China. I wound up sitting in the first pew. The service's opening bell sounded. I turned and verified that I was the youngest white person in Saint Sernin's by several decades. I wondered how the older Catholics here dealt with Saint Sernin's kneelers, which had no cushion. They were so monstrously hard it felt as though I were genuflecting on a diamond reef. After the penitential rite, I turned around again and counted my fellow parishioners attending Sunday Mass at the largest Romanesque church in Europe. There were fourteen of us, counting Henri.

IV.

A wide array of New Testament commentators have imagined that the apostle Luke refers to as "Simon, who was called the Zealot," was also a member of one of the ancient world's most reckless and vicious revolutionary movements: the Zealots. As the fundamentalists' fundamentalists, the Zealots were blamed by Josephus (who personally knew and despised many of them) as having been so deranged, intransigent, and "vile beyond belief" as to have essentially caused the Roman destruction of Jerusalem during the Jewish War.* A few popular Christian histories have pointed to the socio-revolutionary piquancy of the Twelve Apostles containing both an anti-Roman Zealot named Simon and a Roman tax collector named Matthew. The delighted underlying assumption is that the persuasive force of Jesus's message was able to ally two men conditioned to hate each other.

Unfortunately, this is bunk as both history and analysis. "Simon, who was called the Zealot," was not and could not have been a member of the Zealot party, which did not exist until

---

* Many of Josephus's charges against the Zealots are almost certainly exaggerated. For instance, they probably did not actually drink the blood of the men and women he claims they killed and violated in Jerusalem.

more than three decades after Jesus's death. It is distantly possible one of the apostles later became a member of the Zealot party, but there are no traditions to indicate that and quite a few to indicate the opposite. (Josephus does refer at one point to two Zealots—brothers, in fact—named Simon and Judas, but these are assuredly not Jewish Christian apostles.) In all likelihood, Simon's epithet, the "Zealot" or "zealous," was needed to distinguish him from the Twelve's more famous Simon, Simon Peter.

There is little evidence that Jewish "zealousness" prior to the 40s and 50s was primarily focused on opposition to Palestine's Roman occupation or that this kind of zealousness was akin to extremist nationalism.* Later in the first century, with the rise of the Zealots and other extremist Jewish groups, zealousness and nationalism more closely aligned. According to Josephus, Ananus ben Ananus, the former high priest of Jerusalem, gave a public speech in the mid-60s that used the Zealots' fanatical nationalism as the primary strike against them. (While this speech is almost certainly Josephus's invention, it is probably accurate in its reflection of the high priestly class's opinion of the Zealots.) "The Romans," Ananus pointed out, "never went beyond the bounds set [in the Temple] for unbelievers, never trampled on one of our sacred customs, but reverently gazed from a distance at the walls of the Sanctuary." As for the Zealots, Ananus said, they "stroll where they like in the Inner Sanctuary, their hands still reeking with the slaughter of their countrymen!" The Romans were not ideal masters, as Ananus admitted,

---

* One exception to this is the Jewish uprising inspired by Judas of Galilee (or Gamala) in 6 CE, which had highly nationalist overtones. This uprising was a response to the census carried out by the Roman governor of Syria and the concomitant Roman annexation of Judaea. Judas's son, Menahem, led a group that at one point in *The Jewish War* is referred to by Josephus as comprising Zealots. This appears to be Josephus's mistake. Elsewhere in the text, Menahem's group is identified as the Sicarii, also extremist, but not formally associated with the Zealot party and sometimes, according to Josephus, at war with it. Menahem and Josephus began the Jewish War ostensibly on the same side but quickly became enemies.

but life under Roman rule was far better than "subservience to the scum of our own nation." Soon after this speech, the Zealots helped engineer the savage murder of Ananus ben Ananus. "I should not be far wrong," Josephus wrote, "if I said that the fall of the City began with Ananus' death."*

In the less politically volatile time of Jesus, a "zealous man" was probably akin to the type of person Paul had been when he was a Pharisee known as Saul. Zealous men of this type understood themselves as the guardians of the Law and habitual minders of those obligated to obey it. This did not necessarily mean they were dragging Law-breakers before the authorities and handing out rocks for stoning. More likely, the efforts of little-*z* zealots were grounded in public-shaming efforts. As the scholar Richard Horsley writes, "What little evidence there is suggests that 'zeal for the Law' was an individual, not a collective, feeling about the importance of other Jews' faithful observance of the precepts of the Torah." Horsley notes that even in the literature of the Qumran community, the most fanatically zealous Jews of their era, the word "zeal" "occurs with striking infrequency."

It is nonetheless uncharacteristic of Luke to allow a word like "zealot," which had unsavory implications, to find its way into his gospel, much less into the circle of the Twelve. Elsewhere in the gospel, he takes pains to disassociate Jesus from hot-button political movements and words. Take the Greek word *lestes* ("bandit" or "brigand"), which appears several times, and in several contexts, in the gospel tradition. In common Greek usage, "bandit" was used to denote simple highway robbers and thieves. The problem this type of banditry posed was always present for Jews, especially those who conducted business between cities, as Jesus's parable of the Good Samaritan famously establishes. After the mid-40s, however, when social

---

* Josephus's sympathetic portrait of Ananus in *The Jewish War* is inconsistent with his portrait of Ananus in his later *Antiquities of the Jews,* where Ananus is criticized for his ruthless dispatching of James the brother of Jesus.

strife in Roman Palestine spiraled out of control, the word took on subtler, more political insinuations. This is evident from Josephus, who called banditry "the chief curse of the country" and viewed just about anyone who caused trouble in Palestine after the mid-40s as "bandits," regardless of whether their troublemaking had criminal or political intent. (Once or twice in *The Jewish War,* Josephus is unable to resist using "bandit" as a synonym for "Zealot.") Just how highly charged "bandits" became after the Jewish War is apparent in Luke's refusal to use the word in his account of Jesus's trial and crucifixion, wherein we meet three men who obviously *were* supposed to be bandits in the pre-40s sense of the word.

The first, Barabbas, is the criminal whose release the people of Jerusalem demand in Jesus's stead. Luke vaguely describes Barabbas as a man "put in prison for an insurrection that had taken place in the city, and for murder," which actually makes him sound more like a "bandit" in the later, more Josephusian sense of the word—an irony Luke might have been consciously playing with. The symbolic convenience of a man whose name means "son of the Father" being freed in place of the Son of the Father has long been a matter of vexation to thoughtful Christians. In the third century, Origen was arguing that it had been added to the gospel by heretics. Origen had a point: Why on earth would the people of Jerusalem select Barabbas over Jesus? The former was a murderer and bandit; the latter was someone whose good works many had seen and who days before entered the city on a wave of adulation. In light of this, it seems obvious that the scene is the gospel writers' response to later Jewish attitudes about Jesus.

The other two are the men Luke tells us were crucified beside Jesus. One of them berates Jesus from the cross, but his friend rebukes him, saying they were both "condemned justly." For this admission, Jesus tells the so-called good thief, "Today you will be with me in Paradise." The New Revised Standard Version refers to these men as "criminals," but the Greek word Luke uses is more akin to "wrongdoer." Mark and Matthew both refer to Jesus's co-crucified as "bandits," while John, altogether uninterested in these men, refers merely to "two others." All the evangelists were writing for people in temporal proximity to the Jewish War. Luke was apparently highly conscious of how the various groups of criminals and revolutionaries who brought so much strife on Romans and Jews alike might have blended together in the minds of his audience, much in the way Josephus was guilty of blending these groups together in his account of the Jewish War. Luke seems to have worried about the revolutionary message it would have sent to the Gentile and especially Roman members of his audience if Jesus was depicted as having been crucified between two "bandits."

One possible explanation for how "Zealot" might have slipped Luke's notice: Mark's "Simon the Cananaean" was a garbled attempt to obfuscate the semantic connection between an apostle widely known as "Simon the zealous" and the Zealot party. Matthew understood Mark's goal and preserved "Simon the Cananaean." Luke did not understand Mark's goal and corrected "Simon the Cananaean" to "Simon the zealous." Perhaps Luke simply failed to regard the term "Zealot" as being as politically incendiary as "bandit," but Galilee, where Christianity began, was deeply associated with the Zealot party, members of which were sometimes called Galileans. If, however, Luke did slip by referring to Simon as Simon the Zealous, it was a strange and uncharacteristically sloppy slip.

Mark likely purposefully tried to avoid associating Jesus with the Zealots; he was wise to. Among the Zealots' accomplishments during the half decade in which they were politically active were a handful of victories against Roman troops, the seizure of the Temple Mount, the destruction of the Romans' department of records, the burning of numerous Herodian temples, the looting of the Temple's supply of sacred lumber to build siege engines, the massacre of Jerusalem's priestly class, the setting up of what Josephus described as "sham courts and faked trials," and the fervent instigation of a religious and class war. Only seven years before the Zealots rose up, the Romans were faced with another violent uprising in a similarly far-flung province: Roman Britain. In this case, the Romans' chief opponent was Boudicca, queen of the Iceni tribe. The revolt she led resulted in the deaths of several thousand Roman soldiers and as many as eighty thousand Iceni, including Boudicca, who committed suicide rather than suffer the humiliation of capture.

The savage Roman experience against the Iceni helped determine the harshness with which they responded to the first stirrings of revolt in Palestine, which, of course, only strengthened the hand of the Zealots and extremists. In a strangely poetic coincidence, Simon the Zealot was later imagined by Christian storytellers as having been in Britain—and, in some legends, crucified by the Romans—around the time of the Icenian revolt against Rome. For their part, the Zealots ended the war they helped start by following the path of Boudicca and committing mass suicide at Masada with what remained of the equally radical Sicarii. Anyone who visits that godforsaken place today is unpleasantly reminded that the most fanatical of the Zealots are regarded as heroes by many in modern Israel, despite the Zealots' disastrous role in helping to bring Palestinian Judaism to its knees.

V.

Simon the Zealot was not a Zealot, and Jude Thaddaeus was not Jude. Then again, Jude might not have been Jude. Other than Thaddaeus, the New Testament contains several potential Judes. One is "Judas of James" from the apostolic lists of Luke and Acts. One is John's "Judas (not Iscariot)." One is the author of the Letter of Jude. All three might be the same person. They might be two people. They might be three different people. Fitting that Jude Thaddaeus became the patron saint of lost causes: discerning his real identity is as lost as New Testament causes get.

We can be virtually certain of one Jude's existence, though, and that is Jude the brother of Jesus. The scholar Richard Bauckham has done extensive work on early Christianity's opaque relationship to the brothers of Jesus. He argues that "brothers of the Lord" was a special title used by Jewish Christians of first- and second-century Palestine to refer to Jesus's blood brothers. Furthermore, he believes, this title was roughly (and briefly) akin in prominence to "apostle," even though it likely indicated a different degree of ecclesiastical authority and its use was not nearly as widespread.

According to Bauckham, Jewish Christianity developed other phrasal titles to describe the descendants of Jesus and his brothers, one of which was the curious phrase "humanly speaking" (also translated as "according to the flesh"). Here, for instance, is Eusebius describing the aftermath of the destruction of Jerusalem and the resultant flight of its Christian communities: "There is a firm tradition that those of the apostles and disciples of the Lord who were still alive assembled from all parts together with those who, humanly speaking, were kinsmen of the Lord—for most of them were still living."

The phrase turns up again in a fragment of Hegesippus, which survives thanks to Eusebius's extensive citation. Here, we learn that "the grandsons" of Jesus's brother Jude, "who was said to be his brother, humanly speaking," were "informed against" by mysterious parties and dragged before the emperor Domitian, "who was afraid of the advent of Christ as Herod had been."

> Domitian asked them whether they were descended from David, and they admitted it. Then he asked them what property they owned and what funds they had at their disposal. They replied that they had only 9,000 denari* between then, half belonging to each; this, they said, was not available in cash, but was the esti-

_____
* In the time of Jesus, a worker typically earned a single denarius per day.

mated value of only thirty-three *plethra** of land, from which they raised the money to pay their taxes and the wherewithal to support themselves by their own toil.

In his subsequent gloss of Hegesippus, Eusebius described how the grandsons of Jude showed Domitian their farmer's calluses "as proof of their toil." When Domitian asked them about "Christ and His Kingdom—what it was like, and where and when it would appear," the grandsons of Jude patiently explained to the emperor that Christ's kingdom "was not of this world or anywhere on earth but angelic and in heaven." Domitian, apparently relieved that the ethereal portents of Christianity were nothing to worry about, released Jude's grandsons and "issued orders terminating the persecution of the Church." After this, Jude's grandsons—Jesus's grandnephews—"became leaders of the churches, both because they had borne testimony and because they were of the Lord's family."

Needless to say, this is extremely interesting information. While it is doubtful that the grandsons of Jude ever had a meeting with Domitian—much less that Domitian called off his persecution of Christians due to their testimony—the rough outlines of the story may have a vague historical basis. The aspects of the story that Bauckham regards as something other than simple hagiography include the fact that Jude's grandsons were landowning but not particularly wealthy farmers (probably in Galilee),† that they fell under Roman suspicion due to their descent from David, and that they were well-known among their fellow Jewish Christians in Palestine.

---

* Between a quarter and half an acre.

† The Letter of James, purportedly written by the granduncle of Jude's farmer grandsons, makes time to rail against rich exploitative farmers: "Listen! The wages of the laborers who mowed your fields, which you kept back by fraud, cry out, and the cries of the harvesters have reached the ears of the Lord of hosts." In light of this passage, how easy it is to imagine the grandsons of Jude proudly exhibiting their calluses to an emperor!

Eusebius turned again to Hegesippus to describe the fate of Jesus's other brother, Simon, or Simeon, who following the death of James the brother of Jesus became the second bishop of the Jerusalem church and who was frequently confused with Simon the Zealot in early Christian legend. According to Hegesippus, Simon was charged by "heretical sects" with "being a descendant of David and a Christian" and brought before the Roman authorities. Jude's grandsons were, of course, said to have been hauled in on a similar charge. In Hegesippus's account, Atticus, the provincial governor of Judaea, tortured Simon "for days on end" despite Simon's advanced age of 120. Having miraculously survived this torture, Simon was then crucified.

Despite this story's obviously fantastical elements, Bauckham believes there may be something to the notion that a rival "heretical" Christian sect betrayed Simon to the Romans. Hegesippus claimed that a Jewish Christian named Thebuthis, angered that he was not ceded leadership of the Jerusalem church after the death of James the brother of Jesus, went on to corrupt the Christianity of Palestine, which had hitherto "not yet been seduced by listening to [the] nonsense" of heretics. Out of Thebuthis's apostasy, Hegesippus wrote, sprouted "seven sects" in which "every man [introduced] his own opinion in his own particular way. From these came false Christs, false prophets, false apostles, who split the unity of the Church by poisonous suggestions against God and against His Christ." While this information is too polemical to take seriously as history, it may point to friction within first-century Jewish Christian communities. After all, a fine way to destroy a Jewish Christian community in Palestine would have been to tell the Roman authorities that all who descended from David and Jesus were messianic insurrectionists. An internally divided Jewish Christian church, with one sect eagerly reporting on the other, might also have discouraged a notionally sympathetic Gentile church from extending the hand of fellowship. Add to this the destruction of Jerusalem and the consequent flight of Jewish Christianity's leaders into exile, and a clear—and tragic—picture emerges: a community ripped apart from within and clobbered by all sides, despite its vaunted connection to Jesus's own brothers.

Hegesippus's stories about Jesus's grandnephews and brother falling into Roman dragnets due to their Davidic descent is further supported by the testimony of a Christian traveler named Julius Africanus, who lived from roughly 160 to 240 and spent time in Palestine. But for a few stray citations in Eusebius, Julius's writings have disappeared, even though he was well known among his contemporaries and apparently corresponded with Origen.

Julius employed yet another phrase to describe Jesus's relatives, which appears nowhere else in ancient Christian literature: *desposynoi,* which is Greek for "those who belong to the master," in Bauckham's translation. According to Julius, the *desposynoi* "took pride in preserving the memory of their aristocratic [i.e., Davidic] origin" to such a degree that a few preserved "private records" documenting their bloodlines. One of the *desposynoi's* annoyances concerned the discrepancy between the genealogical lists in Matthew and Luke that detail Jesus's descent from David. If those who claimed to be Jesus's relatives made it part of their mission to lobby for their Davidic genealogy, it is easy to see why certain Romans mistook Jesus's relatives for messianic troublemakers—and why the Gentile church might have gradually sought to distance itself from them. (How exactly Jesus descended from David was of so little concern to the Gentile church that it placidly accepted scripture that contradicted itself on the issue.)

Even so, the church and the synagogue were not easily separated prior to the destruction of Jerusalem, and rancor between Christians and Jews—and between Gentile Christians and Jewish Christians—became increasingly prominent after 70. It affects even Matthew's gospel, which is otherwise sympathetic to Jews and Jewish Christians. By the time the gospels were written, Jerusalem was in ruins, the nation of Israel had been crushed by

Rome, and Jewish diaspora communities were in disarray. Why the Temple had been destroyed, and what that meant for Jews, became a question about who Jesus was and what he promised. For decades after the Jewish War, Jewish scribes adopted a mission to refute the Christian notion that Jews had been judged by God for rejecting Jesus. It was, apparently, an intellectually consuming mission: there are no more proper works of Jewish history, and no proper Jewish historians, until a thousand years later. Little record exists *at all* of what went on within Judaism for roughly 150 years, so dense was the fog that lowered upon the faith after the razing of the Temple. One mission of Gentile Christianity, meanwhile, became appropriating Jewish scriptural writings to prove that Jews *had* been judged by God, whether they knew it or not, for rejecting Jesus. This eternal humiliation eventually came to affect the descendants of Jesus and their Jewish Christian communities.

The little evidence that exists suggests that members of Jesus's family maintained their prominence in the Jewish Christian churches of Palestine, and the (eventually restored) mother church in Jerusalem, until the second century. While the destruction of Jerusalem severely damaged Jewish Christianity, it did not destroy it. What finally destroyed Jewish Christianity was the Second Revolt* against Rome in 132, which was led by Simon Bar Kosiba, whom the influential rabbi Akiva had suggested might be the Messiah (after which Simon took the name Bar Kokhba, or "Son of the Star").

His revolt began as a response to Hadrian's determination to remake Jerusalem into a great Roman city. In pursuing this goal, Hadrian disregarded several centuries of freely available and highly cautionary historical precedent. Hadrian thought little of Judaism, but almost certainly he did not intend to trigger the Second Revolt. For his part, Bar Kokhba was not merely

---

* It was, technically, the third Jewish revolt against Rome; the actual second revolt mostly took place in Diaspora communities rather than in Palestine proper.

a nationalist but one of the finest guerrilla fighters of his time. The Second Revolt, unlike the lunatic free-for-all of the First Revolt, was a continuously and horrendously fought four-year-long military campaign. More than half a million Jewish rebels were destroyed, along with almost one thousand Jewish villages, and when it was over, not a single synagogue was left standing.

Tradition maintains that the Jewish Christian church had returned to Jerusalem before the Second Revolt began, and, according to Justin Martyr, those who refused to defy Jesus and accept Simon Bar Kokhba as their messiah were killed. While it would be interesting to learn precisely how many Jewish Christians blasphemed Jesus and fought alongside Simon, it could not have been many: the psychological appeal of Jewish independence was already a fading memory to most Jewish Christians, whatever their precise beliefs. When the Second Revolt was finally put down, Jews and Jewish Christians alike lost access to Jerusalem, which was renamed Aelia Capitolina and dedicated to the three principal gods venerated on the Capitoline Hill in Rome: Jupiter, Juno, and Minerva. Circumcision was forbidden, as was reading the Torah. No one who had been circumcised was allowed to set foot in Jerusalem for fifty years—and then only on a temporary basis. Consequently, the next Christians to step into Jerusalem in the mid-second century were Gentiles, led by a bishop apparently named Mark. After Constantine, Gentile Christians maintained their hold on the world's most Jewish city for centuries. A newly entrenched and radically cautious rabbinical power structure emerged from the ashes of the Jews' disastrous revolts against Rome, and one of the things it did was continue the formal exclusion of Jewish Christians from its synagogues.

Aside from a few scattered mentions in the work of the church fathers, Jewish Christianity begins to fade from history after the Second Revolt. When the church fathers do deign to mention Jewish Christians, it is mostly with overt disapproval or (as with Jerome) neutral half interest. The fate of Jesus's descendants is even sadder for being so unknown. Richard Bauckham writes, "If we knew more about Christianity in Egypt, Arabia, Phoenicia, east Syria, and Mesopotamia the impression [of Palestine-derived Christianity] might be different."

Why there is not more information about the influence of the relatives of Jesus has been said by some to be the greatest riddle of early Christianity. Yet Christians failed to preserve and in many cases destroyed the work of countless early Christian writers, including that of Papias, Irenaeus, Origen, and Hegesippus. The likely Gentile Christian response to work that emphasized the enduring influence of Jesus's family's descendants is not terribly difficult to imagine. Recognizing Jesus's family endangered the doctrine of the virgin birth, placed the exceptionality of Jesus himself at risk, and unhappily reminded Gentile Christians that at the beginning there was *only* Jewish Christianity. The strange thing is that several church fathers spent time in Palestine and could conceivably have sought out the living relatives of Jesus. This includes Origen, Eusebius, Epiphanius, and, especially, Jerome, who lived for many years in Bethlehem. As Bauckham notes, none of them seem to have had "the slightest interest in doing so." The later family members of Jesus were products of a culture defined by the strength of family ties and members of a church whose leadership structure was apparently determined by bloodline succession. How these men and women were allowed to become historical phantoms would be the greatest riddle of early Christianity were it not so patently obvious why the Gentile church would have wanted them all to vanish without a trace.

VI.

Saint Sernin's was one of the few churches I had visited with an apostolic reliquary that it did virtually nothing to advertise. To the left of the chancel was a gated ticket area. Beyond the gate was a winding two-level ambulatory lined with marble bas-relief carvings and a series of almost ludicrously ornate bays, chapels, and reliquaries. The sublevel contained the lower crypt, where I could see the reliquary of Simon and Jude. As I paid my two euros to access the crypts, I looked around in vain for some sign or notice that brought attention to Saint Sernin's apostolic heritage.

This ambulatory was once known for its holy relics display, and within the chapels I encountered an array of impressively carved and beautifully painted wooden reliquaries—they looked like Christian dollhouses—dating from the seventeenth century, most of which contained the relics of various Toulousian bishops. An eight-foot-high wall separated the ambulatory from the upper crypt, which circled the main altar from above. Above the upper crypt's entrance, printed in gold letters on black lintel, were the words HIC SUNT VIGILES QUI CUSTODIUNT CIVITATEM, or "Here are the watchmen who guard the city."

Saint Sernin's had once boasted Europe's finest array of relics. Alas, during the French Revolution angry mobs thinned out its collection. The most beautiful surviving relic was a small enameled reliquary, made in the twelfth century, called the Limoges Box, which was said to contain a piece of *la Vraie Croix*. The bright, Technicolor images depicted on the Limoges Box told the story of how this piece of the True Cross was found and how it later made its way to Toulouse. The floor in the upper crypt was slate gray, the marble pillars were cloudy gray, and most of the art was unnerving: everywhere I turned, the inert eyes of some coldly beatific martyr stared through me. I missed the reliquary of Saint Sernin himself on my way into the upper crypt but found it on my way out; EX OSSIBUS ST. SATURNIN was written above it. A large gold statue depicted Sernin as a man whom doting cherubs rushed to dress. His actual sarcophagus, however, was as small as a piece of carry-on baggage.

I waded into the tepid darkness of the lower crypt, which was not dug until the fourteenth century. The handrail along the stairs—a length of thick nautical rope—had a glassy, oily smoothness I attributed to the passage of tens of thousands of hands. It was several degrees cooler and duller in the lower crypt. The first thing I noticed was a bright red fire extinguisher with a complicated black nozzle, even though this dark, damp, stony space seemed roughly as flammable as a lake. In the middle of the crypt was a marble pillar as old as the basilica itself. The crypt's chandeliers had been hung from their chains just a hair too low; many of their misty white lightbulbs had long burned out. I had the sudden feeling of being inside a medieval Christian boy's first attempt at a spook house.

The reliquary bays were found around the edges of the lower crypt; all were lit by small spotlights. It turned out that Simon and Jude were not the only apostles whose relics Saint Sernin's claimed to have. The lower crypt also contained chapels devoted to Philip and both of the Twelve's Jameses, though their collections, I was later told, were comparatively meager. Likewise, Simon's and Jude's relics had other repositories around the world: some are held by Saint Peter's in Rome, and one of Simon's arms was said to have been kept in a monastery in Cologne, Germany, which was unfortunately destroyed by Allied bombing during World War II. In any event, the lower crypt's chapel bays were brutally plain and closed off to entry by a black metal gate. The sarcophagi were relatively plain, too, resembling small, primitive, gold arks with triangular tops held up by slender pillars. The sarcophagus of Philip and the James here referred to as "the Lesser" was balanced (I hoped temporarily) on wooden sawhorses. Simon and Jude's sarcophagus lid looked to have been cut, not very skillfully, from an imperfectly veined piece of marble.

My nostrils were clogged with the stench of wet gravel. I stood before the plain, carved-out hollow that contained Simon and Jude's unexciting reliquary, trying and failing to experience something that could be described as an emotion. A few other tourists wandered down into the crypt but never stayed for long. I asked some of the crypt's visitors if they spoke English. The usual response was a quick scan around the small dark crypt, a queasy smile, an alarmed wave, and a hasty retreat back up the stairs.

Eventually, two young Americans came down. Two young Americans always come down. I faded back into the crypt's far corner to give them room and eavesdrop. The man was tall and fit, with hair so gleaming and brown it seemed like an accessory picked to match his outfit. He wore a lilac soft-collared polo shirt, canvas shorts, and leather sandals that showed off the seashell perfection of his toenails. His wife (they wore wedding rings) was wearing a loose white blouse, and her hair had been pulled into a ponytail of polished chestnut lustrousness. They both seemed freshly toothbrushed and unnaturally clean, like Mr. and Mrs. Leisure Traveler on their way to a travel magazine cover shoot.

While standing before the reliquary of Simon and Jude, the man said, "Who are Simon and Jude again?"

The woman, already walking to the next chapel, said, "Jude wrote the Letter of Jude."

The man did not move. "What's that about?"

"It's the shortest book of the New Testament."

"How long is it?"

"Like a page and a half or something."

"Oh, really? I'll read it, then."

"I wouldn't bother. It's really boring."

"How can a page and a half be boring?"

Good question. The Letter of Jude, despite being only twenty-five verses long, is the book of the New Testament most historically neglected by Christian thinkers and scholars alike. For this, there are many reasons. It is, for one, among the most textually unstable New Testament documents; verses 22 and 23[*]

---

[*] Here they are: "And have mercy on some who are wavering; save others by snatching from out of the fire; and have mercy on still others with fear, hating even the tunic defiled by their bodies."

have been described as "the most corrupt passages in New Testament literature." Richard Bauckham, the Letter of Jude's great modern champion, argues that Jude is one of the most concentrated and overt works of exegesis in the New Testament: virtually every line of Jude refers, however sneakily, to another text. Copyists and scribes unable to read the mind of Jude's author spent centuries trying to figure out what he was trying to say, which frequently put them at cross-purposes, with one copyist "correcting" the interpretation of another until the original meaning was lost.

Resistance to the Letter of Jude is ancient. One problem is that verses 14 and 15 contain direct quotations from *1 Enoch,* a first-century Jewish midrashic text, purportedly written by the father of Methuselah, whose canonicity only two branches of the Ethiopian Orthodox Church accepts. Several early Christian works are familiar with *1 Enoch*—it was, in one historian's words, "part of the mental furniture of the generation of Jesus and his disciples"—but Jude is the lone New Testament work to cite it directly. The issues posed by a canonical work citing a noncanonical work in a manner that suggests the former's spiritual endorsement of the latter are obvious. Jude also refers to a story in which the Devil wrangles over Moses's body. This derives from an apocryphal Jewish work called *The Assumption of Moses,* which survives only in an incomplete Latin text. The author of Jude was merely using a popular story to arrive at a greater point, but, again, there are real scriptural and spiritual issues at stake when a canonical work of scripture refers to a text that no longer formally exists.

From an average reader's perspective, the explanation for why this strange letter has been neglected seems relatively straightforward: reading Jude feels like being cornered by someone jabbing you in the chest with his finger while calling you a skeeze. A sample passage: "For certain intruders have stolen in among you, people who long ago were designated for this condemnation as ungodly, who pervert the grace of our God into licentiousness and deny our only Master and Lord, Jesus Christ. . . . [T]hese dreamers also defile the flesh, reject authority, and slander the glorious ones."

The author of the Letter of Jude identifies himself as "Judas, a servant of Jesus Christ, and brother of James." Scholarly opinion on its authorship and time of composition varies greatly. Bauckham believes the author was Jude the brother of Jesus, who, he proposes, might have completed the text as early as 50 CE. Most scholars, however, regard the text as pseudonymous and estimate its composition date around 90. On the surface, Jude is a ranting text about sexually or ethically dangerous intruders. Like the Letter of James, Jude says virtually nothing about Jesus; unlike the Letter of James, Jude mentions the apostles but in a way that makes them feel like members of a generation past. As with all the pastoral New Testament letters, the situation Jude is determined to address feels painfully specific to its author's community. In this respect, Jude feels even more low ceilinged and sectarian than the three letters of John.

Bauckham argues that Jude, in its abandonment of "reasoned discussion" and focus on "attacking [its] opponent's moral character," is a "typically Jewish Christian" text. If so, we can read between the lines fairly easily and conclude that Jewish Christianity was not always a pleasant faith. Its practitioners were apparently obsessed with the end of the world and demanded unbending obedience to a morality of their own envisioning. Communities that seek vindication of their beliefs at all costs are rarely happy, much less long-lived, and strains of Jewish Christianity appear to have been as eager to find fault with others as Gentile Christianity at its worst. Paul's strategy in dealing with ethical lapses among his communities was notably different. Rather than condemn opponents to "punishment of eternal fire," Paul actually tried to reason and think his way through a community's problems. That Jude is not even very explicit about the nature of the problems tormenting his community does not help his case. Like the literature of John, Jude's letter has almost no persuasive missionary value at all, unless your mission is to persuade one neighbor to string up the other. Intimations of sects first debut in Christianity within the pastoral letters of Jude, Peter, and John, and it is largely from these letters that the Christian disasters of heretic hunting and inquisition can be ignobly traced. It is sadly revealing that the New Testament contains a multitude more warnings against competing Christian understandings than it does against pagan beliefs.

I introduced myself to the American couple. They happened to be in Toulouse—where the woman, whose name was Beth, had been an exchange student during high school—on their honeymoon. Step one of their honeymoon (a week in Paris) was over. Step two (ten days in the South of France) had just gotten under way.

"How's your French?" I asked Beth.

"My French is bad," she said. "I'm actually embarrassed I remember so little."

They were from New York City, they said at first, but it later came out they were actually from Rowayton, Connecticut. The man, whose name was Michael, worked in finance in Stamford and, given the last few months of economic upheaval, said he regarded the continuing existence of his job as a minor miracle. I decided I liked Michael; I had already decided I liked Beth. Eventually, I asked Beth and Michael if they were Christians. They were. Liberal Christians, Beth was quick to say. She had actually taken several Bible-as-literature classes during college at Cornell, though claimed to remember most of what she had learned even more poorly than her French.

We talked about Simon Peter and Simon the Zealot and Judas of James and Jude Thaddaeus. Beth and I talked at length about the Letter of Jude, of which Michael finally said, with a laugh, "Yeah, that does sound pretty awful." When I said something about Paul's not having been an apostle, Michael jumped in to say, "But Paul was an apostle."

"Actually," I said, "he wasn't."

Michael was smiling. "Are you sure?"

"He's right," Beth said. "Well, it depends. I think he's called an Apostle Not of the Twelve. Like Mark and Luke and Barnabas."

A person visiting a Christian church who knew something about Christianity. It had taken me four years, but I finally found her.

MATTHEW

Monastery of Armenian Brotherhood: Kurmanty, Kyrgyzstan

ANDREI & SERGEI • THE CATALAN ATLAS • *HO TELONES* • LEVI SON OF ALPHAEUS • *THE GOSPEL OF THE NAZARENES* • HOT LAKE • "DEMONSTRATIONS IN THE SCRIPTURES" • CONSERVATIVE JESUS • SPIDER FIGHT • "MAY GOD LET YOU FIND HIM"

I.

Before we left Bishkek, the capital of Kyrgyzstan, in search of a lost apostolic reliquary, Andrei, my guide and translator, wanted me to meet his friend Sergei, whom Andrei described as the "most learned" person he knew. Sergei was also a devoted Christian, prone to leaving Kyrgyzstan for months at a time to study in a Russian monastery outside Moscow. While there, Andrei said, Sergei meditated and did his penances.

Andrei and I were walking alongside a wildly overgrown park on the outskirts of Bishkek, on our way to Sergei's apartment. "Why penances?" I asked.

Andrei smiled. "Sergei sins like no other." Sergei had converted to Islam to marry his Uzbek wife, who by Andrei's lights was a wonderful person—beautiful, smart, and liberal-minded. I was more curious to learn how Sergei's formal conversion to Islam affected his study of Christianity at the Russian monastery he habitually fled to.

"I doubt they know," Andrei said. "Well, maybe they do. He's very open about things. But he's not actually a Muslim. He's still very Christian. He converted only for his wife's family's approval. His wife doesn't care one way or the other." Andrei paused. Then: "My girlfriend can't stand Sergei. Well, I mean to say, she loves him, because I love him, but she doesn't admire his . . . duality."

"His duality?"

"That's what she said. In Russian, of course."

I met Andrei through an American friend whom Andrei had guided across Kyrgyzstan the previous year. Andrei was ethnically Russian, blond, in his early twenties, and smart. He claimed to have learned English from watching episodes of *Entourage* over and over again. I had been in Bishkek for two days now; tomorrow Andrei and I would leave for Issyk-Kul (literally, Hot Lake), the high-altitude jewel of Kyrgyzstan's mountainous ecosystem, on the shores of which local archaeologists claimed to have found the remains of an Armenian monastery that dated anywhere from the sixth to the fourteenth century. Supposedly, within this monastery, there had once been a tomb or reliquary devoted to the apostle and evangelist Matthew.

As we walked through Sergei's neighborhood, many people, Russians and Kyrgyz alike, called out to Andrei by name. He called back to all with a sporting wave. Wherever we went in Bishkek, we met people Andrei knew, including yesterday, at the bazaar, when we bumped into a middle-aged Kyrgyz man Andrei once worked for. Andrei and the man shook hands, fake smiling, their teeth bared in vaguely simian hostility. When the man hurried away, I asked Andrei what all that counterfeit friendliness had been about.

It turned out that Andrei had once worked as a translator for a pornographic Web site owned by the Kyrgyz man. That the thin, balding, deracinated ghoul I had just met was a pornographer did not at all surprise me. Andrei described the man's latest venture: buying apartments all around Bishkek for his stable of Webcam girls to live in and occasionally diddle themselves for an attentive regional audience. "It's been very successful," Andrei said. So why did the man seem to dislike Andrei so much? "I quit working for him last year, and I was his best, most reliable producer. It's not so simple to explain in English why I quit. I guess I would say my soul was being killed? Is that right? Can I say that?"

Yes, I told him. He could say that.

"I got really good at writing porn," Andrei went on. "I would simply steal stories from English-language Web sites and translate them into Russian, with certain . . . adjustments, since there are some cultural differences, you understand. For the first five months, it was a lot of fun, and I made a lot of money, both for him and myself. Unfortunately, for the next five months, I wanted to die."

We entered Sergei's apartment building, which like all Soviet apartment buildings resembled a fissiparous block of concrete with rows of windows chiseled into it. Sergei, who lived on the third floor, must have seen us coming down the street, for when we turned on the third-story corner of his walk-up, he was standing in the jamb of his apartment's open door with a shy smile on his face. One side of his head had been gulagishly shaved, and his chin and jawline were covered in fresh cuts that glistened like tiny bloodred berries. Sergei looked as though he had fallen out of a Dostoyevsky novel. Actually, he looked as if he had barely survived his fall from a Dostoyevsky novel. The cuts on his face were the result of a tumble he had taken on his bicycle a few hours before. The haircut, I eventually gathered, was just general Sergei weirdosity. "Please, please," he said, "come in."

He apologized for the mess, even though his apartment was not messy. He was living here alone, he said, while he and his wife worked out some "problems." Andrei was translating by now, because 70 percent of everything Sergei said was an enigmatic mixture of Russian and English. From the gleam in his zirconium eyes, it was clear that Sergei had spent a large portion of the day drinking.

We walked into his living room. A soft monastic chant was playing from a small Russian-made boom box. Sergei asked me if I liked the music. I said I did. He spoke slowly and deliberately, as though relearning the meaning of each word on the fly: "I enjoy. The meditative music." Sergei had a yoga mat in the middle of his living room floor, which was not something you typically saw in Central Asia. I asked about it, too. "Yes," Sergei said. "I enjoy the yoga. However. Here it is forbidden. For Christians. This is true. For America, too. Yes?"

"I think," I said, now speaking as slowly and deliberately as Sergei. "That very conservative American Christians. Discourage yoga. But for most Christians. I do not believe. It is a problem."

Sergei tsk-ed. "The Russian monks think yoga is . . ." He looked over at Andrei and asked him to supply a certain English word.

Andrei did so: "Pagan." Stress on the first syllable.

Sergei looked back at me. "The Russian monks. Think yoga. Is pagan." Stress on the second syllable.

I asked Sergei what he did for a living.

"I am English teacher." When Sergei smiled, I realized I, too, was allowed to smile at the thought of this man teaching English. Sergei put up his hands in mock surrender. "So yes. Maybe I don't speak so good. But I read very well. I understand okay."

"Sergei speaks five languages," Andrei, who spoke merely three, said.

Sergei had another thing you rarely saw in private Central Asian homes: bookshelves bowed with the weight of something other than the leather-bound collected works of the same five Russian titans. Sergei had actual paperbacks worn from consultation, as well as several dozen hardcovers. I saw titles in English, Russian, French, Kyrgyz, and Uzbek. "I read more books," Sergei said, as I looked his library over, "than any professor in Bishkek." Just today Sergei had purchased a new Russian translation of the New Testament, which he showed me and which, as I paged through it, allowed me to marvel anew at the fascinating, transgalactic-warlord wrongness of the Russian word for God: *Bog*. Sergei was proudest, however, of his one-hundred-year-old Slavonic Bible, which no one was allowed to touch, lest it disintegrate further. It was a gift, Sergei said, from a Russian monk who was much beloved by him. When he tried to describe their relationship, he again had to consult Andrei.

"Mentor," Andrei said.

"Yes. My mentor. Please, please, come to kitchen."

On Sergei's kitchen table were several small sacks of spices and herbs. Some, he said, were from Afghanistan, some from Chechnya, some from Ingushetia, some from Siberia, and some from the slopes of Kyrgyzstan's Tien Shan Mountains. He sliced up an apple ("Kyrgyzstan has. The most delicious apples. In the world") and boiled water for tea. The apple slices were, as promised, delicious, and I was reminded how much I missed Central Asian melon and fruit. I was a Peace Corps volunteer in Uzbekistan in the mid-1990s and, in the early years of the twenty-first century, frequently traveled back and forth to Uzbekistan as I wrote my first book.

Everything in Sergei's sad, tidy little apartment had a double function: his hot plate was also his water boiler, his kitchen table was also his ironing board, his couch was also his bed, his vodka glasses were also his tea cups. As he handed me my tea (also delicious, and flavored with a clove-like herb he claimed was a family secret), I realized how hungry for conversation and company this lonely, brittle man was. We sat down in his shadowy living room, while outside the orange light of dusk was turning soft and shaggy. Next to where I sat, Sergei had a framed picture of Tsar Nicholas II and his daughters, which I made the mistake of asking him about. While Andrei sighed, Sergei lamented the many crimes of the Bolshevik Revolution, the most devious of which, he said, was the murder of Nicholas, whom Sergei described as the greatest, noblest defender Russia and Russian Christianity ever had.* Sergei said he wept when the bones of Nicholas and his family were finally interred in the Peter and Paul Cathedral in St. Petersburg in 1998; he wept again, he said, two years later, when the Russian Orthodox Church canonized Nicholas. Sergei spent the next twenty minutes describing his monastery outside Moscow, which he said was the most beautiful place in the world—or at least the most beautiful place he had seen. ("Maybe," he said, "California is more beautiful.") His monastery allowed him pure study, pure meditation. This I believed. The spiritual traditions of Russian Orthodoxy are not distinguished by their openness to novelty. Insight came through careful—one might even say slavish—adherence to established rituals and thought patterns.

"When will you return to your monastery?" I asked Sergei.

"Next summer," he said. Which could not come soon enough. Whenever he was in Bishkek, he said, he drank too much and pined after too many women.

"You are a man of big dreams," Andrei said, "and big appetites." Then he repeated this in Russian.

An abashed Sergei shook his head. "Yes. This is true, unfortunately." Then he looked at me. "Are you Catholic?"

"No," I said.

"Are you Christian?"

"I'm not."

He looked accusingly over at Andrei, as though he had been misled by him, and turned back to me. "But Andrei say. You seek Matthew."

"'Seek' isn't really the word I'd use. What I'd like to do is see the remains of the monastery where Matthew's relics were supposedly kept."

---

* At least since the reign of Ivan the Terrible in the sixteenth century, the tsarist secret police drew many of its members from Orthodox monasteries. The ease with which state-sponsored monks could conflate the enemies of the state with the enemies of *Bog* would have dreadful consequences throughout subsequent Russian history.

"Why do you want this?" he asked, puzzled.

"I'm writing a book about the tombs of the Twelve Apostles."

Nodding gravely, Sergei took this in. "And how did you learn of this monastery?"

Andrei's translation services went into overdrive as I described how, in 2006, while living in Rome, I saw a BBC piece online about an archaeologist named Vladimir Ploskih, an ethnic Russian of Kyrgyz citizenship who ... But Sergei stopped me. Yes, yes. He knew all about Ploskih, a member in good standing of the Kyrgyz Academy of Sciences. Sergei also knew about the so-called Catalan Atlas, which was created in the late fourteenth century by apparently Jewish cartographers in Majorca, Spain. The atlas, which had many legendary flourishes, placed at "Ysikol" (obviously Issyk-Kul) something it called "the monastery of Armenian Brotherhood," within which, purportedly, the relics of Matthew were once placed. Ploskih claimed to have unearthed not only portions of this monastery but also evidence of a more ancient settlement, all of which was underwater. Among Ploskih's smaller discoveries were a Christian tombstone with an Uighur inscription and a piece of pottery decorated with what he described as a Star of David–like shape, which he interpreted as possible evidence of ancient Jewish or Jewish Christian activity in the area.

As I sat in Rome, the whole thing sounded far-fetched, but I nonetheless tracked down Ploskih's e-mail and wrote him a letter in English in which I expressed my hope to join him as a journalist on his next expedition to the area. I received back a short letter, in Russian, from one of Ploskih's assistants, politely declining. I later learned that the expedition was not state funded; rather, it was overseen by a few professional historians and archaeologists but was mostly staffed by passionate local history buffs.

That Christians existed in some number throughout Asia and Central Asia during medieval times, up to and around the fourteenth century, is undeniable. That the forces of Armenian

Christianity launched a far-flung missionary effort is also fairly well established. (Armenian missionaries are believed to have initially Christianized *Iceland,* of all places.) That Ploskih's expedition discovered some kind of underwater archaeological marvel in the waters of Issyk-Kul was also clear, even though it had nothing to do with ancient Christianity. Nevertheless, the Catalan Atlas was the only shred of historical evidence that placed an ancient Armenian monastery on the shores of Issyk-Kul. That such an anomalous place could have remained completely hidden until 2006 seemed unlikely. I thus asked Sergei, who had read so many books, if he gave the legend of the Monastery of Armenian Brotherhood any credence.

Instead of answering, he said, "You know there was other monastery there. Russian monastery." As Sergei elaborated on this, he switched over to Russian, and Andrei began a running translation: "Okay, so he's saying that an Orthodox monastery, a Russian monastery, was built, at the order of the tsar, on the shore of Issyk-Kul, in the late nineteenth century, very close to where the Armenian monastery is supposed to be. And he's saying this monastery was built because, you see, the Russians back then were very smart. They wanted to come into Central Asia, so they sent out their priests to build churches, seminaries, monasteries. That way, when the Muslims attacked Russian Christians, as the tsar knew they would, Russia had a justification to invade."

"The French did the same thing in Southeast Asia," I said. "Missionaries first, gunboats second."

Then Sergei said, in English, "You know about the punishment squads?"

"I don't know," I said. "What are they?"

Sergei was slumped back in his chair. Andrei listened to him drone on for a moment. "Yes, okay," Andrei said. "I know about this, too. 'Punishment squads,' you see, were what the tsar called the Russian and Ukrainian soldiers he sent to Central Asia. And now Sergei's saying that these punishment squads 'disciplined' all the naughty Kyrgyz who resisted."

"Naughty Kyrgyz?"

"That's what Sergei calls them. He says the punishment squads were prepared to rid the earth of all Uzbeks and Kyrgyz and Turkmen to make room for Russian people here, to make a second homeland. The only thing that saved the local people, Sergei says, was the Bolshevik Revolution. Without the revolution there would be no Kyrgyz anymore, and this would be Russian territory."

I was quiet for a moment. "It sounds a little bit like ethnic cleansing. I'd think Sergei, as a Muslim, would be sensitive to that issue."

When Andrei translated this, Sergei laughed and said something quick and dismissive. Andrei: "He says he doesn't approve or disapprove. He says it's simply history."

"So what happened to this Russian monastery?"

Sergei talked on. "It was destroyed in 1916," Andrei translated, "by Kyrgyz bandits. They killed all the monks but two. In Karakol, Sergei says, we can visit the Orthodox church and see a statue of Mary that was very dear to the monks there. Every year, he says, on the anniversary of the monastery's destruction, the statue weeps tears of blood." Andrei stopped translating, even though Sergei was still talking, and looked at me, obviously troubled. "Do you think it's true?"

"What—about the blood-crying statue?"

"Yeah," Andrei said.

I had already learned that Andrei was not a religious person, so I did not worry about offending him when I said that this blood-crying Mary statue was probably the opposite of true.

Sergei, who had finally stopped talking and was in the process of hand rolling a cigarette, asked what we were talking about. Andrei told him. Sergei lit up, took a meditative drag, and expelled some pungently cumulus smoke. He said, "You do not believe. The statue of Mary. Weeps blood."

"Sorry," I said. "But no. I don't."

Sergei frowned and ashed his cigarette into his empty tea

glass. Once he got back to his monastery, he said, he would read up on the matter and get back to me.

II.

Legitimizing agents and locales were imagined to lurk behind the composition of the other gospels: Mark had Rome and Peter; Luke had Paul; and John had Ephesus. One would think that early Christians would have similarly wanted to know with whom the apostle and evangelist Matthew associated and where he decided to live. Yet tradition is largely silent on these points. As far as can be known, no early Christian community claimed Matthew as its founder. Matthew did not much register in the minds of the church fathers and barely stirred the imaginations of early Christian storytellers. Even the allegorical symbol assigned to Matthew the evangelist is a dreary tautology: while Mark gets to be symbolized by a lion, John by an eagle, and Luke by an ox, Matthew's symbol is a man.*

In their lists of the Twelve, Mark and Luke list merely Matthew's name, but Matthew's list refers to someone most translations render as "Matthew the tax collector," which is probably why Matthew was eventually attached to the gospel that bears his name. In the ninth chapter, we find Jesus in Capernaum, the

---

* These evangelistic symbols, known as the Tetramorph, were standardized by Jerome around the turn of the fifth century. Jerome's source for the Tetramorph was difficult imagery in Ezekiel: "As for the appearance of their faces: the four had the face of a human being, the face of a lion on the right side, the face of an ox on the left side, and the face of an eagle" (all of which was later used by the author of Revelation to describe the "four living creatures" that attend the throne of Jesus). Jerome assigned the lion to Mark because his gospel opens with John the Baptist, which reminded Jerome of a "lion roaring in the wilderness." John was assigned the eagle due to the gospel's soaring nature. Luke was assigned the ox because his gospel opens with Zechariah offering incense in the sanctuary of the Lord, and the ox was a sacrificial animal. Matthew was assigned the human being—Jerome symbolically upgraded this figure to an angel—because his gospel opens with Joseph's angelic visitation.

citizens of which he has recently astounded by healing a para-
lytic man. "As Jesus was walking along," the gospel writer tells us,
"he saw a man called Matthew sitting at the tax booth; and he
said to him, 'Follow me.' And he got up and followed him."

That Matthew was a tax collector is one of the oldest,
strongest traditions about him. According to the scholar Joseph
Fitzmyer, however, the Greek words *ho telones,* which are typically translated as "the tax collector" (and, in older translations,
"the publican"), are not correct. The Greek term for "tax collector" never appears in the New Testament. Also mistaken is the
popular image of Matthew as a quisling of the Roman Empire.
What Matthew's gospel technically indicates is not a tax collector but a toll collector or customs officer in charge of procuring
what Fitzmyer describes as "indirect taxes": tolls, tariffs, and customs on all goods passing by his booth in Capernaum.

Thanks to Julius Caesar, the "publican" model of Roman tax
collection—whereby a moneyed member of the equestrian class
squeezed provincial peasants for poll and land taxes—ceased to
function within Palestine around 44 BCE. During the lifetime of
Jesus, poll and land taxes in Judaea, Idumaea, and Samaria were
collected by agents of the local prefect; indirect taxes such as
tolls, tariffs, and customs, meanwhile, were administered by a
chief toll collector who most likely came into his position by way
of a public auction. What made this system so gapingly open to
corruption was the Roman practice of compelling a chief toll
collector to pay his jurisdiction's expected taxes ahead of time,
from his own pocket, which he then recouped via a network of
toll and tax farmers who sat eagle-eyed in their tax booths, much
like the Matthew of tradition. Anyone who actually lived in first-
century Galilee would have regarded a toll collector as the creature of the local Jewish tetrarch Herod Antipas, not as an agent
of the Roman occupation, which most Galileans could pretend
did not affect them, as there is no record of a significant Roman
military presence in Galilee until much later in the first century.

Mark's and Luke's accounts of the calling of the Capernau-

mian "tax collector" are similar to Matthew's, but for one thing:
in both accounts, the man Jesus calls is referred to as Levi. (Mark
calls him "Levi son of Alphaeus," indicating a familial connection to James son of Alphaeus that the later Luke chose to leave
unnoted and unexplored.) All three accounts of the calling of
Matthew/Levi are followed by a jump cut to a dinner party at
which Jesus is the apparent guest of honor. Mark tells us that
the party was held at Levi's house and that "many tax collectors
and sinners were also sitting with Jesus—for there were many
who followed him." Somehow the local Pharisees get wind of
this scandalous dinner party and ask Jesus's disciples, "Why does
he eat with tax collectors and sinners?" Jesus overhears the question and answers the Pharisees directly: "Those who are well
have no need of a physician, but those who are sick; I have come
to call not the righteous but sinners." Meanwhile, in Luke's version, Levi throws a "grand banquet" for Jesus "in his house," at
which "there was a great crowd of tax collectors and others sitting at the table." Matthew's account of the party does not mention it being thrown by the toll collector recently called by Jesus,
but many of the elements in Mark and Luke are present.

A late scene in Luke shows Jesus having dinner at the house
of yet another toll collector, one Zacchaeus, who works as the
chief toll collector in Jericho. When the people of Jericho complain, Jesus again makes a public comment about the necessity
of his attending to the sinful. In Matthew, Jesus announces that
toll collectors and prostitutes are likelier to enter the Kingdom
of God than those who disobey their fathers; he also commends
toll collectors and prostitutes for believing in the proclamation
of John the Baptist. Luke, too, makes special note of the toll collectors who had been baptized by John.

Obviously, Jesus was remembered as having made some pro-
nouncement concerning toll collectors that ran counter to their
popular social standing in Palestine, and there seems to have
been a communal memory from the ministry of Jesus that had
him consorting with toll collectors personally. That so many of

Jesus's parables involve wealth, and its various social derange-
ments, helps contextualize why toll collectors are figures of such
specialized treatment in the gospels. Eventually, the apostle Matthew became the patron saint of all moneyed trades: accoun-
tants, bankers, tax collectors, and customs officers. In many
traditional representations, he is often shown clutching (or
standing on) a bag of coins, bringing him dangerously close into
symbolic brotherhood with Judas, who is sometimes depicted
holding coins as well.

The earliest copies of Mark contain numerous textual variations as to which disciple Jesus called from the tax booth—in
some texts, the called disciple is James son of Alphaeus—leading
one scholar to judge the assumed historicity of this scene as
"problematic" at best. While both Mark and Luke include the call
of Levi from his tax booth, they do not include Levi in their lists
of the Twelve, which seems to suggest that Levi was regarded by
these gospel writers as a fully fledged disciple of Jesus but not
as a member of the Twelve. While several church fathers (Origen and Clement of Alexandria among them) regarded Matthew
and Levi as different disciples, tradition has generally evolved
to accept that the toll-collecting man Jesus summoned from his
booth had two names: Matthew (his Greek name) and Levi (his
Semitic name). But Matthew is not a Greek name—*Matthaios,*
as his name is rendered in Greek, is a shortened form of the
Hebrew name Mattityah or Mattityahu, which means "gift of
Yahweh"—and not many first-century Jews are known to have
used two Semitic names in this manner.

The conservative scholars W. F. Albright and C. S. Mann
argue that "Levi" was not a personal name but a tribal designation that was eventually overwritten as a personal name.
According to this notion, Mark and Luke misunderstood a tradition in which Matthew the Levite was called from his tax booth
and rendered the scene as the call of Levi. Other scholars have
proposed that the author of Matthew's gospel, familiar with a
tradition in which the apostle named Matthew was a toll col-

lector, confused by Mark's treatment of the call of Levi, and not knowing what to do with Mark's assertion that Levi was a son of Alphaeus, swapped Levi's name for Matthew's. If this happened early in the history of Matthew's composition—before it had achieved literary fixity, say, but after it had become associated with Matthew—the decision makes good sense, as it added to the gospel an extra degree of authenticity.

Consequently, most early mentions of Matthew the apostle are related to his having written one of the gospels, though Irenaeus and Clement of Alexandria both briefly mention him in the context of having evangelized in Judaea. According to Eusebius, the early-second-century Christian writer Papias wrote, "Matthew compiled the sayings [*logia*] in the Aramaic language, and everyone translated them as well as he could." A curious and revealing note of defensiveness on the part of Papias is detectable here. Matthew's "sayings" text appears to have been questioned for its interpretive divergences, which Papias apparently tried to attribute to translational difficulties. What Papias meant by "sayings," however, has never been clear. The relationship these texts, which Papias attributed to both Mark and Matthew, had to the canonical gospels is unknown. They might have been early versions of the canonical gospels, but they might also have had little in common with the canonical gospels.

In Clement of Alexandria's *Paedagogus,* a tract on Christian ethics written around the turn of the third century, the apostle Matthew is put forth as an exemplar of the moderate, restrained type of living Clement most cherished in his fellow Christians. Clement believed that the "most suitable" foods were those "fit for immediate use without fire" and argued that an overreliance on cooked meat could lead to a "Belly-demon," which in Clement's mind was "the worst and most abandoned of demons." Clement went on: "It is far better to be happy than to have a demon dwelling with us. And happiness is found in the practice of virtue. Accordingly, the apostle Matthew partook of seeds, and nuts, and vegetables, without flesh."

That Matthew was thought to be vegetarian is a more historically interesting assertion than it might initially seem. One ancient source pegs James the brother of Jesus as vegetarian, and several ultra-ascetic sects of early Jewish Christianity, including one branch of Ebionites, were purported vegetarians. Irenaeus, meanwhile, wrote that Matthew originally wrote his gospel "in the language of the Hebrews" and, in *Against Heresies,* discussed a group of Christians who "use the gospel according to Matthew only." Origen, too, noted that Matthew's gospel "was published for believers of Jewish origin, and was composed in Aramaic." Virtually all of the church fathers believed that Matthew was the first gospel to have been written and that it had originally been written in either Hebrew or Aramaic expressly for Jews. These baseline assumptions endured for roughly fifteen hundred years, until their first serious questioning in the nineteenth century. Nonetheless, from all this we see second- and third-century Christian thinkers recognizing that the obvious Jewishness of Matthew's gospel was related to the Jewishness of its original audience. We see, too, that many church fathers regarded this fact with at least mild discomfort.

By the late fourth century, many assumptions about Matthew and his gospel had become institutionalized. Jerome, one of the few Latin writers who spent considerable time among Eastern Christians, confidently noted that Matthew wrote his gospel in Judaea for "those of the circumcision who believed." He also maintained the gospel had been translated into Greek from Hebrew by parties unknown. According to Jerome, Matthew followed "the authority" of the Hebrew version of Jewish scripture rather than the Greek Septuagint. Jerome even claimed to have had "the opportunity to copy" the original Hebrew version of Matthew's gospel, which he said he received from "Nazarenes" living in modern-day Aleppo.

The majority of Jerome's assertions about Matthew's Hebrew provenance have effectively been disproven. Most scholars now believe that Jerome was at best exaggerating his familiarity with the "original" Hebrew version of Matthew. (Jerome made claims in his work of having fully translated works he had only partially translated and to have seen other works that might have never actually existed.) What most scholars assume is that the gospel Jerome claimed to have fully translated, while related to Matthew, was neither an original version of nor even a gloss on Matthew. It was, rather, a specific gospel, written in a Semitic language and apparently used by Nazarene Christians. Christian fascination with this "original" copy of the Gospel According to Matthew, nonetheless, endured well into the medieval era, with Jacobus de Voragine relating a legend of how a copy "written" in Matthew's "own hand" was discovered among the bones of Barnabas and was used to heal any ill person who came into contact with it.

Unlike his fellow apostle and evangelist John, Matthew was imagined to have written very few other works, whether canonical or apocryphal. One text, today known as *The Gospel of Pseudo-Matthew,* is an eighth- or ninth-century Latin conflation of the *Protoevangelium of James* and *The Infancy Gospel of Thomas.* It was evidently written to bolster the cult of Mary, and one of its authors or editors attached to it a spurious letter of prefatory endorsement from Jerome, who, funnily enough, wrote at length against the *Protoevangelium of James* during his lifetime. *The Book of Thomas the Contender,* a Coptic "sayings" text from the third century that emphasizes the importance of sexual abstinence, purports to have been written by either Matthew or Matthias, as there was rampant confusion among early Christian storytellers about which of these two was which.

A legend contained in *Pseudo-Abdias* has Matthew journeying to Ethiopia and staying with the Ethiopian treasurer whom Philip converted to Christianity in Acts of the Apostles. There Matthew runs afoul of a pagan king named Aeglippus, whose two serpent-wielding sorcerers, Zaroës and Arfaxat, Matthew battles. In short order, Matthew overcomes the pair and chases them into Iran, where they later run afoul of Simon and Jude.

With his magicians defeated, Aeglippus and his family promptly convert to Christianity. According to this legend, Matthew thus established the Ethiopian church. The legend concludes by noting how Matthew lived in Ethiopia for years, until being stabbed in the back by an agent of Aeglippus's brother, whom Matthew forbade to marry a young nun.

III.

I had last visited Central Asia in the spring of 2003. At that time, in a hotel bar in Tashkent, Uzbekistan, I fell into a conversation with a Belgian who worked for the International Monetary Fund. This man hated Uzbekistan—hated being there, hated working there, hated the government, hated the police, and hated the political situation. (It would get worse.) But this man was careful to note how much he loved Kyrgyzstan, to which he traveled as often as he could. "Now that," he told me, "is a country."

I had visited Kyrgyzstan a couple times in my travels through Central Asia, and I, too, had adored my time amid its mountains and among its almost unflaggingly welcoming people. The Kyrgyz were tough without being overly aggressive—and quite unhappy, many of them, but not in a way that became your problem. Since my last visit to Kyrgyzstan, however, much had changed, including the overthrow of two despotic governments. There had been the occasional talk of civil war, angry protests against an American military base, and increasingly strychnine relations with neighboring Uzbekistan. One of the young men who worked at my hotel, an ethnic Uzbek, had told me, when I tried out my disintegratingly rusty language skills on him, "You know, Kyrgyz and Uzbeks—we are no longer brothers right now."

Considering Kyrgyzstan's internal political turmoil, I had been expecting to find the country I so loved transformed into a minor police state. When Andrei and I left Bishkek around

7:00 a.m., in a car piloted by our hired driver, Igor, no one stopped us. We came to no checkpoints. In Tashkent in 2003, you were stopped at least three times while trying to leave the city limits—even the checkpoints had checkpoints. As Bishkek disappeared behind us, I blathered something to Andrei about how the lack of checkpoints seemed to me indicative of Kyrgyz culture's greater openness.

"There are *plenty* of checkpoints in the south," Andrei said. "Down there, whole villages are surrounded by tanks." Andrei gazed out the window for a moment. "But you know," he said, turning to me, "maybe if we had more checkpoints, we wouldn't have so many revolutions."

The Kyrgyz Tulip Revolution, which occurred in 2005, succeeded in ridding Kyrgyzstan of President Askar Akayev and his vampirically embezzling family. In my first book, I referred to Akayev, a former physics professor and the first president of independent Kyrgyzstan, as "the most liberal" leader of post-Soviet Central Asia. When the Kyrgyz people started pushing back against the Akayev regime in 2004, they were astonished to discover that few members of its beleaguered police or internal security forces had any heart left to defend the system. Kyrgyz protesters eventually found themselves standing in the drawing room of Kyrgyzstan's presidential palace, which like ours is called the White House. When Akayev's personal diaries were discovered (the man himself had fled to Russia), the genuinely shocking extent to which he had been enriching himself on the backs of his impoverished countrymen was revealed to all.

Akayev was succeeded by Kurmanbek Bakiyev, whose strongest support came from southern Kyrgyzstan. Bakiyev's many broken promises, a high national unemployment rate, a kidney-punched economy, and, eventually, race riots involving Uzbeks and Kyrgyz in the south led to widespread protests and weeks of violent unrest. (The flame-blackened husk of the prosecutor's office, stormed by protesters as a symbol of all that was wrong with the regime, still marred Bishkek's Ala-Too Square.) Bakiyev, who resigned in 2010 and fled to Belarus, was replaced by his foreign minister Roza Otunbayeva, a major opposition figure during the Tulip Revolution and, by most accounts, a relatively decent human being (though ten years from now I might be lamenting my credulous admiration of her as well). Of President Otunbayeva, Andrei said, "She won't be allowed to seek reelection, so obviously she's trying to steal as much as she can right now."

I was disappointed to hear bad things about Otunbayeva, if only because Kyrgyzstan badly needed and deserved a break. Igor perked up when we began to discuss Otunbayeva, for he had an opinion on her, too. I did not put much faith in Igor's opinions. Any of them. He affected great offense whenever I put on my seat belt, for instance, claiming he was such a fine driver I would not need to wear it, and later asked Andrei if I was in the CIA. The only CD Igor had in his car was something called *Hans Zimmer Presents,* even though none of the songs (the *Hawaii Five-O* theme song, the *Chariots of Fire* theme song, the *X-Files* theme song, Spandau Ballet's "True") had anything to do with Hans Zimmer.

While Igor declaimed his opinion on Otunbayeva, Andrei translated by saying, "And now he's going on about a bunch of bullshit, basically." As intrigued as I was by Igor, I would have recommended his driving services only to my most implacable enemies. Igor loved hunting through the tracks of *Hans Zimmer Presents* when he was passing another car. In fact, he saved all of his most complicated, attention-requiring in-car maneuvers (rolling down his window, turning around to talk to me) for when he was passing another car, preferably around a blind turn.

When we were a few miles outside Bishkek, Igor told Andrei he could arrange a prostitute for me and insisted Andrei ask me if I wanted one. It was troubling but not really surprising to learn that of all the Americans Igor had driven, all but two "went crazy," in his words, for local prostitutes. When Andrei made it clear I had no interest in prostitutes, Igor asked him if he thought I was gay. "If he is gay," Igor said before a stunned Andrei could answer, "we have a big problem." When Andrei told me all this later that day, part of me wanted to tell Igor I was a gay CIA agent here to break up prostitution rings run by freelance drivers, but my fear of being beaten to death roadside with a tire iron prevailed.

The day before, it had snowed for hours in and around Bishkek. The spectacular mountains all around us were covered in snow and invisible against a bleach-white sky. As we drove on, the morning grew warmer, and little by little the lower reaches of the mountains developed patches and then swaths of evergreen. At the base of the mountains were little huddled collections of smokestacks and boxy industrial buildings. By 9:00 a.m., huge clouds had risen up behind the mountains. Later, the clouds shifted and shrouded the mountaintops like ragged, broken halos. Some of the higher mountains managed to pierce the cloud layer, creating wounds of intense blue. In a few hours' time, we had our first glimpse of Issyk-Kul. Initially, I could see only a curved, scythe-like section of the lake. As more of it came into sight, it was a prairie of plate glass sparkling in the sun.

The Kyrgyz government takes Issyk-Kul's "ecological habitat" status fairly seriously, as can be seen when one enters the lake's officially protected environs and passes beneath a grand arched gate marked BIOSPHERE ENTRANCE. At 450 kilometers in diameter, Issyk-Kul is the tenth-largest lake in the world. Its name (Hot Lake) derives from the curious fact that it never freezes, no matter how cold the winter or how many meters of snow lay piled on its surrounding panorama of mountains. It has been theorized that the bubonic plague that wiped out 50 percent of Europe in the fourteenth century might have been spread by merchants who stopped at an important Silk Road way station found on the shores of Issyk-Kul—and what an unfortunate historical association for such a lovely, lonely place. We were driving along the lake's edge now, where the little resorts had an almost Chesapeakean tidiness. Andrei told me that if we had

been here a month ago, we could have seen Bishkek's elite out on
the lake in their sailboats. The water, now that we were closer to
the shoreline, seemed motionless, autumn still, and gray.

Soon we were driving down a road lined on both sides by
tall, perfectly spaced poplar trees. Sometimes the trees broke to
reveal small tucked-away villages or Muslim cemeteries. Igor
was swerving a lot, for on the road were more animals than
cars. Among the creatures we almost hit: several sheep, a cow,
two horses, and a goat. Among the creatures we actually hit: a
chicken, two crows, and a dog. (The dog lived. The chicken did
not. The fate of the crows was unclear.) At one point, Igor had to
stop and get out of the car to shoo away a dozen horses standing
in the middle of the road, one of which turned and hissed at Igor
when he smacked her on the backside. Andrei and I watched
this confrontation with great amusement from the safety of our
SUV.

Most of the villages we passed were little more than one-
building-deep rows of roadside homes. You could sprint from
one end to the other of most of these villages in twenty seconds
flat. You could stand in the middle of these villages and physically count the number of people who lived in them.

The village we thought we were looking for was once called
Svetly Mys, which means "Bright Cape" in Russian. Like most
places throughout Central Asia, Svetly Mys had been granted
a new name after the collapse of the Soviet Union. It was now
called Ak Bolun, which means something like "White Knight" in
Kyrgyz. Although Ak Bolun was found two miles away from the
shore of Issyk-Kul, its former Russian name suggests it had once
been closer to the water's edge. After talking to some villagers,
we learned we were looking not for Svetly Mys or Ak Bolun at
all but rather for a nearby village called Kurmanty, which was
also the name of the small river that divided Kurmanty from Ak
Bolun. The people of Ak Bolun were adamant that Kurmanty
was where all the recent excavation work had taken place. Before
our search for the Monastery of Armenian Brotherhood formally

began, we decided to drive to Karakol, the regional capital, for lunch.

Karakol's boulevards were wide and Soviet—Venetian canals filled with cement. It was obvious the town attracted tourists and foreigners: many of the signs were in English, and a small percentage of its ATMs actually worked. As we pulled up to the restaurant Andrei wanted to visit, I saw that it specialized in *balikh* (fish). I had learned the hard way that one's best option when confronted with a seafood restaurant in landlocked Central Asia was to fake a heart attack and sneak back to your hotel when your friends ran off to find an ambulance, but Andrei assured me that the fish was all fresh caught from Issyk-Kul, which, he said, "wasn't that polluted."

Inside, Andrei and Igor ordered far too much food, the standout of which was an aromatic bucket of fish soup. Overeating was the Kyrgyz way, as this was a land whose national hero, Manas, is said to have eaten an entire sheep at birth and two dozen sheep for his twelfth birthday. After lunch, our search began in earnest for the Monastery of Armenian Brotherhood. Thanks to a guide friend of Andrei's, we knew a few things about the excavation site. One was that the supposed catacombs that once led into the vanished monastery were all that had been excavated and all that could be explored. We also knew that the land on which the ancient monastery had supposedly been located was sold about a year ago, which meant the excavation site was now considered private property. We knew the entrance to the catacombs was "on the left" when heading toward Issyk-Kul and was said to be visible from the "main road." Finally, we knew a member of the archaeological dig team had planted a large wooden cross near the entrance to the catacombs. As it turned out, though, everything we thought we knew about the excavation site was at least a little wrong.

We stopped in the literal center of Kurmanty and learned it had precisely two kinds of citizens at home in the middle of the day: the awe-inspiringly old and the informationally unharvestable young. Neither had the faintest idea where the old monastery excavation site was located; most claimed to have never heard of it. This seemed odd. The supposed monastery site was mentioned in many books, including several Central Asian guidebooks. I had passed through the Issyk-Kul area once before and heard talk of Matthew's supposed resting place from a freelance guide who offered to take me there, which later led to my first thoughts of writing a book about apostolic tombs. Also, BBC International had come here and done a story on the excavation site. I did not understand how an international news crew or Western guidebook writers could pass through these small, eleemosynary villages, asking about apostles and monasteries, and not gloriously implant themselves within local memory for the next three generations.

After a short, old, grinning woman with a mouthful of gold teeth told us she had never heard anything about any excavation in the village in which she had spent her entire life, I asked Andrei to rephrase his question. Instantly, Andrei turned to me. "What do you mean? I already asked her about the monastery."

"But did you mention Matthew?"

"Yeah," he said, "of course I did."

"Matthew the apostle."

He laughed. "I don't think she knows anything."

I looked at the woman, who shrugged as though on cue. "This is really weird," I said.

"I agree it's strange. But if she doesn't know, she doesn't know."

We walked back to Igor's SUV and drove on down a dirt road. We had been asking around for an hour by this point, and Igor was getting angry. Andrei provided a running translation: "He says the Kyrgyz are ignorant. That's their problem, he says. They don't understand good Russian anymore. He says maybe if they didn't change the names of all their villages, people here would feel some connection to their past."

At this I sighed. "That's pretty rich, coming from a Russian."

Andrei sighed, too. "It's what he says. Don't shoot the messenger."

We pulled up beside a middle-aged, unhappy-looking woman walking along the road carrying a small, stuffed suitcase. She claimed to know of a sign, found a little farther down the road, that made official note of the monastery. Close to where the road passed by the Kurmanty River, we found the sign she spoke of: SIT [sic] OF KORMENTU [sic?] ANCIENT SETTLEMENT. We turned onto the indicated road, Igor still grumbling about the hopelessness of our quest. Ahead we saw some Kyrgyz children pushing one another across the road in wheelbarrows. Igor had a fascinating response to this, which was to gun his engine and steer the SUV toward the children. I advised him never to do anything like that again when I was a passenger in his car and promised that if he did, I would not be paying him. Igor said nothing to me for the rest of the day.

We followed the road but came across no second "Ancient Settlement" sign. To encounter a sign that announced the existence of something that turned out to not exist would not be the weirdest thing ever to happen to me in Central Asia, a land of seven-year-old hitchhikers and hotels and restaurants whose windows were affixed with both Visa and MasterCard stickers and yet refused to accept either Visa or MasterCard. At a bend in the road, we saw an old Kyrgyz woman wearing a bright red head scarf gathering up twigs in a field. Igor had stopped the SUV and was approaching the woman before Andrei had his seat belt unbuckled. I got out, too, half expecting Igor to punch her in the head. Instead, I heard him greet the woman with a polite "Assalom aleikum." Predictably, she had never heard of any "ancient settlement" found along this road. When we got back in the SUV, Andrei said we should drive down to the end of the road anyway. "What good are old people," a clearly frustrated Andrei said, "when they don't *know* anything?"

We found at the end of the road an old Soviet factory so completely abandoned it seemed more like a first-person-shooter multiplayer map than a place that had ever been a functional site of manufacture. The area was surrounded by collapsed chain-link fence and pieces of concrete that looked catapulted in by an invading medieval army. The factory was found on the lakeshore. In back, near some unloading docks, the tetanusly rusted arm of a broken crane sagged into the water, reminding me that perhaps no force in world history had done more for the cause of rigorous waterfront destruction than Communism. I marveled for a moment at the sight of the factory's padlocked side door, beside which was a bank of broken open windows. Walking back to the SUV, I cut through some high grass and stepped in a pile of still-warm horse manure several times larger than my foot. I did my best to clean my filthy shoe in the waters of Issyk-Kul while incoming ducks sailed over fast and low. I could hear Igor laughing from inside his SUV.

Andrei had an idea. We should, he said, drive back up the road to the midpoint between the factory and Kurmanty, get out of the SUV, and walk in opposite directions until we found the catacombs' entrance. This was better than my idea, which was to physically assault Igor.

The off-road landscape at the midpoint was surprisingly rolling, with swampy glade-like areas tucked unseen between the hills. I had with me a burner cell phone that I bought in Bishkek and used it to stay in touch with Andrei while we fanned out in search of the entrance to the catacombs.

When we got far enough away from the SUV, I said, "Igor is a dickhead. Hearing him complain about Kyrgyz not able to speak Russian well . . . does that motherfucker speak Kyrgyz at all?"

"But the people we met didn't speak Russian very well."

"Are you offended by that?"

"Not really. It would be good for us if they did, though."

"Do you see anything? Anything at all?"

"I see nothing that resembles an old monastery or catacombs."

"We're supposed to be able to see it from the road, right?"

"That's what my friend told me."

"..."

"..."

"*Now* what do you see?"

"Nothing. I'm peeing."

"Great. I see some frogs. I see a swamp."

"I see a swamp as well."

"The BBC did a segment on this stupid monastery! Why is it so hard to find?"

"I have no answer."

"Do the hills you're walking on have these odd markings on them?"

"Yes. They're not markings. They're paths the cows use to walk along the hillside."

"Oh. Indeed they are. Okay. Now I'm actually watching a cow spray diarrhea out of its ass."

"My advice is to stand back."

"Thanks."

"..."

"..."

"So. No catacombs here. No ruins. No ancient settlement."

"Meet you back at the truck?"

"Okay."

We decided to head to our hotel in Karakol and come back the following day. Near the main highway, however, we saw a young Kyrgyz guy on a motorcycle. "Stop!" Andrei said to Igor. Apparently, Andrei had a feeling about this young man, which handsomely paid off. Not only did he know of the monastery and its catacombs, but he knew roughly where it was located. We were on the wrong road, he said. The road we wanted was the second unpaved road down from the main highway—the road, in other words, that did not advertise its ancient settlement. The young man said we would have to drive down this road a mile or so, after which we would see a trailer. The excavation-site catacombs were somewhere beyond that trailer.

We did as instructed and drove down a bumpy, unpaved road, past a sheep market and a couple tiny houses, and finally saw, in a miniature valley just below a grassy escarpment, the trailer the young man mentioned. We left the SUV, followed the road down, and stopped when we came to a padlocked gate, on either side of which was barbed-wire fencing. The trailer looked as though it had gone unused since Kyrgyz independence. Its windows were transparent plastic that had been taped in place, but the tape had come loose, which meant the plastic windows were flapping in and out of their frames. The trailer was the centerpiece of a surrounding little farm. Here were three endlessly grass-chewing cows, and here was a goat walking up to the gate and bleating, as though to warn us away from entering.

Andrei stepped closer to the barbed wire and discovered a section of it could be parted wide enough for us to squeeze through. We did not discuss whether we should squeeze through. I held the barbed wire open, and he did the same for me. We were now officially trespassing on private property. "In America," Andrei asked, "could we be shot for doing something like this?"

"Actually," I said, "yeah, we could."

"Here you just get the shit beaten out of you."

We thought we found the entrance to the catacombs when we saw a relatively fancy wooden canopy on the edge of the farm. This turned out to be a cooking pit of some sort. We followed the one path we could find, which carried us along a peaceful inlet of Issyk-Kul. Ducks kicked beside us. Big orange fish slalomed through the tall cattails along the shore. This seemed another world altogether, one onto which the catastrophe of twentieth-century Communism had not crash-landed. Across the inlet, which became as wide as a river, we saw two Kyrgyz shepherds. They saw us, too. In fact, they were watching us. Andrei said, "They're probably thinking, 'What are those assholes doing over there?'"

The path led around two large mammillated hills and to a

delta where the inlet split in two. In other words, nowhere. We walked back to the SUV and found Igor engaged in conversation with an older, mustached Kyrgyz man, whose principal interest derived from the fact that he was the first man I had ever encountered wearing a coat and tie while on horseback. The old man, who spoke Russian extremely well, knew about the monastery and knew about the recent excavation. "They were here last April," he said, with reassuring specificity. He promised the catacomb entrance was indeed back there somewhere and went so far as to draw for us a map in the dirt. Andrei and I ducked back through the gap in the barbed-wire fence and tried again.

Just past the inlet's delta, Andrei rushed ahead of me, saying he knew exactly where the catacombs were. I let him go, only to get lost on one of the mammillated hills we had seen earlier, both of which were jungles of tall and finger-cuttingly sharp yellow grass. I had more or less given up on finding the catacombs when I heard Andrei, rooting around on the other hill, shout, "I found it!" He had almost fallen into the entrance, which was not an entrance so much as a hole that looked dynamited into the hillside. Someone had partially covered this entrance with branches and leaves. We looked inside, but it was forbidding and terrifying in the way actual real-life darkness is forbidding and terrifying. Andrei asked if I had a flashlight.

"Sorry," I said. "I don't."

"You should have a flashlight."

"Really? It's not like I've been visiting apostolic tombs for the last several years."

"I understand American sarcasm, you know," Andrei said, and ducked inside.

I followed him in, squatting to keep from hitting my head on the ceiling. Almost immediately we both stopped. Fifty feet ahead of us: a shaft of light. To our immediate left: a passageway that led into deeper darkness. To our immediate right: the same. I had been in plenty of catacombs before. These were not the friendly and torch-lit catacombs one found in suburban Rome. This was a cramped, hostile, dirt-floored, spider- and millipede-infested space as uninterested in its own history as it was in our exploratory comfort.

Outside the sun was setting along the edge of a bruise-colored sky. We decided to return, with a flashlight, the next morning.

IV.

Whoever he was, the author of the Gospel According to Matthew had some skill with Greek and felt an obvious comfort and familiarity with Jewish scripture. Most scholars thus regard the gospel's author as an educated—and probably pharisaically trained—member of the Jewish Diaspora. In this sense, the Gospel According to Matthew has quite a bit in common with the writings of Paul, possibly because its author, like Paul, hailed from a Pharisaic background. Both Paul and the author of Matthew were determined to portray the mission, life, and death of Jesus as the nation of Israel's experience in surrogate form; Matthew was particularly interested in establishing that virtually every recorded act of Jesus had its basis in Jewish scripture. The gospel formulation that runs "Then was fulfilled" occurs fourteen times in Matthew, once in Mark, three times in Luke, and nine times in John.

This parasitic approach to Jewish scripture had intellectually disastrous repercussions, leading later Christian thinkers (and millions of modern Christians) into an inescapable labyrinth of prophecy anytime they peered into scripture. Irenaeus approvingly called this phenomenon the "demonstrations in the Scriptures," and these demonstrations, it turned out, were *everywhere*. Citing proof or demonstration texts has always been a way for Christians to establish the airtight validity of their beliefs. They do not appear to have bothered to imagine how easily someone

with a piece of scripture next to him could craft a story that "fulfilled" what the cited scripture appeared to predict.*

There were other rhetorical methods by which first-century
Jews and Jewish Christians put Jewish scripture to work. One
method was called *halakha,* which was legalistically inclined,
reveled in commentary and specifics, and tended toward long-
winded extrapolation—Paul's method, generally speaking. The
method of the Qumran community (see page 372) was closer
to a *pesher,* or commentary, which lined up chunks of Jewish
scripture (sometimes unrelated pieces of scripture that had been
grouped thematically) for the purpose of illuminating the social,
legal, or cosmic issue at hand. The *midrash,* which was used by
many first- and second-century Jewish teachers, was probably
the loosest of all these interpretive methods, as it allowed a
speaker or writer to explore pieces of Jewish scripture through
parable, homily, and metaphor, sometimes in surprising or coun-
terintuitive ways.

In writing his gospel, Matthew's author seems to have
combined the loose midrashic approach with that of a textually intense pesher. When Jesus is approached by the disciples
in Matthew and asked why he speaks in parables, for instance,
Jesus responds, "The reason I speak in parables is that 'seeing

---

* The weirdest moment in Matthew—possibly the weirdest moment in the entire
gospel tradition—is described in Matthew 27:53. As Jesus dies on the cross, we are
told, nearby "tombs . . . were opened, and many bodies of the saints who had fallen
asleep were raised. After his resurrection they came out of the tombs and entered the
holy city and appeared to many." In other words, an unspecified but large number of
unnamed prophets and holy figures from the traditions of Judaism sprang to life and
zombied their way through Jerusalem. The astonishing so-called Risen Ones never
come up again in the New Testament, which rattled Christian cages for generations.
Various attempts were made to explain the passage, the most popular—supported
by Tertullian, Augustine, and John Chrysostom, among others—being that Matthew
described not a literal raising but a spiritual one. The likeliest source of this strange
passage? Of course, Jewish scripture. Ezekiel 37:12: "Thus says the Lord God: I am
going to open your graves, and bring you up from your graves, O my people; and I
will bring you back to the land of Israel."

they do not perceive, and hearing they do not listen, nor do they understand.'" To put it another way, when asked why he uses midrashic tools, Jesus responds with a pesher on a passage from Isaiah. Matthew's Jesus, more teacher than miracle worker, is much like the author of Matthew himself: metaphorically gifted but legalistically rigid, devoted to scriptural authority while aware of human needs that scripture does not explicitly address, seemingly open-minded but also an unbending traditionalist.

A major concern for the author of Matthew was the Kingdom of Heaven, even though what exactly Jesus meant by the Kingdom of Heaven remains danglingly up for debate. By all available evidence, the first Christians understood the Kingdom as the coming of a Jewish-run world in which all the vexations that plagued the Jews—occupation, poverty, and disease (not for nothing did Jesus heal)—would be vanquished from the earth. To this end, Matthew mentions the imminence of the end numerous times and the "weeping" that will occur. Luke's and Mark's discussions of the Kingdom often feel uncertain and hedging—Luke seems to suggest at one point that it develops *within* a believer—and in John's gospel we see overmuch individual belief in the Kingdom lampooned in the figure of Nicodemus, the Sanhedrin's secret Jesus partisan, who is depicted as being so obsessed with signs of the coming Kingdom that he does nothing in particular to reify its arrival. Matthew's author is by far the clearest of any of the gospel writers on what he thinks the Kingdom of Heaven means, and discipleship is a prominent part of that message.

For Matthew, Jesus is both the fulfillment and the embodiment of Israel itself. But he is also something new on this earth, something that escapes Israel's ethno-gravitational pull. Even though Matthew's Jesus tells the disciples during his ministry, "Go nowhere among the Gentiles," in the middle of the gospel Matthew cites the prophet Isaiah as the source of these words of Jesus: "And in his name the Gentiles will hope." Matthew's Jesus also declaims during the Last Supper that "this good news of

the kingdom will be proclaimed throughout the world, as a testimony to all the nations, and then the end will come." After his
resurrection, Jesus unambiguously tells the Eleven, "Go therefore
and make disciples of all nations, baptizing them in the name of
the Father and of the Son and of the Holy Spirit, and teaching
them to obey everything that I have commanded you."

The degree to which such conflicting sentiment reflects the
beliefs of the historical Jesus cannot be known, but it can almost
certainly be traced to the community for which Matthew wrote
his gospel. Matthew contains several internal clues that indicate
its author, like the author of the Gospel According to John, was
directing his words to a troubled community in need of guidance on key issues. It would seem that one of the most pressing
issues for Matthew's community was tension between Jewish
and Gentile Christians.

If the Jesus of Matthew's gospel seems torn as to whether
his disciples should seek Jew or Gentile, this is probably due to
the issue's remaining unsettled within Matthew's community.
Antioch (in modern-day Syria) is often assumed to be where
Matthew was written, and the likely situation faced by Christians in that city would align with what Matthew's gospel indi-
rectly depicts: a prosperous, ethnically mongrel, Greek-speaking
community with strong ties to Jewish Christianity. Matthew's
community was probably not self-destructing, as John's was,
and appears to have agreed on many basic principles. But if
some in Matthew's community sought to make disciples of all
nations and others believed Jesus was the perfect fulfillment of
Israel—both postulations contained in the Gospel According to
Matthew—the nature of its internal disagreements can easily be
imagined.

Matthew is the only evangelist to use the word "church,"
which is significant. He is also the only evangelist to use the
world "Gentile." It may be that to Matthew the church brought
into being by Jesus's followers *was* the Kingdom of Heaven,
and the only way to enter it was through official disciples of

the church. From Matthew's emphasis on Jesus's fulfillment of Jewish scripture to the long speeches he gives Jesus that stress the importance of upright behavior, we see a gospel whose main argumentative thrust is for continuance of tradition and community well-being. "Therefore whoever breaks one of the least of these commandments," Matthew's Jesus tells us, "and teaches others to do the same, will be called least in the kingdom of heaven."

Yet Matthew's was not a strictly egalitarian community, and the Jesus of this gospel lingers on the concepts of reward and punishment ("the angels will come out and separate the evil from the righteous and throw them into the furnace of fire") to a much greater extent than the other gospels. (John, by contrast, simply writes off everyone who doesn't belong to his community as hopelessly irredeemable.) Matthew, however, expects a higher code of conduct from the disciples of Jesus, even if "the kingdom of heaven," as his Jesus says at one point, "is like a net that was thrown into the sea and caught fish of every kind."

Throughout Jewish religious history—throughout the history of all religions—there is abiding tension between traditionalists and modernizers. Modernizers were probably the first monotheists, because the earliest forms of Jewish worship were demonstrably polytheistic, strains of which remain embedded in the Hebrew Bible. Traditionalists such as the Maccabees overthrew the Seleucid modernizers seeking to bring Judaism into a place of accommodation with Hellenism, and traditionalists like the Zealots drove a dagger into the corrupted heart of a collaborationist and thus modernizing Temple aristocracy. When Christianity began to win more pagan converts in the second century, staunch pagan traditionalists such as Tacitus and Celsus were horrified.* The argument between traditionalism and modern-

---

* Tacitus believed the Roman Empire had become too inclusive for its own moral good, a place where "all things hideous and shameful from every part of the world meet and become popular." Celsus's more explicit argument against Christianity

ization lives on today within Judaism, Christianity, and Islam. It is and will always be an argument about the past and the future, about the pressures of inheritance and the desire for constancy. Although this ageless argument might twist and turn to unlikely effect (with a great modernizer such as Paul being adored by the traditionalists of today), the argument itself will never resolve. It will never fade away. It will emerge over and over again, with different parties wearing similar masks, for every spiritually engaged community is forced to confront the inevitability of newly arisen beliefs and the drifting tectonic plates of assumed morality.

The Jesus of the gospels is often viewed as a modernizer, but the Jesus of Matthew is a conservative traditionalist in most matters. The Gospel According to Matthew is most emphatic of all the gospels on one issue in particular: Jesus upholds the Law.* When we see Jesus debate the Pharisees on various interpretive matters in the gospels, the temptation for modern readers is to see Jesus as a fearless hypocrisy smasher, an iconoclast putting the conservative, pettifogging Pharisees of his time in their place. In the socioreligious context of the first century, however, the Pharisees were seen as promulgators of many newfangled interpretations of scripture—including one alarming belief having to do with bodily resurrection. But when Jesus calls the Pharisees hypocrites, which he does on seven occasions in Matthew, it is not because they fail to practice what they preach; on

---

sounds not unlike the conservative American argument against, say, immigrants not learning English: "We are citizens of a particular empire with a particular set of laws, and it behooves the Christians to at least recognize their duties within the present context."

* A revealing example concerns Jewish dietary law. In Mark, Jesus claims, "It is what comes out of a person that defiles." According to Mark, Jesus thus declared all foods clean. Matthew, who was clearly working off a similar tradition concerning eating and defilement, has Jesus claim that "evil intentions" are what defile a person; "to eat with unwashed hands," Jesus goes on, "does not defile." Jewish dietary law remains in effect for the Jesus of Matthew.

the contrary, it is because they are not living up to the Law as laid down by Moses. John's Jesus nukes any lingering loyalty to the Law because John's community felt it no longer applied to them. Matthew's Jesus honors the decrees of Moses because his community apparently needed the Law to bind together Jew and Gentile under terms both could understand and accept. In the end, that is what the gospels are: accidental autobiographies of the communities, and authors, that produced them.

The Law, according to Matthew, was the foundation by which disciples of Jesus would be judged. When one considers the type of community for which Matthew was writing—a community comprising Jew and Gentile, deeply familiar with the Law, and desperately attempting to satisfy extremists on both sides of the issue—Matthew becomes a carefully positioned mediating document, even though many of the positions it takes are conservative. In this sense, it is the most fascinating and moving gospel, for the type of Christian community it went to such pains to comfort and promote proved to be early Christianity's most fragile.

V.

The next morning, we went to a bazaar in Karakol to find and purchase a flashlight. With no flashlights available, we were forced to settle for a Chinese-made miner-style headlamp. The debate quickly began: Which of us would be forced to wear the headlamp inside the catacomb? Andrei said he should not be made to wear such a ridiculous thing within his home country; someone he knew might see him. I would wear the headlamp.

Before heading back to Kurmanty, Andrei suggested we stop in at the local Russian Orthodox church to see if any of the priests there knew anything about the lost Armenian monastery and its purported Matthew reliquary. Karakol's Orthodox church was well over a hundred years old and made almost entirely of wood; it was a point of local pride that only a few hundred nails were holding the place together. The paint-scoured, faded building had once been highly colorful, Andrei said, but only its turban-shaped onion domes and lintels retained any pigment more vivid than gray. As though to compensate, its surrounding metal gate had been freshly painted, as had the grounds' benches, both done up in garish, glow-stick blues and greens. We walked up to the church door, on which was a sign. "'No photo or video,'" Andrei said, translating it. "'Do not shake hands with anyone. Do not put your hands in your pocket.'"

"Wow," I said.

"'Do not sit cross-legged.'"

"Understood."

"'No women in pants, skirts, or open dresses. No hats for men. No lipstick.'"

"No *lipstick*?"

"'Women must wear head scarves.'"

"Got it."

"'No bathing suits.'"

"Now you're just making shit up."

"Again, 'No bathing suits.' It says so here."

Inside was the bare, forlorn world of Russian Christianity. There were no pews, and only on days of service did anyone bring in the fold-out chairs for parishioners. The floor was orange and warped; when I closed my eyes and walked along, it felt more as if I were walking on the natural unevenness of a hillside path than any man-made interior. A fair number of old, blobby parishioners were staggering on varicose legs from icon to icon. It was genuinely awful to think of the decades of emotional deprivation Russian Christians had endured, and in a way I admired the tenacity of their faith. These people had the devastated stature of tragic heroes.

Russian Christianity, a brazen imitation of Byzantine Christianity, was nearly destroyed by the Mongols in the early thirteenth century and almost destroyed again after the Bolshevik Revolution. The faith of every Russian Christian was determined by a sense of inevitable opposition—the terror of encirclement, of potential destruction. It was a faith of obedience and strictness, with a view of God as imperial as it was mystical. Nothing Jewish remained in this faith. Some Greek and Roman traces remained, but these were often ornamental, such as the Russian love of icons. Not a few Russian Christian traditions were repellent to non-Russian Christians, such as drinking holy water. Such a viscerally unpleasant thing for a former altar boy to contemplate! The holy water into which I had dunked my fingers as a boy was always a mineral lukewarm pool, as potable as engine coolant.

We walked to the middle of the church, where there stood a lectern with an icon that appeared to depict Jesus raising Lazarus. The image was unclear, and Andrei did not have the necessary command of liturgical calligraphic nineteenth-century Russian, or enough familiarity with the New Testament, to figure it out. This was the first time Andrei had been in a church in fifteen years. "My mother believes in her soul," he said, "but she never had me baptized. They say that those who are not baptized are not under God's protection."

"I don't think that's true."

"Are you baptized?"

"Well. Yeah."

"Ah," he said. "I see. Then I think this is easy for you to say."

A Russian woman who obviously worked at the church walked by us. She was wearing a polka-dot head scarf and had oversized welder's glasses and a mouthful of gold teeth. Her face was unlined but obviously old; this was a woman who had spent a large portion of her life being cold indoors. I nudged Andrei to ask if she knew anything about the Monastery of Armenian Brotherhood.

He approached her. The first thing Andrei said was that I was writing a book on the Twelve Apostles. The moment Andrei said this, the woman's eyes shot over to me suspiciously. At the moment she started to speak, Andrei said, quietly, "This woman is weird." She spoke for a while. Andrei, finally, translated: "She has no right, she says, to open her mouth about this matter without the priest's permission. Even if she knew about it, which she doesn't, to speak of it would be a sin."

"A sin? You're kidding me."

I must have smiled, because she spoke again, harshly. Andrei duly translated: "And now she's saying this may be a laughing matter to you but to her this is quite serious. Only a priest can give you correct information."

"Please," I said, "apologize to her for me."

"I don't think she cares. Or that it will help. Igor told me that the priest here is a very stern man."

"Yeah, no shit. Is the priest here?"

"He's not. He's in Bishkek."

"Can you ask her if she's even heard of Matthew's reliquary being found near here?"

Andrei asked her, and she had the same answer: "I can speak only if I get the blessing of the priest. Without that blessing, I cannot speak." With that, she marched off.

"She was not helpful," Andrei said. "Sergei would have found a way to talk to that lady. He would have mentioned the names of respected monks in Russia, and she would have talked."

Back at the catacombs, I was standing beside a lake that never froze while snow fell on the mountains from a bright blue sky. No wonder Mongols worshipped mountains. Yet the air was sunny, crisp—a cup of hot tea with a fresh ice cube dropped in it. When we reached the barbed-wire gate, Andrei pointed out that someone had been here after us yesterday, tidying up: the hole in the fence through which we had slipped was bent back into place. We nevertheless made the hole again and climbed through. The animals, this time, turned weirdly restive, and for several seconds we believed we were going to be charged by one of the cows. Rather than follow yesterday's trail through the ornery bestiary, we decided to walk around the farm and approach the catacombs from a different angle. There was no trail over here, so instead we followed the path of some recently mown hay.

I found myself wondering who had purchased this property and why the local people seemed not to regard these catacombs as having any historical or cultural importance. When I lived in Rome, a new discovery in Saint Paul Outside-the-Walls was a Reuters-making news event. Even the first mentions of Matthew's relics here had reached me through a Google alert. But now, years later? Nothing. Nothing to mark this place as significant in any way. It had to be the only potential apostolic site in the world to be so ill-tended and forgotten. Even Hakeldama had its visitors.

We walked over the hills, which the previous night's rain had transformed into dunes of wet grass. From the surrounding swamps came the song of bullfrogs—dozens of broken bows dragged along rusty violin strings. When we reached the entrance, Andrei changed his mind: he would wear the headlamp. Once we climbed into the catacombs and could actually see what was inside, it became instantly clear that one of the mysterious tunnels that led off into darkness stopped due to collapse, while the other led into an open area big enough for us to stand in. Revealed by the light of Andrei's headlamp, this catacomb was so defiantly unremarkable I started to laugh.

Matthew's relics were found elsewhere in this world. Some are kept in the Cathedral of San Matteo in Salerno, Italy (according to legend, they were transported there from Ethiopia in the eleventh century), and others are held by Saint Mary Major in Rome. Contrary to many travel guides' breathless imagining of how Matthew might have wound up in Kyrgyzstan ("Could Matthew have traveled to Central Asia and died there?"), there was never any legend that had Matthew physically perishing in this land. The legend held merely that Armenian Christians brought with them a collection of purported Matthew relics. All mentions of the Ploskih excavation's having found a sarcophagus that might have housed Matthew's body were ridiculous. Assuming that Matthew's relics did find their way into the hands of Armenian missionaries, it goes against all sense that the body of an apostle would be entrusted to Christians launching themselves into a part of the world unknown to most Christians. Whatever relics this legendary Armenian monastery was supposed to have held, they would almost certainly have been small and few in number.

Meanwhile, the abundance of spiders Andrei and I were encountering within the catacombs would have powered down the nervous system of even the mildest arachnophobe. Every time I picked a spider out of my hair, I felt another hypodermically legging its way along my neck. We walked from one end of the tunnels to the other and back again, cursing the spiders the entire way. When Andrei flicked a millipede at me, I put a spider in his hair. After that, not surprisingly, he decided we had seen enough. We pushed out of the catacombs and sat on the hillside, pointing out our best guesses as to where the legendary Monastery of Armenian Brotherhood might have been. My imagined locations were all in the middle of the lake. Andrei frowned. "Like Atlantis?" he asked.

"Yes," I said. "Exactly like Atlantis."

Andrei plucked a wet piece of grass from the hillside and put it into his mouth. I did not tell him that he still had a spider in his hair. He said nothing for a while. Then: "That doesn't sound very likely."

"No," I said. "It doesn't."

VI.

A few days later, back in Bishkek, we visited Holy Trinity Cathedral, the city's largest Russian Orthodox church. I did not have an appointment, but as luck would have it, standing just inside the gate was Yuri Anastasian, who served as a kind of information minister for the cathedral. He was in the middle of what appeared to be a friendly, animated conversation with a Kyrgyz woman. He was wearing a puffy winter vest with a red long-sleeve thermal T-shirt underneath. Brown-gray hair, beard, thick glasses—Yuri looked a little like a pre-Islamic Cat Stevens in Adidas track pants. During a lull in his conversation, Andrei and I introduced ourselves and asked about the ancient monastery in Kurmanty. Instantly, Yuri began to nod. He had been to Kurmanty several times, he said, and had even worked to create a handmade, highly detailed map of the lost monastery by talking to the area's oldest people.

Yuri meant the Russian monastery, I realized. I told him I was talking about not the Russian monastery destroyed in 1916 but rather the Monastery of Armenian Brotherhood.

"There's only one monastery at Kurmanty," Yuri said. "Or Svetly Mys. It was actually located in Svetly Mys."

"Ah," I said. "So the Monastery of Armenian Brotherhood is . . . what?"

Yuri was by now amused; I was not the first person to come calling with such questions. "The Catalan Atlas," he said, "is the only source that mentions that monastery's connection to Matthew. There was no monastery in that area before the tenth century, in my opinion. And any monastery to appear there after the tenth century would have been a Russian monastery, not an Armenian monastery. We have no reason to think that an old Catalonian map is correct in its information."

I asked him about the catacombs.

"There are two opinions on the catacombs," Yuri said, with a growingly professorial mien. "One view is that they belong to the ancient monastery. The other view is that they were dug by the Russian brothers in the nineteenth century. The scientists who went there found something, but they didn't find any shrine. Did you hear they'd found a shrine?"

"I did," I said.

He shook his head. "A lot of people who 'find' things at Svetly Mys are looking to start their careers. Much of what has been 'found' at Svetly Mys is, in my opinion, fabricated."

"So no Matthew reliquary," I said.

"Probably no," he said. "Probably it's not true. Probably it's a mistake." But he had heard strange things about Svetly Mys all the same. "Some people claim to have seen the spirits of the Russian monks killed by bandits. A journalist, for instance, a non-religious woman, who stayed out near the lake, told me she saw some ghostly monks pass by in front of her, near the seashore, at night. Others claim to have seen a big glowing cross over the water, where the monastery had once been."

I asked Yuri if he believed any of that.

He smiled. "I myself have never seen such things."

Andrei asked Yuri if maybe the catacombs were older than the Russian monastery; I could tell he wanted our trip to have been based on something less pathetic than a misunderstanding.

"Those tunnels," Yuri said, "you've been inside, yes? Then you see they are already collapsing. It's very rainy in Svetly Mys. The winds meet there, additionally. There is no way any catacombs from the eighth century would have endured in that place. So Russian monks dug them, probably in the late nineteenth century. Any information that says otherwise is from archaeologists and scientists who are tainted by their need for money and sensation. That is my opinion. You see, I am interested in history, in what's true, not in what I would like to be true."

The Kyrgyz woman he had been speaking to when we arrived used this opportunity to introduce herself. She spoke English and told us she was a trained psychologist; she was also a Muslim who attended mosque and prayed daily. Nevertheless, she came to this cathedral several times a week because of the "spiritual openness" of the men and women she met here. She thanked Allah for guiding her toward such people as Yuri. "Look around," she said, looking around. "Isn't this a pleasant place to sit and think?"

"Yes," I said. "It certainly seems like it."

Andrei asked her how long she had been coming here.

"Years," she said. "Today I was bringing Yuri some poems

that I like." She turned to me. "As a writer, you should appreciate that."

At this, I reached out, my hand over my heart, and shook hands with her. "I do appreciate that," I said.

She looked at me. "Are you an American?"

"I am."

"I love Americans," she said. "Do you want to know why?"

I did, if only because the number of times a Muslim had asked me if I wanted to know why she loved Americans had just increased by 100 percent.

"Because Americans can be many things, many ethnicities, and many religions, just like the Kyrgyz people. Because Americans, like Kyrgyz, are free people." Then she took my hand. "You are looking for Matthew?"

"Yes," I said. "I am. Or I was."

"May God let you find him," she said. I tried to retrieve my hand, but she was not yet done: her fingers warmly tightened. "May God straighten your road. May God put the wind at your back. May God allow the rain to come down softly. And may God bring us together again."

JAMES SON OF ZEBEDEE

Cathedral of Santiago de Compostela: Santiago, Spain

NO SENSE • BLISTERS • A BAROQUE TRAIN STATION •
STORIES & FOOTPRINTS

I.

What Christianity promises, I do not understand. What its god could possibly want, I have never been able to imagine, not even when I was a Christian. Augustine once wrote of wanting to "comprehend my comprehender," and this was the boldly searching Christianity I have always been drawn to. It was easy to mock certain strains of modern American Christianity, which had become, at their emotional core, white-person Rastafarianism—a way for an aggrieved and self-conscious subculture to barricade itself in righteous anger. If nothing else, such Christians were reminders of the bio-evolutionary basis of the roughly ten-thousand-year-old phenomenon of moralistic monotheism, the genetic development of which is traceable to the rise of agriculture, the relaxation of nomadism, and the resultant fears of cultural contamination. Our primitive propensity toward faith begins as the tribal impulse to exclude, as the amplifier of genetically encoded fears. Yet anyone who derived meaning from art has no business claiming not to understand meaning derived from religion. Stories are part-time religions; readers are temporary fundamentalists. My religion makes no sense and does not help me. Therefore I pursue it.

My friend Gideon and I walked five hundred miles across Spain along the oldest Christian pilgrimage route in Europe. Our destination was the Cathedral of Santiago de Compostela in Santiago, Spain. To become a pilgrim is to live at the speed of thought, to transform movement into ritual, to sacralize the very space through which one walks. When we set out, both of us had vague hopes of something transformative happening. All I learned was walking fifteen-mile days locks one deep within oneself. To avoid any solitary confinement, Gideon and I talked about writing, about our careers, about blisters; about women we loved, women we wanted to love, and women we wished had loved us. In our five weeks of spending literally twenty-four hours a day in sweaty proximity, Gideon and I got into three arguments. One was about money. Two were about religion, the only subject capable of taking two young men who loved each other, two young men who agreed on almost everything, and turning them into silent, cold-eyed strangers eating *bocadillos* on either side of a path in the loneliest middle of the Spanish Meseta.

Gideon rightly wanted me to know that it should not be so easy to brush aside any area of human inquiry, especially one that many intelligent people had let consume them. But I knew Christians are not and never have been one thing. There have been Jesus Christians, Paul Christians, Origen Christians, and Augustine Christians; law-and-order Christians, sensualist Christians, bloodthirsty Christians, and godly Christians. The most attractive thing about Christianity has always been its ability to provide a spiritual roof over so many different heads. I knew, too, that most Christians longed only for reassurance that the last room into which we all walk would be filled with a great and motionless light. It was so simple and yet for many so complicated: needing this reassurance did not necessitate denying another his.

I knew I would not take medical, legal, family, or hygienic advice from anyone who lived two thousand years ago. And yet

I live in a world in which billions of people regard the cosmologies of our intellectual ancestors as plausible, even true. Men and women who did not know whether the moon was a dragon's eye or a piece of frozen water determined the nature and identity of a being who both is telepathically privy to our most intimate sins and superintends the distant collapse of black holes. Putting one's faith in such primitivism was obvious madness. Yet Shakespeare knew nothing of developmental psychology, political theory, economics, or the genome, and I gladly put a different kind of faith in him. Storytelling has and always will have a corrective power less fragile than that of faith—less fragile because it is not vulnerable to mere fact. This was, I am afraid, my walk through Spain: thirty-six days of arduously yes-but thoughts. Nothing is more predictable, more unpredictable, more agelessly, familiarly alien, than the human mind. We want. We long. We imagine. We fight. We gather. We love. We hate. We lie. We believe.

II.

We have arrived at Santiago de Compostela, which Gideon thinks looks like a baroque train station. Every five minutes, a new group of pilgrims enters the plaza and collapses on the rough paving stones in front of the cathedral. They arrive wearing knee braces and bandages; some are on crutches; everyone limps. I am limping, as is Gideon. Our fellow pilgrims unshoulder their backpacks and drop their walking sticks. They are sweating and tired, and almost all of them are crying. Gideon and I cried, too, on the way in, because we knew we were grasping the same dirty laundry we had when we first set out. We know we are the same but do not want to be the same.

The faces of those around me are slack with dumb, incommunicable wonder. No pilgrim has much to say in her collapse moment. Everyone is looking at the cathedral, and it is quite a cathedral. Huge, several magnitudes larger than anything else around it. In the Vatican complex, Saint Peter's is like Everest.

Santiago de Compostela is different; it is freestanding and solitary; it is Kilimanjaro. Its mothy, dun-colored facade is covered
in yellowy moss. In the central spot of pedestaled glory, which
most basilicas and cathedrals reserve for Jesus, stands James son
of Zebedee, brother of John, the first of the Twelve to be martyred. Known as *Matamoros*, or Saint James the Moor Slayer—a
Galilean Jew resurrected as a medieval Christian knight—who
helped rid Spain of infidel Muslims. Symbolized by the pilgrim
staff, the floppy sun hat, the seashell. According to tradition, and
tradition alone, James preached in Spain in the first century,
but a Spanish vision of Mary the mother of Jesus sent him back
to Roman Palestine, back to Jerusalem, and to this: "About that
time King Herod laid violent hands upon some who belonged
to the church. He had James, the brother of John, killed with the
sword." So says Acts 12:1. "King Herod" must have been Herod
Agrippa, because he was the only Herodian ruler to have had
jurisdiction over Jerusalem in the early 40s. Somehow James's
remains found their way back to his flock in Galicia, in western
Spain, whose native pre-Christian religions believed the living
sun nightly expired in the waters of the Atlantic. The location of
James's tomb was eventually, and improbably, forgotten. When
the tomb was rediscovered in the ninth century, by yet another
ambitious Christian bishop, Santiago de Compostela* was built
in James's honor.

In his letter to the Romans, Paul mentions wanting to go to
Spain, seeing that his "ambition" is to "proclaim the good news"
in places where word of Jesus has not yet spread, "so that I do
not build on someone else's foundation." If one of the Twelve
Apostles was preaching Christ Jesus resurrected among Spaniards, Paul was unaware of it. As to whether Paul himself reached
Spain, no one knows—how little we know, really, about any of
this—but there is no record of Christian activity in Spain until

---

* The name, a Latin corruption, means "field of the star."

more than a century after Paul and James had left this earth. No record, but stories.

I do not regard the stories about James son of Zebedee, or any stories about any apostle, as merely stories. All beliefs have moral insinuations, and all representations have political repercussions. James the infidel slayer was adapted for propagandistic use by the Franco regime, after all. I do not believe a discernible form of "good" or acceptable or authentic Christianity stands behind these stories. Christianity, like Judaism before it and Islam after it, has always been and will always be a less than ideal way to understand the world and our place within it. At the same time, I know there is no purely rational way of understanding the world. A thousand irrational spasms daily derange us all. God is part of the same formless reality as thought, as real as all bits of data that float invisibly through this world, somehow creating output. In this sense, all that moves through us is real. To explain the realness of that which we cannot see, we turn to stories left behind by evangelistic writers, working behind their complicated veils of anonymity. The footprints they left behind lead us to places we long to be led.

High above me, on a colonnaded veranda on the right side of the cathedral, a police officer slowly stalks, carrying what appears to be a sniper rifle. I move closer to the church, ant-like in its presence, moving toward it in ant time. The closer I get, the more majestically eroded it seems. The overgrown yellow moss all over its facade feels cool and lush and soft. I place my hand flush against the marble.

Nothing in this world suggests our overtures toward God are either wanted or needed. Someday this building will fall and the civilization around it. It is only our stories that lay balms across our impermanence. I have a longer story to tell about Gideon's and my walk and suddenly wonder what would happen if I chose not to tell it, to transform it. What if a story was enough for a thing to be?

GLOSSARY OF PEOPLE AND TERMS

Apocrypha: A collection of anonymous Christian writings from the first five hundred years of the faith. Most survive due to happenstance, because many apocryphal writings were condemned and destroyed by the early church.

Athanasius (ca. 298–373 CE): Alexandrian bishop. Instrumental in defending the concept of the Trinity.

Augustine of Hippo (354–430 CE): Greatest theologian and philosopher of the Western church. Pioneer of the memoir.

Celsus (ca. 2nd century CE): Philosopher and pagan critic of Christianity.

Christology: Field of theological inquiry concerned with the relationship of Jesus to his divinity.

Clement of Alexandria (ca. 150–215 CE): Theologian and educator. Helped accommodate Christian thinking to concepts drawn from Hellenistic philosophy. Influenced Origen, early Christianity's greatest theologian.

Clement of Rome (?–ca. 100 CE): Roman bishop. Purportedly wrote *1 Clement,* one of the earliest surviving examples of noncanonical Christian literature.

Epiphanius of Salamis (ca. 315–403 CE): Theologian and heresiologist.

Essenes: Ascetic Jewish sect active from the second century BCE to the first century CE. Wiped out by the Romans during the Jewish War.

Eusebius of Caesarea (ca. 260–ca. 340 CE): Historian. Wrote the earliest surviving history of the Christian church.

Hasmonaean Dynasty: Autonomous Jewish dynasty. Founded after the Maccabaean revolt against the Seleucids. Ruled Judaea and parts beyond from 140 BCE to 37 BCE.

Hegesippus (ca. 110–ca. 190 CE): Chronicler and historian responsible for a five-volume work of Christian history, which survives only in a handful of outside citations. Thought to have had strong historical connection to the traditions of Jewish Christianity.

Ignatius of Antioch (ca. 40–ca. 110 CE): Bishop and martyr.

Irenaeus of Lyon (?–ca. 200 CE): Bishop, heresiologist, and polemicist.

Jacobus de Voragine (ca. 1230–1298): Archbishop of Genoa and medieval Christian chronicler.

Jerome (ca. 347–420 CE): Theologian and translator.

The Jewish War (66–73 CE): Also called the First Jewish-Roman War. Ended with the destruction of the Second Temple.

John Chrysostom (ca. 347–407 CE): Preacher and bishop. Instrumental in deepening Christian hostility toward both paganism and Judaism.

Josephus (37–ca. 100 CE): Jewish historian and defector to the Romans during the Jewish War. His histories are the source of much of our information about first-century Palestine outside the New Testament.

Justin Martyr (ca. 100–ca. 165 CE): Early Christian apologist and martyr.

Maccabaean Revolt (167–160 BCE): Jewish revolt against the Seleucids. Its leaders founded the Hasmonaean dynasty.

Marcionism: After Marcion (ca. 85–ca. 165), a heterodox Christian who assembled his own proto–New Testament. Regarded the Jewish God as inferior to the Christian God.

Nag Hammadi: Egyptian city where an important cache of early heterodox Christian texts was discovered in 1945.

Origen (ca. 184–ca. 254 CE): Christianity's first great theologian. Among the first to fuse Greek philosophical concepts onto Christian thinking. Later branded a heretic by the Catholic Church.

Papias of Hierapolis (?–155 CE): Bishop and chronicler. Apparently wrote a quintology titled *Expositions of the Sayings of the Lord,* none of whose volumes are extant. His work survives only through limited citations by other early Christian writers.

Polycarp (ca. 69–ca. 155): Bishop and martyr. Alleged to have known John the apostle.

Pseudo-Clementine Literature: Collection of second-century Jewish Christian pseudepigrapha. Purportedly written by Clement of Rome.

Qumran: Archaeological site in Palestine. Where a collection of nearly one thousand texts used by the Essenes, and today known as the Dead Sea Scrolls, were collected between 1946 and 1956.

Second Revolt (132–136 CE): Also known as the Bar Kokhba Revolt. Was the last and most severe Jewish rebellion against Rome.

Seleucid Dynasty (305–63 BCE): Founded by Seleucus, former infantry general of Alexander the Great. Major force in the cultural Hellenization of the Near East.

Septuagint: The Greek translation of the Hebrew Bible. What most of the authors of the New Testament knew as holy scripture.

Synoptic Gospels: Matthew, Mark, and Luke. From *synoptic,* or "seen together," due to their obvious similarities and reliance on similar traditions.

Syriac Christianity: Form of Christianity with perhaps the strongest historical ties to Palestinian Christianity, that is, the Christianity of Jesus's earliest followers.

Tertullian (ca. 160–ca. 225 CE): First great theologian of the Latin-speaking world. Ferocious heresiologist. Eventually joined heterodox Christian cult.

ACKNOWLEDGMENTS

Thank you to Jay Rubenstein, Dana Prescott, John Thavis, Arman Schwartz, Suzy Hansen, Andrei Bondarev, and Gideon Lewis-Kraus for accompanying me on my apostolic travels. Thank you, too, to everyone who spoke to me, especially Hal Taussig, who was the first.

Thank you to the American Academy in Rome, the Black Mountain Institute at UNLV (especially Carol Harter and Richard Wiley), and the John Simon Guggenheim Memorial Foundation for their support during the writing of this book.

Thank you to John Alford, Jamie Quatro, Dan Josefson, Pauls Toutonghi, and William Heyward for early, helpful reads of this book, and to Hendrik Dey for his scholarly expertise.

Thank you to Ronnie Scott, Ted Genoways, and Bill Buford and Jason Wilson for publishing sections of this book in, respectively, *The Lifted Brow*, *Virginia Quarterly Review*, and *The Best American Travel Writing 2010*.

Thank you to Dan Frank, Walter Donohue, and, as always, Andrew Miller for editorial faith and support.

Thank you to my family and friends.

Thank you to Trisha Miller, my heart's Pantokrator.

Thank you to my daughter, Mina, who taught me there are things greater than finishing a book.

BIBLIOGRAPHY

The Acts of the Apostles. Translation and commentary by Joseph A. Fitzmyer. Anchor Bible 31. New York: Doubleday, 1998.

Armstrong, Karen. *A History of God: The 4,000-Year Quest of Judaism, Christianity, and Islam.* 1993. Reprint, New York: Ballantine Books, 1994.

———. *Jerusalem: One City, Three Faiths.* New York: Alfred A. Knopf, 1996.

Athanasius. *On the Incarnation.* Translated and edited by C. S. M. V. 1944. Reprint, Crestwood, N.Y.: St. Vladimir's Seminary Press, 1996.

Augstein, Rudolf. *Jesus Son of Man.* Translated by Hugh Young. New York: Urizen Books, 1977.

Augustine. *Confessions.* Translated by Henry Chadwick. 1991. Reprint, Oxford: Oxford University Press, 1992.

———. *Select Letters.* Translated by James Houston Baxter. 1930. Rev. ed. Cambridge, Mass.: Harvard University Press, 2006.

Barnett, Paul. *The Birth of Christianity: The First Twenty Years.* Grand Rapids: William B. Eerdmans, 2005.

Bauckham, Richard. *Jesus and the Eyewitnesses: The Gospels as Eyewitness Testimony.* Grand Rapids: William B. Eerdmans, 2006.

———. *Jude and the Relatives of Jesus in the Early Church.* 1990. Reprint, London: T & T Clark International, 2004.

Benedict XVI. *The Apostles.* Huntington, Ind.: Our Sunday Visitor, 2007.

———. *The Fathers of the Church: From Clement of Rome to Augustine of Hippo.* Edited and annotated by Joseph T. Lienhard. Grand Rapids: William B. Eerdmans, 2009.

Bhaskaran, Vijayan P. *The Legacy of St. Thomas: Apostle of India.* Mumbai: St. Pauls, 2007.

Boman, Thorleif. *Hebrew Thought Compared with Greek.* Translated by Jules L. Moreau. 1960. Reprint, New York: W. W. Norton, 1970.

Borg, Marcus J., and John Dominic Crossan. *The Last Week: A Day-by-Day Account of Jesus's Final Week in Jerusalem.* San Francisco: HarperSanFrancisco, 2006.

Bowen, Elizabeth. *A Time in Rome*. 1959. Reprint, London: Vintage Books, 2003.

Brown, Raymond E. *The Churches the Apostles Left Behind*. Mahwah, N.J.: Paulist Press, 1994.

———. *The Community of the Beloved Disciple: The Life, Loves, and Hates of an Individual Church in New Testament Times*. Mahwah, N.J.: Paulist Press, 1979.

———. *The Death of the Messiah: From Gethsemane to the Grave: A Commentary on the Passion Narratives in the Four Gospels*. Vols. 1 and 2. 1994. Reprint, New York: Doubleday, 1998.

———. *An Introduction to New Testament Christology*. Mahwah, N.J.: Paulist Press, 1994.

Brown, Raymond E., Karl P. Donfried, and John Reumann, eds. *Peter in the New Testament*. Minneapolis: Augsburg, 1973.

Buyukkolanci, Mustafa. *The Life and Monument of St. John*. Selçuk: Efes 2000 Foundation [*sic*], 2001.

Carson, Anne. *Glass, Irony, and God*. New York: New Directions, 1995.

———. *Plainwater: Essays and Poetry*. 1995. Reprint, New York: Vintage Books, 2000.

Castelli, Elizabeth A., and Hal Taussig, eds. *Reimagining Christian Origins: A Colloquium Honoring Burton L. Mack*. Valley Forge, Pa.: Trinity Press International, 1996.

Celsus. *On the True Doctrine: A Discourse Against the Christians*. Translated by R. Joseph Hoffmann. New York: Oxford University Press, 1987.

Chilton, Bruce. *Rabbi Jesus: An Intimate Biography*. 2000. Reprint, New York: Doubleday, 2002.

———. *Rabbi Paul: An Intellectual Biography*. 1994. Reprint, New York: Doubleday, 1995.

The Complete Dead Sea Scrolls in English. Translated by Geza Vermes. New York: Penguin, 2012. The community responsible for the Dead Sea Scrolls was almost certainly a group known as the Essenes, an apocalyptic, pistic, ablution-obsessed, and apparently very testy group who withdrew from Jewish society after the Maccabaean revolt of 166 BCE and lived in several highly organized communities in the desert around the Dead Sea. (The Essenes are believed to have resented, in the words of one scholar, the Maccabaean rebels' Obamaian shift "from being charismatic rulers of the people to being adaptable real politicians," as well as the fact that a traditionally nonpriestly family had taken over the high priesthood.) The ancient writer who had the most to say about the Essenes was Josephus. In his *Life,* he admitted to spending time in the desert with an ascetic hermit named Bannus, very likely a former Essene, and in *The Jewish War* described the Essenes as "peculiarly attached to each other . . . They possess no one city but everywhere have large colonies." Not much else was known about them until the late 1940s, when a number of their scrolls—now called the Dead Sea Scrolls—were discovered in the spectacularly spooky caves at Khirbet Qumran about nine miles south of Jericho. The Qumran community, as it is known, is thought to have lived in this area for around two hundred years. Many questions concerning this community remain unresolved: Was the Qumran community's collection of recovered scrolls a comprehensive library or a hastily gathered and just-as-hastily hidden cache of documents? If Essenism was so opposed to the encroachment of Hellenism, why are so many of its texts in Greek? Was the Qumran settlement a working community, a hostel for like-minded travelers, or a monastery of some kind? Was the community there a klatch of self-obsessed fanatics or representative of the larger beliefs of Essenism? Did this community have anything in common with early Christianity? This forces one back to the question of how reliable the gospel accounts of early Christian history really are. Whether one believes they are accurate generally, completely, or not very, there can be no doubt that part of the gospels' intent was to accommodate. Not to obfuscate, or to betray theological principals, but to provide enough room for those teetering on the brink of belief to fall across the threshold of the faith being advocated. What is so striking about the work of the Qumran community is that it is not at all accommodating. The reason the Dead Sea Scrolls are not accommodating is they were never edited. Instead, they were hidden by people who never had the opportunity to go back for them, for the simple reason that they were killed during the Jewish War. (According to Josephus, the Romans were especially brutal when dealing with the Essenes, "subjecting them to every torture yet invented.") One is thus left with a surprising realization: until the discovery of the Dead Sea Scrolls, all of the surviving work that covers the time of Jesus—which is to say, the gospels, Acts, Paul's letters, and Josephus—was written by those seeking accommoda-

tion. The earliest, preedited forms the first Christian writings took
may well have resembled the Qumran writings in their spiritual
extremism. Were we to have any access to those writings, the link-
ages between the Dead Sea Scrolls and early Christianity might be
clearer and more startling.

*The Contendings of the Apostles: Being the Histories of the Lives and
Martyrdoms and Deaths of the Twelve Apostles and Evangelists.*
Translated by E. A. Wallis Budge. London: Oxford University
Press, 1935.

Corn, Alfred, ed. *Incarnation: Contemporary Writers on the New Testament.* 1990. Reprint, New York: Penguin Books, 1991.

Crossan, John Dominic. *The Birth of Christianity: Discovering What
Really Happened Immediately After the Execution of Jesus.* 1998.
Reprint, New York: HarperCollins, 1999.

———. *Who Killed Jesus? Exposing the Roots of Anti-Semitism in the
Gospel Story of the Death of Jesus.* San Francisco: HarperSanFrancisco, 1995.

Culpepper, R. Alan. *John: The Son of Zebedee, the Life of a Legend.* 1994.
Reprint, Minneapolis: Fortress Press, 2000.

Culpepper, R. Alan, and C. Clifton Black, eds. *Exploring the Gospel of
John.* Louisville, Ky.: Westminster/John Knox Press, 1996.

Dante. *The Divine Comedy.* Translated by Clive James. New York: Live-
right, 2013.

DeConick, April D. *The Thirteenth Apostle: What the Gospel of Judas
Really Says.* London: Continuum, 2007.

De Quincey, Thomas. *Judas Iscariot and Other Writings.* Edinburgh:
Adam and Charles Black, 1863.

*The Didache, The Epistle of Barnabas, The Epistles and the Martyrdom
of St. Polycarp, The Fragments of Papias, The Epistle to Diognetus.*
Translated by James A. Kleist. New York: Newman Press, 1948.

D'Souza, Herman. *In the Steps of St. Thomas.* 1952. Rev. ed. Madras:
Disciples of St. Thomas, 2009.

Ehrman, Bart D. *Lost Christianities: The Battles for Scripture and the
Faiths We Never Knew.* 2003. Reprint, Oxford: Oxford University
Press, 2005.

———. *The Orthodox Corruption of Scripture: The Effect of Early Christological Controversies on the Text of the New Testament.* New York:
Oxford University Press, 1993.

———. *Peter, Paul, and Mary Magdalene: The Followers of Jesus in History and Legend.* New York: Oxford University Press, 2006.

Eisenman, Robert. *James the Brother of Jesus: The Key to Unlocking the Secrets of Early Christianity and the Dead Sea Scrolls*. 1997. Reprint, New York: Penguin Books, 1998.

Elliott, J. K., ed. *The Apocryphal New Testament*. 2005. Reprint, Oxford: Clarendon Press, 2006.

The Epistles of John. Translation and commentary by Raymond E. Brown. Anchor Bible 30. New York: Doubleday, 1982.

The Epistles of St. Clement of Rome and St. Ignatius of Antioch. Translated by James A. Kleist. Mahwah, N.J.: Paulist Press, 1946.

Eusebius. *The History of the Church*. Translated by G. A. Williamson. Edited by Andrew Louth. 1965. Rev. ed. London: Penguin Books, 1989.

Finegan, Jack. *The Archeology of the New Testament: The Life of Jesus and the Beginning of the Early Church*. 1969. Reprint, Princeton, N.J.: Princeton University Press, 1978.

Fredriksen, Paula. *From Jesus to Christ: The Origins of the New Testament Images of Jesus*. New Haven, Conn.: Yale University Press, 1988.

Freeman, Charles. *A New History of Early Christianity*. New Haven, Conn.: Yale University Press, 2009.

Frykenberg, Robert Eric. *Christianity in India: From Beginnings to the Present*. 2008. Reprint, Oxford: Oxford University Press, 2010.

Galatians. Translation and commentary by J. Louis Martyn. Anchor Bible 33. New York: Doubleday, 1997.

Gascoigne, Bamber. *A Brief History of Christianity*. London: Constable & Robinson, 2003. Reprint of the 1977 edition, titled *The Christians*.

Gibbon, Edward. *The History of the Decline and Fall of the Roman Empire*. Edited and abridged by David Womersley. London: Penguin Books, 2000.

The Gospel According to John I–XII. Translation and commentary by Raymond E. Brown. Anchor Bible 29. New York: Doubleday, 1966.

The Gospel According to John XIII–XXI. Translation and commentary by Raymond E. Brown. Anchor Bible 29A. New York: Doubleday, 1970.

The Gospel According to Luke I–IX. Translation and commentary by Joseph A. Fitzmyer. Anchor Bible 28. New York: Doubleday, 1981.

The Gospel According to Luke X–XXIV. Translation and commentary by Joseph A. Fitzmyer. Anchor Bible 28A. New York: Doubleday, 1985.

Goulder, Michael. *St. Paul Versus St. Peter: A Tale of Two Missions*. Louisville, Ky.: Westminster/John Knox Press, 1994.

Graham-Dixon, Andrew. *Caravaggio: A Life Sacred and Profane*. New York: W. W. Norton, 2011.

Grant, Michael. *History of Rome*. New York: Charles Scribner's Sons, 1978.

Greenwood, F. W. P. *Lives of the Twelve Apostles with Explanatory Notes*. Boston: Hilliard, Gray, Little, and Wilkins, 1828.

Hamburger, Jeffrey F. *St. John the Divine: The Deified Evangelist in Medieval Art and Theology*. Berkeley: University of California Press, 2002.

Hansen, Brooks. *John the Baptizer: A Novel*. New York: W. W. Norton, 2009.

Hardy, Edward R., ed. *Christology of the Later Fathers*. Philadelphia: Westminster Press, 1954.

Hawkin, David J. *The Johannine World: Reflections on the Theology of the Fourth Gospel and Contemporary Society*. Albany: State University of New York Press, 1996.

Hengel, Martin. *Judaism and Hellenism: Studies in Their Encounter in Palestine in the Early Hellenistic Period*. Translated by John Bowman. 1974. Reprint, Eugene, Ore.: Wipf and Stock, 2003.

———. *The Son of God: The Origin of Christology and the History of Jewish Hellenistic Religion*. Translated by John Bowden. Minneapolis: Fortress Press, 1976.

Hibbard, Howard. *Bernini*. 1965. Reprint, London: Penguin Books, 1990.

Hippolytus. *On the Apostolic Tradition*. Translated by Alistair Stewart-Sykes. Crestwood, N.Y.: St. Vladimir's Seminary Press, 2001.

Holland, Tom. *Rubicon: The Last Years of the Roman Republic*. 2003. Reprint, New York: Anchor Books, 2005.

Holmes, Michael W. *The Apostolic Fathers: Greek Texts and English Translations*. 1992. Rev. ed. Grand Rapids: Baker Books, 1999.

The Holy Bible: New Revised Standard Version. New York: Oxford University Press, 1989.

Horsley, Richard A. *Galilee: History, Politics, People*. Valley Forge, Pa.: Trinity Press International, 1995.

———. *Jesus and the Spiral of Violence: Popular Jewish Resistance in Roman Palestine*. 1987. Reprint, Minneapolis: Fortress Press, 1993.

———, ed. *Christian Origins: A People's History of Christianity*. Minneapolis: Fortress Press, 2005.

Horsley, Richard A., and Neil Asher Silberman. *The Message and the Kingdom: How Jesus and Paul Ignited a Revolution and Trans-*

formed the Ancient World. 1997. Reprint, Minneapolis: Fortress Press, 2002.

Hughes, Robert. *Rome: A Cultural, Visual, and Personal History.* New York: Alfred A. Knopf, 2011.

Irenaeus. *Against the Heresies.* Translated by Dominic J. Unger, with further revisions by John J. Dillon. New York: Newman Press, 1992.
————. *On the Apostolic Preaching.* Translated by John Behr. Crestwood, N.Y.: St. Vladimir's Seminary Press, 1997.

Jacobus de Voragine. *The Golden Legend: Readings on the Saints.* Vols. 1 and 2. Translated by William Granger Ryan. Princeton, N.J.: Princeton University Press, 2002.

Jeffers, James S. *The Greco-Roman World of the New Testament Era: Exploring the Background of Early Christianity.* Downers Grove, Ill.: InterVarsity Press, 1999.

Jenkins, Philip. *Jesus Wars: How Four Patriarchs, Three Queens, and Two Emperors Decided What Christians Would Believe for the Next 1,500 Years.* 2010. Reprint, New York: HarperCollins, 2011.

Johnson, Luke Timothy. *The Real Jesus: The Misguided Quest for the Historical Jesus and the Truth of the Traditional Gospels.* 1996. Reprint, San Francisco: HarperSanFrancisco, 1997.

Johnson, Paul. *A History of Christianity.* 1976. Reprint, New York: Touchstone, 1995.
————. *A History of the Jews.* New York: Harper & Row, 1987.

Josephus. *The Jewish War.* Translated by G. A. Williamson. 1959. Revised by E. Mary Smallwood. New York: Penguin, 1981. A quick note about the work of Josephus, who, like Paul, was a defector to a cause he initially fought. In 63 CE, when he was a Pharisee still only in his twenties, he traveled to Rome to lobby the emperor Nero for the release of some Jewish priests. He returned to Palestine in 66 CE quite astonished by the power and reach of the Roman Empire. Shortly after his return home, unfortunately, the Jewish revolt against Rome began. Josephus, believing the rebellion would fail, claimed he reluctantly served as the military commandant of Galilee against the Romans, though in actual fact he appears to have been attempting to quell the rebellion from within on behalf of the Temple's high-priestly authorities. (His various accounts of his actions during the war are difficult to reconcile with one another.) Whatever the case, when the fortifications of Josephus's fortress, Jotapata, collapsed, he and many of his comrades fled and took shelter in a cave, which was eventually surrounded by the Romans. Josephus's initial impulse was to surrender. Not because he was a coward (he performed with guile throughout the siege of his fortress, at least according to him) but because he knew that much of what was driving the Jewish War was the fanaticism of the Jewish Zealots he despised. Josephus was encouraged in his wish to surrender when it was communicated to him by the Romans that he would be spared if he emerged from the cave. Yet Josephus's comrades made it quite clear they would kill Josephus if he gave himself up. And so Josephus and his comrades pledged to commit mass suicide rather than surrender. At their commander's suggestion, the men drew lots to determine the order in which they would die, with one person killing the next until the last alive finally killed himself. Josephus somehow managed to ensure that he drew the last lot. All went according to plan: Josephus's comrades killed each other, one after another. Eventually, the young general was left alive with his final remaining soldier; both agreed they had no strong wish to die after all. Josephus was soon captured by the Romans but proved his worth in intelligence and insight into his fellow Jews' strategies and desires. He remained a prisoner, however, until the commanding Roman officer in Judaea, Vespasian, whose notice Josephus had caught when he predicted to Vespasian that he would eventually sit on the Roman throne, left Palestine to fulfill his imperial destiny. Working now as the official translator of Vespasian's son Titus, Josephus attempted to persuade the Zealots barricaded within the city of Jerusalem to surrender, but the sight of the man many Zealots regarded as a traitor tearfully beseeching them from behind enemy lines put steel in their backs. After Jerusalem was destroyed, Josephus salvaged a few devotional items from the wreckage of the Temple, intervened to save three friends from crucifixion, and halted the Roman deportation and enslavement of several dozen others, including his brother. Josephus returned to Rome, and Titus placed him on a pension as an official historian. Eventually, he became a Roman citizen and was adopted into Titus's imperial family, the Flavians, earning him the name Titus Flavius Josephus. It was in Rome that he wrote his histories, a short autobiography (notable for being the first known work of its kind to survive into the modern age), and a tract against a dead Jew-hating Alexandrian academic named

Apion. As a Roman apologist to the Jews and a Jewish apologist to the Romans, Josephus displays a fascinating split in his sympathies as a historian and writer. This dividedness—to say nothing of Josephus's anfractuous morality—is why so much of his work is to be treated with caution.

———. *The Works of Josephus.* Translated by William Whiston. Peabody, Mass.: Hendrickson, 1987.

Kazin, Alfred. *God and the American Writer.* 1997. Reprint, New York: Vintage Books, 1998.

Kelly, J. N. D. *Early Christian Doctrines.* Rev. ed. New York: Harper & Row, 1978.

———. *Jerome: His Life, Writings, and Controversies.* 1975. Reprint, Peabody, Mass.: Hendrickson, 2000.

Krosney, Herbert. *The Lost Gospel: The Quest for the Gospel of Judas Iscariot.* Washington, D.C.: National Geographic, 2006.

Kugel, James L. *The Bible as It Was.* Cambridge, Mass.: Belknap Press, 1997.

Kysar, Robert. *John: The Maverick Gospel.* Rev. ed. Louisville, Ky.: Westminster/John Knox Press, 1993.

Lampe, Peter. *From Paul to Valentinus: Christians at Rome in the First Two Centuries.* Translated by Michael Steinhauser. Edited by Marshall D. Johnson. Minneapolis: Fortress Press, 2003.

Lane, Belden C. *The Solace of Fierce Landscapes: Exploring Desert and Mountain Spirituality.* New York: Oxford University Press, 1998.

Lewis-Kraus, Gideon. *A Sense of Direction: Pilgrimage for the Restless and Hopeful.* New York: Riverhead, 2012.

Longenecker, Richard N. *Biblical Exegesis in the Apostolic Period.* 2nd ed. Grand Rapids: William B. Eerdmans, 1999.

MacArthur, John. *Twelve Ordinary Men: How the Master Shaped His Disciples for Greatness, and What He Wants to Do with You.* Nashville: Thomas Nelson, 2002.

MacCulloch, Diarmaid. *Christianity: The First Three Thousand Years.* New York: Viking, 2010.

———. *Silence: A Christian History.* New York: Viking, 2013.

MacDonald, Dennis Ronald. *The Acts of Andrew and The Acts of Andrew and Matthias in the City of the Cannibals.* Atlanta: Scholars Press, 1990.

Mack, Burton L. *Who Wrote the New Testament? The Making of Christian Myth.* San Francisco: HarperSanFrancisco, 1995.

Malina, Bruce. *The New Testament World: Insights from Cultural Anthropology.* 3rd ed. Louisville, Ky.: Westminster/John Knox Press, 2001.

Martin, Michael. *The Case Against Christianity.* Philadelphia: Temple University Press, 1991.

Matthew. Translation and commentary by W. F. Albright and C. S. Mann. Anchor Bible 26. New York: Doubleday, 1971.

Meeks, Wayne A. *The First Urban Christians: The Social World of the Apostle Paul.* 1983. Rev. ed. New Haven, Conn.: Yale University Press, 2003.

———. *The Moral World of the First Christians.* Philadelphia: Westminster Press, 1986.

———, ed. *The Writings of St. Paul.* New York: W. W. Norton, 1972.

Melczer, William. *The Pilgrim's Guide to Santiago de Compostela.* New York: Italica Press, 1993.

Metzger, Bruce M. *The Canon of the New Testament: Its Origin, Development, and Significance.* 1987. Reprint, Oxford: Clarendon Press, 1997.

Metzger, Bruce M., and Michael D. Coogan, eds. *The Oxford Companion to the Bible.* New York: Oxford University Press, 1993.

Meyer, Marvin. *The Gospel of Thomas: The Hidden Sayings of Jesus.* San Francisco: HarperSanFrancisco, 1992.

Milavec, Aaron. *The Didache: Text, Translation, Analysis, and Commentary.* Collegeville, Minn.: Liturgical Press, 2003.

Miles, Jack. *Christ: A Crisis in the Life of God.* 2001. Reprint, New York: Vintage Books, 2002.

———. *God: A Biography.* New York: Alfred A. Knopf, 1995.

Most, Glenn W. *Doubting Thomas.* Cambridge, Mass.: Harvard University Press, 2005.

Murray, Peter, and Linda Murray, eds. *The Oxford Companion to Christian Art and Architecture.* Oxford: Oxford University Press, 1996.

Origen. *Contra Celsum.* Translated by Henry Chadwick. 1953. Rev. ed. Cambridge, U.K.: Cambridge University Press, 1980.

———. *An Exhortation to Martyrdom, Prayer, and Selected Works.* Translated and introduction by Rowan A. Greer. Mahwah, N.J.: Paulist Press, 1979.

Osborn, Eric. *Irenaeus of Lyons.* 2001. Reprint, Cambridge, U.K.: Cambridge University Press, 2005. Irenaeus casts a long shadow on early Christianity. Along with salvaging the reputation of the Fourth Gospel, Irenaeus helped rescue the Gospel According to

Luke and the Acts of the Apostles from their association with Marcionism. More than that, Irenaeus provided early Christianity with its most crucial voice in determining what would and would not later be recognized as orthodoxy. Despite this, very little is known of him. Exactly two of Irenaeus's works have survived, and then only in (incomplete) Latin and (complete) Armenian translations. Everything else is either fragmentary or preserved in the work of Eusebius. He was probably born no later than 130, at some point replaced the martyred bishop Pothinus at Lyon, and later traveled to Rome to mediate the dispute about when Asian Christians, known as Quartodecimans, celebrated Easter. Thanks to Irenaeus—whose name, fittingly in this case, means "peace"— the Quartodecimans were not excommunicated. It is believed that one of the reasons Irenaeus's work did not survive was due to his belief, which Paul shared, that the world was soon coming to an end. He was one of the last prominent Christian intellectuals to make such an argument, which might have been a source of embarrassment to Christians of the defiantly sturdy fourth and fifth centuries.

Paffenroth, Kim. *Judas: Images of the Lost Disciple*. Louisville, Ky.: Westminster/John Knox Press, 2001.

Pagels, Elaine. *The Gnostic Gospels*. 1979. Reprint, New York: Vintage Books, 1989.

Painter, John. *Just James: The Brother of Jesus in History and Tradition*. 1997. Reprint, Edinburgh: T & T Clark, 1999.

Perkins, Pheme. *Peter: Apostle for the Whole Church*. 1994. Reprint, Minneapolis: Fortress Press, 2000.

Peterson, F. Paul. *Peter's Tomb Recently Discovered in Jerusalem!* 1960.

Polo, Marco. *The Travels of Marco Polo*. Translated by W. Marsden. Revised by T. Wright. Newly revised and edited by Peter Harris. New York: Alfred A. Knopf, 2008. Revision of the 1908 edition.

Price, Reynolds. *Three Gospels*. New York: Scribner, 1996.

Pritz, Ray A. *Nazarene Jewish Christianity: From the End of the New Testament Period Until Its Disappearance in the Fourth Century*. 1988. Rev. ed. Jerusalem: Hebrew University Magnes Press, 2010.

Pseudo-Dionysius. *The Complete Works*. Translated by Colm Luibheid with collaboration from Paul Rorem. Mahwah, N.J.: Paulist Press, 1987.

Roberts, Alexander, and James Donaldson, eds. *Ante-Nicene Christian*

Library: Translations of the Writings of the Fathers, Down to A.D. *325.* Vols. 1–26. Edinburgh: T & T Clark, 1867–1885.

Robinson, James M., ed. *The Nag Hammadi Library in English.* 1978. Rev. ed. New York: HarperCollins, 1990.

Rollston, Christopher A., ed. *The Gospels According to Michael Goulder: A North American Response.* Harrisburg, Pa.: Trinity Press International, 2002.

Rudolph, Conrad. *Pilgrimage to the End of the World: The Road to Santiago de Compostela.* Chicago: University of Chicago Press, 2004.

Ruffin, C. Bernard. *The Twelve: The Lives of the Apostles After Calvary.* Huntington, Ind.: Our Sunday Visitor, 1997.

Sanders, E. P. *Paul and Palestinian Judaism.* Minneapolis: Fortress Press, 1977.

Schnackenburg, Rudolf. *Jesus in the Gospels: A Biblical Christology.* Translated by O. C. Dean Jr. Louisville, Ky.: Westminster/John Knox Press, 1995.

Scotti, R. A. *Basilica: The Splendor and the Scandal: Building St. Peter's.* New York: Viking, 2006.

Stegemann, Ekkehard W., and Wolfgang Stegemann. *The Jesus Movement: A Social History of Its First Century.* Translated by O. C. Dean Jr. Minneapolis: Fortress Press, 1999.

Stewart, Robert B., ed. *The Resurrection of Jesus: John Dominic Crossan and N. T. Wright in Dialogue.* Minneapolis: Fortress Press, 2006.

Suetonius. *The Twelve Caesars.* Translated by Robert Graves. 1957. Revised by Michael Grant. London: Penguin Books, 1979.

Tacitus. *The Annals and The Histories.* Translated by Alfred John Church and William Jackson Brodribb. Edited by Moses Hadas. New York: Modern Library, 2003.

Taussig, Hal. *Jesus Before God: The Prayer Life of the Historical Jesus.* Santa Rosa, Calif.: Polebridge Press, 1999.

Tertullian. *Apology and De Spectaculis.* Translated by T. R. Glover. Cambridge, Mass.: Harvard University Press, 1931.

———. *Five Books Against Marcion.* Translated and edited by Alexander Roberts. Calgary, Alb.: Theophania, 2010.

———. *Treatises on Penance: On Penitence and on Purity.* Translated by William P. Le Saint. Ramsey, N.J.: Newman Press, 1959.

The Travels of Sir John Mandeville. Translated by C. W. R. D. Moseley. London: Penguin Books, 1983.

Twain, Mark. *The Innocents Abroad.* 1869. Reprint, New York: Penguin Books, 2002.

Visser, Margaret. *The Geometry of Love: Space, Time, Mystery, and Meaning in an Ordinary Church.* New York: North Point Press, 2000.

Walsh, John Evangelist. *The Bones of Saint Peter: A Fascinating Account of the Search for the Apostle's Body.* London: Victor Gollancz, 1982.

Wills, Garry. *Saint Augustine.* New York: Viking, 1999.

Wilson, A. N. *Jesus: A Life.* New York: W. W. Norton, 1992.

————. *Paul: The Mind of the Apostle.* New York: W. W. Norton, 1997.

Wink, Walter. *John the Baptist in the Gospel Tradition.* 1968. Reprint, Eugene, Ore.: Wipf and Stock, 2000.

Witherington, Ben, III. *John's Wisdom: A Commentary on the Fourth Gospel.* Louisville, Ky.: Westminster/John Knox Press, 1995.

————. *What Have They Done with Jesus? Beyond Strange Theories and Bad History—Why We Can Trust the Bible.* San Francisco: HarperSanFrancisco, 2006.

Wright, N. T. *The Challenge of Jesus: Rediscovering Who Jesus Was and Is.* Downers Grove, Ill.: InterVarsity Press, 1999.

————. *Who Was Jesus?* 1992. Reprint, Grand Rapids: William B. Eerdmans, 2001.

Wroe, Ann. *Pontius Pilate.* New York: Random House, 1999.

INDEX

Page numbers in *italics* refer to illustrations.

ALSO BY

TOM BISSELL

CHASING THE SEA
Lost Among the Ghosts of Empire in Central Asia

In 1996, Tom Bissell went to Uzbekistan as a naïve Peace Corps volunteer. Though he lasted only a few months before illness and personal crisis forced him home, Bissell found himself entranced by this remote land. Five years later he returned to explore the shrinking Aral Sea, destroyed by Soviet irrigation policies. Joining up with an exuberant translator named Rustam, Bissell slips more than once through the clutches of the Uzbek police as he makes his often wild way to the devastated sea. In *Chasing the Sea*, Bissell combines the story of his travels with a beguiling chronicle of Uzbekistan's striking culture and long history of violent subjugation by despots from Jenghiz Khan to Joseph Stalin. Alternately amusing and sobering, this is a gripping portrait of a fascinating place.

Travel

ALSO AVAILABLE

The Father of All Things
God Lives in St. Petersburg
Extra Lives

VINTAGE BOOKS
Available wherever books are sold.
www.vintagebooks.com